Strengthening Language Education Through ICT Integration:

Bridging SDG4 With Digital Innovation

Peter Ilic
University of Aizu, Japan

IGI Global
Scientific Publishing
Publishing Tomorrow's Research Today

Vice President of Editorial	Melissa Wagner
Director of Acquisitions	Mikaela Felty
Director of Book Development	Jocelynn Hessler
Production Manager	Mike Brehm
Cover Design	Jose Rosado

Published in the United States of America by
IGI Global Scientific Publishing
701 East Chocolate Avenue
Hershey, PA, 17033, USA
Tel: 717-533-8845
Fax: 717-533-7115
Website: https://www.igi-global.com E-mail: cust@igi-global.com

Library of Congress Cataloging-in-Publication Data

Names: Ilic, Peter, 1967- editor
Title: Strengthening language education through ICT integration : bridging SDG4 with digital innovation / edited by Peter Ilic.
Description: Hershey, PA : IGI Global Scientific Publishing, [2026] | Includes bibliographical references and index. | Summary: "This book seeks to address a critical gap in current research and practice by examining the intersection of three vital domains: Information and Communication Technology (ICT), language education, and UN Sustainable Development Goal 4 (SDG4)"-- Provided by publisher.
Identifiers: LCCN 2025014129 (print) | LCCN 2025014130 (ebook) | ISBN 9798337308012 hardcover | ISBN 9798337308029 paperback | ISBN 9798337308036 ebook
Subjects: LCSH: Sustainable Development Goals (Project) | Language and languages--Study and teaching--Technological innovations | Language and languages--Computer-assisted instruction | LCGFT: Essays
Classification: LCC P53.855 .S77 2026 (print) | LCC P53.855 (ebook)
LC record available at https://lccn.loc.gov/2025014129
LC ebook record available at https://lccn.loc.gov/2025014130

British Cataloguing in Publication Data
A Cataloguing in Publication record for this book is available from the British Library.

Table of Contents

Detailed Table of Contents

Sustainable Development Goal 4 (SDG4) aims to ensure inclusive and equitable quality education and promote lifelong learning opportunities for all. However, achieving this ambitious goal requires more than traditional approaches. Innovation plays a crucial role in bridging the gap between the current state of education and the ambitious targets set by SDG4. It can transform teaching and learning practices, improve access to education, and enhance the relevance and quality of educational outcomes. While innovation holds immense promise for achieving SDG4, there are also challenges that need to be addressed. By embracing technology, fostering pedagogical innovation, and creating supportive policies, one can transform education systems and ensure that all learners have access to quality education and lifelong learning opportunities. This chapter delves into the intersection of SDG4 and innovation, examining how technology and policy can be leveraged to enhance the quality of education and promote digital learning.

The integration of information and communication technology (ICT) into language education has transformed traditional teaching methodologies by enhancing the educational experience and creating more personalized learning environments. Particularly, the inclusion of digital tools, virtual classrooms, and artificial intelligence-driven tutors have revolutionized how learners acquire language skills. However, challenges such as digital literacy gaps, limited access to technology, and insufficient professional development hinder the full potential of ICT in language education. By aligning ICT integration with the principles of inclusive and equitable education as outlined in the United Nations Sustainable Development Goal 4 (SDG 4), this chapter highlights the need for institutional support, professional training, and culturally responsive approaches to ensure that ICT serves as an effective tool for fostering linguistic diversity, global communication, and lifelong learning opportunities for all.

This study systematically reviews 44 Web of Science-indexed articles to examine the integration of artificial intelligence (AI) in foreign language education within higher education. Findings indicate that AI implementation in this field is a recent trend, with research activity increasing notably since 2022, especially in countries such as People's Republic of China and Ukraine. Key areas explored include teacher competence, ethical implications, AI tools for feedback, and assessment practices. AI demonstrates strong potential in enhancing language skills, particularly writing, speaking, vocabulary, and grammar. Despite its growing presence, AI research in this domain remains limited. The review identifies the need for greater collaboration, professional development, and ethical considerations. Furthermore, the study aligns with Sustainable Development Goal 4, underscoring AI's capacity to support inclusive and quality education.

The rapid advancement of Information and Communication Technology (ICT) offers unprecedented opportunities to enhance traditional language teaching. However, its integration into pedagogical practices often encounters significant challenges. This chapter delves into the complexities of transitioning from traditional methods to ICT-enhanced teaching, focusing on maintaining educational quality and respecting cultural sensitivities. Through an analytical lens, it explores barriers such as resistance to change, infrastructural limitations, lack of teacher training, and the need for culturally responsive materials. The chapter concludes with strategies to overcome these challenges, fostering an inclusive and effective ICT-enabled language learning environment.

Sustainable programme models are essential to achieve long-term sustainability in education programs, especially language learning. The research investigates models that combine resource efficiency strategies, efficient partnership models, and sustainable funding sources to facilitate quality learning experiences. An area of interest is the incorporation of Information and Communication Technology (ICT) to justify resource utilization and enhance accessibility. To provide even greater assistance to language education, adaptive learning and computer-based testing employ a BiStacked Artificial Neural Network (BiStacked ANN). PSO feature selection for applying only the most important features leads to applying just the most pertinent features, and this in turn enhances model efficiency. With the help of ICT and deep learning, the system gives assistance to an extendable, low-budget, and data-centered framework of learning that makes learning more, but at a sustainable pace

Pedagogical barriers exert significant impact on successful integration of ICT in education, hindering the effective utilization of technology for instructional purposes. Pedagogical barriers are recognized and categorized using an Improved Fuzzy C-Means (IFCM) clustering technique, reducing uncertainty in the processing of education data. 120 in-service teachers were sampled, focusing on their ICT experience, challenges, and awareness of sustainability. Preprocessing techniques like normalization and Ant Colony Optimization-based feature selection were employed to prepare the dataset for clustering. IFCM partitioned the teachers successfully on the basis of challenges, labeling predominant hindrances as inadequate technical training, institutional limitation, and resistance to change. The findings provide policymakers and teachers with clear advice on implementing strategic interventions for mitigating the mentioned barriers to boost ICT takeup in schools

In this study, we conducted a comparative analysis of the NIRF performance scores of the five oldest Indian Institutes of Management (IIMs) in India. The five IIMs were selected and data was collected over the past five years (2017-2021). The results show that all five IIMs have consistently performed well in the NIRF rankings, with IIM Ahmedabad consistently topping the rankings in the management category. The study also highlights the strong correlation between various NIRF parameters and their impact on overall NIRF performance scores. In conclusion, valuable insights into the performance of the five oldest IIMs in India, as assessed by the NIRF. Our findings demonstrate that these institutions continue to maintain high standards of quality in terms of teaching, research, and industry engagement. The results can be useful for institutions and stakeholders in higher education to better understand the NIRF ranking methodology and to develop strategies for improvement.

The Internet is increasingly integral part of our pupils' lives. From birth, children are exposed to technological advances, making technology a natural element of their daily life. Therefore, Information and Communication Technologies (hereinafter ICT) need to be present in the classroom, but in a thoughtful and coherent manner. ICTs have introduced significant changes in business practices, production processes, administration, ways of working, or employee training. However, in the education system, on the other hand, there has been little to no transformation in how education is managed, how young people learn, or in the methodologies employed in teaching. This chapter focuses on analysing the use of social networking and other web applications as effective tools for the improvement of English teaching in different fields. This research aims to formalise experiences and provide a practical reflection on how specific ICT tools can be used to drive changes in students' learning approaches, aligning with the objectives of SDG4.

We are currently living in the age of communication, a period that has transformed how society acquires knowledge. This change is also evident in the way we teach subjects across all levels, starting from Primary Education. 21st century students exemplify what is known as the multiple knowledge society. These learners, often referred to as "digital natives", were born into the communication era, teachers who must adapt their teaching methods to meet the needs of these new learners. To address this, this chapter focuses on a series of workshops utilising digital resources to enhance English language instruction. This initiative is part of a pilot project designed for third-cycle Primary Education students in Spain, aligning with the goals of SDG4. Such is the pervasive role of ICTs that a new term, Learning and Knowledge Technologies (LKT), has emerged within the field of education, evolving directly from ICTs. The goal of LKT is to guide the use of ICTs in a formative way. The purpose of ICTs is to help both students and teachers acquire better and more effective learning.

This chapter presents the development of educational resources to enrich the practice of prepositions of motion in English from a technological perspective. Web augmented reality technology is used to show animations that exemplify the use of prepositions in scenarios that combine virtual and objective elements. The representation of the situations has been carried out following recommendations obtained through generative artificial intelligence and the consultation of specialized literature on the subject of propositions in the English language. The educational resources developed can be used from any mobile device with Internet access and a camera, so it is possible to generate many scenarios and situations that encourage the practice of prepositions of motion. In this way, it is possible to address conditions that combine multiple elements, both real and virtual, favoring the teaching practice and

Preface

1. OVERVIEW OF THE SUBJECT MATTER

Strengthening Language Education Through ICT Integration: Bridging SDG4 With Digital Innovation examines how digital innovation and language education intersect with the Sustainable Development Goal 4 (SDG 4) mandate to ensure inclusive and equitable quality education. Contemporary language education increasingly relies on information and communication technologies (ICT) to deliver instruction, support multilingual learners and develop cross-cultural skills. The chapters assembled in this volume explore this landscape through several lenses. They examine digital transformations in education and map the opportunities and limitations of e-learning platforms, virtual/augmented reality, artificial intelligence (AI) tools and data-driven analytics (Chapters 1–6); investigate national and regional case studies of ICT integration in tertiary education (Chapter 7) and performance measurement systems (Chapter 8); and evaluate technology-enhanced language teaching in secondary and primary contexts (Chapters 9–10). The closing chapter demonstrates how generative AI and web-based augmented reality can create comprehensive learning resources for complex grammatical structures. Across these diverse studies, the volume stresses that digital technology must be thoughtfully implemented to advance SDG 4 rather than exacerbate inequalities.

2. POSITIONING THE TOPIC IN TODAY'S WORLD

The education sector is undergoing rapid digitalization. The United Nations notes that the rise of digital societies requires technology to be embedded in education so that learners acquire relevant, high-quality skills for a rapidly evolving labor market. Yet progress is uneven: in 2024 more than one fifth of primary schools still lacked basic services and roughly half lacked computers or internet for pedagogical purposes. During the COVID-19 pandemic, countries without robust ICT infrastructure suffered the most severe learning losses; up to one-third of students worldwide were left without access to education. These disruptions underscored that digital technology is now a social necessity for upholding the right to education. UNESCO therefore promotes digital innovation to expand access and enhance inclusion, building open and resilient learning systems and focusing on the digital literacy of teachers and students. The organization emphasizes a humanistic, rights-based approach that centers marginalized groups – women and girls, low-income populations, people with disabilities and linguistic minorities – ensuring that technology serves as a common good.

Technology can both bridge and widen educational divides. On one hand, digital platforms support second-language acquisition and provide multilingual open educational resources. For example, the Bloom Library hosts over 11 000 books in more than 500 languages and StoryWeaver offers 45 000 books in 323 languages, with over 60 % of them in indigenous tongues. Machine-translation projects and blended-learning courses deliver language training to refugees and migrants. On the other hand, digital content is often dominated by a few major languages; 92 % of the resources in the OER Commons are in English, and mass open online courses predominantly use English. Technology-based solutions are not always adapted to local contexts, potentially reinforcing inequalities. These global realities highlight why the contributions in this book – which analyze both technological innovations and the barriers to their adoption – are timely and relevant.

3. TARGET AUDIENCE

This book is designed for a multidisciplinary audience committed to advancing language education in line with SDG 4. Educational administrators and policy-makers will find evidence-based analyses of how national strategies and institutional practices influence the efficacy of ICT integration, including analyses of performance metrics and policy frameworks. Researchers and graduate students in applied linguistics, educational technology, and data science will value the systematic reviews, bibliometric analyses, deep-learning models and clustering algorithms presented across the chapters. Language teachers and curriculum designers can draw on practical case studies from higher-education, secondary, and primary classrooms, which illustrate how AI tutors, social media tools and blended-learning workshops can support communicative competence. Educational technologists and software developers will gain insight into how generative AI, augmented reality and open-source resources can be harnessed to create accessible learning materials. International organizations and NGOs concerned with educational equity and sustainable development will appreciate how the chapters situate technological innovations within broader debates on digital inclusion, gender equity, and regional disparities.

4. THE IMPORTANCE OF EACH CHAPTER

Chapter 1, Bridging SDG4 with Innovation for Quality Education, by Ananya Pandey of the School of Law, Christ University, Bangalore, India, explores how digital innovation can serve as a catalyst for achieving Sustainable Development Goal 4 (SDG4), which aims to ensure inclusive and equitable quality education for all by 2030. The research presents a comprehensive analysis of digital transformation in education, examining both opportunities and challenges inherent in implementing educational technologies. Pandey articulates SDG4's foundation through three core principles: (1) education as a fundamental human right, (2) education as a public good essential for developing critical thinking, and (3) the intrinsic link between universal education and gender equality.

The chapter investigates a range of digital innovations, e-learning platforms, eBooks, virtual and augmented reality, artificial intelligence systems, and online learning environments, that are reshaping educational delivery globally. The work's distinct contribution lies in its balanced and realistic assessment of digital education's potential without resorting to technological determinism. A critical concern raised is the widening digital divide, especially affecting marginalized communities; for example, nine out of ten young women in the world's poorest countries lack internet access. This highlights the paradox that, without equitable infrastructure, digital technologies may inadvertently reinforce educational inequalities.

The chapter's policy governance section discusses how public-private partnerships can foster sustainable digital education ecosystems. It underscores that realizing the goals of SDG4 requires coordinated efforts among governments, international organizations, educational institutions, and private sector actors. By avoiding technological idealism and focusing on systems-level change, the chapter contributes valid insights into how innovation can support rather than undermine quality education.

Chapter 2, Advancing Information and Communication Technology Integration in Language Education to Quality Education, by Kelly M. Torres of The Chicago School, United States, presents a comprehensive examination of how Information and Communication Technology (ICT) integration serves as a transformative force in language education while directly supporting the United Nations' Sustainable Development Goal 4 (SDG4), which aims to ensure inclusive, equitable, and quality education for all. Torres effectively bridges theoretical foundations and practical applications, illustrating how digital tools, ranging from AI-powered language tutors to virtual reality environments, fundamentally reshape traditional pedagogical models by enabling more personalized, accessible, and engaging learning experiences.

The chapter's distinctive contribution is its structured framework for understanding ICT integration, organized around three interrelated pillars: technology-enhanced pedagogy, educator capacity building, and sustainable implementation practices. Rather than offering a simple catalogue of technological benefits, Torres underscores the importance of the human element, how professional development and ongoing support empower educators to meaningfully incorporate these tools into their teaching. The discussion emphasizes that effective ICT adoption must go beyond surface-level engagement to include culturally responsive pedagogy, digital literacy training, and institutional strategies for long-term sustainability.

Torres highlights ICT's promise but acknowledges challenges. Notably, the chapter offers valuable insights into how ICT can democratize access to language learning for marginalized communities, while simultaneously equipping learners with essential 21st-century skills such as digital fluency and intercultural communication. By linking technological innovation with broader goals of educational equity and global inclusion, Torres demonstrates that ICT integration, when approached thoughtfully and strategically, is not merely an instructional enhancement but a vital mechanism for realizing the inclusive vision articulated in SDG4.

Chapter 3, Analyzing Artificial Intelligence Utilization in Foreign Language Education in Higher Education, by Dr. Ülkü Ülker of Dicle University (Ziya Gökalp Education Faculty), Turkey, presents a comprehensive systematic review of how artificial intelligence (AI) is being applied in foreign language education within higher education contexts. Based on 44 open-access studies drawn from the Web of Science Core Collection, the chapter investigates global research trends from 2019 to 2024, analyzing publication patterns, research methodologies, disciplinary concentrations, and the application of AI across the four core language skills.

Ülker's findings reveal that writing is the most commonly studied skill, and that mixed-methods research dominates the field. The analysis also uncovers notable geographic trends, with China and Ukraine identified as leading contributors to this area of scholarship, while simultaneously highlighting a persistent lack of international collaboration. The chapter categorizes the key thematic areas of AI-driven language education research, including pedagogical innovation, ethical considerations, teacher preparedness, and technological integration. These are framed in relation to the broader goals of Sustainable Development, with a particular emphasis on SDG 4 (Quality Education).

A unique strength of this chapter lies in its integration of bibliometric and content analysis techniques, enhanced by AI tools such as ChatGPT, Gemini, and Perplexity. These tools are leveraged to support SDG mapping and the visualization of emerging research trends, offering a methodologically rigorous foundation for scholars and policymakers alike. By aligning empirical insights with global development objectives, Ülker provides a perspective on how AI can shape the future of equitable and effective language education in higher education.

Chapter 4, Reimagining Language Teaching and Transforming Traditional Language Teaching with ICT Integration, by Seema Yadav of the Bhopal School of Social Sciences, India, examines the potential of artificial intelligence (AI) in enhancing foreign language acquisition within the Indian higher education context. The chapter offers a comprehensive analysis of AI's multifaceted contributions, from intelligent tutoring systems and natural language processing to personalized feedback and adaptive learning environments. Emphasizing India's vast linguistic diversity and rapidly evolving educational infrastructure, Yadav argues that AI holds substantial promise for democratizing language education and reducing socio-economic and geographic disparities.

A notable strength of this chapter is its critical engagement with the ethical, pedagogical, and infrastructural barriers to AI adoption. Yadav explores challenges such as the digital divide, insufficient teacher training, and data privacy concerns, grounding these issues in the Indian context. Rather than treating AI as a replacement for traditional instruction, the chapter advocates for its thoughtful integration to enrich existing pedagogical practices and make language learning more responsive to learners' needs.

Drawing on practical examples and policy perspectives, Yadav illustrates how AI-enhanced language education can foster more equitable and learner-centered outcomes. By aligning technological innovations with educational equity goals, the chapter contributes valuable insights into how ICT integration can reshape traditional language instruction to better serve a linguistically and socioeconomically diverse student population.

Chapter 5, Smart Education: A Deep Learning Approach for Sustainable Language Learning, by Usharani Bhimavarapu of the Department of Computer Science and Engineering at Koneru Lakshmaiah Education Foundation, India, presents a sophisticated computational framework for sustainable language education through the integration of deep learning methodologies within Information and Communication Technology (ICT) environments. The chapter introduces an adaptive learning model that combines a BiStacked Artificial Neural Network (BiStacked ANN) with Particle Swarm Optimization (PSO) for feature selection, aimed at enhancing personalized instruction while optimizing computational and educational resources.

Using user interaction data from 162,650 learners across 1,115 courses on the XuetangX.com platform, Bhimavarapu demonstrates how advanced machine learning techniques can drive adaptive, scalable, and efficient language learning systems. The BiStacked ANN model achieves a predictive accuracy of 92.3%, significantly outperforming traditional neural network models and other baseline machine learning algorithms. The PSO-based feature selection mechanism further improves the system by reducing computational complexity without sacrificing performance, making it suitable for deployment on large-scale educational platforms.

The unique contribution of this chapter lies in its seamless synthesis of computational intelligence and sustainable education. Bhimavarapu highlights how deep learning can be harnessed not only to improve educational outcomes but also to promote efficient use of resources, aligning the technological model with broader sustainability goals. By integrating artificial intelligence with sustainable design, the chapter offers a forward-looking approach to language learning that is both data-driven and environmentally conscious.

Chapter 6, Pedagogical Barriers to ICT Use: A Data-Driven Clustering Approach, by Usharani Bhimavarapu of the Department of Computer Science and Engineering at Koneru Lakshmaiah Education Foundation, India, applies an Improved Fuzzy C-Means (IFCM) clustering technique in combination with Ant Colony Optimization to analyze pedagogical barriers to ICT integration among 120 in-service teachers. Moving beyond traditional qualitative assessment, the chapter adopts a computational intelligence framework to systematically classify barriers based on variables such as ICT experience, sustainability awareness, and implementation challenges in educational contexts.

The study identifies three primary clusters of pedagogical barriers: insufficient technical training, institutional constraints, and resistance to pedagogical change. Notably, the fuzzy clustering approach allows the analysis to account for the overlapping and non-binary nature of these barriers, providing a more nuanced understanding than conventional classification methods. This is particularly relevant in education, where teacher challenges often span multiple categories and vary by context.

A demographic breakdown further enriches the analysis, revealing how variables such as years of teaching experience, type of institution, and prior ICT exposure influence teachers' readiness and ability to adopt digital tools in language education. These insights contribute to a more targeted approach for policymakers and institutional leaders aiming to overcome resistance and promote sustainable ICT integration. By combining data-driven clustering with actionable recommendations, Bhimavarapu offers a valuable methodological and practical contribution to the discourse on technology adoption in pedagogical practice.

Chapter 7, A Comparative Analysis of NIRF Performance Scores among the Oldest 5 IIMs in India, by Neeraj Sharma of the Department of Management Studies at Graphic Era (Deemed to be University), India; Rupesh Kumar of Jindal Global Business School, O.P. Jindal Global University, India; and Anurag Singh of BITS Dubai Campus, United Arab Emirates, presents a detailed comparative study of the National Institutional Ranking Framework (NIRF) performance scores across India's five oldest Indian Institutes of Management (IIMs), Ahmedabad, Bangalore, Calcutta,

Lucknow, and Indore, over the period from 2018 to 2022. Employing a factorial research design and ANOVA-based quantitative methodology, the authors analyze institutional performance across five key NIRF dimensions: Teaching, Learning & Resources (TLR), Research & Professional Practice (RP), Graduation Outcomes (GO), Outreach & Inclusivity (OI), and Peer Perception (PR).

The chapter's unique contribution lies in situating this institutional analysis within the broader policy discourse surrounding Sustainable Development Goal 4 (SDG 4), with a focus on how existing NIRF indicators reflect, or fail to reflect, digital innovation and language education capabilities. The findings reveal considerable variability in performance both across institutions and between metrics. While IIM Ahmedabad and IIM Bangalore consistently top the rankings, IIM Indore, and IIM Lucknow exhibit relative weaknesses, particularly in the areas of research output and peer perception.

Beyond quantitative trends, Kumar provides a critical assessment of the NIRF methodology itself, pointing to structural blind spots including limited attention to linguistic inclusivity, digital accessibility, and the integration of ICT in pedagogy. The chapter also incorporates qualitative case studies illustrating how IIMs have adopted digital systems in areas such as library services, administrative functions, and course delivery, particularly in response to the pandemic. The analysis critiques systemic biases embedded in the ranking framework, such as the urban-centric weighting, perception-driven favorability toward legacy institutions, and insufficient normalization for differences in institutional scale and resources.

The chapter concludes with specific policy recommendations for both individual IIMs and national-level ranking bodies. These include calls for the integration of multilingual education indicators, stronger digital equity metrics, and more nuanced frameworks that align ranking methodologies with the innovation-oriented principles of SDG 4. In doing so, the authors contribute to an important reevaluation of how institutional performance is measured and how it might better reflect the potentiality of technology in higher education.

Chapter 8, Integrating ICTs to Deliver Quality EFL Education in a Spanish Secondary Education Classroom, by Isabel María García of the Centro Universitario de la Defensa de San Javier, Spain, provides a comprehensive examination of Information and Communication Technology (ICT) integration in English as a Foreign Language (EFL) education within the Spanish secondary school context, with a particular focus on aligning with Sustainable Development Goal 4 (SDG 4): ensuring inclusive and equitable quality education. García explores how social networking and web-based applications can serve as pedagogical tools to bridge the persistent gap between societal technological advancement and its effective use in classroom instruction.

The theoretical framework of the chapter is anchored in two key hypotheses: first, that education must mirror the digital transformation occurring in modern workplaces to better prepare students for adult life; and second, that successful ICT integration requires not just technical competence but also pedagogical training to ensure that digital tools enhance rather than simply replicate traditional learning experiences.

The chapter's unique contribution lies in García's detailed and practical analysis of specific digital platforms and their pedagogical affordances. Tools such as Delicious (for organizing learning resources), WebQuests (to promote constructivist learning), Flickr (for visual literacy), Moodle (as a comprehensive learning management system), ThatQuiz (for assessment), discussion forums (for collaborative learning), Twitter (for concise communication), and Google Docs (for collaborative writing) are all evaluated not only for their functionality but for their pedagogical impact in supporting language acquisition.

Rather than advocating for superficial digitization, García emphasizes the importance of systemic change, highlighting that consequential ICT integration demands sustained teacher professional development, institutional commitment, and methodological innovation. The chapter offers a holistic vision of how technology can be leveraged to create authentic, student-centered, and communicative language learning environments. By moving beyond tool-based instruction to focus on transformative practice, García contributes a model for technology-enhanced EFL education that supports 21st-century learning objectives and global communicative competence.

Chapter 9, Utilizing Digital Resources in an EFL Primary Education Class to Implement SDG4 Objective, by Antonio Daniel Juan Rubio of Universidad de Granada, Spain, investigates the role of digital resource integration in English as a Foreign Language (EFL) instruction for third-cycle primary school students in Granada. The study is explicitly framed around the Sustainable Development Goal 4 (SDG 4) mandate to ensure quality education and reflects a broader pedagogical shift from Information and Communication Technologies (ICT) to Learning and Knowledge Technologies (LKT). This transition emphasizes technology as a support system for cultivating "learning to learn" competencies rather than simply mediating content delivery.

Grounded in Howard Gardner's Theory of Multiple Intelligences, the chapter argues that digital tools can accommodate a range of cognitive strengths and learning styles, thereby moving beyond the limitations of 20th-century pedagogies focused on rote memorization and passive instruction. Rubio also addresses the generational divide between "Digital Natives", students who are naturally immersed in technology, and "Digital Immigrants", educators required to adapt to evolving digital platforms. This dynamic, the chapter notes, shapes classroom engagement, pedagogical effectiveness, and overall learning outcomes.

The chapter's unique contribution lies in its detailed pilot project comprising a sequence of digital workshops targeting all four core language skills: listening, reading, speaking, and writing. Each skill area is supported by paired digital tools, such as Listen and Write combined with Voki for listening comprehension, Storybird with Reading Planet for reading development, Voxopop with Skype for oral communication, and Dvolver Moviemaker with Wordle for writing instruction. These activities are aligned with both Spanish educational policy and the European Union's digital competence frameworks, providing a concrete, curriculum-aligned model for meaningful technology integration in early language education.

By emphasizing communicative competence, learner autonomy, and the practical application of digital tools within legislative guidelines, Rubio contributes a scalable approach for primary educators seeking to implement SDG 4 in linguistically and digitally enriched classroom environments.

Chapter 10, Development of Educational Resources Aimed at Learning Prepositions of Movement in the English Language Using Generative Artificial Intelligence, by Anabelem Soberanes-Martín, José Luis Castillo-Mendoza, and Edgar Serrano-Pérez of Universidad Autónoma del Estado de México, Mexico, presents an innovative pedagogical approach that combines Generative Artificial Intelligence (GAI) and Web Augmented Reality (WebAR) to address the long-standing challenge of teaching English prepositions of movement to second language learners.

The study targets a particularly complex area of English grammar, spatial prepositions such as "across," "through," "under," and "over", which are often taught using static, two-dimensional representations that fail to convey the dynamic, three-dimensional nature of movement these terms describe. The unique contribution of this work lies in its strategic integration of GAI and WebAR to create immersive and contextualized learning environments that enhance grammatical comprehension through real-world simulation.

Using ChatGPT to generate linguistic parameters and program code, alongside A-Frame technology to construct interactive AR animations, the authors provide a replicable model that enables educators to develop advanced instructional materials without needing extensive technical expertise or costly infrastructure. The mobile-first, WebAR approach enhances accessibility for learners from diverse socio-economic backgrounds, making the project particularly relevant for addressing equity concerns central to SDG 4.

Empirical validation was conducted using the System Usability Scale (SUS), with data collected from 88 students and 5 teachers across three higher education institutions. The results, average scores of 91.66 for students and 89.74 for teachers, fall within the "excellent" usability category, confirming the platform's effectiveness in delivering pedagogically sound and user-friendly learning experiences.

This chapter offers a constructive framework for language educators seeking to harness the potential of emerging technologies to improve grammar instruction. By prioritizing both accessibility and pedagogical rigor, the authors demonstrate how thoughtful GAI-AR integration can redefine traditional approaches to language education while promoting the broad and innovative values at the heart of SDG 4.

5. CONCLUSION AND CONTRIBUTION TO THE FIELD

By bringing together diverse research on ICT-enhanced language education, this volume offers a holistic appraisal of how digital innovation can support SDG 4. The chapters not only showcase cutting-edge technologies but also interrogate their pedagogical value, ethical implications, and sustainability. The studies emphasize that digital tools must be accompanied by capacity building for educators, institutional support and policy frameworks that address infrastructure gaps and digital divides. Insights from deep-learning models and clustering analyses reveal patterns in learner engagement and barriers to adoption, while cross-country case studies illustrate how context shapes technology use. Examples of generative AI and augmented reality demonstrate how emerging technologies can create inclusive, mobile-friendly resources for complex language skills.

Collectively, the book reinforces the idea that technology is not a panacea but a catalyst when aligned with human rights and equity principles. It underscores the imperative to design technology-enhanced language education that is contextually appropriate, linguistically accessible to all learners, echoing UNESCO's call for digital innovation to be leveraged as a common good. By bridging rigorous research with practical applications, this volume contributes to the global dialogue on how to harness ICT to make quality language education more sustainable in the digital age.

Chapter 1
Bridging SDG4 With Innovation for Quality Education:
A Way Foreward

Ananya Pandey
https://orcid.org/0000-0002-2419-6314
Christ University, Bangalore, India

ABSTRACT

Sustainable Development Goal 4 (SDG4) aims to ensure inclusive and equitable quality education and promote lifelong learning opportunities for all. However, achieving this ambitious goal requires more than traditional approaches. Innovation plays a crucial role in bridging the gap between the current state of education and the ambitious targets set by SDG4. It can transform teaching and learning practices, improve access to education, and enhance the relevance and quality of educational outcomes. While innovation holds immense promise for achieving SDG4, there are also challenges that need to be addressed. By embracing technology, fostering pedagogical innovation, and creating supportive policies, one can transform education systems and ensure that all learners have access to quality education and lifelong learning opportunities. This chapter delves into the intersection of SDG4 and innovation, examining how technology and policy can be leveraged to enhance the quality of education and promote digital learning.

DOI: 10.4018/979-8-3373-0801-2.ch001

INTRODUCTION

"A plan of action for people, planet, and prosperity" is what the 2030 Agenda for Sustainable Development is. There are seventeen Sustainable Development Goals (SDGs) in all. These objectives, which have social, economic, and environmental components, are inseparable (Jain, 2020). The fourth Sustainable Development Goal aims to "ensure inclusive and equitable quality education and promote lifelong learning opportunities for all." This objective, which highlights the transformational potential of education in creating a sustainable and just world, is a key force for good change (Ferguson et al., 2018). In terms of both access and quality, this objective promotes the lessening of imbalances and disparities in education. It acknowledges that everyone, but particularly vulnerable groups including impoverished children, children living in rural regions, people with disabilities, indigenous people, and refugee children, require access to high-quality education (Saini et al., 2023). Due to its transformative impact on the other SDGs, this goal is extremely important. The provision of high-quality education to all children is essential to sustainable development. When children are given the resources, they need to reach their full potential, they grow up to be successful individuals who can contribute to their communities and end the cycle of poverty (McGreal, 2017). Socioeconomic mobility upward is made possible by education.

In the current technology era, digital transformation in education is quickly becoming a trend. In addition to optimizing instructional activities, the use of contemporary technological solutions offers real-world advantages to educators, learners, and educational establishments (Haleem et al., 2022). The process of integrating digital technologies into teaching, learning, and educational administration is known as "digital transformation" in education. This entails strengthening training participants' and students' learning experiences, refining teaching strategies, and updating learning support resources (McCarthy et al., 2023). Digital transformation involves more than just transferring information to internet platforms or digitizing course materials; it also generates new methods for teaching. It makes individualized learning routes possible, improves teacher-student connection, and boosts school administration effectiveness (Joseph et al., 2024). This contributes to the development of an adaptable, practical learning environment where students can access information at any time and from any location. Platforms such as EdX, Udemy, and Coursera are excellent illustrations of how education is changing digitally (Likovič & Rojko, 2022). Instead of attending traditional classes, students can take courses at any time and from any location. These platforms provide a wide range of learning materials, such as assignments, online tests, and video lectures, enabling students to arrange their study schedules and places whichever best suits their needs while maximizing their ability to absorb information (Taylor, 2002).

However, in an era of rapid technological advancement, ensuring inclusive, equitable, and quality education (SDG 4) remains a challenge, especially for underserved communities. Traditional education models often struggle to adapt to the evolving digital landscape, leading to disparities in access, engagement, and learning outcomes (Rosa, 2017). Despite the potential of digital innovation—such as AI-driven personalized learning, immersive technologies, and data-driven educational strategies—many schools and learners face barriers including inadequate infrastructure, digital literacy gaps, and limited access to quality digital content (Laak & Aru, 2024). Keeping in view the above perspective, this chapter aims to provide a comprehensive analysis of how digital innovation can serve as a catalyst for achieving SDG4, ensuring inclusive, equitable, and quality education for all.

UNDERSTANDING SDG 4: QUALITY EDUCATION FOR ALL

SDG4 is based on three fundamental ideas. *Firstly*, a basic human right and an enabling right is education. In order to implement this right, nations must guarantee that all people, regardless of gender, disability, social status, or economic background, have free, mandatory access to inclusive, equitable, and high-quality education and learning (Ashley, 2016). In addition to fostering friendship, tolerance, understanding, and peace, education should strive for the whole development of the human personality (Savolainen & Torney-Purta, 2011). *Secondly*, education should foster curiosity, bravery, and resilience while empowering people with critical thinking, creative, and collaborative skills in addition to basic literacy and numeracy abilities. The state bears the responsibility for education, which is a public good (Tracey et al., 2016). Since education is a shared communal enterprise, it involves an inclusive process of formulating and implementing public policies, in which key roles are played by civil society, educators, the private sector, communities, families, youth, and children (Ghaus-Pasha, 2005). The state plays a crucial role in establishing and enforcing norms and standards. *Lastly*, the right to universal education is linked to gender equality. A right-based strategy that guarantees that men and women, boys and girls, not only have equal access to and completion of educational cycles, but also get equal empowerment in and via education is necessary to achieve gender equality (Peppin Vaughan, 2016).

ROLE OF DIGITAL TECHNOLOGY IN EDUCATION

Education innovation is not a well-defined phrase. The spirit of innovation education is an openness to seeing challenges from new perspectives and approaching them in novel ways. It is an acknowledgment that one do not have all of the answers and are open to new ways to improve, such as information transfer methods combined with novel teaching strategies (Serdyukov, 2017). Innovation in education comes from identifying problems, observing and learning from others, developing new approaches to solve these difficulties, and iterating on them when these experiments do not produce the desired outcomes (Diallo, 2014). One of the primary ways that technology improves the learning experience is through the utilization of digital resources (Lebler, 2012). E-books, online films, and interactive simulations are examples of digital resources that give students easy and quick access to a plethora of information. This can help to make the learning process more engaging and dynamic while also increasing student involvement and motivation (Haleem et al., 2022). Another way that technology improves the learning experience is the usage of online learning platforms. Online learning platforms like Blackboard, Moodle, and Canvas make it easy for students to access course materials, communicate with their lecturers and classmates, and complete assignments and evaluations (Parveen & Ramzan, 2024). This can help make the learning process more adaptable. Technology is also being used to improve the learning experience by utilizing virtual and augmented reality (Lee, 2012). Virtual and augmented reality can offer students an immersive and dynamic learning experience while also simulating real-world events like field excursions and laboratory research. This can help to make the learning process more engaging and dynamic while also increasing student involvement and motivation (Zhao et al., 2023). The use of artificial intelligence (AI) and machine learning is another method in which technology improves learning experiences. Artificial intelligence and machine learning can be used to tailor the learning experience for each student by creating individualized learning routes and feedback (Fitria, 2021). Gamification is another example of how technology is being utilized to improve the learning experience. Gamification is the use of game-like elements, such as points, badges, and leaderboards, to make the learning experience more interesting and participatory. This can make the learning experience more enjoyable and engaging while also increasing student involvement and motivation (Smiderle et al., 2020). Some of the digital innovations in education are described below.

E-Learning

E-learning is an educational technique that uses information and communication technology (ICT) to deliver educational content and resources through online platforms (Bates, 2005). Unlike traditional education in physical classrooms, e-learning allows students to access training materials, participate in activities, and interact with instructional materials using electronic devices such as computers, mobile phones, and even Virtual or Augmented Reality (VR, AR) (Culduz, 2024).

In recent years, e-learning has grown dramatically, owing to a variety of factors like societal digitalization and a growing desire for customizable and easily accessible training, among others (Wong, 2007). This phenomenon indicates not just a shift in how knowledge is communicated and learned, but also an effective reaction to the changing demands of today's digitalized society (Verhoef et al., 2021). E-learning enables teachers to improve their teaching methods by incorporating new technologies and novel educational approaches. This allows them to provide more engaging and effective learning experiences (Mohammed et al., 2017).

eBooks

eBooks have opened the doors of education to the entire world, allowing students to easily access course materials regardless of their location. Furthermore, they contribute significantly to closing the educational gap between pupils from wealthy and lower socioeconomic backgrounds (Hadaya & Hanif, 2019). eBooks are also simple to translate into many languages, which helps to break down language barriers and level the playing field in education regardless of how diverse the student population is (Brigula, 2017). eBooks have opened the doors of education to the entire world, allowing students to easily access course materials regardless of their location. Furthermore, they contribute significantly to closing the educational gap between pupils from wealthy and lower socioeconomic backgrounds (Davidson & Carliner, 2014). eBooks are also simple to translate into many languages, which helps to break down language barriers and level the playing field in education regardless of how diverse the student population is (Alotaibi & Salamah, 2023).

Online Learning Platforms

Online platforms provide a vast choice of courses to suit various interests and career goals. Students can explore their passions and gain skills relevant to the modern job market in a variety of fields, including coding, digital marketing, soft skills, and the creative arts (Sofi-Karim et al., 2023). Various examples of online learning platforms include Moodle, Google Classroom, Unacademy, Udemy and the like.

Virtual and Augmented Reality

Knowledge transfer, which is the foundation of contemporary education, is critical in today's society. Information and communication technology are becoming increasingly important in the teaching and learning processes (Ghaznavi et al., 2011). Virtual reality, augmented reality, and 3D technologies are now used in all sectors that involve educational activities. These technologies have assisted learners worldwide in internalizing complicated issues, applying knowledge to problem solving, and engaging with diverse cultures in the natural sciences, social sciences, and humanities (Alkhawaldeh & Khasawneh, 2023). Virtual reality is a computer-generated simulation that affects our perceptions of reality. In its most basic form, virtual reality is a world filled with synthetic sights and objects that appear to be real (Gudoniene, & Rutkauskiene, 2019). Individuals can experience other worlds to their own and believe them to be genuine by using particular technology gadgets such as glasses or helmets. Because virtual reality produces parallel realities that feel very real, it has been utilized in education to help pupils learn complicated subjects and form friendships across cultural boundaries (Sala, 2021). Virtual reality can help to educate respect for cultural variety and increase acceptance of differences. Virtual reality is transforming the education business, including the job of teachers (Boyles, 2017). Before the COVID-19 epidemic, teachers utilized less technology and taught in a face-to-face setting. Today, with the emphasis on virtual education environments, teachers want to focus on facilitating the transmission of material to pupils via technology. As a result, virtual reality enables students and teachers to explore content together and create collaborative knowledge (Kesim & Ozarslan, 2012).

Augmented reality has had a significant impact on education by making it feasible to improve learning processes in the classroom. Augmented reality, for example, has piqued the interest of geometry teachers since it helps them to illustrate basic concepts like perimeters, areas, and diameters (Pelagros et al., 2017). Augmented reality is a sophisticated combination of technologies that enable people to perceive an important aspect of the world using technological devices that collect information from their surroundings, such as mobile phones and tablets (Jumani et al., 20220. In general, augmented reality overlays sights, sounds, movies, and graphics onto a given environment. Augmented reality incorporates key components such as cameras and sensors, computation, projection, and reflection (Kaufmann, 2003).

Artificial Intelligence and Machine Learning

AI-powered instructional technology, apps, and platforms are sweeping the education landscape. Machine learning has grown popular in teaching. These technologies are growing more popular. Their applications are visible in the form of interactive textbooks and assessment tools (Huang & Khan, 2021). Educational tools can help students study more effectively when used properly. One example would be the usage of AI-powered language translation. Such improvements allow students from many backgrounds to participate in lectures (Tiwari, 2023). One of the most significant advantages of AI and Machine Learning in education is the capacity to tailor learning experiences. Traditional schools frequently use a one-size-fits-all approach, despite the fact that no two pupils learn the same way (Luan & Tsai, 2021). AI addresses this by tailoring information and pacing to each student's learning style and pace. Consider a math lesson in which each student receives practice problems based on their present level of understanding (Nafea, 2018). If a student grasps a concept fast, AI might assign more difficult assignments to keep them interested. If a learner struggles with a concept, AI can provide extra explanations and smaller exercises until they understand the material (Popenici & Kerr, 2017). AI has a significant impact on how assessments and evaluations are conducted in education. Historically, teachers have spent a significant amount of time marking assignments and tests (Chen et al., 2020). AI-powered grading systems can assess and evaluate student replies fast and accurately. This not only saves teachers time, but also allows students to receive speedier feedback on their work (Ouyang & Jiao, 2021). Formative assessments, which measure students' progress during a course, gain significantly from AI. By continuously monitoring student performance data, AI can detect areas where students are suffering and provide further assistance (Limna et al., 2022). This real-time feedback enables teachers to tailor their teaching tactics to better match the requirements of their students, ensuring that no one falls behind. Contrary to expectations that AI will replace instructors, its genuine promise rests in improving their talents (Zhai et al., 2021). AI can help educators manage administrative work and provide individualized support to pupils. In lesson planning, AI-powered technologies can provide teaching materials and resources that are suited to specific learning objectives (Fitria, 2021). These technologies sift through large volumes of instructional content and recommend the most relevant and successful resources for instructors to use in the classroom (Eyyam & Yaratan, 2014). AI can help with classroom management by automating mundane chores like attendance and scheduling. This automation enables teachers to spend more time teaching and interacting with students, resulting in a more engaging and productive learning environment (Rahm, 2023).

CHALLENGES AND ETHICAL CONSIDERATIONS

The challenges and ethical considerations in digital education navigate the delicate landscape in which technology and education meet, addressing the ethical factors that define the digital learning experience. Some of the significant hurdles are described below.

Digital Divide

Access to technology has become an absolute requirement for a great education anywhere in the world. Even in a world that appears to be completely digitized for many, there is still a considerable digital divide between cultures, which disproportionately impacts marginalized populations, particularly in rural areas of low-income countries (Nemer, 2015). This issue exacerbates educational inequality and perpetuates poverty cycles in developing countries. The digital divide in education has far-reaching implications (Parsons & Hick, 2008). It not only limits students' daily access to information, but it also has an impact on the overall level of education they receive over time (Livingstone & Helsper, 2007). The epidemic has increased this divide furthermore, as only educational systems with digital skills can adapt to a totally digital learning environment (Molina, 2003). This left millions of pupils behind, making the problem more severe than ever. According to UNICEF research, nine out of ten young women and adolescent girls in the world's poorest countries lack internet access. The most evident manifestation of the digital divide is a lack of access to critical technology (Elahi, 2020). This includes PCs, iPads, and an Internet connection. In many low-income and isolated places, kids may lack access to even the most basic technology instruments needed for modern education (Tarman, 2003). Beyond mere access, there is a considerable divide in digital literacy, or the capacity to utilize technology efficiently. Many children in underserved neighborhoods lack the necessary abilities to traverse digital platforms, limiting their capacity to benefit from online educational resources (Cruz-Jesus et al., 2016). The global digital divide has far-reaching ramifications for education, influencing everything from access to learning resources to educational attainment. These outcomes include unemployment, poverty, regional environmental pressure, access to healthcare, and the possibility of proper education for the next generation (Moore et al., 2018).

Privacy and Security

Online learning platforms capture a large quantity of personal information from students, including names, addresses, contact information, academic records, and, in some cases, biometric data (Stahl & Karger, 2016). This sensitive information, which is frequently held online, makes it an ideal target for fraudsters. Data breaches, such as illegal access or theft of personal information, are a serious threat to students' privacy and security (Kumar et al., 2019). Furthermore, sharing student data with third-party service providers for analytics, marketing, or research raises worries about data misuse, illegal access, and the possibility that data will be sold or used for malevolent reasons (Amo et al., 2020). These challenges underscore the need of online learning platforms implementing comprehensive data protection mechanisms and being transparent about their data management policies (Kamenskih, 2022). Several factors increase the vulnerability of online education platforms to data breaches and security problems. This includes: weak cyber infrastructure where many educational institutions lack adequate cybersecurity protections, making them vulnerable to assault (Burov et al., 2020). Also, lack of awareness where the students and teachers frequently have insufficient knowledge of cybersecurity best practices, rendering them vulnerable to phishing and social engineering attacks (Alexei & Alexei, 2021). Furthermore, third-party risks include the usage of third-party service providers increases security concerns because data breaches at these providers can affect student information. Regulatory compliance is inclusive of navigating the complicated environment of data privacy requirements can be difficult for educational institutions, increasing the likelihood of noncompliance (Burov et al., 2020).

Training and Adaptation to Advancements

Inadequate digital abilities and technical challenges can impede successful learning outcomes. Maintaining engagement in a digital setting can be challenging due to the lack of personalized connection compared to traditional training approaches (Haleem et al., 2022).

POLICY GOVERNANCE FOR SUSTAINABLE DIGITAL EDUCATION

Many higher education institutions are straining to provide excellent, cost-effective education and research while simultaneously maintaining and enhancing their infrastructure. A public-private partnership (PPPs) could be the best alternative for non-core educational services including real estate, buildings, and front/back-office management (Patrinos, 2023). These agreements could take the shape of an operating contract/management agreement, a ground lease/facility lease, an availability payment, or a demand-risk concession (Robertson & Verger, 2012). Education benefits from private sector participation because it provides new viewpoints, innovative instructional methods, and technological integration (Rose, 2013). PPPs allow schools and colleges to leverage the private sector's experience in curriculum creation, teacher training, pedagogy, and instructional design. This leads to higher teaching quality, better learning experiences, and better academic results (Davies & Hentschke, 2006). PPPs promote the integration of industry-relevant skills and vocational training, bring industry experience and contacts, and expand internship and placement possibilities, allowing educational programs to better correspond with changing job market demands (Verger et al., 2016). This relationship provides students with practical skills, improves employability, and contributes to national economic growth by developing a trained workforce. PPPs divide risk and reward between the public and private sectors (Pillay et al., 2013). Governments can transfer financial and operational risks to private partners, easing the load on public coffers. At the same time, private partners can be compensated through revenue-sharing arrangements or performance-based contracts, which aligns their interests with operational excellence (Wang, 1999).

Furthermore, Governments and international organizations play an important role in expanding digital education by developing regulations, sponsoring initiatives, and assuring equal access to technology (Mhlongo et al., 2023). Governments create digital curricula, invest in infrastructure, and train teachers to bring technology into the classroom. International organizations such as UNESCO and the World Bank promote global digital literacy programs, advocate for inclusive education, and foster international collaboration (Kapur et al., 2018). They also help to close the digital gap by encouraging inexpensive internet access and open educational resources. By collaborating, these organizations build a more accessible, innovative, and future-ready education system that empowers students worldwide (Jhurry & Rampersad, 2022).

CONCLUSION

In the pursuit of Sustainable Development Goal 4 (SDG4), which calls for inclusive and equitable quality education for everyone, innovation emerges as a revolutionary force. Digital technology and novel pedagogies are transforming learning by breaking down obstacles to accessibility, affordability, and inclusivity. The integration of artificial intelligence, virtual learning environments, and adaptive learning tools personalizes education, meets various learning needs, and provides educators with data-driven insights. Furthermore, digital platforms offer remote learning, which strengthens education during times of disaster, such as the COVID-19 epidemic. However, while technology has enormous potential, the digital divide remains a major issue. Disparities in access to digital infrastructure, internet connectivity, and technology literacy can exacerbate rather than alleviate existing inequities. To truly link innovation with SDG4, governments, legislators, and stakeholders must collaborate to provide equal access to digital resources, especially in underprivileged areas. Investments in teacher training, curriculum reform, and digital literacy programs are critical for reaping the benefits of technology-driven education. Furthermore, ethical concerns about data privacy, digital well-being, and the responsible use of AI in education must be highlighted. Traditional teaching approaches should be supplemented and enhanced by innovation, resulting in a balanced, student-centered learning environment. By cultivating a culture of constant innovation and inclusivity, one can leverage digital horizons to create a future in which great education is available to all, helping individuals and communities to prosper in an increasingly knowledge-driven world. Achieving SDG4 through innovation is more than a technological challenge; it is a societal obligation that necessitates dedication, teamwork, and a vision for a more equal educational landscape.

REFERENCES

Alexei, L. A., & Alexei, A. (2021). Cyber security threat analysis in higher education institutions as a result of distance learning. *International Journal of Scientific and Technology Research*, (3), 128–133.

Alkhawaldeh, M. A., & Khasawneh, M. A. S. (2023). Exploring virtual reality as a transformative tool for enhancing learning abilities in students with disabilities. *Journal of Namibian Studies: History Politics Culture*, *35*, 861–882.

Alotaibi, H., & Salamah, D. (2023). The impact of translation apps on translation students' performance. *Education and Information Technologies*, *28*(8), 10709–10729. DOI: 10.1007/s10639-023-11578-y

Amo, D., Torres, R., Canaleta, X., Herrero-Martín, J., Rodríguez-Merino, C., & Fonseca, D. (2020, October). Seven principles to foster privacy and security in educational tools: Local Educational Data Analytics. In *Eighth International Conference on Technological Ecosystems for Enhancing Multiculturality* (pp. 730-737). DOI: 10.1145/3434780.3436637

Ashley, S. L. (2016). Unpacking an over-packed agenda for the marginalized: Problematizing sustainable development goal 4, targets 4.6 and 4.7. *Andragoške studije*, (2), 9-19.

Bates, A. W. (2005). Technology, e-learning and distance education.

Boyles, B. (2017). Virtual reality and augmented reality in education. *Center For Teaching Excellence, United States Military Academy, West Point, Ny, 67.*

Bringula, R. P. (2017). Influence of usage of e-books, online educational materials, and other programming books and students' profiles on adoption of printed programming textbooks. *Program*, *51*(4), 441–457. DOI: 10.1108/PROG-06-2015-0046

Burov, O., Lytvynova, S., Lavrov, E., Krylova-Grek, Y., Orliyk, O., Petrenko, S., . . . Tkachenko, O. M. (2020). Cybersecurity in educational networks. In *Intelligent Human Systems Integration 2020: Proceedings of the 3rd International Conference on Intelligent Human Systems Integration (IHSI 2020): Integrating People and Intelligent Systems, February 19-21, 2020, Modena, Italy* (pp. 359-364). Springer International Publishing. DOI: 10.1007/978-3-030-39512-4_56

Burov, O. Y., Butnik-Siversky, O. B., Orliuk, O., & Horska, K. A. (2020). Cybersecurity and innovative digital educational environment. *Інформаційні технології і засоби навчання, 6*(80), 414-430.

Chen, L., Chen, P., & Lin, Z. (2020). Artificial intelligence in education: A review. *IEEE Access : Practical Innovations, Open Solutions, 8*, 75264–75278. DOI: 10.1109/ACCESS.2020.2988510

Cruz-Jesus, F., Vicente, M. R., Bacao, F., & Oliveira, T. (2016). The education-related digital divide: An analysis for the EU-28. *Computers in Human Behavior, 56*, 72–82. DOI: 10.1016/j.chb.2015.11.027

Culduz, M. (2024). Benefits and Challenges of E-Learning, Online Education, and Distance Learning. In *Incorporating the Human Element in Online Teaching and Learning* (pp. 1–27). IGI Global. DOI: 10.4018/979-8-3693-4131-5.ch001

Davidson, A. L., & Carliner, S. (2014). E-books for educational uses. *Handbook of research on educational communications and technology*, 713-722.

Davies, B., & Hentschke, G. (2006). Public–private partnerships in education: Insights from the field. *School Leadership & Management, 26*(3), 205–226. DOI: 10.1080/13632430600736977

Diallo, A. (2014). *The Use of Technology to Enhance The Learning Experience of ESL Students*. Online Submission.

Elahi, F. (2020). *Digital inclusion: Bridging divides*. Cumberland Lodge.

Eyyam, R., & Yaratan, H. S. (2014). Impact of use of technology in mathematics lessons on student achievement and attitudes. *Social Behavior and Personality, 42*(1), 31S–42S. DOI: 10.2224/sbp.2014.42.0.S31

Ferguson, T., Iliško, D., Roofe, C., & Hill, S. (2018). *SDG4–Quality Education: Inclusivity, Equity and Lifelong Learning for All*. Emerald Publishing Limited. DOI: 10.1108/9781787694231

Fitria, T. N. (2021, Dec). Artificial intelligence (AI) in education: Using AI tools for teaching and learning process. In *Prosiding Seminar Nasional & Call for Paper STIE AAS* (Vol. 4, No. 1, pp. 134-147).

Ghaus-Pasha, A. (2005, May). Role of civil society organizations in governance. In *Kertas Persidangan 6th Global Forum on Reinventing Government Towards Participatory and Transparent Governance. Seoul* (pp. 24-27).

Ghaznavi, M. R., Keikha, A., & Yaghoubi, N. M. (2011). The Impact of Information and Communication Technology (ICT) on Educational Improvement. *International Education Studies, 4*(2), 116–125. DOI: 10.5539/ies.v4n2p116

Gudoniene, D., & Rutkauskiene, D. (2019). Virtual and augmented reality in education. *Baltic Journal of Modern Computing*, *7*(2), 293–300. DOI: 10.22364/bjmc.2019.7.2.07

Hadaya, A., & Hanif, M. (2019). The Impact of Using the Interactive E-Book on Students' Learning Outcomes. *International Journal of Instruction*, *12*(2), 709–722. DOI: 10.29333/iji.2019.12245a

Haleem, A., Javaid, M., Qadri, M. A., & Suman, R. (2022). Understanding the role of digital technologies in education: A review. *Sustainable operations and computers, 3*, 275-285.

Huang, Y., & Khan, S. M. (2021). Advances in AI and machine learning for education research. *Computational Psychometrics: New Methodologies for a New Generation of Digital Learning and Assessment: With Examples in R and Python*, 195-208.

Jain, E. (2020). A review study on sustainable development goals: Un 2030 Agenda. *Our Heritage*, *68*(5), 1–13.

Jhurry, D., & Rampersad, R. D. (2022). From online learning to digital transformation. *Quality Assuring Unknown Territory, 57.*

Joseph, O., Onwuzulike, O., & Shitu, K. (2024). Digital transformation in education: Strategies for effective implementation. *World Journal of Advanced Research and Reviews.*, *2*.DOI: .30574/wjarr

Jumani, A. K., Siddique, W. A., Laghari, A. A., Abro, A., & Khan, A. A. (2022). Virtual reality and augmented reality for education. In *Multimedia computing systems and virtual reality* (pp. 189–210). CRC Press. DOI: 10.1201/9781003196686-9

Kamenskih, A. (2022). The analysis of security and privacy risks in smart education environments. *Journal of Smart Cities and Society*, *1*(1), 17–29. DOI: 10.3233/SCS-210114

Kapur, R., Byfield, V., Del Frate, F., Higgins, M., & Jagannathan, S. (2018). The digital transformation of education. *Earth observation open science and innovation*, 25-41.

Kaufmann, H. (2003). Collaborative augmented reality in education. *Institute of Software Technology and Interactive Systems, Vienna University of Technology*, 2-4.

Kesim, M., & Ozarslan, Y. (2012). Augmented reality in education: Current technologies and the potential for education. *Procedia: Social and Behavioral Sciences*, *47*, 297–302. DOI: 10.1016/j.sbspro.2012.06.654

Kumar, P. C., Chetty, M., Clegg, T. L., & Vitak, J. (2019, May). Privacy and security considerations for digital technology use in elementary schools. In *Proceedings of the 2019 CHI Conference on Human Factors in Computing Systems* (pp. 1-13). DOI: 10.1145/3290605.3300537

Laak, K. J., & Aru, J. (2024). AI and personalized learning: bridging the gap with modern educational goals. *arXiv preprint arXiv:2404.02798.*

Lebler, D. (2012). Technology and students' musicking: Enhancing the learning experience. *Theory into Practice*, *51*(3), 204–211. DOI: 10.1080/00405841.2012.690302

Lee, K. (2012). The Future of Learning and Training in Augmented Reality. *InSight: A Journal of Scholarly Teaching, 7*, 31-42.

Likovič, A., & Rojko, K. (2022). E-Learning and a Case Study of Coursera and edX Online Platforms. *Research in Social Change*, *14*(1), 94–120. DOI: 10.2478/rsc-2022-0008

Limna, P., Jakwatanatham, S., Siripipattanakul, S., Kaewpuang, P., & Sriboonruang, P. (2022). A review of artificial intelligence (AI) in education during the digital era. *Advance Knowledge for Executives*, *1*(1), 1–9.

Livingstone, S., & Helsper, E. (2007). Gradations in digital inclusion: Children, young people and the digital divide. *New Media & Society*, *9*(4), 671–696. DOI: 10.1177/1461444807080335

Luan, H., & Tsai, C. C. (2021). A review of using machine learning approaches for precision education. *Journal of Educational Technology & Society*, *24*(1), 250–266.

McCarthy, A. M., Maor, D., McConney, A., & Cavanaugh, C. (2023). Digital transformation in education: Critical components for leaders of system change. *Social Sciences & Humanities Open*, *8*(1), 100479. DOI: 10.1016/j.ssaho.2023.100479

McGreal, R. (2017). Special report on the role of open educational resources in supporting the sustainable development goal 4: Quality education challenges and opportunities. *International Review of Research in Open and Distance Learning*, *18*(7). Advance online publication. DOI: 10.19173/irrodl.v18i7.3541

Mhlongo, S., Mbatha, K., Ramatsetse, B., & Dlamini, R. (2023). Challenges, opportunities, and prospects of adopting and using smart digital technologies in learning environments: An iterative review. *Heliyon*, *9*(6), e16348. DOI: 10.1016/j.heliyon.2023.e16348 PMID: 37274691

Mohammed, A., Kumar, S., Saleh, B. M., & Shuaibu, A. (2017). E-learning: A tool for enhancing teaching and learning in educational institutes. *International Journal of Computer Science and Information Technologies*, *8*(2), 217–221.

Molina, A. (2003). The digital divide: The need for a global e-inclusion movement. *Technology Analysis and Strategic Management*, *15*(1), 137–152. DOI: 10.1080/0953732032000046105

Moore, R., Vitale, D., & Stawinoga, N. (2018). The digital divide and educational equity. *Insights in Education and Work*, 1-10.

Nafea, I. T. (2018). Machine learning in educational technology. *Machine learning-advanced techniques and emerging applications*, 175-183.

Nemer, D. (2015). From digital divide to digital inclusion and beyond. *The Journal of Community Informatics*, *11*(1). DOI: 10.15353/joci.v11i1.2857

Ouyang, F., & Jiao, P. (2021). Artificial intelligence in education: The three paradigms. *Computers and Education: Artificial Intelligence*, *2*, 100020. DOI: 10.1016/j.caeai.2021.100020

Parsons, C., & Hick, S. F. (2008). Moving from the digital divide to digital inclusion. *Currents: Scholarship in the Human Services, 7*(2).

Parveen, D. S., & Ramzan, S. I. (2024). The role of digital technologies in education: Benefits and challenges. *Int. Res. J. Adv. Eng. Manag*, *2*, 2029–2037.

Patrinos, A. (2023). *Designing effective public-private partnerships in education.*

Pelargos, P. E., Nagasawa, D. T., Lagman, C., Tenn, S., Demos, J. V., Lee, S. J., Bui, T. T., Barnette, N. E., Bhatt, N. S., Ung, N., Bari, A., Martin, N. A., & Yang, I. (2017). Utilizing virtual and augmented reality for educational and clinical enhancements in neurosurgery. *Journal of Clinical Neuroscience*, *35*, 1–4. DOI: 10.1016/j.jocn.2016.09.002 PMID: 28137372

Peppin Vaughan, R. (2016). Gender equality and education in the Sustainable Development Goals.

Pillay, H., Watters, J. J., & Hoff, L. (2013). Critical attributes of public-private partnerships: A case study in vocational education. *International Journal of Adult Vocational Education and Technology*, *4*(1), 31–45. DOI: 10.4018/javet.2013010103

Popenici, S. A., & Kerr, S. (2017). Exploring the impact of artificial intelligence on teaching and learning in higher education. *Research and Practice in Technology Enhanced Learning*, *12*(1), 22. DOI: 10.1186/s41039-017-0062-8 PMID: 30595727

Rahm, L. (2023). Education, automation and AI: A genealogy of alternative futures. *Learning, Media and Technology, 48*(1), 6–24. DOI: 10.1080/17439884.2021.1977948

Robertson, S. L., & Verger, A. (2012). Governing education through public private partnerships. In *Public private partnerships in education*. Edward Elgar Publishing. DOI: 10.4337/9780857930699.00009

Rosa, W. (2017). Goal 4: Ensure inclusive and equitable quality education and promote lifelong learning opportunities for all. *A New Era in Global Health: Nursing and the United Nations 2030 Agenda for Sustainable Development, 283.*

Rose, P. (2013). Achieving Education for All through public–private partnerships? In *Achieving Education for All through Public–Private Partnerships?* (pp. 1–11). Routledge. DOI: 10.4324/9781315879383

Saini, M., Sengupta, E., Singh, M., Singh, H., & Singh, J. (2023). Sustainable Development Goal for Quality Education (SDG 4): A study on SDG 4 to extract the pattern of association among the indicators of SDG 4 employing a genetic algorithm. *Education and Information Technologies, 28*(2), 2031–2069. DOI: 10.1007/s10639-022-11265-4 PMID: 35975216

Sala, N. (2021). Virtual reality, augmented reality, and mixed reality in education: A brief overview. *Current and prospective applications of virtual reality in higher education*, 48-73.

Savolainen, K., & Torney-Purta, J. (2011). Modes of discourse about education, peace and human rights in the 1974 UNESCO Recommendation. *Prospects, 41*(4), 581–596. DOI: 10.1007/s11125-011-9209-3

Serdyukov, P. (2017). Innovation in education: what works, what doesn't, and what to do about it?. *Journal of research in innovative teaching & learning, 10*(1), 4-33.

Smiderle, R., Rigo, S. J., Marques, L. B., Peçanha de Miranda Coelho, J. A., & Jaques, P. A. (2020). The impact of gamification on students' learning, engagement and behavior based on their personality traits. *Smart Learning Environments, 7*(1), 3. DOI: 10.1186/s40561-019-0098-x

Sofi-Karim, M., Bali, A. O., & Rached, K. (2023). Online education via media platforms and applications as an innovative teaching method. *Education and Information Technologies, 28*(1), 507–523. DOI: 10.1007/s10639-022-11188-0 PMID: 35791317

Stahl, W. M., & Karger, J. (2016). Student Data Privacy, Digital Learning, and Special Education: Challenges at the Intersection of Policy and Practice. *Journal of Special Education Leadership, 29*(2), 79–88.

Tarman, B. (2003). *The Digital Divide in Education.* Online Submission.

Taylor, R. W. (2002). Pros and cons of online learning–a faculty perspective. *Journal of European Industrial Training, 26*(1), 24–37. DOI: 10.1108/03090590210415876

Tiwari, R. (2023). The integration of AI and machine learning in education and its potential to personalize and improve student learning experiences. *International Journal of Scientific Research in Engineering and Management, 7.*

Tracey, B., Florian, K., & Marc, F. (2016). *Educational research and innovation education governance in action lessons from case studies: Lessons from case studies.* OECD Publishing.

Verger, A., Bona, L. X., & Zancajo, A. (2016). What is the role and impact of public-private partnerships in education? A realistic evaluation of the Chilean education quasi-market. *Comparative Education Review, 60*(2), 223–248. DOI: 10.1086/685557

Verhoef, P. C., Broekhuizen, T., Bart, Y., Bhattacharya, A., Dong, J. Q., Fabian, N., & Haenlein, M. (2021). Digital transformation: A multidisciplinary reflection and research agenda. *Journal of Business Research, 122*, 889–901. DOI: 10.1016/j.jbusres.2019.09.022

Wang, Y. (1999, Nov). Public-private partnerships in health and education: Conceptual issues and options. In *A Manuscript Prepared for Manila Social Policy Forum: The New Social Agenda for East, Southeast and Central Asia. Joint ADB-World Bank Conference* (pp. 9-12).

Wong, D. (2007). A critical literature review on e-learning limitations. *Journal for the Advancement of Science and Arts, 2*(1), 55–62.

Zhai, X., Chu, X., Chai, C. S., Jong, M. S. Y., Istenic, A., Spector, M., Liu, J.-B., Yuan, J., & Li, Y. (2021). A Review of Artificial Intelligence (AI) in Education from 2010 to 2020. *Complexity, 2021*(1), 8812542. DOI: 10.1155/2021/8812542

Zhao, X., Ren, Y., & Cheah, K. S. (2023). Leading Virtual Reality (VR) and Augmented Reality (AR) in education: Bibliometric and content analysis from the web of science (2018–2022). *SAGE Open, 13*(3), 21582440231190821. DOI: 10.1177/21582440231190821

KEY TERMS AND DEFINITIONS

21st Century Skills: The term "21st Century Skills" refers to a wide range of abilities, behaviors, and knowledge that are necessary for success in the complicated, rapidly evolving, and technologically advanced world of today. Critical thinking, creativity, communication, teamwork, digital literacy, problem-solving, flexibility, global awareness, and emotional intelligence are all highlighted in these abilities, which go beyond conventional academic knowledge. These competences become essential in preparing students for active and responsible citizenship in a global society as well as for employment, as educational systems around the world align with Sustainable Development Goal 4. By incorporating 21st Century Skills into curricula, educators may make education more relevant, transformative, and future-ready by ensuring that students are prepared to overcome obstacles, create across disciplines, and flourish in a variety of settings.

Blended Learning: An educational strategy known as blended learning mixes traditional in-person classroom instruction with virtual or online learning opportunities. With the help of this hybrid model, which combines the advantages of face-to-face engagement and technological flexibility, students can interact with the material at their own pace while still receiving peer and teacher support. There are several ways to implement blended learning, including flipped classrooms, rotating models, and enriched virtual environments. Because it encourages accessibility, customisation, and active learning, it works especially well for meeting the demands of a wide range of learners. In line with Sustainable Development Goal 4's focus on inclusive and high-quality education for everyone, blended learning promotes deeper comprehension, ongoing evaluation, and skill development by fusing digital tools and multimedia materials with traditional pedagogy.

Digital Learning Ecosystem: Digital Learning Ecosystems refer to interconnected, dynamic networks of digital tools, platforms, content, and stakeholders that collectively support and enhance the teaching and learning process. These ecosystems integrate technologies such as Learning Management Systems (LMS), virtual classrooms, artificial intelligence (AI), educational apps, and digital content repositories, enabling flexible, personalized, and collaborative learning experiences. They encompass interactions among students, educators, institutions, and technology providers, fostering continuous learning across formal and informal environments. A well-structured digital learning ecosystem ensures accessibility, inclusivity, and adaptability, aligning with the goals of SDG 4 by promoting equitable and lifelong learning opportunities. These ecosystems also encourage innovation in pedagogy, real-time assessment, and data-driven decision-making. Importantly, they bridge geographic and socio-economic gaps by providing remote learning solutions and democratizing access to quality education. In the context of the Fourth Industrial Revolution, digital learning ecosystems are pivotal in preparing learners with 21st-century skills and fostering global educational resilience and sustainability.

EdTech (Educational Technology): EdTech (Educational Technology) refers to the integration of digital tools, technologies, and platforms into teaching and learning processes to enhance educational outcomes. It encompasses a wide range of applications, from interactive whiteboards, virtual classrooms, and learning management systems (LMS) to artificial intelligence (AI), gamified learning, virtual reality (VR), and mobile learning apps. EdTech supports personalized learning by allowing educators to tailor instruction to individual student needs, monitor progress in real-time, and provide adaptive feedback. It facilitates access to education in remote and underserved areas, thus promoting equity and inclusivity in alignment with SDG 4. Moreover, it empowers both educators and learners by fostering engagement, collaboration, and creativity in the learning environment. As education systems evolve to meet the demands of the 21st century, EdTech plays a pivotal role in transforming traditional models of education into more flexible, interactive, and learner-centered formats that support lifelong learning and global educational goals.

Educational Innovation: Educational innovation refers to the purposeful implementation of new ideas, methods, tools, and practices aimed at improving teaching, learning, assessment, and educational management. It encompasses both technological advancements—such as digital learning platforms, artificial intelligence, and virtual classrooms—and pedagogical reforms, including learner-centered approaches, flipped classrooms, and experiential learning models. The core objective of educational innovation is to enhance the quality, relevance, accessibility, and equity of education across diverse learning environments. In the context of Sustainable Development Goal 4 (SDG 4), educational innovation plays a critical role in ensuring inclusive and equitable quality education. It addresses challenges such as outdated curricula, teacher shortages, unequal access, and the need for personalized learning. Innovations can range from simple classroom strategies that engage students in critical thinking, to large-scale systemic reforms involving education policy, infrastructure, and professional development. Importantly, educational innovation is not confined to high-tech solutions. It also includes social innovations like community-based learning, inclusive teaching practices, and culturally responsive education that resonate with local needs. For innovation to be effective, it must be sustainable, scalable, and evidence-based, while keeping learners' needs at the centre. Ultimately, educational innovation supports the transformation of education systems to better prepare learners for the demands of the 21st century and beyond.

Equity in Education: The idea and practice of ensuring that all students, irrespective of their socioeconomic background, gender, ethnicity, disability, location, or other conditions, have access to the tools, opportunities, and support they require to realize their full potential is known as equity in education. In contrast to equality, which gives every student the same resources, equity acknowledges that every person has unique obstacles to overcome and, as a result, needs varying degrees of assistance to achieve. It entails locating and eliminating institutionalized prejudices, discriminatory behaviors, and impediments in educational systems. Fairness in educational procedures and results is emphasized by equity, which guarantees that underprivileged and marginalized groups are not only included but also given more authority. Achieving educational equity is essential to creating inclusive, just, and resilient societies in the framework of Sustainable Development Goal 4 (SDG 4).

Inclusive Innovation: Inclusive education is an approach that ensures all learners, regardless of their abilities, backgrounds, identities, or socio-economic status, have equal access to quality education within mainstream learning environments. It is grounded in the principles of equity, non-discrimination, and respect for diversity. Inclusive education does not segregate or isolate students based on disabilities, language, gender, ethnicity, or other differences; rather, it adapts teaching methods, curricula, and learning environments to accommodate varied learning needs. This approach promotes a sense of belonging, active participation, and academic success for every student by fostering supportive and flexible classrooms. Teachers play a critical role by using differentiated instruction, assistive technologies, and inclusive assessment practices. Inclusive education aligns with the objectives of SDG 4 by ensuring no learner is left behind. It contributes to social cohesion, empathy, and lifelong learning, preparing students to thrive in diverse societies and contribute meaningfully to inclusive and sustainable development.

Lifelong Learning: Lifelong Learning refers to the continuous, voluntary, and self-motivated pursuit of knowledge for personal or professional development throughout an individual's life. It transcends formal education and encompasses informal and non-formal modes of learning, such as community engagement, workplace training, online courses, and experiential learning. This concept is central to Sustainable Development Goal 4, which emphasizes inclusive and equitable education and the promotion of lifelong learning opportunities for all. In a rapidly changing world shaped by technological advances, globalization, and shifting labor markets, lifelong learning equips individuals with the skills, adaptability, and resilience needed to remain relevant and empowered. It fosters a culture of curiosity, critical thinking, and innovation, enabling people to respond to societal challenges, participate actively in civic life, and improve their quality of life. Ultimately, lifelong learning supports human development by recognizing that education is not confined to childhood or classrooms but is a lifelong endeavor.

Pedagogical Transformation: The term "pedagogical transformation" describes the substantial and intentional change in teaching methods, techniques, and attitudes that results in more effective, inclusive, and engaging learning environments. It adopts learner-centered practices that put an emphasis on active learning, critical thinking, teamwork, and practical problem-solving, going beyond conventional teacher-centered approaches. Digital technology integration, cutting-edge assessment instruments, and adaptable learning paradigms like blended or flipped classrooms are frequently the driving forces behind this change. By modifying materials and approaches to accommodate various learning requirements and environments, pedagogical transformation also celebrates the diversity of learners. By making learning more fair, accessible, and relevant in the knowledge society of the twenty-first century, it plays a critical role in guaranteeing high-quality education within the framework of SDG 4.

SDG 4 (Quality Education): Sustainable Development Goal 4 (SDG 4), as outlined by the United Nations, aims to "ensure inclusive and equitable quality education and promote lifelong learning opportunities for all" by 2030. It recognizes education as a fundamental human right and a driving force for sustainable development, social inclusion, and economic growth. SDG 4 emphasizes that access to education must go beyond mere enrolment in schools—it must ensure that learners acquire the knowledge, skills, values, and competencies necessary to lead productive lives and contribute positively to society. The goal encompasses a wide range of targets, including universal primary and secondary education, early childhood development, vocational training, equal access to higher education, elimination of gender disparities, and education for sustainable development and global citizenship. It also calls for improved educational infrastructure, trained teachers, and safe, inclusive learning environments. Importantly, SDG 4 promotes lifelong learning, recognizing that education must continue throughout an individual's life to adapt to evolving personal, societal, and technological changes. In today's digital era, innovation and equity are crucial to delivering quality education, especially for marginalized groups. Achieving SDG 4 is seen as foundational to the realization of all other SDGs, as education empowers individuals to break the cycle of poverty and build resilient, informed communities.

Chapter 2 Advancing Information and Communication Technology Integration in Language Education to Quality Education

Kelly M. Torres
https://orcid.org/0000-0003-4374-6366
The Chicago School, USA

ABSTRACT

The integration of information and communication technology (ICT) into language education has transformed traditional teaching methodologies by enhancing the educational experience and creating more personalized learning environments. Particularly, the inclusion of digital tools, virtual classrooms, and artificial intelligence-driven tutors have revolutionized how learners acquire language skills. However, challenges such as digital literacy gaps, limited access to technology, and insufficient professional development hinder the full potential of ICT in language education. By aligning ICT integration with the principles of inclusive and equitable education as outlined in the United Nations Sustainable Development Goal 4 (SDG 4), this chapter highlights the need for institutional support, professional training, and culturally responsive approaches to ensure that ICT serves as an effective tool for fostering linguistic diversity, global communication, and lifelong learning opportunities for all.

DOI: 10.4018/979-8-3373-0801-2.ch002

INTRODUCTION

The integration of information and communication technology (ICT) into education has revolutionized learning environments, providing innovative solutions to address challenges across the globe regarding accessibility, equity, and quality of education. ICT has especially impacted the way in which students learn and educators facilitate instruction. These tools are particularly impactful in language classrooms in assisting learners in the development of foreign and second language skills. Language education, which plays a pivotal role in fostering lifelong learning and global citizenship, has tremendously benefited from the inclusion of ICT tools through the enhancement of teaching methodologies and student engagement (Singer et al., 2023). This chapter provides an overview of the relationship between ICT, language education, and the United Nations Sustainable Development Goal 4 (SDG 4), which seeks to ensure inclusive and equitable quality education while promoting lifelong learning opportunities for all individuals. Specifically, this chapter focus highlights the positive impact of developing a professional development framework to equip language educators with the skills and knowledge necessary to leverage ICT effectively. Particularly, the initiative of the chapter is to emphasize the importance of technology-enhanced pedagogy, capacity building, and sustainable practices to achieve meaningful educational outcomes. These areas are vital given that language education is a fundamental aspect of lifelong learning, global citizenship, and cultural exchange.

Moreover, language education provides individuals with the skills needed to communicate effectively, access global knowledge, and participate in intercultural dialogue (Hassain, 2024). However, conventional language education methods often struggle to address the diverse needs of learners, particularly those in underserved or marginalized communities. ICT presents a powerful avenue to bridge this gap by offering adaptive, interactive, and scalable learning solutions for educators across diverse levels of education. Innovative technologies (e.g., artificial intelligence language tutors, language apps) have the potential to support learners with personalized and engaging experiences. Personalized language learning has continuously demonstrated success in providing targeted language interventions allowing for educators to respond to individual student needs (Chen et al., 2021). By leveraging ICT in language education, educators can enhance learning experiences, promote digital inclusion, and contribute to a more equitable and accessible global education system. This chapter will provide an overview of the significance of ICT and its implementation globally within language education.

United Nations Sustainable Development Goal 4

To provide a blueprint for achieving a more equitable and sustainable future, the United Nations developed 17 goals focused on ending poverty, protecting the planet, and addressing inequalities with the goal of creating a more peaceful and prosperous world for everyone. Ultimately, these goals seek to address global challenges and establish peace and justice (The United Nations, n.d.). Although the 17 goals are interconnected, they each focus on a specific area and are considered equally important. The United Nations Sustainable Development Goal 4 (SDG 4) seeks to ensure inclusive and equitable quality education while promoting lifelong learning opportunities for all individuals. Particularly, this goal emphasizes the inequalities found in education across the globe and pledges to leave no one behind (Rothe et al., 2022). Indeed, Ramaswamy et al. (2021) proposed that the integration of the United Nations sustainability goals into teaching and learning provides unique opportunities for shaping the educational landscape to transform and improve society through internationalization. However, the United Nations (n.d.) expressed challenges associated with ICT implementation due to individuals possessing low skill levels which create barriers in the implementation of universal and meaningful connectivity. Addressing this challenge requires a multi-faceted approach that focuses on education, accessibility, and support centered on implementing targeted training programs and user-friendly technology. Costa et al. (2023) postulated that educational technology provides a framework for improving teaching and learning processes and promoting the achievement of SDG 4. Principally, educational technology is instrumental in allowing learners access to education and improving their academic performance.

In the context of ICT-integrated language education, SDG 4 plays a crucial role in shaping policies, strategies, and innovations that aim to enhance access, equity, and quality in learning. Rothe et al. (2022) contended that creating programming that is mainstreamed across contexts avoids worsening existing inequalities by increasing digital development. By leveraging digital tools and technology-enhanced methodologies, ICT integration in language education directly aligns with the United Nation's mission to reduce educational barriers and create more inclusive learning environments (United Nations, n.d.). The United Nations (n.d.) shared that quality education is lacking in many places across the world and that primary and secondary completion rates are increasing but at uneven paces. Providing language education access to students can further promote the United Nation's goal of ensuring continuous learning opportunities for all learners. Haleem et al. (2022) contended that digital technologies resulted in a paradigm shift in education emerging as powerful tools that can help achieve the United Nation's SDG 4 goal. Saini et al. (2023) described SDG4 as being at the forefront of global initiatives in promoting sustainable growth through high quality education. One of the most significant ways ICT contributes to SDG 4 is by expanding access to language learning for diverse populations, including those in remote or underserved areas. For example, digital platforms, mobile applications, and open educational resources (OER) enable learners to engage with language education regardless of geographical or socioeconomic limitations. Toke (2023) emphasized that lifelong learning requires leveraging transformative learning tools such as ICT in order to advance the goal of providing inclusive and accessible quality education to everyone. This sentiment was further expressed by the Central Institute of Educational Technology (n.d.) who shared that ICT serves as a valuable resource for creating personalized instruction and enabling educators to offer more inclusive and effective instructional approaches. This is particularly relevant for marginalized groups, including refugees, individuals with disabilities, and those from low-income backgrounds, who may otherwise face challenges in accessing traditional classroom instruction. Research indicates that technology integration can enable developing countries to skip over some stages of income equality and achieve its goal of inclusive education (Asongu et al., 2021; Andreou & Koutsampelas, 2015). ICT-facilitated language learning helps bridge these gaps by providing flexible, cost-effective, and scalable solutions that ensure broader participation in education.

In addition to accessibility, ICT enhances the quality of language education by fostering innovative pedagogical approaches. The Central Institute of Educational Technology (n.d.) asserted ICT tools empower educators to facilitate instruction focused on intricate language concepts in an engaging and meaningful way while encouraging active participation. Interactive tools such as artificial intelligence (AI)-powered tutoring systems, gamified learning experiences, and adaptive assessments personalize instruction to meet learners' individual needs. These digital innovations support differentiated learning, allowing students to progress at their own pace while receiving real-time feedback. Moreover, technology enables the integration of multimedia content, virtual exchanges, and collaborative platforms, enriching the language learning experience by making it more immersive and engaging. ICT integration also contributes to lifelong learning (Valverde-Berrocoso et al., 2021), which is another key aspect of SDG 4. Digital literacy and technological proficiency are essential skills in the modern workforce, and integrating ICT into language education equips learners with competencies that extend beyond language acquisition. By fostering self-directed learning habits and providing continuous access to educational resources, technology-driven language education encourages learners to develop skills that support ongoing personal and professional growth. Despite the transformative potential of ICT in advancing SDG 4, challenges remain, including disparities in digital access, the need for teacher training, and resistance to change in educational institutions (Alenezi et al., 2023; Ghazali et al., 2024; Ofosu-

Asare, 2024; Timotheou et al., 2022; Treve, 2021). Addressing these issues requires multi-stakeholder collaboration, policy advocacy, and investment in infrastructure to safeguard that digital education initiatives are sustainable and equitable. However, Huong (2021) warned that ICT integration requires many changes within the classroom (e.g., student willingness, teacher implementation) that can negatively impact technology use even with institutional buy-in.

Governments, educational institutions, and technology developers must work together to implement policies that support digital inclusion, fund teacher professional development, and create adaptable ICT-based solutions tailored to diverse learning needs. Further, accomplishing the sustainability development goals involves technological understanding and implementation (Saini et al., 2023). Still, the integration of ICT in language education serves as a powerful mechanism for advancing SDG 4 by promoting accessibility, enhancing pedagogical quality, and fostering lifelong learning. While challenges persist, strategic investments and collaborative efforts can help harness the full potential of digital education in ensuring equitable, high-quality learning opportunities. As ICT continues to evolve, its role in achieving SDG 4 will become increasingly vital, reinforcing the global commitment to inclusive and sustainable education. Ramaswamy et al. (2021) conveyed that there are practical intersections between the United Nation Sustainable Development Goals and internationalization allowing for a global challenge within education to create a better world for all. The success of achieving this goal may rely on the inclusion of ICT perspectives (Angelaki et al., 2023)

ICT AND LANGUAGE EDUCATION

Saini et al. (2023) described 21st century education encapsulating technology and active learning that extends beyond traditional teacher-centric models of teaching. The integration ICT into education has significantly transformed learning environments, providing innovative solutions to enhance accessibility, equity, and quality of education. ICT includes skills related to computing, software, and applications and systems. ICT has become more favorable with language educators since it encompasses the use of computers, videos, the internet, and other relevant forms of technology (Huong, 2021). Language education, as a cornerstone for fostering lifelong learning and global citizenship, has benefited immensely from ICT tools that enhance teaching methodologies and student engagement (Singer et al., 2023).

SDG 4 underscores the importance of inclusivity, quality, and equity in education, addressing barriers such as socioeconomic disparities, gender inequalities, and language marginalization. Language education is a critical vehicle for promoting intercultural understanding, personal empowerment, and access to global knowledge.

However, traditional language education methods often fail to reach underserved populations or address diverse learning needs (Osipova & Lao, 2022). However, ICT offers powerful solutions to these challenges by increasing accessibility, enabling personalization, and fostering learner engagement. Online platforms and digital tools make remote learning possible for marginalized and rural populations, while adaptive technologies cater to individual learning styles and paces. Additionally, multimedia tools, including video content and gamification, create interactive and engaging language learning experiences. Nevertheless, when considering ICT education, digital literacy components and infrastructure are both equally imperative for successful integration (Angelaki et al., 2023).

The use of ICT in language education has introduced new opportunities for both learners and educators by fostering interactive and immersive learning environments. Blake (2013) outlined how digital platforms, such as language learning apps and virtual classrooms, provide learners with access to extensive resources, including grammar exercises, pronunciation tools, and interactive lessons. Online tools such as Duolingo, Babbel, and Rosetta Stone utilize gamification and AI-driven learning paths to personalize instruction and maintain learner motivation. Poudel (2022) listed motivation as a major advantage of educational technologies in capturing learners' interest and concentration toward the lesson. Researchers highlighted the benefits of AI generated tools in creating personalized instruction but caution that these platforms cannot substitute human language teachers (Baskara, 2023). Additionally, video conferencing and collaborative platforms have enabled real-time language practice with native speakers across the globe. For example, tools like Zoom, Microsoft Teams, and Google Meet support synchronous learning, allowing students to engage in live discussions, practice pronunciation, and receive immediate feedback. Researchers have continuously reported the value of offering virtual exchange programs and online language partnerships in order to further enhance learners' exposure to authentic language use, reinforcing their communicative competence (Barbosa & Ferreira-Lopes, 2021; Brautlacht et al., 2022; Duffy et al., 2020; O'Dowd, 2018; Zhou, 2023). Another key advancement is the integration of artificial intelligence (AI) and machine learning in language instruction. AI-driven chatbots and virtual tutors provide learners with instant feedback on their language use, improving grammar, vocabulary, and pronunciation. These tools can simulate real-life conversations, helping students develop practical communication skills. Moreover, speech recognition technology enhances pronunciation practice, allowing students to refine their speaking abilities through automated assessments.

Beyond individual learning, ICT also supports differentiated instruction and inclusive education (Johler & Krumsvik, 2022; Palieraki & Koutrouba, 2021). Adaptive learning platforms use data analytics to tailor lessons according to individual progress, ensuring that students receive instruction aligned with their proficiency levels. This is particularly beneficial for multilingual and special needs learners, as AI-powered tools can offer customized support, including text-to-speech applications, real-time translation, and accessible learning formats. Despite these advancements, Canese et al. (2023) shared that challenges still remain in integrating ICT effectively into language education. They indicated that issues such as the digital divide and insufficient teacher training hinder the widespread adoption of technology-enhanced language learning. As a result, many educators struggle to navigate digital tools due to limited technical expertise, emphasizing the need for targeted professional development programs.

Learner Benefits

Although ICT implementation can face many barriers, the integration of these tools has resulted in many benefits for language learners. Particularly, the integration of ICT into language education is widely recognized for its potential to enhance learning experiences and outcomes (Abraham et al., 2022; Alobaid, 2020; Becirovic et al., 2021; Ghavifekr & Rosdy, 2015; Naghdipour, 2022; Vargas-Montoya et al., 2023). Prior research highlights several key benefits of ICT for learners including increased accessibility, personalized learning, engagement, and skill development. As conveyed by Chin (2021), personalized education has become more popular given the emphasize of designing pedagogical approaches that focus on individual differences in the acquisition of content. One of the most significant advantages of ICT in language education is its ability to improve accessibility for diverse learners, including those from marginalized or underserved communities. Digital platforms and mobile applications provide opportunities for students to engage with language learning materials regardless of geographic location or socioeconomic background (Cheng & Parker, 2023; National Center for Education Statistics, n.d.). Additionally, ICT enables learners with disabilities to access tailored support through assistive technologies, such as text-to-speech software and captioned videos resulting in more inclusive learning environments (Laabidi et al., 2014; Fernández-Batanero et al., 2022; Vincent et al., 2024).

ICT allows for adaptive learning experiences, catering to individual learner needs and preferences. AI-driven platforms and learning management systems (LMS) are great examples of how this technology uses data analytics to assess learner progress and adjust instructional content accordingly (Alotaibi, 2024; Halkiopoulos & Gkintoni, 2024). This personalization supports differentiated instruction, enabling learners to advance at their own pace and focus on areas that require improvement while reinforcing previously learned concepts. Researchers have further found that gamification features, such as progress tracking and achievement badges, further reinforce motivation and self-directed learning (Grabner-Hagan & Kingsley, 2023;

Luo, 2024; Nilubol & Sitthikikul, 2023). Research suggests that ICT-integrated language learning environments enhance student engagement through interactive and multimedia-based instruction. Researchers additionally discovered that the use of virtual reality (VR) and augmented reality (AR) applications provide immersive experiences that facilitate real-world language practice, reducing communication anxiety and improving language retention (Ai et al., 2024; Dhimolea et al., 2022; Salamah et al., 2024; Shi et al., 2024). Chen (2022) suggested that public speaking is the most anxiety provoking activity found in language classrooms. Utilizing tools such as VR eliminates performance pressures experienced by learners by allowing them to practice speech production in a low-anxiety environment. Further, Chen (2022) found that instructor feedback generated through AI reduces learners' public speaking anxiety levels. Through the inclusion of these tools, educators create supportive learning environments in which students feel comfortable practicing their language skills through accessible and personalized learning experiences. Integrating feedback loops can also provide continuous language exposure which ultimately enhances the learning experience. Chen et al. (2021) emphasized that personalized learning is a prevailing focus within the realm of educational technology in developing meaningful classroom environments that encompass a focus on learner pace, approaches, objectives, content, and activities. Similarly, online discussion forums, video conferencing tools, and collaborative platforms foster peer interaction and authentic language use, creating a dynamic and participatory learner centered atmosphere (Alsayer, 2023; Chen, 2023; Muir et al., 2022; Qi & Derakhshan, 2024).

Beyond language proficiency, ICT integration promotes essential digital literacy and critical thinking skills. As learners navigate online resources, analyze multimedia content, and engage in virtual communication, they develop competencies that are increasingly valuable in academic and professional settings (Akour & Alenezi, 2022). Additionally, exposure to diverse online learning communities fosters cross-cultural understanding, preparing students to engage in a globalized world (Shonfeld et al., 2021). ICT enables continuous and lifelong learning opportunities by providing learners with flexible and self-directed study options. Educators further utilize a range of resources including mobile-assisted language learning applications, podcasts, and digital repositories in order to allow students to practice language skills outside formal educational settings, reinforcing language acquisition through consistent exposure and practice (Guo et al., 2021; Lowean et al., 2019; Sendag et al., 2024). Moreover, access to open educational resources (OER) and online language communities encourages autonomous learning, empowering students to take ownership of their educational journey (Benson, 2022). Combining these resources and technologies into language environments ultimately creates a robust environment that contributes to higher acquisition of target languages.

Recent research has also continuously emphasized the importance of culturally responsive integration of ICT into education as a means to improve educational equity and learning outcomes (Msambwa et al., 2024; Timotheou et al., 2022; Vargas-Montoya et al., 2023). Specifically, Han et al. (2024) realized the importance of aligning digital tools with students' linguistic and cultural backgrounds since this results in them experiencing deeper engagement and higher levels of motivation and comprehension. Further, ICT platforms that allow for multilingual content, localized examples, and culturally relevant instructional materials support differentiated instruction and reduce marginalization in diverse classrooms. In addition to fostering inclusivity, these tools also enhance cultural interaction within learning environments by enabling cross-border collaboration, digital storytelling, and virtual exchanges, which all expose students to diverse worldviews and encourage global citizenship. For example, web-based platforms such as ePals or video conferencing tools like Zoom, WhatsApp, and Teams all allow for the facilitation of real-time intercultural dialogue, allowing learners to reflect critically on their own identities while developing empathy and intercultural competence (Lin, 2018; Zhang & Zhou, 2023). When ICT is implemented with cultural responsiveness in mind, it increases inclusivity and relevance and also promotes cultural preservation and exchange, which are vital for education in a globalized society.

PEDAGOGICAL INNOVATIONS

Extensive research further supports the role of ICT in language education. Numerous studies have shown that ICT integration enhances pedagogical effectiveness by enabling innovative teaching methods, such as digital storytelling, gamification, and VR tools, all of which enhance learners' levels of motivation and improve their levels of language acquisition (Akram et al., 2022; Bereczki & Kárpái, 2021). Moreover, ICT facilitates differentiated instruction, addressing the diverse needs of learners. Despite these advantages, significant barriers persist, including insufficient infrastructure, lack of teacher training, and the digital divide. For example, educators often struggle to select and implement appropriate technologies due to limited technical knowledge. Addressing these barriers through targeted professional development is essential for educators to realize the full potential of ICT in advancing language education. Nevertheless, the integration of ICT in language education has paved the way for groundbreaking pedagogical innovations that enhance both teaching and learning experiences. One major innovation is the pedagogical approach of game-based learning which incorporates gamified elements (e.g., leaderboards, achievement badges, and progress tracking) throughout the learning process. The implementation of gamification into classrooms has significantly increased learner motivation and engagement (Baah et al., 2023; Garcia-López et al., 2023; Kaya, 2023; Oliveria et al., 2022; Xu et al., 2021). Language learning apps, including Drops and Memrise, utilize game-based strategies to reinforce vocabulary acquisition and language retention in a fun and interactive way. These platforms provide fun ways to learn language moving away from mundane, rote-based learning strategies.

Further, AI-driven language tutors, such as ChatGPT and ELSA Speak, provide learners with real-time feedback, personalized lesson plans, and adaptive learning pathways. These tools analyze user progress and tailor content to meet individual needs, ensuring an effective and customized learning experience. Other types of immersive technologies, such as VR language labs and AR-enhanced textbooks, create authentic learning environments where students can practice language skills in simulated real-world scenarios. These tools allow for the utilization of mobile learning since students can use their phones to scan textbooks and other AR materials to receive information about course topics. Applications that include Mondly VR also enable learners to engage in lifelike conversations and build confidence in their speaking abilities. Additional ICT models such as flipped learning help to engage students with digital content (e.g., instructional videos, interactive exercises) before attending class. This approach allows educators to use in-class time for active learning strategies, such as group discussions and role-playing exercises, fostering deeper understanding and practical application of language skills. ICT also fosters global collaboration through discussion forums, virtual language exchanges, and social media platforms. Providing practical opportunities for language practice is essential for skill development. Global access to language learners across the world is accessible through technology as well. Students can connect with peers worldwide, participate in joint projects, and gain exposure to diverse linguistic and cultural contexts, promoting cross-cultural competence. Research supports ICT integration in language education as a means to enhance pedagogical effectiveness. Studies have consistently demonstrated that ICT enables innovative teaching methods (e.g., digital storytelling, gamification, VR), which significantly improves learners' motivation and language acquisition levels (Akram et al., 2022; Bereczki & Kárpái, 2021). Additionally, ICT facilitates differentiated instruction, catering to the diverse needs of learners and promoting inclusive education. Despite these advantages, challenges such as insufficient infrastructure, lack of teacher training, and the digital divide persist, hindering effective ICT implementation (Goel & Vishnoi, 2022).

To address these challenges, Goel and Vishnoi (2022) presented a framework consisting of three pillars which include technology-enhanced pedagogy, capacity building, and sustainable practices. The first pillar focuses on providing educators with practical knowledge of ICT tools and methods. Key activities that promote this knowledge include workshops and webinars focused on using tools that include Duolingo, Kahoot!, and Quizlet for interactive learning, guidance on embedding

ICT into language curricula, and sharing case studies of successful ICT integration. The second pillar, capacity building, ensures that educators possess the skills and confidence needed to sustain ICT use. Strategies to teach these skillsets include train-the-trainer programs that prepare educators as mentors, continuous professional development opportunities with micro-credentials for mastering ICT applications, and the creation of online communities for collaborative knowledge sharing. The third pillar, sustainable practices, emphasizes long-term impact through policy advocacy, promotion of low-cost and energy-efficient technologies, and the establishment of evaluation frameworks to measure the effectiveness of ICT in language education. Expanding on the proposed framework, it is important to consider how fostering a supportive network ensures the successful integration of ICT in language education. Networks involve the collaboration of policymakers, educational institutions, technology developers, and local communities in addressing systemic challenges such as the digital divide and uneven access to infrastructure (Imran, 2022). Policymakers particularly play a pivotal role in creating environments by prioritizing funding for ICT resources, establishing policies that incentivize technology adoption, and integrating ICT into national language education standards. Indeed, Kwihangana (2024) conveyed that policymakers have the power to leverage technological affordances that result in the improvement of quality and accessible education. At the institutional level, school administrators and education leaders must champion ICT initiatives by providing ongoing support to educators and investing in infrastructure that facilitates access to digital tools. These collaborative efforts result in a united force that is dedicated to ICT implementation across all educational levels and formats.

CULTURALLY RESPONSIVE ICT INTEGRATION

Language education is inherently linked to cultural identity and diversity. Indeed, Hassain (2024) proclaimed that cultural diversity is a significant aspect of language classrooms. As a result, in order to ensure relevance and inclusivity, ICT tools must be adapted to local contexts. Designing language learning applications that incorporate local dialects, traditions, and cultural nuances enhances learner engagement and promotes a sense of belonging (Lu & Xie, 2022). Moreover, considering the local and global uses of the target language further positions learners to balance the local uses of the language verses global competence on how the language is produced across the globe in diverse settings (Low, 2025). Engaging with local communities and stakeholders ensures that ICT solutions remain both technologically innovative and culturally meaningful.

The role of culturally responsive approaches in ICT integration is another essential aspect of curricula development. Language education is inherently linked to cultural identity and diversity and educators must consider how to adapt ICT tools to local contexts to ensure relevance and inclusivity (Lu & Xie, 2022). For instance, designing language learning applications that incorporate local dialects, traditions, and cultural nuances can significantly enhance learner engagement and promote a sense of belonging. By combining ICT with human language teachers, students receive targeted practice opportunities, access to authentic language resources, and educator feedback focused on dialect and cultural differences (Baskara & Mukarto, 2023) Collaboration with local communities and stakeholders ensures that ICT solutions are not only technologically innovative but are also culturally meaningful. Digital literacy extends beyond technical skills, encompassing the ability to critically evaluate online content, navigate digital platforms responsibly, and leverage ICT for creative and collaborative learning (Ahmed & Roche, 2021). Ultimately, building digital literacy bridges the gap between access and effective use, ensuring that ICT becomes a transformative force rather than a superficial addition to language education. Working with community leaders and educators across the global allow for the development of culturally sensitive language materials.

PROFESSIONAL DEVELOPMENT

Researchers have discovered that educators consider ICT valuable for language education but feel discomfort in their application of these tools (Pitambar, 2021). To overcome barriers to ICT adoption, targeted professional development for educators is essential. Many educators struggle to select and implement appropriate technologies due to limited technical knowledge. A structured professional development framework consisting of the three pillars of technology-enhanced pedagogy, capacity building, and sustainable practices assists in bridging this gap. Kwihangana (2022) found that ICT policies shape the digital identities of educators positioning them to advocate for technology integration in achieving ICT-supported pedagogical goals. Yet, educational systems are often slow to respond to technological innovations resulting in a lack of teacher preparedness and knowledge in implementing new tools (Gutiérrez-Martín, 2022). For instance, research focused on gamification in language learning consistently results in positive student academic gains (Evurulobi et al., 2024; Liu, 2024; Pinto et al., 2021; Shen et al., 2024; Shortt et al., 2021). An example of how to integrate gamification into language classes is through the use of the app Duolingo. This app provides gamified language lessons that adapt to a learner's proficiency levels and allows for practice of vocabulary acquisition, grammar comprehension, and pronunciation practice. The app's built-in rewards system further motivates students to stay consistent while receiving immediate feedback. Ultimately, students who use this app receive additional supports in their independent language learning processes and educators can integrate this app for classroom-based reinforcement. Another example of gamification that is trending in educational settings is Kahoot! This interactive quiz platform engages students through live competitive games and self-paced challenges. Educators can customize quizzes to reinforce vocabulary, grammar, and cultural knowledge, or they can access the platform's extensive library of existing quizzes that are tailored to different languages and lessons. The platform offers a lively, fast-paced format that motivates students' active participation and peer collaboration. By competing in a low-stakes environment that is conducive to the meaningful practice of language skills, students gain mastery of course content through independent and collaborative competitions. Other tools such as Quizlet help support language development through customizable flashcards, quizzes, and games that promote repetition and recall of previously taught concepts. This platform includes features such as "Learn" and "Match," which include both rote learning and timed challenges. Students also have access to the platform's audio functions for listening practice and pronunciation reinforcement.

Effective technology-enhanced pedagogy also includes strategies such as blended learning, flipped classrooms, and project-based language activities that leverage ICT to extend learning beyond traditional settings. For example, students might collaborate on Google Docs to create a story, use Padlet to build a vocabulary wall, or engage in language exchanges via a video conferencing platform. Ultimately, the integration of ICT tools into language curricula empowers educators to design more immersive, interactive, and adaptable learning experiences through a diverse range of tools and experiences. Teachers who embrace technology create vibrant language learning environments where students build confidence, competence, and cultural understanding (Hassain, 2024; Ozdemi & Papi, 2021; Teng et al., 2021). These skills are all deemed essential for communicating in an increasingly diverse globalized world.

One effective strategy for guiding educators in the development of these skills is through the implementation of train-the-trainer programs. These programs empower experienced educators to become mentors for their peers resulting in increased knowledge development and self-confidence in their understanding of technology integration. This training model allows trainees to gain competence through mentored experiences that are on-going and cost-effective (Raghavan et al., 2024; Suhrheinrich, 2011). Utilizing this approach results in the development of individual expertise through a scalable and sustainable training model where knowledge is continuously shared and expanded within the school or institution. Fostering a community of in-house experts, further results in a reduction of reliance on external training while promoting collaboration and peer support. In addition to initial training sessions, continuous professional development opportunities are vital in keeping educators up to date with emerging technological trends and pedagogical strategies. Many of these programs are structured in concise micro-credentialing and certification course models in order to provide educators with targeted, practical learning experiences that validate their ICT competencies. These bite-sized, flexible learning pathways emphasis specific skills making professional growth more accessible and manageable alongside their teachers' professional responsibilities. Tooley and Hood (2021) described micro-credentials as containing discrete competencies for immediate implementation into practice.

Other professional development opportunities available to educators are participating in professional learning communities, social media groups, and educator discussion forums to gain access to spaces for continuous dialogue, knowledge exchange, and technology troubleshooting support. Common platforms for these interactions include Edutopia, Twitter's #EdTechChat, and International Society for Technology in Education (ISTE) forums since they enable educators to share best practices, discover new tools, and reflect on challenges together. These forums for vital for extending global connections that promote innovative teaching approaches, foster cross-cultural insights, and reinforce that educators are part of a broader, supportive community working towards the same goal of promoting student learning through effective technology integration.

Establishing sustainable practices in ICT integration is similarly crucial in ensuring the long-term impact and accessibility of technology in education. One key approach to this focus involves developing policies that advocate low-cost and energy-efficient technologies. Prioritizing affordable and sustainable solutions (e.g., open-source educational software, cloud-based platforms) permits institutions to extend access to technology for a broader range of learners while minimizing environmental impact (Ahmed et al., 2021; Goel & Vishnoi, 2022; Wang et al., 2021). This approach is especially important in under-resourced areas, where equitable access to technology can bridge digital divides and empower more students to engage in ICT-enhanced learning experiences resulting in sustained learning outcomes. For long-term sustainability, institutions should also embed ICT adoption strategies into their overarching educational policies.

Leaders who align technological integration with institutional goals make certain that employees understand that digital tools are not perceived as temporary enhancements but as essential components of the learning environment. To augment this view, leaders' technology budgets need to include funding for infrastructure, professional development for educators, and maintenance plans for digital resources. Moreover, promoting inclusive access and practices is vital to guarantee that all students including those from diverse socioeconomic backgrounds, those with disabilities, and multilingual learners can fully engage with digital tools creating more equitable learning environments. This approach may involve incorporating accessibility features, offering offline learning alternatives, and ensuring resources are adaptable for a variety of devices and connectivity levels. To ensure these practices remain effective, periodic assessments and feedback mechanisms are essential. Incorporating both educator and student feedback in these measures provides a more well-rounded overview of technology effectiveness (Consoli et al., 2023). Furthermore, institutions should establish clear evaluation frameworks that measure the effectiveness of ICT in enhancing language education. Technology acceptance models promote an understanding of technology integration in schools (Msambwa et al., 2024). Researchers investigating the impacts of technology frameworks often collect data centered on these frameworks and metrics including student performance data, teacher feedback, technology usage reports, and student engagement. Regular technology evaluation helps identify what works, what needs improvement, and where resources should be reallocated. Additionally, feedback loops that involve incorporating insights from students, educators, and technology support teams make certain that technology strategies remain responsive to the evolving needs of the learning community. This iterative and collaborative approach fosters a culture of continuous improvement, keeping ICT-enhanced language education aligned with pedagogical goals and emerging technological advancements. The combination of cost-effective technology policies, long-term strategic planning, and data-driven evaluation ascertains that institutions create a sustainable, adaptable, and inclusive foundation for technology-enhanced learning. Essentially, this approach is vital in guaranteeing that ICT integration is not merely a temporary innovation but a lasting transformation that supports equitable, high-quality language education for future generations.

CHALLENGES AND SOLUTIONS

The integration of ICT in language education presents numerous opportunities for enhancing learning outcomes. Poudel (2022) proclaimed that three major benefits include providing authentic language experiences, creating a co-operative and collaborative learning environment, and integrating opportunities that allow for effective teaching and learning. However, technology integration is not without its challenges at both the institutional and classrooms levels. In fact, educators often face several challenges in effectively implementing new technologies resulting in a lack of technology integration within their curricula. Educator frustration likewise stems from a lacking of training of new technological tools. Indeed, Howard et al.

(2021) stated that access and training are insufficient in technology implementation. As such, ensuring that educators possess the skills and confidence necessary for sustained ICT use is vital to the success of technology-enhanced pedagogy. One of the primary challenges is limited digital literacy and an inadequate understanding of how to implement new innovative tools to benefit learner performance. A recent example is that many language educators have experienced challenges in relation to the significant impact that advanced tools such as AI (e.g., ChatGPT) have had on language education (Yang, 2024). Rahimi and Sevilla-Pavón (2024) contended that insufficient readiness of AI integration and an efficient understanding of how to integrate these types of tools to facilitate innovative teaching have created unique educator challenges. Training opportunities that identify how AI can benefit learners could reduce the challenges and frustrations educators feel toward these tools. Basically, educators can learn to embrace AI instead of viewing it as a competitor to education. Providing educators access to meaningful experiences in their application of AI is valuable in restructuring their beliefs about integrating AI into language curriculum. For example, Mutammimah et al. (2024) discovered that teachers' perspectives of ChatGPT significantly impacted their use of this tool in their classes. They discovered that teachers who possessed more positive attitudes toward AI use were more likely to find it valuable in the language learning process. To address this concern, continuous professional development programs should focus on digital literacy, instructional design, and the effective use of language learning technologies with a specific emphasis on how to embrace these tools for language development.

Another major barrier is inadequate access to resources and infrastructure, particularly in underfunded regions where institutions struggle with limited internet connectivity, outdated software, and a lack of modern hardware (Mustafa et al., 2024). These regions also struggle with accessing additional funds needed to overcome these challenges. This result in a digital divide that limits equitable opportunities for technology integration. To mitigate this situation, institutions and governments should prioritize funding initiatives to improve ICT infrastructure. Particularly, they can offer region specific grants that allow for technology implementation and training. Additionally, educators can incorporate low-tech solutions such as downloadable lesson materials, offline apps, and SMS-based learning tools to support students with limited internet access. Open educational resources and free digital platforms further offer cost-effective alternatives for language instruction. However, similar to incorporating other types of instructional materials, Rice and Ortiz (2021) cautioned that educators should carefully evaluate these types of materials prior to integrating them into their learning environments. They indicated four areas of consideration for evaluating online materials including their quality, accessibility, accountability to standards and data privacy, and flexibility in promoting active engagement.

Resistance to change and pedagogical adaptation is another challenge found across educational settings since many educators may be reluctant to adopt ICT due to unfamiliarity, fear of technology replacing traditional methods, or skepticism about its effectiveness. Interestingly, Alanoglu et al. (2022) reported that teachers' philosophies of education negatively impact their levels of digital literacy and resistance to change. Yet, many educators work and live within digital societies in which technology permeates all aspects of their daily lives. Gutiérrez-Martin et al. (2022) discovered that higher importance is placed on media and information literacy professional development than ICT training. A blended learning approach, which integrates both traditional and digital methodologies, can help educators gradually adopt technology at a comfortable pace and develop more positive perspectives toward ICT integration. Moreover, sharing evidence-based case studies and educator success stories can also demonstrate the positive impact of ICT on student learning outcomes, increasing teacher confidence and motivation. Personalized implementation plans tailored to different teaching styles can further support educators in adapting their pedagogy effectively. Nevertheless, Bingham and Oluwafolakemi (2017) discovered in their research that novice teachers find personalized learning more challenging to implement into their classes. Managing student engagement and digital distractions presents additional difficulties. While ICT tools can enhance engagement, they also introduce distractions such as social media and non-academic online content, which can reduce focus in learning (Vahedi et al., 2019). Detrimental effects of academic distractions are problematic regarding technology resulting in multitasking and decreased attention to classroom instruction (Dontre, 2020). To counteract this challenge, educators should design structured lesson plans with clear digital engagement guidelines, ensuring that technology is used purposefully and meaningfully throughout the class session. For instance, interactive and gamified learning tools can help maintain student interest while reinforcing language skills and reduce off task technology behaviors. Additionally, implementing time management and self-regulation strategies, such as guided online activities, digital break timers, and monitoring tools, can help students stay on task and discourage them for engaging with technology for other reasons during their learning activities.

Finally, assessing language proficiency through ICT-based tools can be complex, as automated grading systems may struggle to evaluate nuanced language skills such as pronunciation, tone, and cultural context. Careful review of students' grades and personalized feedback can offset these errors. Moreover, a combination of automated assessment tools and teacher-led evaluation can ensure a more comprehensive assessment process (Twabu & Nakene-Mginiqi, 2024; Zampirolli et al., 2021). AI-driven feedback tools that provide instant corrections can enhance learning efficiency, while peer review and collaborative learning (e.g., discussion forums, voice recordings, and interactive assignments) can further support students in assessing their own progress. Despite these challenges, strategic solutions can empower educators to overcome barriers and maximize the benefits of technology-enhanced instruction. For instance, as previously mentioned, educational institutions can invest in professional development, leverage low-cost resources, embrace blended learning, and implement structured engagement strategies resulting in educators creating more inclusive, effective, and sustainable ICT-integrated language learning environments. Moving forward Ergado et al. (2021) and Mielikainen (2021) further proposed that institutional support and collaboration among stakeholders are essential in addressing these challenges and ensuring the long-term success of technology-driven language education.

CONCLUDING THOUGHTS

To conclude this chapter, it is imperative to reiterate the importance of integrating ICT into language education since it represents a transformative step toward achieving SDG 4(Tyagi et al., 2020. Unfortunately, Vyas-Doorgapersad (2022) cautioned that ICT on sustainability development goals is not always high but is vital in technological advancement and increasing socio-economic development. By addressing barriers to accessibility, enhancing pedagogical practices, and fostering sustainable solutions, this chapter empowers educators to deliver inclusive and equitable quality education. The proposed solutions similarly offer scalable and adaptable solutions that can drive meaningful progress in language education, benefiting educators and learners alike while advancing the broader mission of sustainable development and global equity. Particularly, the chapter includes insights into the positive impact of ICT on learners in regard to engagement, effective communication, and targeted learning outcomes (Chen et al., 2021; Hassain, 2024; Singer et al., 2023). Furthermore, policy advocacy and research-driven strategies will be crucial in guiding sustainable implementation, ensuring that ICT solutions remain relevant, ethical, and accessible to all learners (Paudel, 2021; Rana & Rana, 2020). As education systems evolve and continue to change, embracing ICT-driven methodologies will become more imperative in enhancing language learning outcomes and contributing to the global mission of sustainable development and social equity. By fostering innovation, inclusivity, and global collaboration, ICT has the power to redefine language education, paving the way for a more equitable and knowledge-driven society.

By addressing barriers to accessibility, enhancing pedagogical practices, and fostering sustainable solutions, Rahimi and Oh (2024) shared that ICT empowers educators to deliver inclusive and equitable quality education. Ultimately, to build on this vision, collaboration between educational institutions, policymakers, and technology developers will be essential to ensure that ICT integration continues to evolve alongside advancements in technology and pedagogy. Partnerships with EdTech companies can facilitate the development of tailored, culturally responsive language learning tools, while government support can provide funding and infrastructure to underserved communities. Additionally, fostering global collaboration through initiatives like cross-border teacher exchanges, shared open educational resources, and multilingual digital content creation can help bridge cultural and linguistic divides. This collective effort can ensure that ICT-enhanced language education remains adaptable to diverse educational contexts, ultimately empowering learners not only to develop linguistic proficiency through impactful learning experiences but also to engage more effectively in a globally connected world.

REFERENCES

Abraham, M., Arficho, Z., Habtemariam, T., & Demissie, A. (2022). Effects of information communication technology-assisted teaching training on English language teachers' pedagogical knowledge and English language proficiency. *Cogent Education*, *9*(1), 2028336. DOI: 10.1080/2331186X.2022.2028336

Ahmed, S. T., & Roche, T. (2021). Making the connection: Examining the relationship between undergraduate students' digital literacy and academic success in an English medium instruction (EMI) university. *Education and Information Technologies*, *24*(4), 4601–4620. DOI: 10.1007/s10639-021-10443-0

Ahmed, Z., Nathaniel, S. P., & Shahbaz, M. (2021). The criticality of information and communication technology and human capital in environmental sustainability: Evidence from Latin American and Caribbean countries. *Journal of Cleaner Production*, *286*, 125529. DOI: 10.1016/j.jclepro.2020.125529

Ai, Y., Hu, Y., & Zhao, E. (2024). Interactive learning: Harnessing technology to alleviate foreign language anxiety in foreign literature education, 1-20. *Interactive Learning Environments*. DOI: 10.1080/10494820.2024.2409990

Akour, M., & Alenezi, M. (2022). Higher education in the era of digital transformation. *Education Sciences*, *12*(11), 784. DOI: 10.3390/educsci12110784

Akram, H., Abdelrady, A. H., Al-Adwan, A. S., & Ramzan, M. (2022). Teachers' perceptions of technology integration in teaching-learning practices: A systematic review. *Frontiers in Psychology*, *13*, 920317. DOI: 10.3389/fpsyg.2022.920317 PMID: 35734463

Alanoglu, M., Aslan, S., & Karabatak, S. (2022). Do teachers' educational philosophies affect their digital literacy? The mediating effect of resistance to change. *Education and Information Technologies*, *27*(3), 3447–3466. DOI: 10.1007/s10639-021-10753-3 PMID: 34602847

Alenezi, M., Wardat, S., & Akour, M. (2023). The need of integrating digital education in higher education: Challenges and opportunities. *Sustainability (Basel)*, *15*(6), 4782. DOI: 10.3390/su15064782

Alobaid, A. (2020). Smar multimedia learning of ICT: Role and impact on language learners' writing fluency – YouTube online English learning resources as an example. *Smart Learning Environments, 24.* https://slejournal.springeropen.com/articles/10.1186/s40561-020-00134-7

Alotaibi, N. S. (2024). The impact of AI and LMS integration on the future of higher education: Opportunities, challenges, and strategies for transformation. *Sustainability (Basel), 16*(23), 10357. DOI: 10.3390/su162310357

Alsayer, A. A. (2023). Learners' experiences in an online environment: An analysis of the impact of international collaboration. *SAGE Open, 13*(4), 21582440231208524. DOI: 10.1177/21582440231208524

Andreou, S. N., & Koutsampelas, C. (2015). Intergenerational mobility and equality of opportunity in higher education in Cyprus. *International Journal of Educational Development, 41*, 80–87. DOI: 10.1016/j.ijedudev.2015.01.003

Angelaki, M. E., Bersimis, F., Karvounidis, T., & Douligeris, C. (2023). Towards more sustainable higher education institutions: Implementing the sustainable development goals and embedding sustainability into the information and computer technology curricula. *Education and Information Technologies, 29*(4), 5079–5113. DOI: 10.1007/s10639-023-12025-8

Asongu, S., Amari, M., Jarboui, A., & Mouakhar, K. ICT dynamics for gender inclusive intermediary education: Minimum poverty and inequality thresholds in developing countries. *Telecommunications Policy, 45*(5). DOI: 10.1016/j.telpol.2021.102125

Baah, C., Govender, I., & Subramaniam, R. (2023). Exploring the role of gamification in motivating students to learn. *Cogent Education, 10*(1), 2210045. DOI: 10.1080/2331186X.2023.2210045

Barbosa, M. W., & Ferreira-Lopes, L. (2021). Emerging trends in telecollaboration and virtual exchange: A bibliometric study. *Educational Review, 75*(3), 558–586. DOI: 10.1080/00131911.2021.1907314

Baskara, R. M., & Mukarto, M. (2023). Exploring the implications of ChatGPT for language learning in higher education. *Indonesian Journal of English Language Teaching and Applied Linguistics, 7*(2), 343–358. https://ijeltal.org/index.php/ijeltal/article/view/1387. DOI: 10.21093/ijeltal.v7i2.1387

Becirovic, S., Brdarevic-Celjo, A. B., & Delic, H. (2021). The use of digital technology in foreign language learning. *Spring Nature, 1*(10), 246. https://pmc.ncbi.nlm.nih.gov/articles/PMC8475434/

Bingham, A. J., & Oluwafolakemi, O. (2017). Staying on track: Examining teachers' experiences in a personalized learning model. *Journal of Ethnographic and Qualitative Research, 12*(2), 75.

Blake, R. J. (2013). *Brave new digital classroom: Technology and foreign language learning* (2nd ed.). Georgetown University Press.

Braudlacht, R. C., Martins, M. L., & Poppi, F. (2022). *Offering 21st century skills training through interactive online collaboration in higher education*. Routledge.

Canese, V., Paez, R., & Amarilla, J. (2023). Critical issues in the English language classroom: ICT and online learning in language education. *International Journal of Technology in Education*, *6*(1), 87–99. DOI: 10.46328/ijte.312

Central Institute of Educational Technology. (n.d.). *ICT for teaching and learning of languages*. https://ciet.ncert.gov.in/

Chen, H. J. (2023). Gather in the metaverse: Learning outcomes, virtual presence, and perceptions of high- and low-achieving pre-service teachers of English as foreign language. *Education and Information Technologies*, *29*(7), 8549–8577. DOI: 10.1007/s10639-023-12135-3

Chen, X., Zou, D., Xie, H., & Cheng, G. (2021). Twenty years of personalized language learning: Topic Modeling and knowledge mapping. *Journal of Educational Technology & Society*, *24*(1), 205–222. https://www.jstor.org/stable/26977868

Chen, Y. C. (2022). Effects of technology-enhanced language learning on reducing EFL learners' public speaking anxiety. *Computer Assisted Language Learning*, *37*(4), 789–813. DOI: 10.1080/09588221.2022.2055083

Cheng, S., & Parker, M. (2023). The role of school socioeconomic status in school-wide technology integration in the U.S. *Contemporary Educational Technology*, *15*(2), 422. DOI: 10.30935/cedtech/13059

Consoli, T., Désiorn, J., & Cattaneo, A. (2023). What is "technology integration" and how is it measured in K-12 education? A systematic review of survey instruments from 2010 to 2021. *Computers & Education*, *197*, 104742. DOI: 10.1016/j.compedu.2023.104742

Costa, A. C. F., Silva, A. M., Espuny, M., Rocha, A. B. T. R., & Oliveira, O. J. (2023). Toward quality education: Contributions of EdTech to the achievement of the fourth United Nations sustainable development goal. *Sustainable Development*. DOI: 10.1002/sd.2742

Dhimolea, T. K., Kaplan-Rakowski, R., & Lin, L. (2022). A systematic review of research on high-immersion virtual reality for language learning. *TechTrends*, *66*(5), 810–824. DOI: 10.1007/s11528-022-00717-w

Dontre, A. J. (2020). The influence of technology on academic distraction: A review. *Human Behavior and Emerging Technologies*. DOI: 10.1002/hbe2.229

Duffy, L. N., Stone, G. A., Townsend, J., & Cathey, J. (2020). Rethinking curriculum internationalization: Virtual exchange as a means to attaining global competencies, developing critical thinking, and experiencing transformative learning. *SCHOLE: A Journal of Leisure Studies and Recreation Education, 37*(1-2), 11-25. DOI: 10.1080/1937156X.2020.1760749

Ergado, A. A., Desta, A., & Mehta, H. (2021). Determining the barriers contributing to ICT implementation by using technology-organization-environment framework in Ethiopian higher educational institutions. *Education and Information Technologies, 26*(3), 3115–3133. DOI: 10.1007/s10639-020-10397-9

Evurulobi, C. I., Dagunduro, A. O., & Ajuwon, O. A. (2024). *Language learning technologies: A review of trends in the USA and globally*. World Journal of Advanced Research and Reviews., DOI: 10.30574/wjarr.2024.23.3.2851

Fernández-Batanero, J. M., Montenegro-Rueda, M., Fernández-Cerero, J., & García-Martínez, I. (2022). Assistive technology for the inclusion of students with disabilities: A systematic review. *Educational Technology Research and Development, 70*(5), 1911–1930. DOI: 10.1007/s11423-022-10127-7

Garcia-López, I. M., Acosta-Gonzaga, E., & Ruiz-Ledesma, E. F. (2023). Investigating the impact of gamification on student motivation, engagement, and performance. *Education Sciences, 13*(8), 813. DOI: 10.3390/educsci13080813

Ghavifekr, S., & Rosdy, W. A. W. (2015). Teaching and learning with technology: Effectiveness of ICT integration in schools. *International Journal of Research in Education and Science, 1*(2), 175–191. https://files.eric.ed.gov/fulltext/EJ1105224 .pdf. DOI: 10.21890/ijres.23596

Ghazali, M., Makrakis, V., Kostoulas-Makrakis, N., Yakob, N., Rashid, R. A. A., Othman, W., & Fitriyanto, N. A. (2024). Predicting teacher's information and communication technology-enabled education for sustainability self-efficacy. *Sustainability (Basel), 16*(3), 5323. DOI: 10.3390/su16135323

Goel, R. K., & Vishnoi, S. (2022). Urbanization and sustainable development for inclusiveness of using ICTs. *Telecommunications Policy, 46*(6), 102311. DOI: 10.1016/j.telpol.2022.102311

Grabner-Hagan, M. M., & Kingsley, T. (2023). From badges to boss challenges: Gamification through need-supporting scaffolded design to instruct and motivate elementary learners. *Computers and Education Open, 4*, 100131. DOI: 10.1016/j.caeo.2023.100131

Guo, P., Jeyaraji, J. J., & Razali, A. B. (2024). A systematic review of collaborative mobile-assisted language learning (C-MALL) practices using bibliometric, content, and scientometric analyses. *Humanities & Social Sciences Communications, 11*(1), 1435. DOI: 10.1057/s41599-024-03940-3

Gutiérrez-Martín. Pinedo-González, R., & Gil-Puente, C. (2022). ICT and media competencies of teachers. Convergence towards an integrated MIL-ICT model. *Media Education Research Journal, 30*(70), 19-30. https://eric.ed.gov/?id=EJ1320974

Haleem, A., Javaid, M., Qadri, M. A., & Suman, R. (2022). Understanding the role of digital technologies in education: A review. *Sustainable Operations and Computers, 3*, 275–285. DOI: 10.1016/j.susoc.2022.05.004

Halkiopoulos, C., & Gkintoni, E. (2024). Leveraging AI in e-learning: Personalized learning and adaptive assessment through cognitive neuropsychology – a systematic analysis. *Electronics (Basel), 13*(18), 3762. DOI: 10.3390/electronics13183762

Han, R., Alibakshai, G., Lu, L., & Labbafi, A. (2024). Digital communication activities and EFL learners' willingness to communicate and engagement: Exploring the intermediate language learners' perceptions. *Heliyon, 10*(3), e25213. DOI: 10.1016/j.heliyon.2024.e25213 PMID: 38333790

Hassain, K. I. (2024). Reviewing the role of culture in English language learning: Challenges and opportunities for educators. *Social Sciences & Humanities Open, 9*, 100781. DOI: 10.1016/j.ssaho.2023.100781

Howard, S. K., Tondeur, J., Ma, J., & Yang, J. (2021). What to teach? Strategies for developing digital competency in preservice teacher training. *Computers & Education, 165*, 104149. DOI: 10.1016/j.compedu.2021.104149

Huong, N. L. T. (2021). Teachers' perceptions of ICT integration in English language teaching at the Vietnamese tertiary level. *European Journal of Contemporary Education, 10*(3), 697–710. https://files.eric.ed.gov/fulltext/EJ1324207.pdf

Imran, A. (2022). Why addressing digital inequality should be a priority. *The Electronic Journal on Information Systems in Developing Countries, 89*(3), e12255. DOI: 10.1002/isd2.12255

Johler, M., & Krumsvik, R. J. (2022). Increasing inclusion through differentiated instruction in a technology-rich primary school in Norway. *International Journal of Primary. Elementary and Early Years Education, 52*(8), 1207–1221. DOI: 10.1080/03004279.2022.2143721

Kaya, O. S., & Ercag, E. (2023). The impact of applying challenge-based gamification program on students' learning outcomes: Academic achievement, motivation, and flow. *Education and Information Technologies*, *28*(8), 10053–10078. DOI: 10.1007/s10639-023-11585-z PMID: 36691635

Kwihangana, F. (2024). Teacher positioning in educational ICT policies: Implications for digital teacher identity development in under-resourced contexts. *Journal of Education Policy*, *40*(2), 242–265. DOI: 10.1080/02680939.2024.2386309

Laabidi, M., Jemni, M., Ayed, L. J. B., Brahim, H. B., & Jemaa, A. B. (2014). Learning technologies for people with disabilities. *Journal of King Saud University. Computer and Information Sciences*, *26*(1), 29–45. DOI: 10.1016/j.jksuci.2013.10.005

Lin, M. (2018). *"I don't even know where Turkey is: Developing intercultural competence through e-pal exchanges. Journal of Global Education and Research, 2*(2), 68-81. 68-81. https://www.doi.org/10.5038/

Liu, G. Z., Fathi, J., & Rahimi, M. (2024). Using digital gamification to improve language achievement, foreign language enjoyment, and ideal L2 self: A case of English as a foreign language learners. *Journal of Computer Assisted Learning*, *40*(4), 1347–1364. DOI: 10.1111/jcal.12954

Loewen, S., Crowther, D., Isbell, D. R., Kim, K. M., Maloney, J., Miller, Z. F., & Rawal, H. (2019). Mobile-assisted language learning: A Duolingo case study. *ReCALL*, *31*(3), 293–311. DOI: 10.1017/S0958344019000065

Low, E. L. (2025). Repositioning the English language teacher education for global competence and local realities: Adopting the cline of glocality. *TESOL Journal*, *16*(1), e70012. DOI: 10.1002/tesj.70012

Lu, D., & Xie, Y. N. (2022). Critical thinking cultivation in TESOL with ICT tools: A systematic review. *Computer Assisted Language Learning*, *37*(1), 222–242. DOI: 10.1080/09588221.2022.2033788

Luo, J. (2024). Validating the impact of gamified technology-enhanced learning environments on motivation and academic performance: Enhancing TELES with digital badges. *Frontiers in Education*, *9*, 1429452. DOI: 10.3389/feduc.2024.1429452

Luo, Z. (2023). The effectiveness of gamified tools for foreign language learning (FLL): A systematic review. *Behavioral Science*, *13*(13), 331. https://pmc.ncbi.nlm.nih.gov/articles/PMC10135444/. DOI: 10.3390/bs13040331 PMID: 37102845

Mielikainen, M. (2021). Towards blended learning: Stakeholders' perspectives on a project-based integrated curriculum in ICT engineering education. *Industry and Higher Education*, *36*(1), 74–85. DOI: 10.1177/0950422221994471

Msambwa, M. M., Daniel, K., & Lianya, C. (2024). Integration of information and communication technology in secondary education for better learning: A systematic literature review. *Social Sciences & Humanities Open*, *10*, 101203. DOI: 10.1016/j.ssaho.2024.101203

Muir, T., Wang, I., Trimble, A., Mainsbridge, C., & Douglas, T. (2022). Using interactive online pedagogical approaches to promote student engagement. *Education Sciences*, *12*(6), 415. DOI: 10.3390/educsci12060415

Mustafa, F., Nguyen, H. T. M., & Goa, X. (2024). The challenges and solutions of technology integration in rural schools: A systematic literature review. *International Journal of Educational Research*, *126*, 102380. DOI: 10.1016/j.ijer.2024.102380

Mutammimah, H., Rejeki, S., Kustini, S., & Amelia, R. (2024). Understanding teachers' perspective toward ChatGPT acceptance in English language teaching. [IJTE]. *International Journal of Technology in Education*, *7*(2), 290–307. DOI: 10.46328/ijte.656

Naghdipour, B. (2022). ICT-enabled informal learning in EFL writing. *Journal of Second Language Writing*, *56*, 100893. DOI: 10.1016/j.jslw.2022.100893

National Center for Education Statistics. (n.d.). *Technology and K-12 education.* https://nces.ed.gov/resources/edtechequity/

Nilubol, K., & Sitthikikul, P. (2023). Gamification: Trends and opportunities in language teaching and learning practices. *PASAA: Journal of Language Teaching and Learning in Thailand, 67,* 378-400. https://files.eric.ed.gov/fulltext/EJ1413891.pdf

O'Dowd, R. (2018). From telecollaboration to virtual exchange: State-of-the-art and the role of UNICollaboration in moving forward. *Journal of Virtual Exchange*, *1*, 1–23. https://eric.ed.gov/?id=ED592404. DOI: 10.14705/rpnet.2018.jve.1

Ofosu-Asare, Y. (2024). Developing classroom ICT teaching techniques, principles and practice for teachers in rural Ghana without access to computers or internet: A framework based on literature review. *International Journal of Information and Learning Technology*, *41*(3), 262–279. DOI: 10.1108/IJILT-04-2023-0045

Oliveira, W., Hamari, J., Joaquim, S., Toda, A. M., Palomino, P. T., Vassileva, J., & Isotani, S. (2022). The effects of personalized gamification on students' flow experience, motivation, and enjoyment. *Smart Learn. Environ.*, *9*(16), 16. DOI: 10.1186/s40561-022-00194-x

Osipova, A. V., & Lao, R. S. (2022). Breaking the cycle of failure for culturally and linguistically diverse learners with exceptional needs: Recommendations for improvement of teacher preparation programs. *Educational Research and Development Journal, 25*(1), 1-25. https://files.eric.ed.gov/fulltext/EJ1360921.pdf

Ozdemire, E., & Papi, M. (2021). Mindsets as sources of L2 speaking anxiety and self-confidence: The case of international teaching assistants in the U.S. *Innovation in Language Learning and Teaching*, *16*(3), 234–248. DOI: 10.1080/17501229.2021.1907750

Palieraki, S., & Koutrouba, K. (2021). Differentiated instruction in information and communications technology teaching and effective learning in primary education. *European Journal of Educational Research*, *10*(3), 1487–1504. DOI: 10.12973/eu-jer.10.3.1487

Pinto, R. D., Peixoto, B., Melo, M., Cabral, L., & Bessa, M. (2021). Foreign language learning gamification using virtual reality – A systematic review of empirical research. *Education Sciences*, *11*(5), 222. DOI: 10.3390/educsci11050222

Pitambar, P. (2021). Information and communication technology in foreign language classes in English: Roles and practices. *International Journal of Technology in Education and Science*, *5*(1), 37–55. DOI: 10.46328/ijtes.179

Poudel, A. P. (2022). Information and communication technology in English language teaching: Some opportunities and challenges. *Journal of Comparative & International Higher Education*, *14*(4), 103–116. https://files.eric.ed.gov/fulltext/EJ1363848.pdf. DOI: 10.32674/jcihe.v14i4.3874

Qi, S., & Derakhshan, A. (2024). Technology-based collaborative learning: EFL learners' social regulation and modifications in their academic emotions and academic performance. *Education and Information Technologies*. DOI: 10.1007/s10639-024-13167-z

Raghavan, R., Fitzsimmons-Craft, E. E., Welch, R. R., Proctor, E. K., Wilson, T., Agras, W. S., & Wilfley, D. E. (2024). Cost-effectiveness of train-the-trainer versus expert consultation training models for implementing interpersonal psychotherapy in college mental health settings: Evidence from a national cluster randomized trail. *Implementation Science : IS*, *19*(55), 55. DOI: 10.1186/s13012-024-01388-2 PMID: 39075590

Rahimi, A. R., & Sevilla-Pavón, A. (2024). The role of ChatGPT readiness in shaping language teachers' language teaching innovation and meeting accountability: A bisymmetric approach. *Computers and Education: Artificial Intelligence*, *7*, 100258. DOI: 10.1016/j.caeai.2024.100258

Rahimi, R. A., & Oh, G. S. (2024). Rethinking the role of educators in the 21st century: Navigating globalization, technology, and pandemics. *Journal of Marketing Analytics*, *12*(2), 182–197. DOI: 10.1057/s41270-024-00303-4

Ramaswamy, M., Marciniuk, D. D., Csonka, V., Coló, L., & Saso, L. (2021). Reimagining internationalization of higher education through the United Nations Sustainable Development Goals for the betterment of society. *Journal of Studies in International Education*, *25*(4), 388–406. DOI: 10.1177/10283153211031046

Rana, K., & Rana, K. (2020). ICT integration in teaching and learning activities in higher education: A case study of Nepal's teacher education. *Malaysian Online Journal of Educational Technology*, *8*(1), 36–47. DOI: 10.17220/mojet.2020.01.003

Rice, M. F., & Ortiz, K. R. (2021). Evaluating digital instructional materials for K-12 online and blended learning. *TechTrends*, *65*(6), 977–992. DOI: 10.1007/s11528-021-00671-z PMID: 34632461

Rothe, F. F., Audenhove, L. V., & Loisen, J. (2022). Digital development inequalities & the sustainable development goals: Whad does "leave-no-one behind" mean for ICT4D? *Information Technology for Development*, *29*(1), 9–26. DOI: 10.1080/02681102.2022.2076640

Saini, M., Sengupta, E., Singh, M., Singh, H., & Singh, J. (2023). Sustainable development goal for quality education (SDG4): A study on SDG4 to extract the pattern of association among the indicators of SDG4 employing a genetic algorithm. *Education and Information Technologies*, *28*(2), 2031–2039. DOI: 10.1007/s10639-022-11265-4 PMID: 35975216

Salamah, U., Zaki, A., Rokhyanto, R., & Razak, F. (2024). Leveraging augmented reality for interactive language learning. *Journal of International of Lingua & Technology*, *3*(3), 499. DOI: 10.55849/jiltech.v3i3.729

Sendag, S., Caner, M., Gedik, N., & Toker, S. (2024). Enhancing language proficiency through mobile extensive listening and podcasting: A multifaceted approached to metacognition and critical thinking. *Thinking Skills and Creativity*, *54*, 101656. DOI: 10.1016/j.tsc.2024.101656

Shen, Z., Lai, M., & Wang, F. (2024). Investigating the influence of gamification on motivation and learning outcomes in online language learning. *Frontiers in Psychology*, *15*, 1295709. DOI: 10.3389/fpsyg.2024.1295709 PMID: 38860036

Shi, J., Sitthiworachart, J., & Hong, J. C. (2024). Supporting project-based learning for students' oral English skill and engagement with immersive virtual reality. *Education and Information Technologies, 29*(11), 14127–14150. DOI: 10.1007/s10639-023-12433-w

Shonfeld, M., Cotnam-Kappel, M., Judge, M., Yeehan Ng, C., Ntebutse, J. G., Williamson-Leadley, S., & Yildiz, M. (2021). Learning in digital environments: A model for cross-cultural alignment. *Educational Technology Research and Development, 69*(4), 2151–2170. DOI: 10.1007/s11423-021-09967-6 PMID: 33654347

Shortt, M., Tilak, S., Kuznetcova, I., Martens, B., & Akinkuolie, B. (2023). Gamification in mobile-assisted language learning: A systematic view of Duolingo literature from public release of 2012 to early 2020. *Computer Assisted Language Learning, 36*(3), 517–554. DOI: 10.1080/09588221.2021.1933540

Singer, J. B., Báez, J. C., & Rios, J. A. (2023). AI creates the message: Integrating AI language learning models into social work education and practice. *Journal of Social Work Education, 59*(2), 294–302. DOI: 10.1080/10437797.2023.2189878

Suhrheinrich, J. (2011). Examining the effectiveness of a train-the-trainer model: Training teachers to use pivotal response training. *Society for Research on Educational Effectiveness,* 1-15.

Teng, M. F., Wang, C., & Wu, J. G. (2021). Metacognitive strategies, language learning motivation, self-efficacy belief, and English achievement during remote learning; A structural equation modelling approach. *RELC Journal, 54*(3), 648–666. DOI: 10.1177/00336882211040268

The United Nations. (n.d.). *Sustainable development goals.* https://www.un.org/sustainabledevelopment/

Timotheou, S., Miliou, O., Dimitriadis, Y., Sobrino, S. V., Giannoutsou, N., Cachia, R., Monés, A. M., & Ioannou, A. (2023). Impacts of digital technologies on education and factors influencing schools' digital capacity and transformation: A literature review. *Education and Information Technologies, 28*(6), 6695–6726. DOI: 10.1007/s10639-022-11431-8 PMID: 36465416

Toke, N. (2023). The role of ICT in achieving the SDG goal of quality education. *Diversity for Social Impact. https://diversity.social/the-role-of-ict-in-achieving-the-sdg-goal-of-quality-education*

Tooley, M., & Hood, J. (2021). Harnessing micro-credentials for teacher growth. A national review of early best practices. *New America.* https://files.eric.ed.gov/fulltext/ED612409.pdf

Treve, M. (2021). What COVID-19 has introduced into education: Challenges facing higher education institutions (HEIs). *Higher Education Pedagogies*, *6*(1), 212–227. DOI: 10.1080/23752696.2021.1951616

Twabu, K., & Nakene-Mginiqi, M. (2024). Developing a design thinking artificial intelligence driven auto-marking/grading system for assessments to reduce the workload of lectures at a higher learning institution in South Africa. *Frontiers in Education*, *9*(16), 1512569. DOI: 10.3389/feduc.2024.1512569

Tyagi, R., Vishwakarma, S., Alexandrovich, Z. S., & Mohammmed, S. (2020). ICT skills for sustainable development goal 4. In L. Filho, A. M. Azul, L. Brandli, P. G. Özuyar, P.G., & T. Wall (Eds), *Quality education. Encyclopedia of the unsustainable development goals*. Springer. DOI: 10.1007/978-3-319-95870-5_39

United Nations. (n.d.). *Goal 4: Ensure inclusive and equitable quality education and promote lifelong learning opportunities for all.* https://sdgs.un.org/goals/goal4

Vahedi, Z., Zannella, L., & Want, S. C. (2019). Students' use of information and communication technologies in the classroom: Uses, restriction, and integration. *Active Learning in Higher Education*, *22*(3), 215–228. DOI: 10.1177/1469787419861926

Valverde-Berrorocoso, J., Fernández-Sánchez, M., Dominguez, F. I. R., & Sosa-Díaz, M. (2021). The educational integration of digital technologies preCovid-19: Lessons for teacher education. *PLoS One*, *16*(8), e0256283. DOI: 10.1371/journal.pone.0256283 PMID: 34411161

Vargas-Montoya, L., Gimenez, G., & Fernández-Gutiérrez, M. (2023). ICT use for learning and students' outcomes: Does the country's development level matter? *Socio-Economic Planning Sciences*, *87*, 101550. DOI: 10.1016/j.seps.2023.101550

Vincent, D. A., Okeowo, R. O., & Ariyo, S. (2024). The use of assistive technology for students with disabilities in technical colleges in Ondo State. *Journal of Educational Research & Practice*, *14*(1), 52–67. DOI: 10.5590/JERAP.2024.14.1.04

Vyas-Doorgapersad, S. (2022). The use of digitalization (ICTs) in achieving sustainable development goals. *Global Journal of Emerging Market Economies*, *14*(2), 265–278. DOI: 10.1177/09749101211067295

Wang, D., Zhou, T., & Wang, M. (2021). Information and communication technology (ICT), digital divide and urbanization: Evidence from Chinese cities. *Technology in Society*, *64*, 101516. DOI: 10.1016/j.techsoc.2020.101516

Xu, J., Lio, A., Dhaliwal, H., Andrei, S., Balakrishnan, S., Nagani, U., & Samadder, S. (2021). Psychological interventions of virtual gamification within academic intrinsic motivation: A systematic review. *Journal of Affective Disorders*, *293*(1), 444–465. DOI: 10.1016/j.jad.2021.06.070 PMID: 34252688

Yang, A. (2024). Challenges and opportunities for foreign language teachers in the era of artificial intelligence. *International Journal of Education and Humanities*, *4*(1), 39–50. DOI: 10.58557/(ijeh).v4i1.202

Zampirolli, F. A., Josko, J. M. B., Venero, M. L. F., Kobayashi, G., Fraga, F. J., Goya, D., & Savegnago, H. R. (2021). An experience of automated assessment in a large-scale introduction programming course. *Computer Applications in Engineering Education*, *29*(5), 1284–1299. DOI: 10.1002/cae.22385

Zhang, X., & Zhou, M. (2023). Information and digital technology-assisted interventions to improve intercultural competence: A meta-analytical review. *Computers & Education*, *194*, 104697. DOI: 10.1016/j.compedu.2022.104697

Zhou, A. (2023). Investigating the impact of online language exchanges on second language speaking and willingness to communicate of Chinese EFL learners: A mixed methods study. *Frontiers in Psychology*, *14*, 1177922. DOI: 10.3389/fpsyg.2023.1177922 PMID: 37251019

ADDITIONAL READING

Abel, V. R., Tondeur, J., & Sang, G. (2022). Teacher perceptions about ICT integration into the classroom instruction. *Education Sciences*, *12*(9), 609. DOI: 10.3390/educsci12090609

Dong, C. (2025). 'Young children nowadays are very smart in ICT' - preschool teachers' perceptions of ICT use. *International Journal of Early Years Education*, *33*(2), 345–358. DOI: 10.1080/09669760.2018.1506318

Feng, L., He, L., & Ding, J. (2023). The association between the perceived teacher support, students ICT self-efficacy, and online English engagement in the blended learning context. *Sustainability (Basel)*, *15*(8), 6839. DOI: 10.3390/su15086839

Jayaprakash, P., & Pillai, R. R. (2021). The role of ICT and effect of national culture on human development. *Journal of Global Information Technology Management*, *24*(3), 183–207. DOI: 10.1080/1097198X.2021.1953319

Jayaprakash, P., & Pillai, R. R. (2022). The role of ICT for sustainable development: A cross-country analysis. *European Journal of Development Research, 34*(1), 225–247. DOI: 10.1057/s41287-021-00369-1

Li, J., Zhu, S., Yang, H. H., & Guo, Q. (2023). Impact of information literacy, self-directed learning skills, and academic emotions on high school students' online learning engagement: A structural equation modeling analysis. *Education and Information Technologies, 28*(10), 13485–13504. DOI: 10.1007/s10639-023-11760-2 PMID: 37361741

Sun, W., & Shi, H. (2024). Fostering success in online English education: Exploring the effects of ICT literacy, online learning self-efficacy, and motivation on deep learning. *Education and Information Technologies, 29*(18), 24899–24920. DOI: 10.1007/s10639-024-12827-4

KEY TERMS AND DEFINITIONS

Digital Technology: comprises electronic tools, systems, devices, and resources that generate, store, or process data.

Information Communication Technology (ICT): tools, systems, and resources that are used to manage, process, and communicate information digitally.

Language Education: the teaching and learning of languages and encompasses the development of reading, writing, speaking, and listening skills.

Learner Engagement: the degree of attention, curiosity, interest, and motivation that students show during the learning process.

Professional Development: focuses on the structured learning experiences and ongoing training that improve an individual's skills, knowledge, and effectiveness in their professional role.

Sustainable Development: the practice of fulfilling current needs while ensuring that future generations have the resources and opportunities necessary to meet their own needs.

Technology-Enhanced Pedagogy: teaching strategies that purposefully integrate digital tools and platforms to improve learning outcomes.

Chapter 3
Analyzing Artificial Intelligence Utilization in Foreign Language Education in Higher Education

Ülkü Ülker
https://orcid.org/0000-0002-5452-4227
Dicle University, Turkey

ABSTRACT

This study systematically reviews 44 Web of Science-indexed articles to examine the integration of artificial intelligence (AI) in foreign language education within higher education. Findings indicate that AI implementation in this field is a recent trend, with research activity increasing notably since 2022, especially in countries such as People's Republic of China and Ukraine. Key areas explored include teacher competence, ethical implications, AI tools for feedback, and assessment practices. AI demonstrates strong potential in enhancing language skills, particularly writing, speaking, vocabulary, and grammar. Despite its growing presence, AI research in this domain remains limited. The review identifies the need for greater collaboration, professional development, and ethical considerations. Furthermore, the study aligns with Sustainable Development Goal 4, underscoring AI's capacity to support inclusive and quality education.

DOI: 10.4018/979-8-3373-0801-2.ch003

INTRODUCTION

The integration of artificial intelligence (AI) into education plays a key role in promoting sustainable practices and achieving the Sustainable Development Goals (SDGs). AI supports accessibility, personalizes learning experiences, and helps adapt curricula to changing societal needs. These capabilities modernize teaching methods and prepare students for a technology-driven world. As a result, the use of AI in foreign language education is gaining increasing attention.

Language learning is a complex process involving both cognitive and social elements. Today, teachers and students are turning to AI tools—especially generative AI (GenAI)—to support this process (Macinska & Vinkler, 2024). These tools offer potential benefits, such as improving speaking practice, providing timely feedback, and tracking learner progress. However, their success depends on how well they are integrated into classroom settings and whether they truly address learners' needs.

To be effective, AI tools must be developed not only with technical knowledge but also with insights from educational research and teaching practice. While AI can support learning outside the classroom, the role of teachers remains essential. Educators provide personalized guidance, emotional support, and meaningful interactions—elements that AI cannot fully replicate (Bastani et al., 2024; Ji et al., 2023). Ideally, AI should complement, not replace, teachers. A balanced partnership between educators and AI can foster collaborative, engaging, and human-centered learning environments (Galaczi & Luckin, 2024).

Despite its potential, the use of AI in language education comes with challenges. Implementing AI tools requires investments in technology, infrastructure, and training. The digital divide continues to limit access in many regions, where students may lack devices, internet access, or digital literacy skills (López-Chila et al., 2024). Ethical concerns—such as data privacy and algorithmic bias—also need careful attention. AI systems must protect learners' data and avoid reinforcing stereotypes or inequalities.

This research aims to analyze how AI is used in foreign language education at the higher education level. The studies included will be identified through a systematic search of the Web of Science Core Collection using selected keywords and criteria. The study will explore the following research questions:

1. What is the distribution of studies by year?
2. What is the distribution of studies across world continents?
3. What is the distribution of studies by Web of Science categories?
4. What is the distribution of studies by scientific research methods?
5. Which variables were examined in these studies?

6. What is the distribution of AI utilization by language skills (reading, writing, listening, speaking)?
7. What is the distribution of Sustainable Development Goals (SDGs) are addressed in the studies?

LITERATURE REVIEW

Foreign Language and Language Learning

A foreign language is defined as one that differs from an individual's native language and is not commonly spoken in their everyday environment (Krashen, 2009; Lambert, 2006). Unlike a second language (L2), a foreign language is typically not used in daily life, and its acquisition occurs mainly through formal education (Ellis, 1997). The main distinction lies in the societal role of the language. For instance, English in Nigeria functions as a second language due to its societal utility, whereas in Arabic-speaking countries or in Türkiye, it is taught as a foreign language (Linguistic – Third Year – Lecture One, n.d.).

Foreign language learning focuses on developing four core skills: speaking, listening, reading, and writing (Brown, 2007). It is a comprehensive process aimed at improving individuals' academic, cultural, and social understanding while enhancing their multilingual competence (The Importance of Foreign Languages, n.d.). Globally, while Chinese is the most spoken language by native speakers, English is the most widely used in international communication, business, and academia (Crystal, 2003; Ethnologue, 2025). Considering these and Ammon's (2010) definition of a global language and its use as a lingua franca, English is the lingua franca of science. As such, English has become a global lingua franca and is widely used in both traditional and digital education contexts (Taskıran & Goksel, 2022).

AI-Powered Tools in Language Learning

Artificial intelligence is fundamentally transforming pedagogical frameworks, learner engagement, and the roles of teachers as instructional designers and facilitators, along with the environments, tools, and resources used in the teaching-learning process—particularly in areas such as critical thinking, personalized learning, and intercultural communication in language education (Zhang & Dong, 2024).

Today, learners benefit from a variety of AI-powered tools that assist with vocabulary acquisition, grammar correction, conversation practice, and personalized instruction (Macinska & Vinkler, 2024). With the development of generative AI (GenAI), these tools have become more accurate and effective, increasingly playing a supportive role in foreign language education. Examples such as multi-perspective text analyses in English literature, personalized learning in Chinese language classes, and VR simulations in Spanish culture classes can be considered concrete evidence of this transformation (Zhang & Dong, 2024). However, research on their pedagogical impact remains ongoing. Figure 1 explains how AI can support the language education.

Figure 1. AI Support for Four Language Skills (Organization for Economic Co-Operation and Development [OECD], 2024)

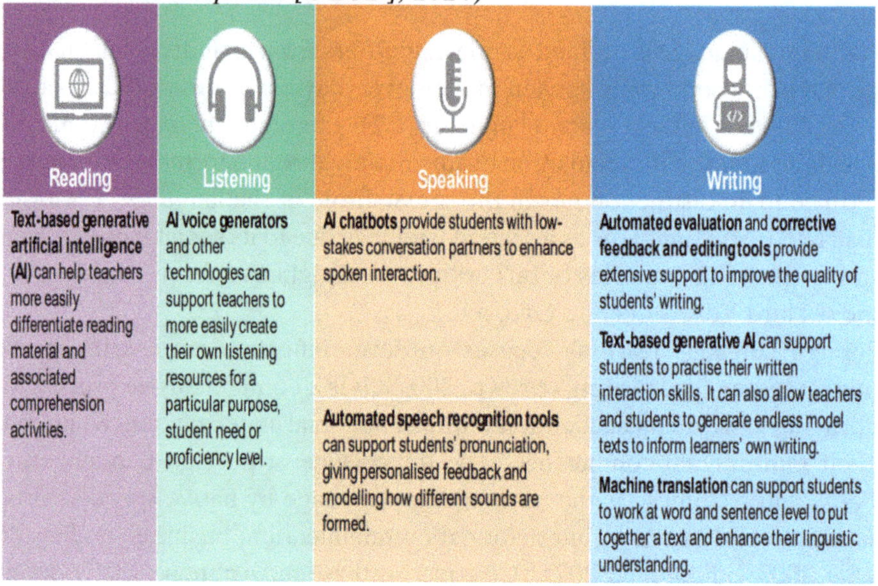

Figure 1 illustrates how AI supports each of the four main language skills. For example, ChatGPT has been shown to improve reading comprehension and inferencing without increasing reading anxiety (Çelik et al., 2024). GenAI is also credited with enhancing the accessibility and effectiveness of language learning (Galaczi, 2023). Artificial intelligence enhances the effectiveness of digital education platforms by supporting key functions such as course delivery, assessment, and content management, while simultaneously boosting student engagement, improving language skills and overall performance, and facilitating the development of communicative competence—the core goal of language learning (Nikonova et al., 2023).

English teachers' perceptions of the potential of artificial intelligence tools like ChatGPT in foreign language teaching and assessment play a pivotal role in shaping their effective use and realizing the benefits of AI in education (Zaiarna et al., 2024). Although AI offers significant advantages in areas such as vocabulary acquisition, grammar instruction, writing support, lesson planning, content creation, task design, and assessment, ongoing concerns remain regarding the appropriateness of AI-generated learning tasks for formal assessment purposes (Zaiarna et al., 2024). Moreover, there is a notable lack of clear guidance and established reliability regarding the effective integration and use of AI tools in language learning (Zaiarna et al., 2024). For instance, although ChatGPT provides valuable assistance in developing writing skills, the quality and consistency of its feedback often fall short compared to that offered by teachers or peers, largely depending on the input commands provided (Kurt & Kurt, 2024). Therefore, the role of teacher support and guidance is essential in enabling students to harness AI as a meaningful and effective feedback mechanism (Kurt & Kurt, 2024).

While generative AI is profoundly reshaping pedagogy, instructional strategies, student engagement, and the broader educational landscape in foreign language education, it simultaneously introduces a range of ethical, cultural, and structural challenges (Zhang & Dong, 2024). Notably, concerns have emerged regarding its potential to exacerbate achievement disparities between privileged and underprivileged student groups, diminish teachers' pedagogical autonomy and creative agency, and accelerate the homogenization of linguistic and cultural expressions (Zhang & Dong, 2024). In addition to these concerns, the integration of AI technologies raises pressing issues related to data privacy, algorithmic bias, academic integrity, and the safeguarding of cultural diversity. Within this evolving context, educators express their concerns about the potential misuse of generative AI for academic dishonesty, including cheating and plagiarism, while students voice skepticism regarding the fairness and transparency of AI-assisted assessment mechanisms (Zhang & Dong, 2024).

In addition to these pedagogical and ethical considerations, the functional limitations and design challenges of AI tools in language education also warrant critical attention. For instance, chatbots—an increasingly utilized AI application in this domain—often fall short in generating context-sensitive and meaningful dialogue, adjusting sentence complexity to align with learners' proficiency levels, and delivering accurate speech recognition and synthesis, all of which can adversely affect user satisfaction (Belda-Medina & Kokošková, 2023). From a technological design standpoint, there is a growing demand for user-friendly interfaces, interactive multimedia features, social media integration, and interface enhancements that promote more human-like interaction (Belda-Medina & Kokošková, 2023). These considerations underscore that the effectiveness of AI integration in language education depends not only on linguistic accuracy and pedagogical alignment but also on the usability and interactional quality of the tools themselves.

Artificial Intelligence in Higher Education

The rapid proliferation of artificial intelligence (AI) across all facets of daily life is driving profound and far-reaching transformations in the field of education. In particular, the integration of AI technologies into classroom environments has gained significant momentum within the educational technology sector, and reflecting this global shift, numerous countries—such as France, Australia, Estonia, South Korea, China, and the United States—have initiated the development of national strategies aimed at leveraging AI to enhance educational systems and practices (Pedró et al., 2019, ss. 34–35).

As national strategies continue to promote the integration of AI into educational systems, it becomes essential to clarify how these technologies function within learning environments. Artificial intelligence is commonly defined as systems capable of processing, modeling, and learning from data (Gillani et al., 2022). In educational settings, AI serves as a tool for analyzing student data in order to generate personalized learning pathways tailored to individual needs (Chen et al., 2020; Vázquez-Parra et al., 2024). Leveraging these capabilities, applications such as adaptive learning platforms and chatbots deliver customized content and support learners through continuous, real-time feedback, thereby enhancing both engagement and instructional effectiveness (Labadze et al., 2023).

High-Level Expert Group on Artificial Intelligence (2018) defines AI as follows:

> *Artificial intelligence (AI) refers to systems designed by humans that, given a complex goal, act in the physical or digital world by perceiving their environment, interpreting the collected structured or unstructured data, reasoning on the knowledge derived from this data and deciding the best action(s) to take (according to pre-defined parameters) to achieve the given goal. AI systems can also be designed to learn to adapt their behavior by analyzing how the environment is affected by their previous actions. As a scientific discipline, AI includes several approaches and techniques, such as machine learning (of which deep learning and reinforcement learning are specific examples), machine reasoning (which includes planning, scheduling, knowledge representation and reasoning, search, and optimization), and robotics (which includes control, perception, sensors and actuators, as well as the integration of all other techniques into cyber-physical systems). (p. 7)*

This definition implies that AI functions as a software-based system capable of autonomously performing predefined tasks. It gathers data from its environment, processes this information, and makes decisions based on programmed algorithms. Once implemented, an AI system can continue to learn and improve independently. These autonomous systems are notable for their ability to save time and reduce labor demands, while also offering potential sustainability benefits. As a result, AI has begun to integrate into various aspects of daily life. The capacity of education systems to effectively harness artificial intelligence is critically important not only for enhancing learning outcomes but also for restructuring educational programs to align with the transformative changes introduced by AI (Pedró et al., 2019, pp. 34–35). Figure 2 shows some impacts of integration AI to higher education systems.

Figure 2. Benefits, Vision, Challenges, and Applications of AI (López-Chila et al., 2024)

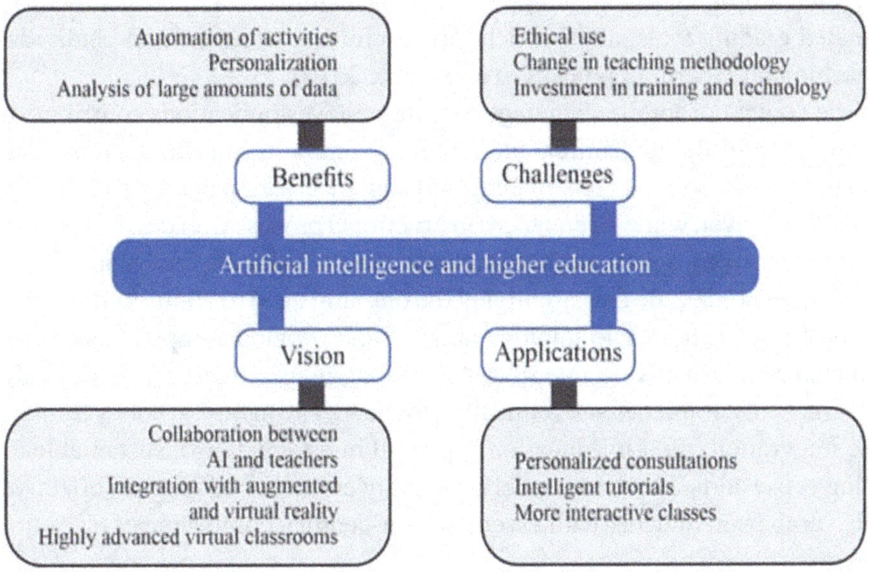

As shown in Figure 2, AI is transforming higher education in multiple areas:

1) Assessment, such as automated evaluation of student's data,
2) Forecasting study outcomes, including predictions of student's current and future situations,
3) Student support, via virtual agents and persuasive digital programs that assist learners,
4) Tutoring, by offering individualized approaches based on students' needs,
5) Learning management, involving analytics for training plans (Crompton & Burke, 2023; Ouyang et al., 2022).

Key advantages of artificial intelligence (AI) in education include student-centered personalization, improved assessment processes, and a reduction in teachers' administrative workload. For instance, adaptive learning systems analyze individual learners' strengths and weaknesses to create customized learning pathways, thereby enhancing academic performance (Holmes et al., 2019). Building on this personalization, AI technologies contribute to achieving Sustainable Development Goal 4: Quality Education, by enabling more inclusive and learner-focused instruction (Ivanytska et al., 2024). Tools such as ChatGPT support teachers in content generation, lesson planning, real-time feedback, and writing assistance, which not only enhance learning outcomes but also alleviate the burden on educators (Ivanytska et al., 2024). Moreover, the broad scope of AI applications in education encompasses intelligent tutoring systems, adaptive learning platforms, virtual instructors, and automated grading tools, all of which serve to further streamline and individualize the teaching and learning process (Yufei et al., 2020).

In the context of foreign language teaching, these applications contribute to the promotion of multilingualism, enable authentic communication, and support various digital tools such as video conferencing and content creation platforms (Ivanytska et al., 2024). However, while AI enhances instructional processes, excessive dependence on these technologies may weaken students' critical thinking and problem-solving skills (Pitts et al., 2025). This highlights the ongoing need to address ethical considerations, ensure responsible implementation, and provide comprehensive training for educators to effectively integrate AI into language education. Ultimately, the development of comprehensive, ethically grounded, and inclusive policy frameworks for the integration of AI in education is pivotal in establishing a sustainable digital learning ecosystem. These frameworks not only enhance pedagogical effectiveness but also empower students with essential 21st-century competencies.

Sustainability in Foreign Language Education

The United Nations Brundtland Commission (1987) defines sustainability as "meeting the needs of the present without compromising the ability of future generations to meet their own needs." The United Nations (2015) adopted 17 Sustainable Development Goals (SDGs) to address global challenges. Figure 3 shows the 17 SDG.

Figure 3. 17 Sustainable Development Goals (Key Sustainability, 2024)

It is obvious with the Figure 3 that sustainability has different dimensions including economic, social and environmental, and it can be defined various ways. In the context of English Language Teaching (ELT), it refers to equipping learners with the knowledge, values, and skills needed for a fairer and more sustainable future (Blue, 2022). Also Cambridge University has developed a sustainability framework for ELT aligned with the 17 SDGs (Cambridge, n.d.). Figure 4 present this framework produced by Cambridge.

Figure 4. Sustainability Framework for ELT (Cambridge, n.d.)

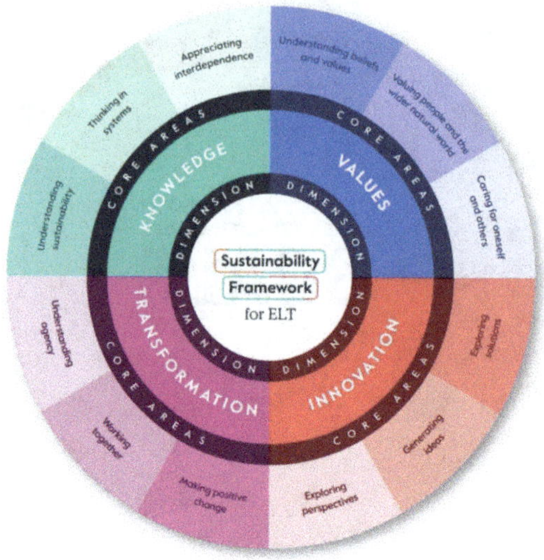

Figure 4 illustrates a sustainability framework for English Language Teaching (ELT) with four core dimensions: knowledge, values, innovation, and transformation, and twelve core areas related to these dimensions. Under the knowledge dimension, the core area of understanding sustainability emphasizes recognizing the environmental, social, and economic dimensions of sustainability (Cambridge, n.d.) that is vital for preparing ELT students to face global issues, fostering communication, critical thinking, problem-solving, empathy, and intercultural competence (Rios, 2023).

In response to the new needs brought about by economic globalization, revamping English language education in universities with AI-supported smart classroom applications, which offer a number of advantages such as personalized learning experiences, real-time feedback, interactive participation, providing a more engaging and effective learning experience, and ensuring the meaningful and effective development of language skills and cultural literacy, is an effective and necessary approach to improving students' language proficiency and cultural literacy (Zhang et al., 2023). This is because AI tools and systems reshape the way students interact with language, literature, and culture by designing personalized, immersive, and multi-perspective learning experiences (Zhang & Dong, 2024). Indeed, AlTwijri and Alghizzi (2024) have shown that AI applications are effective in improving the receptive and productive skills, vocabulary, and intercultural competence of English as a foreign language (EFL) and English as a second language (ESL) learners.

AI and Sustainability in Foreign Language

The use of AI technologies in English as a Foreign Language (EFL) settings is still a relatively recent development, requiring additional research to assess its effects on learners' emotional aspects (AlTwijri & Alghizzi, 2024). Nevertheless, AI's role in promoting sustainable foreign language education can be understood as twofold. On the positive side, it supports SDG 4 (Quality Education) and SDG 10 (Reduced Inequalities) by offering scalable and accessible solutions. For instance, apps like Duolingo use AI to provide personalized language learning, making education more inclusive (Vesselinov & Grego, 2012). AI also reduces resource consumption by minimizing the need for physical infrastructure and printed materials, contributing to environmental sustainability.

However, there are environmental drawbacks. Training large AI models like GPT-3 requires significant energy and produces carbon emissions, potentially conflicting with SDG 13 (Climate Action). For example, GPT-3's training was estimated to emit as much CO_2 as 123 cars annually (Caines et al., 2023; López-Chila et al., 2024; Oliver, 2024). Therefore, it is essential to consider the environmental costs when using AI in education.

In conclusion, when used responsibly, AI can enhance foreign language education by improving accessibility, supporting individual learning needs, and facilitating efficient assessment. These benefits align with the goals of inclusive and sustainable education, particularly SDG 4.

MATERIALS AND METHODS

Research Design

The study was organized according to qualitative principles and conducted with a systematic review approach. According to Gough, Oliver and Thomas (2017), systematic reviews are open, methodical, and reproducible investigations where studies are selected based on specific inclusion and exclusion criteria to address particular issues. These reviews are important as they generate compelling evidence by analyzing quantitative, qualitative, or mixed data (Hemingway & Brereton, 2009). Additionally, systematic reviews, also known as trend analysis studies, help identify research gaps and foster a collective perspective by compiling the findings of the field's research (Serhan & Yahaya, 2022).

Procedure

Why Web of Science?

In the study, the database to be searched for identifying the relevant studies are limited to Web of Science (WOS) core collection, and the scan has been conducted between December 14, 2024 and February 2025. The database is chosen as Web of Science, because it is highly esteemed because it involves prestigious journals in scientific and social fields (Hung & Zhang, 2012).

General View of Foreign Language

According to the screening results, the general view of foreign languages in higher education is as follows: The first scan was conducted on December 14, 2024 in all fields. According to this scan, general results for foreign language in higher education are as follows: At the first step, to examine the general situation, the search terms were determined as ["foreign language" and "higher education"] in all fields. The custom time range was from 1975/01/01 to 2024/12/31. As a result of the latest search on February 2025, a total of 3,671 studies were reached between 1981 and 2024, of which only 1,234 were open access. It can be said that the studies in the field started to gain momentum in 2013 with 118 studies. In addition, in 2017 and the following years, except for 2020, the annual number of studies in the field of foreign languages in higher education is over 300 per year. When these studies were examined according to document types, it was seen that they were distributed as articles, proceeding papers, book chapters, editorial materials, book reviews, retracted publications, meeting abstracts, books, notes, news item, and retraction. However, the WOS metrics show the majority of the studies were in the form of articles (2,597), proceeding paper (955) and book chapters (155). When the 3,671 documents were refined according to WOS categories, it was seen that the results were distributed across 154 different disciplines, with the majority of the disciplines being in the "Education & Educational Research" discipline with 2,310 studies. Also the majority for sustainable development goals is 04 Quality Education with 2,261 research.

Search Restrictions

Search restrictions were implemented as follows:

- The Document panel in the Web of Science Core Collections interface was used and the "All Fields" restriction was applied.

- The search terms were associated with the AND conjunction.
- The "Index Date" restriction was used in the year range. There is no specific starting point was specified for the studies to be included in the review and 2024/12/31 was determined as the cut-off date for indexed date.
- There is no discipline restriction. When the discipline restriction "Education Educational Research" was imposed, it was seen that the studies in the field of "Linguistic" were excluded, but these studies also fit the scope of the subject. In addition, considering the small number of studies under Education & Educational Research (10) when the selection criteria were applied and the reduced data diversity when the disciplinary restriction was imposed, no disciplinary restriction was applied.

Selection Criteria

The selection criteria applied to determine the preliminary studies that will serve the purpose of this research and be included in the systematic review are as follows:

- Document type must be article or review article,
- Retracted publication excluded,
- The language must be English,
- The study must be accessible as open access,
- The study must include artificial intelligence in the main text.

In addition to the selection criteria, since the scan was performed with *All Field* restrictions, the abstracts of the studies in the exported files were examined and the studies that were found not to fit the scope of the study were excluded.

Search Terms

Since only studies focusing on artificial intelligence can be included in this research, the searching term has been expanded in different ways by adding the term "*artificial intelligence*", "*AI*", "*generative* AI", "G*enAI*".

Additionally, three experts in the field of foreign languages were interviewed to gather their perspectives on the searching keywords. They stated that the term "*second language/L2*" is different from the term "*foreign language*" and therefore the use of the term "*foreign language*" is sufficient. In fact, the literature supports this position (Ellis, 1997; Linguistic – Third Year – Lecture One, n.d.). Experts also emphasized that since the term "*foreign language*" is an inclusive term, there is no need to separately scan expressions such as ELT, EFL, FL, IELTS, TEFL, TESOL,

TOFEL. Based on the information provided by the experts, only the term "foreign language" was included in the scan.

Table 1 shows the alternative keywords used to search and identify studies included in the review. You can also see the number of studies reached with the keyword used, based on the specified criteria.

Table 1. Search Terms and Record Counts According to Latest Search

Search Term	**Total Counts (Retracted publications excluded)**	**Document Type: Article or Review Article**	**Language: English**	**Accessibility: Open access**
foreign language (All fields) and higher education (All fields) and artificial intelligence (All fields)	234	168	156 (Studies published in other languages: Russian (9), Chinese (1), German (1), Korean (1))	72
foreign language (All fields) and higher education (All fields) and AI (All fields)	185	155	142 (Studies published in other languages: Russian (9), Spanish (2), Greek (1), Korean (1))	57
foreign language (All fields) and higher education (All fields) and generative AI (All fields)	19	18	18	5
foreign language (All fields) and higher education (All fields) and GenAI (All fields)	1	1	1	1
"foreign language" (All fields) and "higher education" (All fields) and "artificial intelligence" (All fields)	73	59	56 (Studies published in other languages: Russian (2), German (1))	25
"foreign language" (All fields) and "higher education" (All fields) and "AI" (All fields)	63	52	49 (Studies published in other languages: Russian (2), Spanish (1))	19

continued on following page

Table 1. Continued

Search Term	Total Counts (Retracted publications excluded)	Document Type: Article or Review Article	Language: English	Accessibility: Open access
"foreign language" (All fields) and "higher education" (All fields) and "generative AI" (All fields)	9	9	9	3
"foreign language" (All fields) and "higher education" (All fields) and "GenAI" (All fields)	1	1	1	1
Total				**183**
Duplicated				**82**
Out of the scope				**57**
Included				**44**

Table 1 shows the results of a search process, where data from the WOS scan page was exported and sorted by "Document title: A-Z" into an Excel file. After filtering, duplicate records were identified and removed, including studies repeated 8, 6, 4, 3, and 2 times, totaling 82 duplicates. After deleting the duplicates, 101 unique studies remained. These studies were reviewed by examining their titles, abstracts, keywords, and methods to determine relevance to Artificial Intelligence, foreign languages, and higher education. Studies not related to the subject (57) were discarded, leaving 44 studies (see Table Appx 1, for more detail) in included in the research.

Search Dates

Following the initial scan on December 14, additional scans were conducted on January 17, February 7. As a result, studies that were accepted and published within the past year but were uploaded to the electronic database at a later time were also included. Each scan result was compared with the Excel file created for data collection, allowing for the identification of studies that had been delayed in uploading to the electronic platform but were relevant to the scope of the research. These studies were subsequently incorporated into the analysis.

Data Collection Tool

MS Excel form has been prepared as the data collection tool by researcher. Each research question has a column name as themes including: years, world continents, WOS categories / research areas, scientific research methods, variables examined, basic skill areas for language education (reading, writing, listening, speaking), sustainable development goals. Also Web of Science metrics have been used to gather data. The data collection period covers the period between December 2024 and February 2025. During this period, scan files were downloaded at 3 different times.

Data Analysis

Descriptive content analysis has been applied in the examination of the documents. The results obtained from descriptive analysis can be used to identify trends related to a topic and serve as a guide for future studies (Lune & Berg, 2017; Yıldırım & Şimşek, 2018). During the data analysis process, coding can be done by more than one coder or by a single coder at time intervals (Bilgin, 2014, p.16).

The themes are as follows: years, world continents, WOS categories / research areas, scientific research methods, variables examined, basic skill areas for language education (reading, writing, listening, speaking), sustainable development goals. The findings have been recorded in MS Excel form. In addition, Web of Science metrics are used in the analysis of the data.

In this study, a single coder conducted two rounds of coding, with a three-week gap between the first (February 10, 2025) and second (March 10, 2025) coding sessions to assess reliability. Web of Science measurements supported this reliability check. Findings were presented through figures, graphs, or tables, with Napkin AI used to visualize descriptive content analysis results. VOSviewer software was employed for co-authorship and bibliographic coupling analysis, and AI tools such as ChatGPT, Gemini, Perplexity assisted in identifying Sustainable Development Goals (SDGs) for studies lacking this information in their Web of Science records. These three AI tools were selected depending on the researcher's knowledge and skill level. Article abstracts were uploaded to AI tools, and they were asked via a prompt was written to identify the most relevant SDG for each abstract, suggest at least three SDGs, and list them from most to least relevant. The SDGs identified by AI tools were compared with those selected by the researcher for consistency, and AI tools was asked to justify its SDG choices and consider alternative options to ensure result reliability.

Limitations

Open Access studies were chosen as a criterion for supporting sustainable education and ensuring easy access to information in line with the goal of 04 Quality Education. However, this criterion posed a handicap, as studies not registered as open access in the Web of Science (WOS) but offering full-text access through faculty networks were excluded from the research. This limitation reduced the number of studies and the diversity of data, meaning the results may differ if studies providing full-text access were included in the review.

The AI tools as ChatGPT, Gemini, Perplexity that used to identify SDG targets not specified in the WOS records were selected based on the researcher's knowledge and skill level. Results may vary depending on the use of different AI tools or the prompts entered into the AI system. Therefore, the SDG analysis of the 17 studies lacking SDG information in the WOS records may be biased. To minimize bias, analyses were conducted with three different AI tools, and the researcher compared these results with her own analysis.

FINDINGS

This research analyzes the use of AI in foreign language education within higher education, revealing key trends from 3,671 studies published between 1981 and 2024. The majority of studies are articles (2,597), proceeding papers (955), and book chapters (155), with only 1,234 of them being open access, a trend that began in 2006. Notably, only 74 studies address artificial intelligence, with the first mention in 2009. AI-focused studies spiked in 2023 (20 studies) and are expected to rise in 2024 (30 studies), with most being articles (56) and proceeding papers (14). Only 29 of these studies are open access, starting from 2019. The research highlights that AI integration in foreign language education started late, and despite its growth in recent years, its presence remains limited. Ultimately, 44 studies were selected for in-depth analysis.

Distribution by Year

It was observed that the 44 studies included in the research were distributed between 2019 and 2024. The number of studies by year is presented in Figure 5.

Figure 5. Distribution by Year

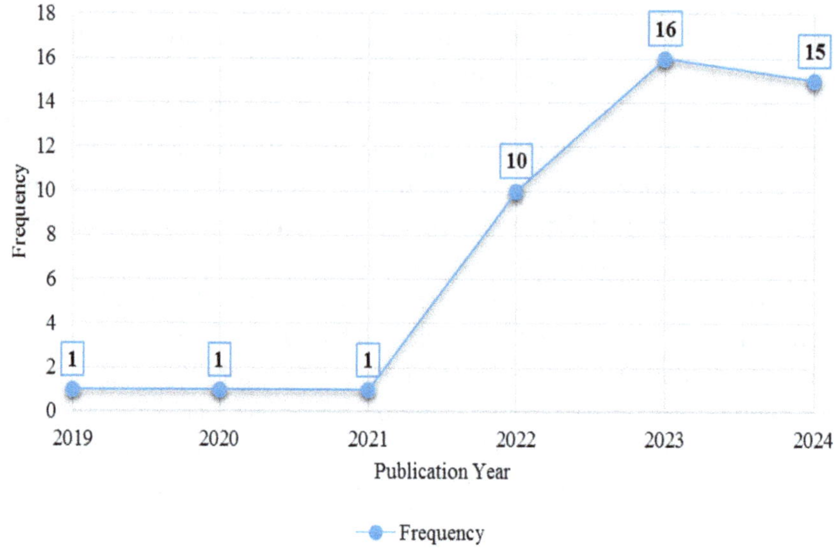

As presented in Figure 5, publications on artificial intelligence in foreign language education in higher education have increased in 2022. Therefore, it can be said that interest in artificial intelligence has increased in 2022 and beyond.

The findings of the analysis conducted to determine which countries on the world continents support this increasing interest and lead in the field are included in the following heading.

Distribution by World Continents

Figure 6 presents the countries according to their continents, along with the frequencies of each one:

Figure 6. Distribution of Studies by World Continent With Countries

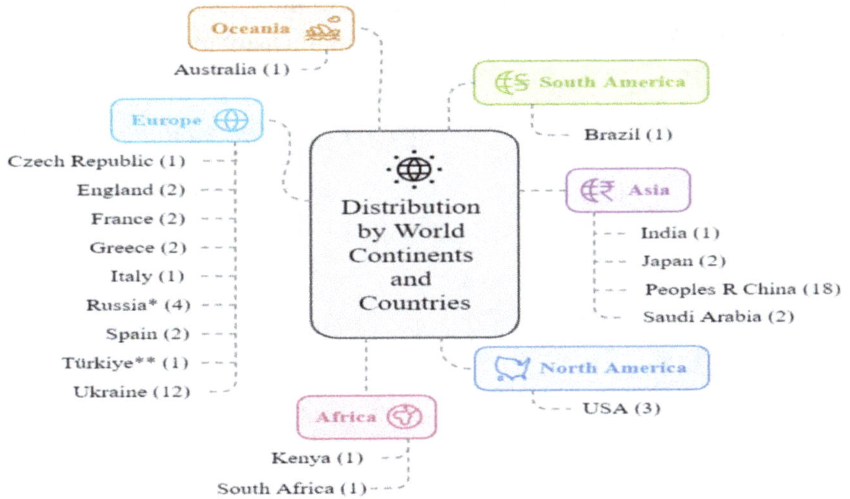

*Russia has been placed under Europe (since a large portion of It's territory is located in Europe, although part is in Asia).
**Türkiye has been placed under Europe (since the study here was carried out in Istanbul, although It's territory is located both Asia and Europe).

The frequencies on the Figure 6 are prepared based on the countries of the authors, and in cases where authors from different countries collaborated in co-authored studies; the same study was added separately to the countries of the contributing authors. So the same study may have been represented more than once on Figure 6.

As presented in Figure 6, 18 different countries were identified that published studies in this field, and it has been observed that studies on artificial intelligence are being carried out in foreign language education in higher education in all continents where active human life is maintained in the world. When the total number of contributions calculated for the Asian (23) and European (27) continents is examined, it can be said that there is no big difference between them about counts, and yet the European continent is the leader in artificial intelligence in foreign language education in higher education.

In the Asian continent, it was revealed that People's Republic of China provided the most contributions with 18 studies while it is Ukraine the most contributed with 12 studies in the European region. Therefore, it can be thought that People's Republic of China and Ukraine focus more on artificial intelligence in foreign language education in higher education and have more researchers working in this field. However, another reason for this situation may be the open access policies adopted by the authors and their institutions, depending on the fees required for open access. The support provided by institutions to authors can facilitate open access publishing and also support an increase in the number of publications in countries.

In order to model cross-country collaboration network on the use of AI in higher education for foreign language education, co-authorship analysis by authors was conducted with the VOSviewer software. The findings are presented in Figure 7.

Figure 7. Co-Authorship Analysis by Authors to Present the Collaboration Network

Figure 7 illustrates three distinct clusters based on a co-authorship analysis conducted using VOSviewer. The analysis of 44 studies identified a total of 162 authors, and by grouping authors with at least two publications, three clusters emerged, with four authors standing out. These four authors contributed at least two studies to the field, while 158 authors contributed only one study. As depicted in Figure 7, only two of these four authors share a collaborative connection, while the other two authors are represented as independent clusters. The two authors with a shared connection work at the same institution in the People's Republic of China, while the author "Yu, Zhonggen" is affiliated with a different institution in People's Republic of China, and "Schetinina, Aleksandra" is based at an institution in Russia. When the analysis criteria were changed to group authors with at least one publication, a graph of thirteen clusters emerged, but these thirteen authors were co-authors of the same publication and were from France, Brazil, and South Africa. Additionally, this study is the only one to show that at most three continents, Europe, South Africa and South America, collaborate. On the other hand, when the criterion was changed to a study with a maximum of ten authors, it was seen that there was a publication with seven authors and the authors were from the USA, Italy and Greece.

The results obtained from the co-authorship analysis on a country basis using the VOSviewer software to model the cross-country collaboration network regarding the use of artificial intelligence in higher education in foreign language education are presented in Figure 8.

Figure 8. Co-Authorship Analysis by Countries to Present the Collaboration Network

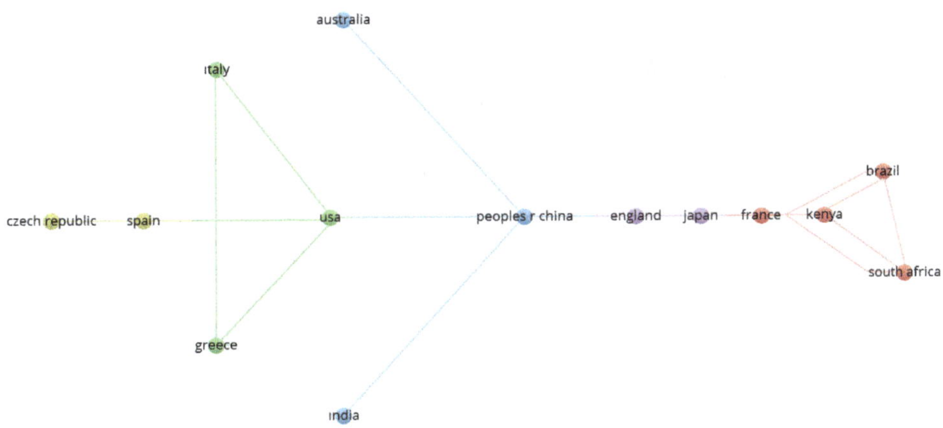

Figure 8 shows that 14 of the 18 countries conducting research on the use of AI in foreign language teaching in higher education have collaborated, and some of these collaborations are intercontinental. Russia, Saudi Arabia, Türkiye, and Ukraine were not listed in the co-authorship analysis by country by VosViewer. This situation has shown that in some countries, not only intercontinental cooperation but also cooperation with countries on the same continent has not developed.

A bibliographic coupling analysis was conducted at the country level to evaluate the connectivity and link strength of topics addressed by authors from each country. The analysis set the minimum criteria of one document per country and five citations per country, using citation counts as the weight for the visualizations. The results are presented in Figure 9.

Figure 9. Bibliographic Coupling Analysis With Country Unit

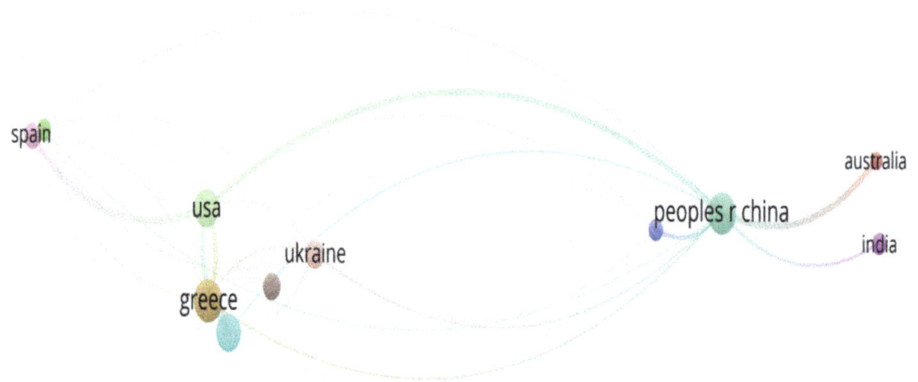

Figure 9 illustrates the relationships among 15 countries based on the selections made for the bibliographic coupling analysis. The topics of focus for authors in these countries, as well as the studies they cite, are interconnected. The citation counts for each country, along with the total link strength, are provided in Table 2.

Table 2. Citations Received by Countries and Total Link Strength

Country	Documents	Citations	Total Link Strength
Australia	1	5	84
Brazil	1	7	285
Czech Republic	1	10	63
England	2	10	138
France	2	8	332
Greece	2	140	191
India	1	10	26
Italy	1	78	182
Japan	2	2	137

continued on following page

Table 2. Continued

Country	Documents	Citations	Total Link Strength
Kenya	1	7	285
People's Republic of China	18	122	291
Russia	4	25	5
Saudi Arabia	2	4	30
South Africa	1	7	285
Spain	2	18	154
Türkiye	1	1	30
Ukraine	12	27	51
USA	3	87	339

An examination of the VOSviewer data presented in Table 2 reveals that Greece, with only two studies, has the highest citation count (140), indicating its influential research in AI for foreign language education. Despite this, Greece ranks seventh in citation similarity with other countries, with a link strength of 191. The United States, contributing three studies, has 87 citations and a link strength of 339, showing strong similarity with Spain. People's Republic of China, with 18 publications, has 122 citations and a link strength of 291, while Australia is most similar to People's Republic of China. Ukraine, with 12 publications, has only 27 citations and a link strength of 51.

The co-authorship analysis reveals no active international collaboration, but highlights interconnected topics and citation patterns among countries, suggesting potential for collaboration, particularly between the U.S., Spain, People's Republic of China, and Australia. This is because bibliographic coupling analysis highlights researchers citing similar work, which can be considered an indicator that these authors share common interests and areas of research. Collaboration between authors with similar knowledge, interests, and focus can contribute to the field's production of compelling work. However, the analysis of 44 open-access studies reveals a lack of cross-country collaboration in the application of AI in foreign language education within higher education. To enhance diverse cultural perspectives, create sustainable educational environments, and foster a global consensus on AI development for education, greater international collaboration is needed.

Distribution by WOS Categories

In order to examine which disciplines the studies produced on the use of AI for foreign language education in higher education belong to, the WOS Categories and Research Areas variables were examined. When reflecting the WOS categories in the table, similar categories are grouped, for example multidisciplinary sciences or social sciences and humanities. The findings are presented in Table 3.

Table 3. WOS Categories Showing Disciplines in Which Research is Conducted

WOS Categories	Frequency
Computer Science, Artificial Intelligence	3
Computer Science, Information Systems	4
Education & Educational Research	8
Environmental Sciences	3
Language & Linguistics	7
Multidisciplinary Sciences (*Chemistry, Engineering, Mathematics, Material Science*)	6
Neurosciences	4
Psychology	4
Social Sciences, Humanities	5

The findings presented in Table 3 indicate that the majority of studies on the use of AI in foreign language education within higher education are classified under the "Education & Educational Research" category, followed by the "Language & Linguistics" category. Additionally, the studies cover a wide range of research fields, including computer science, environmental science, neuroscience, and social science. The analysis reveals that research across these diverse disciplines is primarily aimed at advancing foreign language education.

Distribution by Scientific Research Methods

The scientific research methods of the 44 studies were examined to determine which type of study the interest is directed to. For the legends, please see the Table 4.

Table 4. Distribution of Studies by Scientific Research Methods

Scientific Research Method	Frequency
Literature Review	8
Mixed Research	14
Qualitative Research	
• Case Study	3
• Exploratory	1
Quantitative Research	

continued on following page

Table 4. Continued

Scientific Research Method	**Frequency**
• Experimental	11
• Scale Adaptation	1
• Survey	3
Systematic Review	3
Total	**44**

The 44 studies on AI in foreign language education used various research methods, as summarized in Table 4. Eight studies focused on literature reviews, exploring AI's role and key concepts. Most studies were quantitative (15) or mixed-methods (14), with fewer using qualitative methods (4). This indicates a preference for quantitative or mixed-methods approaches, which provide solid, experience-based insights. Mixed-methods studies strengthen findings by incorporating diverse data. Additionally, three systematic reviews were conducted, synthesizing existing knowledge and identifying research gaps, though these were less common than the other methods.

Distribution of Examined Variables

This thematic analysis organizes the codes into 8 categories related to AI usage, teacher and student engagement, ethical concerns, assessment practices, and the integration of technology into language education. The themes were derived based on the shared focus and nature of the elements in the list, ensuring a more structured and meaningful categorization, and they present the main variables of the 44 researches. The list of themes is as follows: "Enhancing Language Learning with AI (Chatbots, ChatGPT, Digital Tools)", "Teacher Competence, Readiness, Satisfaction", "Ethical Considerations and Academic Integrity", "AI Tools and Feedback", "AI in Assessment and Testing", "Technological Integration and Platforms", "Learners' attributes (Students' cognitive, behavioral, and affective process)", "Technological and Pedagogical Innovations".

Enhancing Language Learning With AI

The variables grouped under this theme are presented in Figure 10.

Figure 10. Variables Related to Enhancing Language Learning With AI

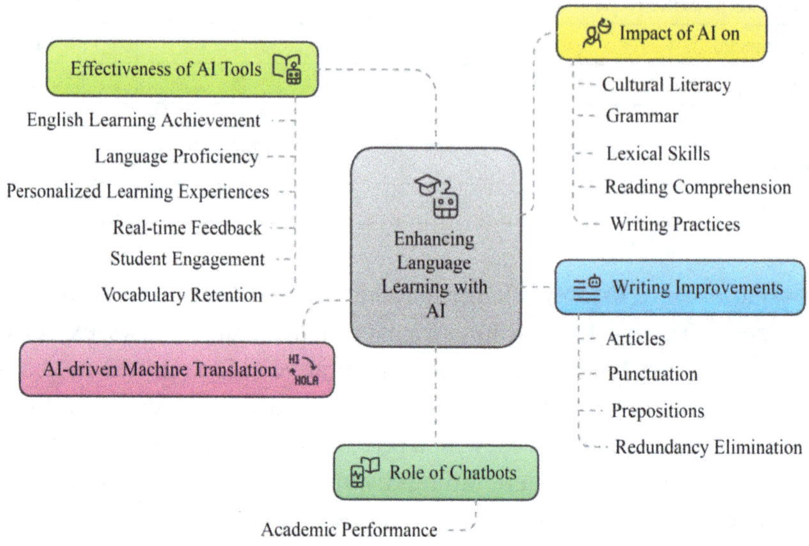

Figure 10 shows variables relevant to research on enhancing foreign language learning in higher education with artificial intelligence. One of the dimensions of the theme is effectiveness of AI tools. Effectiveness of AI on English learning achievement, language proficiency, personalized learning experiences, real-time feedback, student engagement, vocabulary retention is some subheading as variables examined or topics interested in 44 studies. Other dimensions are as follows: impact of AI, writing improvements, role of chatbots, AI-driven machine translation.

Teacher Competence, Readiness, Satisfaction

The variables grouped under this theme are presented in Figure 11.

Figure 11. Variables Related to Teacher Competence, Readiness, Satisfaction

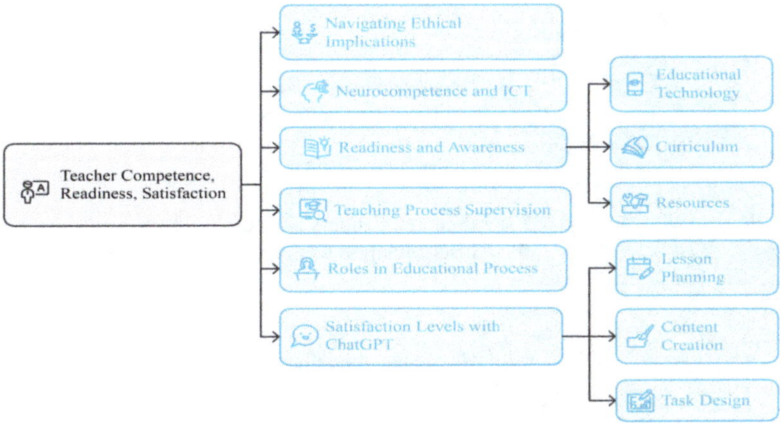

Figure 11 shows variables relevant to research on teacher competence, readiness, satisfaction for foreign language learning in higher education with artificial intelligence. One of the dimensions of the theme is readiness and awareness which has three sub-headings as educational technology, curriculum and resources. In accordance with satisfaction levels with ChatGPT, the sub-variables are lesson planning, content creation and task design. Also navigating the ethical implications, roles in educational supervision, neuro-competence and ICT are the other important variables examined in 44 studies regarding teacher competence, readiness and satisfaction.

Ethical Considerations and Academic Integrity

The variables grouped under this theme are presented in Figure 12.

Figure 12. Variables Related to Ethical Considerations and Academic Integrity

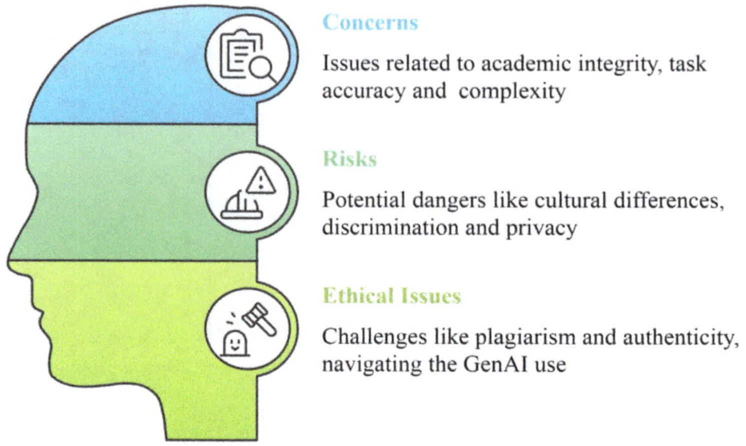

The review of 44 studies on ethical considerations and academic integrity, as shown in Figure 12, is divided into three subheadings. "Concerns" covers academic integrity, task accuracy, and the complexity of tasks generated by ChatGPT. "Risks" highlights issues like cultural differences, discrimination, and privacy. "Ethical Issues" addresses challenges related to plagiarism, authenticity, and the use of Generative AI. These subheadings also suggest language barriers and communication problems, especially in the context of cultural differences, discrimination, and privacy, with variables such as foreign language effects on communication and sustainability discourse falling under these themes.

AI Tools and Feedback

The variables grouped under this theme are presented in Figure 13.

Figure 13. Variables Related to AI Tools and Feedback

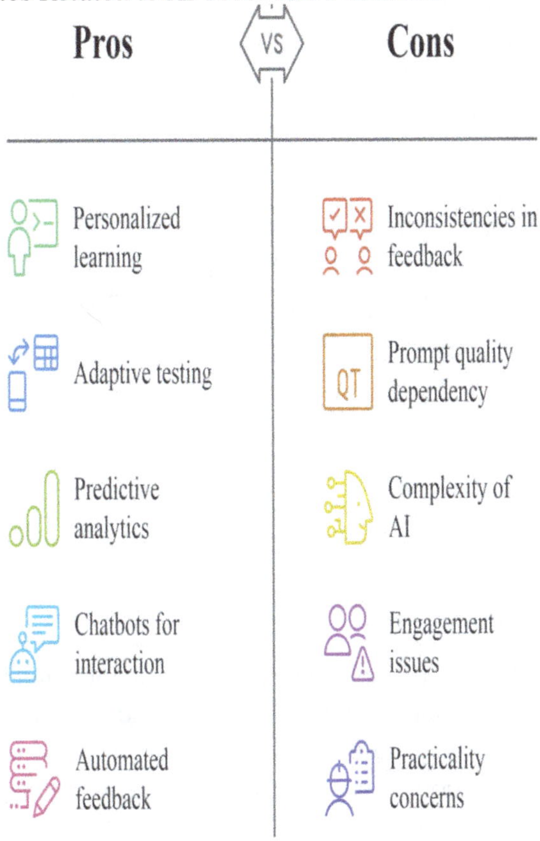

As illustrated in Figure 13, the findings from the review of 44 studies are categorized pros and cons through AI tools and feedback theme. The variables studied in the literature as personalized learning, adaptive testing, predictive analytics, chatbots for interaction, automated feedback are all positive ways of the AI tools and their feedback system. Conversely, certain variables, including inconsistencies in feedback, dependence on prompt quality, the complexity of AI, engagement issues, and practical concerns, highlight the negative aspects of artificial intelligence as discussed in the literature or observed in its use within foreign language education at the higher education level.

AI in Assessment and Testing

The variables grouped under this theme are presented in Figure 14.

Figure 14. Variables Related to AI in Assessment and Testing

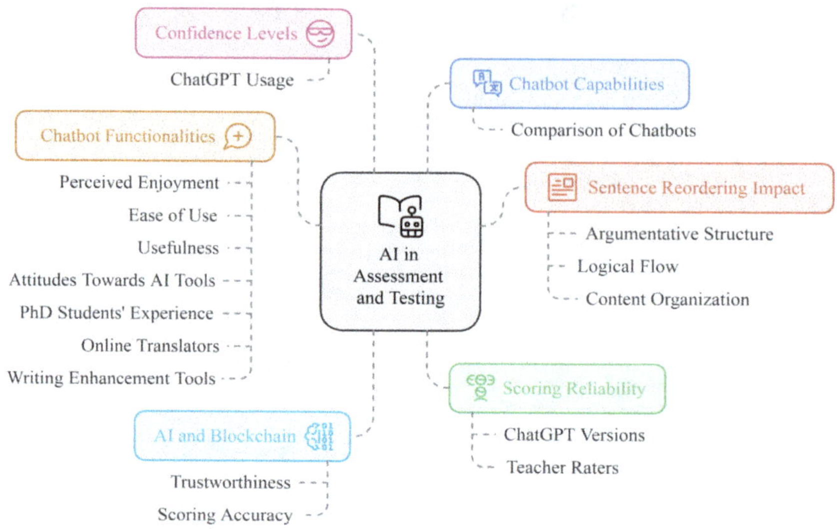

As illustrated in Figure 14, confidence levels, chatbot functionalities, chatbot capabilities, AI and Blockchain, scoring reliability and sentence reordering impact are the main variables investigated by 44 researches included in this study. In this section, it is possible to come across variables such as comparison of chatbots, benefits obtained from chatbots and usage examples, trustworthiness, scoring accuracy, writing enhancement, confidence level of ChatGPT usage. For example, under Scoring reliability, different versions of ChatGPT and teachers' ratings are compared. Thus, it has been seen that the scoring reliability of artificial intelligence has been examined.

Technological Integration and Platforms

The variables grouped under this theme are presented in Figure 15.

Figure 15. Variables Related to Technological Integration and Platforms

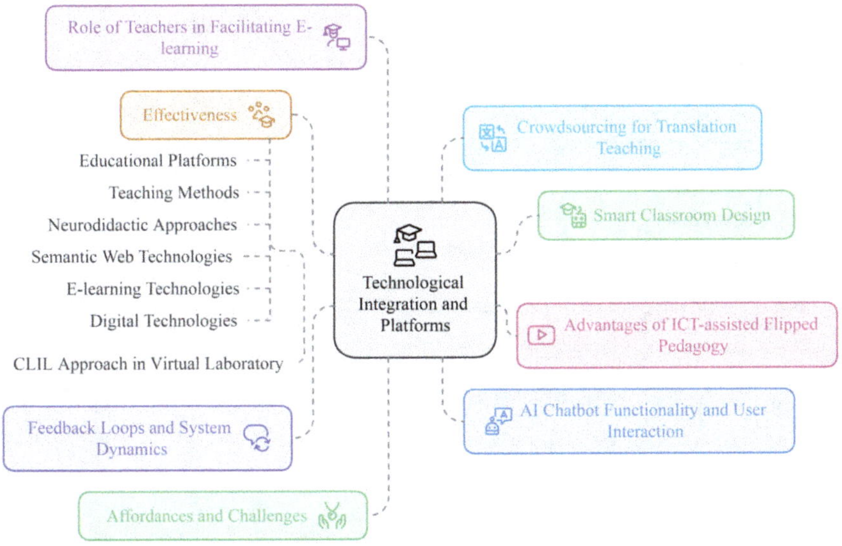

Figure 15 shows the findings from the review of 44 studies, and categorized eight main themes. Technological integration and technological platforms especially mention about smart classroom design, effectiveness, educational platforms, teaching methods, neuro-didactic approaches, semantic web technologies, e-learning technologies, role of teachers in facilitating e-learning, digital technologies, CLIL approach in virtual laboratory, advantages of ICT-assisted flipped pedagogy, AI chatbot functionality and user interaction, crowdsourcing for translation teaching, feedback loops and system dynamics.

Learners' Attributes

The variables grouped under this theme are presented in Figure 16.

Figure 16. Variables Related to Learner Attributes

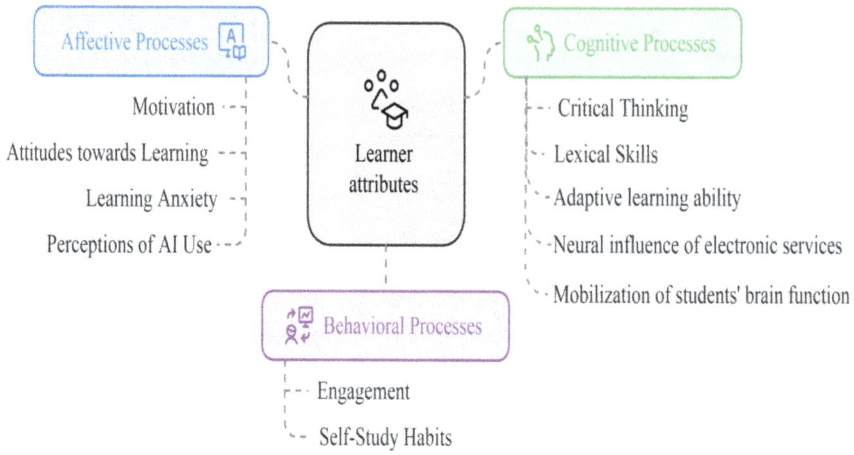

The learners' attributes analyzed in the 44 studies are categorized into three domains: affective, cognitive, and behavioral, as shown in Figure 16. These studies, which explore the use of artificial intelligence in foreign language education at the higher education level, identify several affective student characteristics, including motivation, attitude, anxiety, and perception. In the cognitive domain, the examined variables encompass critical thinking, lexical skills, adaptive learning, the neurological impact of electronic services, and the mobilization of students' brain functions. Finally, the behavioral characteristics investigated in these studies include student engagement and self-study habits.

Technological & Pedagogical Innovations

The variables grouped under this theme are presented in Figure 17.

Figure 17. Variables Related to Technological and Pedagogical Innovations

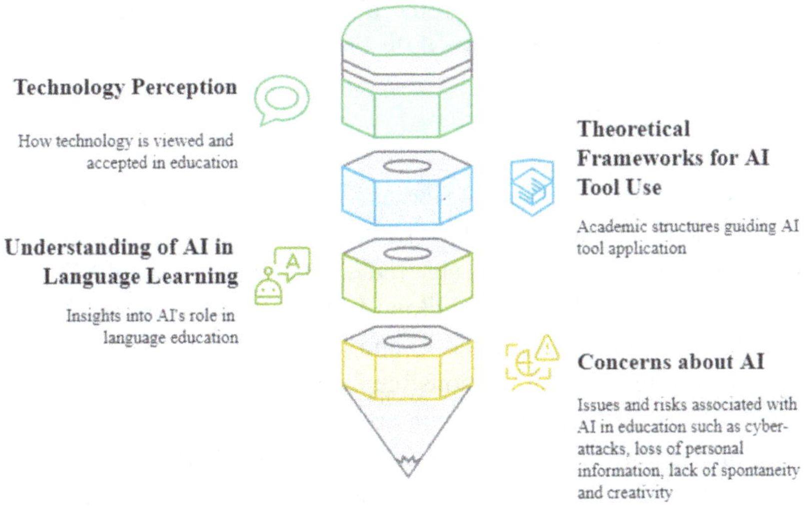

As illustrated in Figure 17, the analysis of 44 studies revealed that another key focus of the studies involving the use of artificial intelligence in foreign language education at the higher education level is the exploration of the technological and pedagogical innovations. The variables explored within this theme are grouped into four main categories: perception of technology, theoretical frameworks regarding the use of artificial intelligence tools, understanding of artificial intelligence in language learning, concerns about artificial intelligence, such as cyberattacks, loss of personal information, spontaneity and lack of creativity.

Distribution of AI Utilization by Language Skills

The analysis of AI's application in higher education, particularly in relation to foundational language skills (reading, writing, listening, and speaking), revealed that AI was most frequently used to develop writing skills (34 studies). Many studies addressed multiple skills, with 12 focusing on AI integration across all four language skills. Of the 44 studies reviewed, 26 emphasized AI's role in supporting reading, 21 focused on speaking, and 14 on listening.

The reviews categorized language skills into receptive (listening, reading) and productive (speaking, writing) skills, highlighting the use of AI for vocabulary acquisition. Studies on writing skills primarily addressed topics like translation, multimedia tasks, academic writing, grammar, and text assessment. For speaking skills, AI was used to improve fluency, pronunciation, speech rate, communicative competence, and productive skills. Research on reading skills focused on reading comprehension and the use of electronic dictionaries, while studies on listening skills explored corpora and receptive skills.

Distribution by SDGs

It was noted that 18 out of the 44 studies included in this review did not specify the sustainable development goal (SDG) in their Web of Science (WOS) records. The remaining 18 studies identified various SDGs. The distribution of SDGs specified in the WOS records is as follows: 03 Good Health and Well-being (2), 04 Quality Education (11), 08 Decent Work and Economic Growth (4), 09 Industry, Innovation and Infrastructure (5), 12 Responsible Consumption and Production (1), and 17 Partnerships for the Goals (4). There are five records in the WOS records that show more than one SDG. Four of these records have SDGs 8, 9, and 17, while one has SDGs 9 and 12. The SDG 04 Quality Education was the most prominent goal with the 11 records.

On the other hand, support was received from artificial intelligence tools such as Chat GPT, Gemini, Perplexity in determining SDGs for 26 studies that did not specify SDGs in WOS records. For each abstract, the tools generated at least three SDGs from most relevant to least. Each time the three of them gave the same results for the first two SDGs, but sometimes not for the third one. The first two codes provided by the AI tools were found to be internally consistent. A comparison with the researcher's codes revealed overlap with the codes initially presented by the AI tools. According to SDGs determined with technological support, the distribution of SDGs in 26 studies is as follows: All 26 studies serve 04 Quality Education SDGs as the first priority. When asked about the second alternative Sustainable Development Goal, most studies served 09 Industry, Innovation and Infrastructure, while a few studies served 10 Reducing Inequality.

Therefore, it can be said that studies addressing AI applications for foreign language education in higher education are intensively aimed at strengthening the quality of education. It is possible to say that research is ongoing for a more sustainable, accessible, universal and inclusive education. In fact, the variables discussed under 4.5 headline of this research is supporting this inference.

DISCUSSION

The research highlights a growing interest in the use of artificial intelligence (AI) in foreign language education, particularly from 2022 onwards. However, this increase may be influenced by the open access criterion in the study. This trend aligns with findings from Zhang and Umeanowai (2025), and researchers like Vincent-Lancrin and van der Vlies (2020), Cardona, Rodriguez and Ishmael (2023) predict that AI's role in education will remain a global focus. Despite this growth, AI integration in foreign language education has been relatively slow compared to other educational technologies. Only a small portion of foreign language education studies (74 out of 3,671) directly address AI, showing that AI has yet to become a central theme in educational research, even as its influence increases in other areas (Zawacki-Richter et al., 2019).

The delayed adoption of AI in foreign language education can be attributed to several factors, including institutional changes, teacher readiness, technological advancements, and individual perceptions. Traditional teaching methods, institutional resistance, inadequate learning environments, lack of teacher training, and limited resources may also explain the slow adoption (Holmes et al., 2019; Kessler, 2018). Additionally, AI is a relatively new technology compared to foreign language education—AI research began in 2009, with open access starting in 2019—helping explain the delayed interest, which has increased since the 2020s (Zawacki-Richter et al., 2019).

The research shows significant contributions from People's Republic of China and Ukraine in AI adoption for foreign language education, with both countries benefiting from policies that support AI education (Eurydice Unit Ukraine, 2025; Peterson et al., 2021). However, the study also highlights the lack of cross-country collaboration in AI-driven language education, emphasizing the need for international cooperation to foster diverse perspectives and best practices. This finding is consistent with Zhang and Umeanowai (2025), but their research identified the USA and UK as the primary contributors, not Ukraine.

Most of the studies in the research were categorized under Education & Educational Research. While the studies primarily stemmed from educational sciences, this could be influenced by the research scope and keywords used. The growing interest in AI in education aligns with Zawacki-Richter et al. (2019), and the results support earlier findings in this area.

The study found that the most commonly used research methods were mixed research, followed by experimental research, which aligns with Wang et al. (2024). This suggests that the empirical need for evidence regarding the effectiveness of AI in language learning, as noted by Woo and Choi (2021), has been addressed. Mixed research, combining quantitative and qualitative data, is a valuable contribution to the field. The high number of experimental designs also offers valuable insights based on applied processes. Unlike this study, Kurvinen et al. (2022) found that case studies were the primary focus in this field, although case studies were also used in this research, aligning with existing literature.

The findings also emphasize that AI adoption in foreign language education is gradual and influenced by factors like institutional changes, teacher preparation, and technological advancements. A primary focus of current studies is improving language proficiency, particularly in writing, through AI integration, as supported by Ivanytska et al. (2024). This focus differs from Kurvinen et al. (2022), who identified AI tool adaptation as the most common focus.

Mallik and Gangopadhyay (2023) noted that studies primarily concentrated on performance assessment, a theme echoed in this research, which also emphasizes AI's role in improving language proficiency. The study categorizes ethical issues under the theme of ethical considerations, addressing risks and academic integrity, which contrasts with Kurvinen et al. (2022), who found a lack of ethical concerns in their review.

The research further identifies key themes, including the enhancement of language skills through AI. Writing skills are most frequently studied, followed by reading, speaking, and listening, reflecting AI's role in supporting productive language skills. Listening is identified as the least explored skill, indicating a research gap and the need for more studies on listening and speaking. This finding is consistent with Mallik and Gangopadhyay (2023), and Macinska and Vinkler (2024) also highlight AI's use in general translation, grammar checking, and dialogue prediction as a writing assistant. Additionally, AI's role in vocabulary acquisition and grammar development is critical, offering personalized learning experiences, as supported by Ivanytska et al. (2024).

The research also shows that AI aligns with the United Nations Sustainable Development Goal (SDG) 04, Quality Education. This alignment emphasizes AI's societal impact, improving access to quality education and supporting global educational goals (United Nations, 2015; United Nations Development Programme, n.d.). AI tools help bridge educational access gaps, especially in under-resourced regions, and successful AI implementation requires addressing social, economic, and environmental dimensions of sustainability (Kryshtanovych et al., 2025; Kurvinen et al., 2022).

CONCLUSION

This study provides a thorough examination of the role of artificial intelligence (AI) in foreign language education within higher education through a systematic review of 44 research papers from the Web of Science (WOS). The primary objective is to assess AI's application in foreign language education at the higher education level, identifying current trends and research gaps. The analysis covers various aspects, including the distribution of research over time, geographical regions, research disciplines, methodologies used, variables explored, AI's impact on the four basic language skills, and its alignment with sustainable development goals (SDGs).

AI's integration into foreign language education has been gradual, particularly in comparison to other educational technologies, though the study reveals a significant rise in AI-related research since 2022. While AI studies in foreign language education represent a small segment of the broader educational research, there is growing interest globally, with notable contributions from Ukraine, and People's Republic of China. However, the study highlights a lack of international collaboration in AI-driven foreign language education.

The research identifies key themes in AI applications, such as teacher competence, ethical concerns, AI tools and feedback, assessment practices, and technological integration. A significant focus is placed on AI's impact on language skills, particularly productive skills like writing, followed by reading, speaking, and listening. AI's role in vocabulary acquisition and grammar development is also frequently explored. These findings suggest that AI has considerable potential to support language learning, especially in writing.

The research further indicates that AI can transform foreign language education by offering personalized learning experiences, enhancing language practice, and contributing to the sustainability of education. Additionally, AI's alignment with SDG 4, which focuses on improving education, is emphasized.

In conclusion, by underscoring AI's transformative potential in shaping the future of foreign language education in higher education. It points to emerging trends, key research areas, and opportunities for collaboration, offering insights for future studies and the continued integration of AI into education. While AI's role in language learning is promising, its integration must be managed carefully to address challenges related to equity, accessibility, and ethics. The successful implementation of AI could lead to a more inclusive, efficient, and sustainable model for language acquisition globally. However, this will require increased collaboration, investment in teacher training, and institutional support to fully realize AI's potential in language education.

ETHICAL CONSIDERATIONS

Depending on the research method, the study does not require to get any ethical permission.

Assistance was obtained from ChatGPT to evaluate the adequacy of the English translations of the texts in accordance with academic style.

FUNDING

There is no funding agency for this research.

NOTES

This research is an original study and has not been published or presented anywhere before.

REFERENCES

AlTwijri, L., & Alghizzi, T. M. (2024). Investigating the integration of artificial intelligence in English as foreign language classes for enhancing learners' affective factors: A systematic review. *Heliyon, 10*(10), e31053. DOI: 10.1016/j.heliyon.2024.e31053 PMID: 38778968

Ammon, U. (2010). World languages: Trends and futures. In Coupland, N. (Ed.), *The Handbook of Language and Globalization* (pp. 101–122). John Wiley & Sons., DOI: 10.1002/9781444324068.ch4

Bastani, H., Bastani, O., Sungu, A., Ge, H., Kabakcı, Ö., & Mariman, R. (2024, Jul 15). *Generative AI can harm learning* (The Wharton School Research Paper). DOI: 10.2139/ssrn.4895486

Belda-Medina, J., & Kokošková, V. (2023). Integrating chatbots in education: Insights from the chatbot-human interaction satisfaction model (CHISM). *International Journal of Educational Technology in Higher Education, 20*(1), 62. DOI: 10.1186/s41239-023-00432-3

Bilgin, N. (2014). *Content analysis techniques and case studies in social* (3rd ed.). Siyasal.

Blue, J. (2022). *Introducing the Sustainability Framework for ELT: free activity cards.* World of better learning. https://www.cambridge.org/elt/blog/2022/09/30/sustainability-framework-elt-activity-cards/

Brown, H. D. (2007). *Principles of language learning and teaching* (5th ed.). Pearson Education.

Caines, A., Benedetto, L., Taslimipoor, S., Davis, C., Gao, Y., Andersen, Ø., Yuan, Z., Elliott, M., Moore, R., Bryant, C., Rei, M., Yannakoudakis, H., Mullooly, A., Nicholls, D., & Buttery, P. (2023). On the application of Large Language Models for language teaching and assessment technology. In J.Stamper, R. Tong, C. Cao, Z. Liu, X. Hu, Y. Lu, J. Liang, H. Khosravi, P. Denny, A. Singh, & C. Broos (Eds.), *Proceedings of the Workshop on Empowering Education with LLMs - the Next-Gen Interface and Content Generation 2023 (AIEDLLM 2023).* Vol.3487. (pp. 173-197). CEUR Workshop Proceedings. DOI: 10.48550/arXiv.2307.08393

Cambridge (n.d.). *The sustainability framework for ELT.* [Infographics]. https://assets.cambridgeenglish.org/events/sustainability-framework-for-elt.pdf?_gl=1*pqow4k*_gcl_au*OTk4OTc3NDI2LjE3NDE2NzY2OTg

Cardona, M. A., Rodriguez, R. J., & Ishmael, K. (2023). *Artificial intelligence and the future of teaching and learning: Insights and recommendations.* U.S. Department of Education, Office of Educational Technology. https://www.ed.gov/sites/ed/files/documents/ai-report/ai-report.pdf

Çelik, F., Yangın Ersanlı, C., & Arslanbay, G. (2024). Does AI simplification of authentic blog texts improve reading comprehension, inferencing, and anxiety? A one-shot intervention in Turkish EFL context. *International Review of Research in Open and Distance Learning*, *25*(3), 287–303. DOI: 10.19173/irrodl.v25i3.7779

Chang, A. C.-S., & Read, J. (2012). The effects of listening support on the listening performance of EFL learners. *TESOL Quarterly*, *40*(2), 375–397. DOI: 10.2307/40264527

Chen, L., Chen, P., & Lin, Z. (2020). Artificial intelligence in education: A review. *IEEE Access : Practical Innovations, Open Solutions*, *8*, 75264–75278. DOI: 10.1109/ACCESS.2020.2988510

Crompton, H., & Burke, D. (2023). Artificial intelligence in higher education: The state of the field. *International Journal of Educational Technology in Higher Education*, *20*(1), 22. DOI: 10.1186/s41239-023-00392-8

Crystal, D. (2003). *English as a global language* (2nd ed.). Cambridge University. DOI: 10.1017/CBO9780511486999

Ellis, R. (1997). *Second language acquisition*. Oxford University.

Etnologue (2025). *What are the top 200 most spoken languages?* https://www.ethnologue.com/insights/ethnologue200/

Eurydice Unit Ukraine. (2025). *Ukraine: Digital transformation of education as a strategic path to resilience and innovation.* Eurydice. https://eurydice.eacea.ec.europa.eu/news/ukraine-digital-transformation-education-strategic-path-resilience-and-innovation

Galaczi, E. (2023). *English language education in the era of generative AI: our perspective.* Cambridge University Press & Assessment. https://www.cambridgeenglish.org/Images/685411-english-language-education-in-the-era-of-generative-ai-our-perspective.pdf

Galaczi, E., & Luckin, R. (2024). *Generative AI and language education: Opportunities, challenges and the need for critical perspectives.* Cambridge University Press & Assesment. https://www.cambridge.org/sites/default/files/media/documents/CPELE_Generative%20AI%20and%20Language%20Education%20Opportunities%20Challenges%20and%20the%20Need%20for%20Critical%20Perspectives_FINAL%20%281%29.pdf

Gillani, N., Eynon, R., Chiabaut, C., & Finkel, K. (2023). Unpacking the "black box" of AI in education. *Journal of Educational Technology & Society, 26*(1), 99–111. DOI: 10.30191/ETS.202301_26(1).0008

Gough, D., Oliver, S., & Thomas, J. (Eds.). (2017). *An introduction to systematic reviews* (2nd ed.). Sage.

Hemingway, P., & Brereton, N. (2009, Apr). *What is a systematic review?* What is ...? series. https://familymedicine.med.wayne.edu/mph/project/what_is_a_systematic_review.pdf

High-Level Expert Group on Artificial Intelligence. (2018). *A definition of AI: Main capabilities and scientific disciplines.* European Commission. https://ec.europa.eu/futurium/en/system/files/ged/ai_hleg_definition_of_ai_18_december_1.pdf

Holmes, W., Bialik, M., & Fadel, C. (2019). *Artificial intelligence in education: Promises and implications for teaching and learning.* Center for Curriculum Redesign (CCR). https://curriculumredesign.org/wp-content/uploads/AIED-Book-Excerpt-CCR.pdf

Hung, J. L., & Zhang, K. (2012). Examining m-learning trends 2003–2008: A categorical meta-trend analysis using text mining techniques. *Journal of Computing in Higher Education, 24*(1), 1–17. DOI: 10.1007/s12528-011-9044-9

Ivanytska, N., Koliasa, O., Kovalevska, T., Matsera, O., & Tkachuk, T. (2024). Analyzing the possibilities of implementation of AI and social networks in teaching foreign language students: Ukrainian universities case study. *Arab World English Journal (AWEJ) Special Issue on ChatGPT,* 306-318. DOI: 10.24093/awej/ChatGPT.21

Ji, H., Han, I., & Ko, Y. (2023). A systematic review of conversational AI in language education: Focusing on the collaboration with human teachers. *Journal of Research on Technology in Education, 55*(1), 48–63. DOI: 10.1080/15391523.2022.2142873

Kessler, G. (2018). Technology and the future of language teaching. *Foreign Language Annals, 51*(1), 205–218. DOI: 10.1111/flan.12318

Key Sustainability. (2024, Jul 24). *United Nations sustainable development goals: Together we can make "sustainable future"*. Commitment towards sustainable future. https://www.keysustainability.com/united-nations-sustainable-development-goals-together-we-can-make-sustainable-future/

Krashen, S. D. (2009). *Principles and practice in second language acquisition.* Pergamon Press. https://www.sdkrashen.com/content/books/principles_and_practice.pdf (Original work published 1982).

Kryshtanovych, S., Bekh, Y., Stadnichenko, O., Shevchenko, Z., Maikher, V., & Liubinska, O. (2025). Education 4.0: Development of the Ukrainian education system in the context of artificial intelligence and information technologies. *Journal of Management World, 2025*(2), 315–319. DOI: 10.53935/jomw.v2024i4.927

Kurt, G., & Kurt, Y. (2024). Enhancing L2 writing skills: ChatGPT as an automated feedback tool. *Journal of Information Technology Education, 23*, 24. DOI: 10.28945/5370

Kurvinen, E., Järvinen, J. P., & Kaila, E. (2022). Artificial intelligence in education–Where are we now? In Carmo, M. (Ed.), *Education and New Developments 2022* (Vol. 2, pp. 391–395). Science Press., DOI: 10.36315/2022v2end087

Labadze, L., Grigolia, M., & Machaidze, L. (2023). Role of AI chatbots in education: Systematic literature review. *International Journal of Educational Technology in Higher Education, 20*(1), 56. DOI: 10.1186/s41239-023-00426-1

Lambert, R. (2006). Foreign language teaching policy. In Brown, K. (Ed.), *Encyclopedia of Language & Linguistics* (2nd ed., pp. 551–558). Elsevier., DOI: 10.1016/B0-08-044854-2/00656-8

Linguistic – Third Year – Lecture One. (n.d.). *Second vs Foreign Language Learning /Acquisition* [Course Notes]. Université Frères Mentouri - Constantine 1. https://fac.umc.edu.dz/fll/images/cours_ang/L3/L3_LING_Lecture%201.pdf

López-Chila, R., Llerena-Izquierdo, J., Sumba-Nacipucha, N., & Cueva-Estrada, J. (2024). Artificial intelligence in higher education: An analysis of existing bibliometrics. *Education Sciences, 14*(1), 47. DOI: 10.3390/educsci14010047

Lune, H., & Berg, B. L. (2017). *Qualitative research methods for the social sciences* (9th ed.). Pearson.

Macinska, S., & Vinkler, A. (2024). *The role of AI in language learning: Research evidence and strategies for success.* Cambridge University Press & Assesment. https://www.cambridge.org/sites/default/files/media/documents/The_Role_of_AI_in_Language_Learning_Research_Evidence_and_Strategies.pdf

Mallik, S., & Gangopadhyay, A. (2023). Proactive and reactive engagement of artificial intelligence methods for education: A review. *Frontiers in Artificial Intelligence*, *6*, 1151391. DOI: 10.3389/frai.2023.1151391 PMID: 37215064

Nikonova, E., Yakhyaeva, K., Pivkina, N., & Schetinina, A. (2023). Using artificial intelligence tools in teaching a foreign language in higher technical institutions. *European Journal of Contemporary Education*, *12*(2), 578–589. DOI: 10.13187/ejced.2023.2.578

Oliver, S. (2024). *AI prompt writing for ELT teachers: 7 ingredients of a successful prompt.* World of better learning. https://www.cambridge.org/elt/blog/2024/03/09/ai-prompt-writing-for-elt-teachers-7-ingredients-of-a-successful-prompt/

Organization for Economic Co-Operation and Development (2024). *How 15-year-olds learn English. Case studies from Finland, Greece, Israel, the Netherlands and Portugal.* PISA, OECD Publishing DOI: 10.1787/a3fcacd5-en

Ouyang, F., Zheng, L., & Jiao, P. (2022). Artificial intelligence in online higher education: A systematic review of empirical research from 2011 to 2020. *Education and Information Technologies*, *27*(6), 7893–7925. DOI: 10.1007/s10639-022-10925-9

Pedró, F., Subosa, M., Rivas, A., & Valverde, P. (2019). *Artificial intelligence in education: Challenges and opportunities for sustainable development.* (Report No. ED-2019/WS/8), UNESCO, https://www.gcedclearinghouse.org/sites/default/files/resources/190175eng.pdf

Peterson, D., Goode, K., & Gehlhaus, D. (2021). *AI education in China and the United States, a comparative assessment.* Center for Security and Emerging Technology (CSET). DOI: 10.51593/20210005

Pitts, G., Marcus, V., & Motamedi, S. (2025). *Student perspectives on the benefits and risks of AI in education*. arXiv. https://doi.org//arXiv.2505.02198DOI: 10.48550

Rios, R. (2023). *Sustainability in the ELT Classroom: Making a positive change in the world.* World of better learning. https://www.cambridge.org/elt/blog/2023/11/02/sustainability-in-the-elt-classroom/

Serhan, S. A. L., & Yahaya, N. (2022). A systematic review and trend analysis of personal learning environments research. *International Journal of Information and Education Technology (IJIET)*, *12*(1), 43–53. DOI: 10.18178/ijiet.2022.12.1.1585

Taskıran, A., & Goksel, N. (2022). Automated feedback and teacher feedback: Writing achievement in learning English as a foreign language at a distance. *Turkish Online Journal of Distance Education*, *23*(2), 120–139. DOI: 10.17718/tojde.1096260

The Importance of Foreign Languages. (n.d.). *The International Union of Youth in Prague Blog.* https://msmstudy.eu/the-importance-of-foreign-languages/

United Nations. (2015). *Transforming our world: the 2030 agenda for sustainable development.* (A/RRES/70/1). https://docs.un.org/en/A/RES/70/1

United Nations Brundtland Commission. (1987). *Report of the world commission on environment and development: Our common future.* (A/42/427). https://www.are.admin.ch/are/en/home/media/publications/sustainable-development/brundtland-report.html#:~:text=It%20developed%20guiding%20principles%20for,and%20production%20in%20the%20North

United Nations Development Programme. (n.d.). *The SDGS in action. Goal 4 quality education.* https://www.undp.org/sustainable-development-goals/quality-education

Vázquez-Parra, J. C., Gonzalez-Gonzalez, C. S., Amézquita-Zamora, J. A., Cotino Arbelo, A. E., Palomino-Gámez, S., & Cruz-Sandoval, M. (2024). Complex thinking and adopting artificial intelligence tools: A study of university students. *Frontiers in Education*, *9*, 1377553. DOI: 10.3389/feduc.2024.1377553

Vesselinov, R., & Grego, J. (2012). *Duolingo effectiveness study final report.* https://www.studocu.vn/vn/document/truong-dai-hoc-ngoai-ngu-tin-hoc-thanh-pho-ho-chi-minh/english-language/duolingo-report-final/62581075

Vincent-Lancrin, S., & Van der Vlies, R. (2020). *Trustworthy artificial intelligence (AI) in education: Promises and challenges.* (OECD Education Working Papers No. 218), OECD Publishing. DOI: 10.1787/19939019

Wang, S., Wang, F., Zhu, Z., Wang, J., Tran, T., & Du, Z. (2024). Artificial intelligence in education: A systematic literature review. *Expert Systems with Applications*, *252*, 124167. DOI: 10.1016/j.eswa.2024.124167

Woo, J. H., & Choi, H. (2021). *Systematic review for AI-based language learning tools*. arXiv. https://doi.org//arXiv.2111.04455DOI: 10.48550

Xiao, Y. (2025). The impact of AI-driven speech recognition on EFL listening comprehension, flow experience, and anxiety: A randomized controlled trial. *Humanities & Social Sciences Communications*, *12*(1), 425. DOI: 10.1057/s41599-025-04672-8

Yıldırım, A., & Şimşek, H. (2018). *Qualitative research methods in the social sciences*. Seçkin.

Yufei, L., Saleh, S., Jiahui, H., & Sayed, S. M. (2020). Review of the application of artificial intelligence in education. *International Journal of Innovation. Creativity and Change*, *12*(8), 548–562. DOI: 10.53333/IJICC2013/12850

Zaiarna, I., Zhyhadlo, O., & Dunaievska, O. (2024). ChatGPT in foreign language teaching and assessment: Exploring EFL instructors' experience. *Information Technologies and Learning Tools, 102*(4), 176–191. DOI: 10.33407/itlt.v102i4.5716

Zawacki-Richter, O., Marín, V. I., Bond, M., & Gouverneur, F. (2019). Systematic review of research on artificial intelligence applications in higher education-where are the educators? *International Journal of Educational Technology in Higher Education, 16*(1), 39. DOI: 10.1186/s41239-019-0171-0

Zhang, X., Sun, J., & Deng, Y. (2023). Design and application of intelligent classroom for English language and literature based on artificial intelligence technology. *Applied Artificial Intelligence, 37*(1), e2216051. DOI: 10.1080/08839514.2023.2216051

Zhang, X., & Umeanowai, K. O. (2025). Exploring the transformative influence of artificial intelligence in EFL context: A comprehensive bibliometric analysis. *Education and Information Technologies, 30*(3), 3183–3198. DOI: 10.1007/s10639-024-12937-z

Zhang, Y., & Dong, C. (2024). Exploring the digital transformation of generative ai-assisted foreign language education: A socio-technical systems perspective based on mixed-methods. *Systems, 12*(11), 462. DOI: 10.3390/systems12110462

ADDITIONAL READING

Alharbi, W. (2023). AI in the foreign language classroom: A pedagogical overview of automated writing assistance tools. *Education Research International, 2023*(1), 4253331. DOI: 10.1155/2023/4253331

European School Education Platform. (2024). *Artificial intelligence as an asset to language learning in Europe*, https://school-education.ec.europa.eu/en/discover/news/artificial-intelligence-asset-language-learning-europe

Liu, M. Y. (2023). Exploring the application of artificial intelligence in foreign language teaching: Challenges and future development. *SHS Web of Conferences, 168,* Article Number: 03025, DOI: 10.1051/shsconf/202316803025

Modern Language Association of America and Conference on College Composition and Communication. (2024). *Building a Culture for Generative AI Literacy in College Language, Literature, and Writing*. Working paper, 3, Modern Language Association of America and Conference on College Composition and Communication. https://aiandwriting.hcommons.org/working-paper-3/

Nikolopoulou, K. (2025). Generative artificial intelligence and sustainable higher education: Mapping the potential. *Journal of Digital Educational Technology*, *5*(1), ep2506. DOI: 10.30935/jdet/15860

Pachava, V., Lasekan, O. A., Méndez-Alarcón, C. M., Pena, M. T. G., & Golla, S. K. (2025). Advancing SDG 4: Harnessing generative AI to transform learning, teaching, and educational equity in higher education. *Journal of Lifestyle and SDGs Review*, *5*(2), e03774. DOI: 10.47172/2965-730X.SDGsReview.v5.n02.pe03774

United Nations Educational, Scientific and Cultural Organization. (2024). *AI competency frameworks for students and teachers.* https://www.unesco.org/en/articles/what-you-need-know-about-unescos-new-ai-competency-frameworks-students-and-teachers

Wang, T., Lund, B. D., Marengo, A., Pagano, A., Mannuru, N. R., Teel, Z. A., & Pange, J. (2023). Exploring the potential impact of artificial intelligence (AI) on international students in higher education: Generative AI, chatbots, analytics, and international student success. *Applied Sciences (Basel, Switzerland)*, *13*(11), 6716. DOI: 10.3390/app13116716

Warschauer, M., & Xu, Y. (2024). Generative AI for language learning: Entering a new era. *Language Learning & Technology*, *28*(2), 1–4. https://hdl.handle.net/10125/73569

Yunina, O. (2023). Artificial intelligence tools in foreign language teaching in higher education institutions. *The Modern Higher Education Review*, *8*(8), 77–90. DOI: 10.28925/2617-5266.2023.85

KEY TERMS AND DEFINITIONS

Artificial Intelligence: Artificial intelligence is a tool that enhances users' expressive capabilities by clarifying their thoughts and fostering intellectual depth through the rapid presentation of diverse perspectives. While this technology offers considerable advantages in terms of efficiency and creativity, commands directed by humans may give rise to ethical concerns and potential challenges. Consequently, artificial intelligence can be viewed as a reflection of humanity's internal struggle.

Bibliographic coupling link: A bibliographic coupling link refers to the connection between two or more research papers that cite the same document. It reflects the relationship between these papers through their shared references, forming a citation network.

Foreign Language: It typically refers to languages that are not commonly encountered in daily life and are not native to the individual's local environment. Unlike a person's native language, a foreign language is not widely spoken in the region where they live, but it can be learned and utilized when necessary.

Higher Education: An advanced educational institution that individuals attend after primary and secondary education to specialize in a specific field. It prepares individuals for social, societal, and economic roles, providing qualifications for a professional career. This education, which can be formal or informal, typically involves adult learners and includes structured teaching aimed at imparting knowledge, skills, and expertise in a particular area of study.

Limitation: These are factors that have the potential to affect the results of the research but cannot be carried out within the scope of the research due to reasons such as time, cost, etc.

Sustainability: Characterized by continuity, self-renewal, and ongoing updates, with the capacity to be carried forward into the future.

Web of Science (WOS): A database that includes prestigious journals with high international recognition and indexes academic research.

APPENDIX

Table 5. List of Articles (Dataset)

ID	WOS ID	DOI Link
1	001245053900022	https://dx.doi.org/10.24093/awej/ChatGPT.21
2	001327933400012	https://dx.doi.org/10.33407/itlt.v102i4.5716
3	000994029600001	https://dx.doi.org/10.1080/08839514.2023.2216051
4	001312598100001	https://dx.doi.org/10.28945/5370
5	001166877100016	https://dx.doi.org/10.18662/brain/14.3/473
6	001366097700001	https://dx.doi.org/10.3390/systems12110462
7	001126749600001	https://dx.doi.org/10.1186/s41239-023-00432-3
8	001241678100001	https://dx.doi.org/10.1016/j.heliyon.2024.e31053
9	001166877200012	https://dx.doi.org/10.18662/brain/14.4/500
10	000824645000001	https://dx.doi.org/10.3390/su14138133
11	001156596500026	https://dx.doi.org/10.34069/AI/2023.71.11.25
12	001166877100029	https://dx.doi.org/10.18662/brain/14.3/486
13	001363951300001	https://dx.doi.org/10.3390/bs14111015
14	001024165100019	https://dx.doi.org/10.13187/ejced.2023.2.578
15	000771425100014	https://dx.doi.org/10.3991/ijet.v17i05.28231
16	001120656300001	https://dx.doi.org/10.1080/2331186X.2023.2282804
17	001196991700001	https://dx.doi.org/10.1057/s41599-024-02904-x
18	000584736900001	https://dx.doi.org/10.3390/app10207022
19	001057338300005	https://dx.doi.org/10.24093/awej/call9.5
20	001165615200004	https://dx.doi.org/10.4018/JOEUC.336277
21	001005041700001	https://dx.doi.org/10.3390/app13116716
22	001100078900001	https://dx.doi.org/10.3389/fpsyg.2023.1258286
23	001006514300001	https://dx.doi.org/10.1016/j.artint.2023.103935
24	000927568900001	https://dx.doi.org/10.4018/IJeC.316823
25	001162162800022	https://dx.doi.org/10.18662/rrem/15.3/770
26	000750744900001	https://dx.doi.org/10.1007/s13748-021-00274-y
27	001250068700025	https://dx.doi.org/10.34069/AI/2024.74.02.25
28	000824051800001	https://dx.doi.org/10.3390/su14137598
29	000836690500044	https://dx.doi.org/10.4018/JITR.298328
30	001196528400019	https://dx.doi.org/10.1371/journal.pone.0297297
31	001103255400001	https://dx.doi.org/10.3389/fpsyg.2023.1261955

continued on following page

Table 5. Continued

ID	WOS ID	DOI Link
32	000884264900003	https://dx.doi.org/10.1155/2022/2776823
33	000856707900018	https://dx.doi.org/10.24093/awej/call8.18
34	000821837300003	https://dx.doi.org/10.1155/2022/8389800
35	000823277700002	https://dx.doi.org/10.18662/brain/13.2/329
36	000781391400001	https://dx.doi.org/10.3390/app12073239
37	001271451000001	https://dx.doi.org/10.5788/34-1-1914
38	000706171100001	https://dx.doi.org/10.3389/fpsyg.2021.679956
39	001293252700004	https://dx.doi.org/10.20535/2410-8286.305061
40	000774491600001	https://dx.doi.org/10.3390/su14063140
41	000465617000004	https://dx.doi.org/10.24093/awej/vol10no1.4
42	001245053900015	https://dx.doi.org/10.24093/awej/ChatGPT.14
43	001192659600001	https://dx.doi.org/10.3390/languages9030078
44	001321854500016	https://dx.doi.org/10.1057/s41599-024-03755-2

Chapter 4
Overcoming Pedagogical Barriers in ICT-Driven Language Education:
Reimagining Language Teaching and Transforming Traditional Language Teaching With ICT Integration

Seema Yadav
https://orcid.org/0000-0002-8477-5895
Bhopal School of Social Sciences, Bhopal, India

ABSTRACT

The rapid advancement of Information and Communication Technology (ICT) offers unprecedented opportunities to enhance traditional language teaching. However, its integration into pedagogical practices often encounters significant challenges. This chapter delves into the complexities of transitioning from traditional methods to ICT-enhanced teaching, focusing on maintaining educational quality and respecting cultural sensitivities. Through an analytical lens, it explores barriers such as resistance to change, infrastructural limitations, lack of teacher training, and the need for culturally responsive materials. The chapter concludes with strategies to overcome these challenges, fostering an inclusive and effective ICT-enabled language learning environment.

DOI: 10.4018/979-8-3373-0801-2.ch004

INTRODUCTION

The UNESCO ICT-Competence Framework for Teachers was created by UNESCO. The competencies that educators require to incorporate information and communication technologies (ICTs) into their professional practice are described in this framework. In order to enable instructors to incorporate ICT in a pedagogically successful manner, the framework attempts to offer guidelines and a fundamental set of credentials for creating courses for pre-service or in-service teachers. The three approaches to teaching technological literacy, knowledge deepening, and knowledge creation, as well as the six facets of a teacher's job knowledge of ICT in education, curriculum assessment, pedagogy, ICT, organization, and administration, and teacher professional learning, intersect to form the necessary competencies (Syifa & Darmahusni, 2019). A curriculum that is built on ICT can be developed, infused, and designed using the ICT Competency Framework for Teachers. It is possible to utilize this framework as the benchmark for incorporating ICT into curriculum creation (Syifa & Darmahusni, 2019). In the twenty-first century, "technology" is a significant topic in a variety of domains, including education. Information, communication, and technology (ICT) integration in education is the use of computer-based communication that is integrated into the regular teaching process in the classroom. Teachers are viewed as the primary users of ICT in the classroom, helping to prepare pupils for the contemporary digital environment (Syifa & Darmahusni, 2019). Information and communication technology's (ICT) quick development has had a significant impact on many facets of human existence, including education. ICT has been incorporated into education to improve the quality of teaching and learning settings (Kibar et al., 2023). Education is no exception, as it plays a vital role in forming society. The swift advancement of information and communication technology (ICT) has had a significant impact on many facets of our lives, including business, law, finance, entertainment, and healthcare (Bohara, 2024). Conventional language instruction emphasizes teacher-centered, structured methods that prioritize vocabulary, grammar, and translation. The Grammar-Translation Method, which emphasizes reading and writing by using direct translation and grammar rules; the Direct Method, which encourages conversation and immersion without translation; and the Audio-Lingual Method, which reinforces language patterns through drills and repetition, are noteworthy approaches. A strategic approach that includes investments in technology infrastructure, teacher training, and a supportive policy environment is necessary to improve ICT integration in ELT classrooms. In the ever-changing landscape of English Language Teaching (ELT), the integration of Information (Kibar et al., 2023) and Communication Technology (ICT) has emerged as a fundamental pedagogical approach. ICT also offers great opportunities to transfer traditional teaching practices, develop ICT skills, access a vast source of information, and, most importantly, the potential for a paradigm shift in recent practices (Bohara, 2024). Opportunities also arise as a result of ICT integration barriers. Rethinking ICT integration and teaching methodology has never been easier thanks to the widespread use of ICT technologies for emergency remote instruction (Canese et al., 2023). With less focus on student interaction and verbal competence, these approaches frequently rely on formal education and rote memorization. Although they are good at building fundamental abilities, they might not have the adaptability required for everyday language use. It is impossible to exaggerate how crucial English language competency is in the modern, globalized world. Since it is a universal language, English is essential to science, technology, the arts, international trade, and diplomacy (Kibar et al., 2023). Information and communications technology's (ICT) explosive growth has opened up a world of options for the education industry. The goal of EFL teachers in the modern educational environment is to employ technology to enhance the way that languages are taught and learned. Investigating the effects of ICT in teaching English as a foreign language is the goal of the current study (Hakim, 2021).

ICT has the potential to propel national advancement, particularly in the area of education. Communication, information, and technology all have a significant impact on education. ICT is one of the learning resources that is frequently utilized in many educational fields since it enhances the effectiveness and efficiency of the learning process. The use of technology in the classroom is essential (Fitria, 2023). The use of information and communication technology (ICT) in the classroom can help to improve, optimize, and assist the dissemination of knowledge. ICT can result in better teaching strategies and higher student learning levels (Thannimalai et al., 2022). The introduction of information and communication technology (ICT) into the classroom has transformed instruction by increasing its efficiency, accessibility, and interactivity. ICT includes a broad range of digital tools and resources that have revolutionized traditional educational processes, such as computers, the internet, multimedia, virtual classrooms, and artificial intelligence. Technology-driven initiatives have replaced traditional chalk-and-talk methods, improving student engagement, enabling personalized learning, and increasing access to high-quality education beyond geographic boundaries. Information and communication technology (ICT) has been widely recognized for its ability to improve speaking and writing abilities in the English language, to the extent that its use in teaching English language fluency has become essential in today's educational setting. As per the contemporary demands of education, the English language has evolved into a communication tool that facilitates national and international connections in a variety of fields, including commerce, science and technology, education, foreign relations, and more (Ndibalema & Mrosso, 2024a). Four competencies pedagogical, social, professional, and individual, are necessary for teachers to master in the field of education. It is explained in pedagogic competence that teachers need to be competent to use and utilize ICT in order to carry out learning. Technology is now used in education to aid in the teaching and learning process (Fitria, 2023). ICT has evolved into an essential tool in education. The activities involved in the learning process change when information technology is incorporated into the classroom. Higher education must offer a learning method that integrates information and communication technologies since it serves as a center for postsecondary education (Fitria, 2023).

Students now have access to a wealth of materials for self-paced learning through digital libraries, e-books, educational apps, and online learning platforms. Additionally, augmented reality and virtual simulations have simplified difficult ideas. Along with encouraging creativity and critical thinking in students, ICT has also made it possible for educators to implement cutting-edge teaching strategies like flipped classrooms, blended learning, and gamified classes (Alonso & Samy, 2018). The significance of ICT in maintaining educational continuity through remote learning solutions was further highlighted by the COVID-19 pandemic. ICT has made data collecting, analysis, and cooperation easier in research and higher education, encouraging multidisciplinary learning and knowledge exchange. Enhancing classroom instruction and learning outcomes is the goal of information and communication technology (henceforth referred to as ICT) devices. The teaching and learning of languages can be effectively facilitated by the use of ICT technologies and methodologies. The more advanced ICT use in language instruction, the more positively it affects students' motivation to learn the language. Students stress the use of ICT in school and its beneficial effects (BARNUCZ & FÓNAI, 2020). the application of ICT (information and communication technology) to ELT in higher education contexts. Promoting greater ICT integration in education, particularly in ELT, would benefit from more frequent training and more robust institutional and governmental policy support for ICT facilities (Hafifah & Sulistyo, 2020a). The field of education has been significantly impacted by the advancement of information and communication technology, or ICT. By working with teachers to design and prepare resources, ICT enables higher-quality lessons. Additionally, ICT improves writing abilities such as grammar, punctuation, spelling, editing, and rewriting. ICTs are seen as a way to help pupils with their challenges and help them develop their writing abilities (Syifa & Darmahusni, 2019).

Additionally, ICT promotes inclusive education by using assistive technologies to meet a range of learning needs. The importance of ICT in education will only increase as technology develops further, forming students who are prepared for the workforce of the twenty-first century and giving them the digital literacy skills they need. To optimize the advantages of ICT in education, however, issues like the digital divide, cybersecurity worries, and the requirement for teacher preparation must be resolved. ICT (information and communication technology) has the ability to completely transform language learning by providing students with unique, personalized, and interactive experiences that surpass conventional approaches. Through the use of digital resources including online platforms, virtual reality (VR), artificial intelligence (AI), and language learning applications, students can participate in self-paced, immersive learning settings that improve language acquisition. ICT facilitates exposure to real-world language use through interactive exercises, multimedia information, and real-time chat and video conferencing with native speakers. Teachers and students in the twenty-first century must be tech-savvy or digitally literate, and able to use ICT technologies and processes as teaching and learning resources. When the Internet, computers, and other telecommunications media began to be employed in educational settings, particularly ELT, in the early 1990s, the term ICT became widely used (Hafifah & Sulistyo, 2020a).

Chatbots and voice recognition software are examples of AI-powered technologies that offer real-time feedback on vocabulary, grammar, and pronunciation, encouraging ongoing development. Additionally, gamification adds interest and motivation to language learning with programs like Babbel and Duolingo. Additionally, ICT supports flipped and blended learning strategies, which allow students to access online materials prior to class and participate in productive practice sessions or conversations during in-person meetings. The abundance of internet resources, such as podcasts, e-books, and audiovisual materials, improves reading, listening, and understanding abilities. Additionally, cloud-based collaboration tools allow students and teachers to interact in real time, making language learning more dynamic and accessible. A potential approach in a world where technology proficiency and language proficiency are essential for successful communication and career advancement is the smooth integration of ICT-based gamification (Ennouari & Houssaini, 2023).

ICT is especially helpful for students with disabilities since assistive technologies, such as text-to-speech and speech-to-text applications, help break down obstacles to communication. In addition to making language learning more effective and interesting, ICT integration helps students from all over the world interact and practice their languages in real-life settings by bridging cultural and geographic divides. To fully realize its transformational potential in language teaching, however, issues like the digital divide, internet accessibility, and the requirement for teacher training in ICT integration must be resolved. Information and communication technology (ICT) integration in language instruction has revolutionized conventional teaching strategies by increasing accessibility, interactivity, and immersion. Conventional methods, such as the syntax-translation, Direct, and Audio-Lingual approaches, emphasize structured education with a focus on vocabulary, syntax, and memorization. However, they frequently lack flexibility and communicative involvement. The rise of ICT, including AI-powered tools, virtual reality, online platforms, and gamified applications, has revolutionized language learning by providing personalized, self-paced experiences that enhance listening, speaking, reading, and writing skills.

Digital tools encourage collaborative learning through cloud-based platforms, provide immediate feedback through chatbots and speech recognition software, and enable real-time connection with native speakers. Furthermore, ICT-driven strategies like blended and flipped learning give students access to digital materials ahead of time, which enhances the significance of classroom interactions. By providing assistive tools for students with impairments, ICT promotes inclusive education in addition to accessibility. To reach its full potential, though, issues like the digital divide, infrastructure constraints, and the requirement for teacher preparation must be resolved. ICT will become more and more important in enhancing the effectiveness, global connectivity, and engagement of language instruction as technology develops.

UNDERSTANDING PEDAGOGICAL BARRIERS IN ICT-DRIVEN LANGUAGE EDUCATION

These days, there is a huge increase in the usage of information and communication technology (ICT) in the classroom. Teachers are increasingly investigating the use and application of ICT as a tool for English Language Teaching (ELT) since they help to create a collaborative and autonomous learning environment (Yumnam, 2021). ICTs, or information and communication technologies, are crucial to developing a fresh and enhanced approach to education. Many studies have been done to look at the benefits of using ICT in language education in general and teaching and learning English as a second language (ESL) in particular. More research is needed to fully understand the drawbacks of ICT use in language instruction, though (Yunus et al., 2013). The process of digitizing education is now irreversible. ICT use in education, however, presents a number of methodological issues while also generating a great deal of controversy and worry (Szyszka et al., 2022). In recent years, technology has become more and more important in education. It makes it possible for teaching and learning processes to be more effective, strategic, interesting, and helpful to students in addition to democratizing access to education and creating more opportunities for cooperation. Because it sees technology as a tool that enhances or facilitates language acquisition and as a significant factor in improving teaching methods and shaping today's dynamic communication practices, language education likewise reflects this importance (Rubio, 2024). Because language education sees technology as a way to improve or help language learning, it is an important part of its role in raising teaching practices and changing the dynamic communication practices of today (Radiamoda et al., 2024). For ICT-driven language education to be implemented successfully and to optimize the advantages of technology in language learning, it is essential to comprehend pedagogical constraints. Resistance to change is one of the biggest problems, and it can come from both students and teachers. A lack of technical expertise, a fear of duplication, or doubts about the efficacy of technology may make many instructors, especially those used to more conventional teaching methods, nervous about incorporating it into their lessons. Some teachers may feel that the shift from traditional classroom instruction to ICT-driven approaches necessitates excessive training and ongoing professional development, which is either unnecessary or stressful. The field of education has been significantly impacted by the advancement of information and communication technology, or ICT. By working with teachers to design and prepare resources, ICT enables higher-quality lessons. Additionally, ICT improves writing abilities such as grammar, punctuation, spelling, editing, and rewriting. ICTs are seen as a way to help pupils with their challenges and help them develop their writing abilities (Syifa & Darmahusni, 2019). The impressive rise in ICT demand in the sphere of education is evidence of how well it works in the teaching and learning process. ICT is important for foreign language development because it exposes students to native speakers' real language and makes the lessons engaging, flexible, and interactive (Khan & Kuddus, 2020).

(Yumnam, 2021) suggests that the majority of educators and students had a favorable attitude toward the use of ICT in English language instruction. (Hafifah & Sulistyo, 2020b) show that the degree of ICT literacy among teachers is significantly correlated with their training, internet usage, and use of ICTs in language instruction. Teachers will become increasingly literate the more often they use ICTs. ICT literacy among teachers is undoubtedly a result of training experiences. Resistance may also result from worries about the dependability of digital resources, the amount of work needed to prepare lessons, and the possibility that non-educational information will divert students. Students, especially those with limited access to technical tools or digital literacy, may also struggle with adaptability. Others, particularly those from disadvantaged families or places with poor internet connectivity, may find it difficult to participate successfully in ICT-based language instruction, even if younger students may pick up digital tools rapidly. Additionally, students who primarily rely on teacher-led instruction may find it challenging to assume greater responsibility for their learning as a result of the transition from passive to participatory, technology-driven learning modes. Students' willingness to embrace ICT in language education can also be hampered by psychological resistance, such as discomfort using AI-driven feedback tools or fear of making mistakes in online interactions. Without addressing these resistance factors, the full potential of ICT in language learning may remain unrealized, limiting its ability to enhance linguistic competence and learner engagement. Targeted interventions, such as teacher training programs, institutional support, student orientation sessions, and strategies to promote a positive attitude towards technology in education, are necessary to overcome these barriers.

INFRASTRUCTURAL LIMITATIONS

The effectiveness of ICT integration in language learning is significantly impacted by the digital divide, which refers to differences in access to technology between different socio-economic groups, urban and rural areas, and developed and developing regions. In many schools and institutions, especially in underprivileged areas, students and teachers may not have access to essential digital tools like computers, tablets, or high-speed internet, making it challenging to implement technology-driven instructional methods. In particular, the digital divide and inadequate access to devices and the internet pose significant pedagogical barriers to ICT-driven language education. Additionally, a significant barrier that prevents students from using AI-driven learning platforms, virtual language exchange programs, and online resources is still poor or inconsistent internet connectivity. Without reliable internet access, students could find it difficult to participate in digital tests, cloud-based collaborative tools, and interactive multimedia content—all of which are crucial for contemporary language instruction. A further barrier to the seamless integration of ICT into pedagogy is the fact that many schools lack the essential infrastructure, such as high-speed networks, smart classrooms, and IT assistance. When teachers are uncertain about the functionality of the necessary digital tools, integrating technology into their class plans can be difficult. Significant investments in technology infrastructure, reasonably priced internet services, and institutional or governmental policies that support fair access to ICT resources are all necessary to remove these infrastructure hurdles. By supplying the required materials, educating educators on technology use, and putting blended learning models into place that take into account students' differing degrees of internet access, schools and colleges can help close the digital divide. Without proper infrastructure, ICT's ability to transform language instruction is restricted, aggravating educational disparities and impeding students' acquisition of critical digital and language skills.

TEACHER TRAINING DEFICITS

Teachers and students in the twenty-first century must be tech-savvy or digitally literate in order to leverage ICT tools and processes as teaching and learning aids. When the Internet, computers, and other telecommunications media began to be employed in educational settings, particularly ELT, in the early 1990s, the term ICT became widely used (Hafifah & Sulistyo, 2020b). The absence of proper teacher preparation and professional development for successfully incorporating technology into pedagogy is one of the main issues facing ICT-driven language teaching. Due to a lack of exposure and training opportunities, many educators, especially those who have historically depended on traditional teaching methods, frequently struggle to adjust to digital tools. Continuous learning is required due to the speed at which technology is developing, yet many instructors find it difficult to access organized professional development programs that give them the tools they need to successfully integrate ICT into language instruction. Without the right training, teachers can use digital resources inefficiently or not at all, which would have little effect on the learning outcomes of their students. Furthermore, the situation is made more difficult by teachers' inadequate knowledge of digital tools, as they might not be familiar with the features of online collaborative platforms, virtual classrooms, artificial intelligence (AI)-based feedback systems, or language learning applications. Teachers are unable to use ICT to provide students with personalized, dynamic, and captivating learning experiences because of this knowledge gap. Furthermore, some teachers might not fully embrace technology-driven approaches because they view ICT as an essential component of language instruction, but rather as an additional tool. It is imperative that institutions provide workshops, practical training sessions, and access to educational materials in order to close this gap and provide educators the self-assurance they need to successfully incorporate technology into their lesson plans. Innovative, student-centered learning environments that promote linguistic competency and digital literacy are hampered by the underutilization of ICT in language education if teacher training deficiencies are not addressed. Language teachers should receive ICT-related training and support centered on resolving digital issues and creating digital content (Radiamoda et al., 2024).

CULTURAL SENSITIVITIES

The risks of cultural homogenization and the challenges of adapting digital tools to local languages and dialects make cultural sensitivity a major obstacle to the successful adoption of ICT-driven language teaching. One significant issue is that a large portion of the standardized digital content used for language learning was created with a Western viewpoint in mind, frequently ignoring the linguistic and cultural variety of students from other areas. When pupils are largely exposed to dominant global cultures while their own language and cultural heritage are marginalized, this might result in cultural homogenization. An approach like this could hinder pupils' ability to acquire language abilities that are culturally relevant and weaken their ties to their own customs, literature, and expressions. Furthermore, regional languages and dialects are frequently under-represented in ICT-based language learning platforms, which favor commonly spoken languages like English, Spanish, or French. Learners from a variety of linguistic backgrounds find it difficult to properly interact with digital content that does not represent their linguistic realities due to this lack of localization. Automated translations and speech recognition software may have trouble understanding complex expressions, colloquial expressions, and dialectical variances, even when ICT tools support multiple languages. This can result in errors and misinterpretations.

Additionally, regional cultural conventions regarding communication methods, gestures, and expressions can vary greatly, so it is crucial that digital language learning materials be modified to acknowledge and take into account these variations. In order to overcome these obstacles, educational institutions, legislators, and tech developers must make a concerted effort to provide digital content that is inclusive of all cultures, integrate regional languages into ICT tools, and promote various representations in language learning resources. ICT-driven language instruction runs the risk of alienating students and eroding the rich linguistic and cultural diversity that language learning aims to maintain if these factors are not taken into account. A number of pedagogical obstacles prevent the successful adoption of ICT-driven language instruction. Since both teachers and students may find it difficult to adjust to technology-integrated learning, resistance to change is a significant obstacle. A lack of technical expertise, doubts about the efficacy of digital tools, or worries about the additional preparation time needed make many educators, particularly those used to traditional techniques, nervous about utilizing them. In a similar vein, students who struggle with ICT-based learning especially those from disadvantaged backgrounds or with low levels of digital literacy—may become psychologically resistant to and uneasy with AI-driven feedback tools. Disparities in learning possibilities are caused by infrastructure constraints, such as the digital divide and insufficient access to gadgets and the internet.

It is challenging to successfully incorporate ICT in many schools and institutions because they lack the requisite technological infrastructure, such as smart classrooms, high-speed internet, and enough digital gadgets, particularly in rural or impoverished locations. Additionally, a significant obstacle is the lack of proper training for teachers, as many of them do not acquire the professional development necessary to integrate technology into their lessons. Teachers who have a limited understanding of digital tools are unable to fully utilize ICT, which results in either underutilization or inadequate implementation. Furthermore, cultural sensitivities provide difficulties because regional languages, dialects, and cultural expressions are sometimes overlooked in favor of standardized digital information that reflects dominant global cultures. This might alienate students whose linguistic and cultural heritage is disregarded and result in cultural homogenization. It is challenging to adapt language learning materials to various linguistic and cultural contexts because many ICT technologies also have localization issues. The creation of culturally inclusive digital material, investments in digital infrastructure, teacher training programs, and laws that guarantee equal access to technology are just a few of the strategic measures needed to address these issues. ICT's transformative potential in language education is still constrained if these obstacles are not removed, which limits its capacity to improve learning inclusivity, engagement, and linguistic competency.

IMPACT ON EDUCATIONAL QUALITY IN ICT-DRIVEN LANGUAGE EDUCATION

Striking the correct balance between academic rigor and technology involvement is one of the major issues in ICT-driven language instruction. Although language learning has become more participatory and accessible thanks to digital technologies and multimedia materials, there is a chance that the focus on involvement will obscure the depth of learning. To keep students interested, gamification, instant incentives, and user-friendly interfaces are given top priority in many ICT-based language learning programs. Although these factors increase motivation, they can also result in surface-level learning, when pupils prioritize task completion above a thorough comprehension of linguistic nuances and structures. Teachers must carefully combine ICT resources with conventional pedagogical approaches to preserve academic rigor, making sure that planned lessons, critical thinking activities, and thorough assessments all complement interactive learning. Virtual language exchange programs and AI-driven chatbots, for instance, offer immersive conversational practice; but, they should be supplemented with formal grammar teaching, writing assignments, and critical conversations regarding language use. Beyond the instant feedback offered by digital platforms, it is also critical to foster metacognitive skills by motivating students to evaluate their learning outcomes, consider their errors, and establish academic objectives. Teachers may design an ICT-integrated learning environment that encourages passion and thorough language competency by finding a balance between student involvement and academic depth. For educators and education policymakers, one of the most recent challenges is integrating cutting-edge artificial intelligence (AI) technology into learning environments. AI chatbots are one of the new and creative Information and Communication Technologies (ICT) technologies made possible by conversational AI (Mageira et al., 2022).

ENSURING EQUITABLE ACCESS TO ICT FOR DIVERSE LEARNERS

One important element affecting the quality of education is still equity in access to ICT-driven language instruction. Inequalities in technical access continue to produce learning gaps, despite the fact that digital tools have the potential to democratize education by making resources accessible to a wider audience. Students from developing nations, rural areas, and disadvantaged families frequently encounter obstacles like poor internet access, a dearth of electronic gadgets, and little exposure to technology in the classroom. A digital divide may arise from these disparities, giving pupils who have access to cutting-edge ICT technologies a competitive edge over those who do not. Targeted efforts at several levels are necessary to provide fair access. Teachers should understand the advantages of technology, stay up to date on its latest developments, prepare themselves to teach tech-savvy students, and above all use it in the classroom to boost student achievement and prepare them for the multimedia technological expansion and digital literacy era (Hafifah & Sulistyo, 2020a). Over time, the development of information and communication technology, or ICT, has greatly benefited education, particularly for educators. ICT is being utilized as a synchronous and asynchronous teaching and learning platform that meets the demands of both educators and students (Ramadass & Shah, 2022).

Governments and educational institutions should make investments in developing mobile-based learning solutions that work even in low-resource situations, giving low-income students access to digital devices, and offering reasonably priced internet services. Additionally, varied learners, including those with disabilities, should be accommodated in the design of digital language learning platforms. For example, ICT tools can be made more accessible to students with visual or hearing impairments by including features like screen readers, speech-to-text capabilities, and adjustable font sizes. In order to ensure that digital resources reflect a variety of linguistic and regional backgrounds rather than just the most widely spoken languages worldwide, equitable ICT integration also entails cultural inclusion. ICT-driven language instruction may exacerbate current inequities rather than lessen them if deliberate measures are not taken to close these gaps.

EVALUATING LANGUAGE LEARNING OUTCOMES IN ICT-INTEGRATED CLASSROOMS

Evaluating language learning outcomes in technology-integrated classrooms is a critical component of assessing the impact of ICT on educational quality. However, assessing language proficiency in ICT-based settings necessitates a comprehensive approach that goes beyond automated assessments. Digital platforms can track vocabulary retention, grammar accuracy, and speaking fluency, but they may not adequately assess higher-order language skills like critical thinking, creative writing, and cultural literacy. In contrast to traditional language instruction, which depends on written assessments and oral examinations, ICT-based education offers a variety of assessment methods, such as AI-powered speech analysis, interactive quizzes, real-time pronunciation feedback, and data-driven progress tracking. Teachers need to use both formative and summative evaluations that combine human-led assessments with technology resources. For instance, teachers need to periodically provide speaking and writing tests to determine students' proficiency in real-world communication, even though AI-driven language analysis can offer immediate feedback on grammar and pronunciation. Teachers can also ascertain if ICT-based instruction results in long-term skill retention and maintained language competency by tracking student performance over time with longitudinal research. Instead of lowering the overall quality of language instruction, teachers can make sure that ICT integration improves it by combining technology-driven and conventional assessment techniques. Universities frequently use ICT and e-learning tools to plan team projects in blended learning, manage the educational process, create different channels of communication and interaction, and assess and evaluate student progress. Students' professional and language skills are also developed through the use of ICT and online learning resources (Samoylenko et al., 2022). Teachers felt that using ICT to improve students' fluency in the English language benefited them in many ways, including developing their speaking and writing abilities and igniting their passion in learning. Writing and speaking are two crucial aspects of effective communication that fluency has been found to possess. In the twenty-first century, these two abilities are essential (Ndibalema & Mrosso, 2024a).

Although ICT-driven language instruction has the potential to revolutionize educational experiences, its effect on the caliber of education will rely on how well it is executed. Students stay motivated while developing profound linguistic proficiency when academic rigor and technology engagement are balanced. All students can benefit from language learning by ensuring equal access to ICT resources, which stops the digital divide from causing educational inequalities. Finally, assessing learning results using both traditional and digital evaluation techniques guarantees that technology complements crucial language learning techniques rather than takes their place. ICT integration has the potential to greatly enhance language instruction by resolving these issues, making it more dynamic, approachable, and successful in preparing students for communication in a globalized world.

ICT-driven language instruction can improve student learning, but how well it is implemented will determine how much of an impact it has on academic quality. A significant obstacle is striking a balance between academic rigor and technological engagement, since digital tools frequently prioritize gamification and interactivity, which, although inspiring, can result in superficial learning. Teachers must incorporate ICT tools with planned lessons, critical thinking activities, and reflective learning techniques to guarantee depth. Equal access to ICT is equally vital since differences in technology resources lead to learning gaps that disadvantage students with impairments, those from rural locations, and those from disadvantaged backgrounds. To solve this, funds must be allocated for accessible internet, device distribution, and inclusive digital platforms that meet a range of regional and language demands. A complete methodology is also required to evaluate language learning results in ICT-integrated schools, integrating human-led evaluations with AI-powered tools to gauge both technical proficiency and higher-order abilities like creative communication and critical thinking. While automated tests can monitor vocabulary, grammar, and pronunciation development, human review is still necessary to evaluate practical language use. Through preserving academic depth, guaranteeing accessibility, and using comprehensive evaluation techniques, ICT-driven language instruction can improve linguistic proficiency, encourage participation, and advance inclusivity, ultimately equipping learners for successful international communication.

STRATEGIES TO OVERCOME PEDAGOGICAL BARRIERS IN ICT-DRIVEN LANGUAGE EDUCATION

Developing a growth mentality in both teachers and students is one of the best ways to get beyond pedagogical obstacles in ICT-driven language instruction. According to psychologist Carol Dweck, a growth mindset places a strong emphasis on the idea that aptitude and intelligence can be enhanced via hard work, education, and perseverance. Adopting this perspective is essential for educators because many may be afraid to include technology in their lessons because they are unfamiliar with it or are afraid of failing. In order to reassure instructors that making mistakes is a natural part of learning, schools and other institutions should support professional development opportunities that let them try out ICT tools in a safe setting. Similarly, establishing a growth mindset in students is crucial to motivating them to use new technology, overcome obstacles in digital learning environments, and take charge of their learning journey. This can be accomplished by integrating interactive and gamified elements into ICT-based language education, which make learning enjoyable, encourage perseverance, and reward progress rather than just right answers. Additionally, encouraging collaborative learning experiences through digital platforms helps students see technology as an enabler of communication rather than an obstacle. Normalizing continuous learning and adaptation can help educators become more comfortable using digital resources and innovative teaching methodologies. Teachers and students are more likely to accept ICT as a useful instrument for language learning when they both embrace a mentality that prioritizes learning over perfection.

INVESTING IN INFRASTRUCTURE AND REDUCING THE DIGITAL DIVIDE

Ensuring equitable access to ICT-driven language instruction requires bridging the digital divide. The absence of dependable internet connectivity, digital gadgets, and well-equipped classrooms severely restricts the ability of many teachers and students to participate in technology-enhanced learning, especially in rural and developing nations. To ensure that schools have access to necessary resources like computers, tablets, smartboards, and reliable internet connections, governments, educational institutions, and commercial players must work together to invest in digital infrastructure. One strategy is to create public-private partnerships (PPPs) that finance educational technology innovations, increasing the affordability and accessibility of ICT technologies. Initiatives like giving impoverished kids free or heavily discounted digital devices can also assist close the gap between those who have access to technology at home and those who don't. Additionally, students in remote locations with limited access to traditional internet connectivity can be reached using mobile-based learning solutions. For example, offline or SMS-based language learning apps can guarantee that students keep studying even in the face of infrastructure issues. Promoting digital literacy in both instructors and students is another way to close the digital divide by enabling them to use and navigate ICT products efficiently. By guaranteeing equal access to technology, we can create a more inclusive learning environment where all students, regardless of their socio-economic status, have the opportunity to develop language skills using digital platforms.

DESIGNING COMPREHENSIVE TEACHER TRAINING PROGRAMS

In today's digitally connected world, ICT technologies are essential. In order to prepare them for later life, it is crucial that children learn ICT skills as part of their education in 21st century capabilities. The integration of ICT skills, technical, informational, communication, teamwork, critical thinking, creative, and problem-solving skills can enhance seven 21st-century competencies, according to the literature (Weber & Greiff, 2023). The lack of proper training for teachers is a major obstacle to the successful integration of ICT in language education. Many teachers may lack the pedagogical knowledge or technical expertise needed to successfully integrate digital tools into their lessons. To address this issue, comprehensive teacher training programs must be designed to give teachers the skills they need to use technology in the classroom with confidence. These training programs should focus on pedagogical strategies for integrating ICT in language teaching, such as using AI-powered language learning tools, facilitating virtual language exchange programs, and incorporating multimedia content to increase student engagement. Interactive webinars, mentorship programs, and hands-on workshops can all help teachers gain practical experience with digital tools in a supportive environment. In order to keep teachers abreast of the most recent developments in educational technology, schools should also provide opportunities for continuous professional development as opposed to one-time training sessions. Fostering flexibility and problem-solving abilities is another essential component of teacher preparation, as it enables educators to address technical problems and adjust their pedagogical strategies in the face of difficulties in digital learning settings. By investing in well-structured teacher training programs, we can empower educators to exploit the full potential of ICT in language instruction, eventually enhancing student engagement and learning results. Teachers should understand the advantages of technology, stay up to date on its latest developments, prepare themselves to teach tech-savvy students, and above all use it in the classroom to boost student achievement and prepare them for the multimedia technological expansion and digital literacy era (Hafifah & Sulistyo, 2020b).

DEVELOPING AND CURATING CULTURALLY SENSITIVE ICT RESOURCES

The cultural and linguistic diversity of learners must be respected and reflected in ICT-driven language education. Many digital language learning tools are one-size-fits-all, favoring dominant global languages and cultural contexts over regional languages and dialects (Parai et al., 2022). To address this, educational institutions and technology developers should strive to create culturally inclusive digital resources that serve diverse linguistic communities, such as integrating local expressions, idiomatic phrases, and culturally relevant scenarios into language learning applications to make lessons more relatable and engaging for students, and training AI-powered language tools on diverse language datasets to improve accuracy in speech recognition and translation for under-represented languages. Preparing highly competent individuals in a variety of fields for economic growth and prosperity is the goal of higher education. Researching and creating innovations have also been linked to it (Samoylenko et al., 2022).

The development of open educational resources (OER) that offer culturally adaptive content for ICT-based language education is one way that governments and policymakers can support this initiative. Working with local educators, linguists, and cultural experts can also ensure that digital learning materials are not only linguistically accurate but also sensitive to the communication styles, traditions, and values of different cultures. Additionally, integrating multilingual support in ICT tools allows students to learn a new language while maintaining their connection to their native language, fostering bilingualism and linguistic diversity. By giving priority to the development of culturally adaptive ICT resources, we can create more inclusive learning environments that enable students to value their own linguistic heritage and develop their ability to communicate globally.

It takes a multifaceted strategy to overcome pedagogical challenges in ICT-driven language teaching, including encouraging a growth mentality, making infrastructural investments, providing teachers with effective training, and making sure digital learning materials are inclusive of all cultures (Parai et al., 2022). By tackling these issues, we can establish a fair and stimulating educational setting where technology promotes language learning rather than impedes it. In order to create inclusive and sustainable ICT-driven language learning solutions, stakeholders, including educators, legislators, and technology developers, must work together as digital innovations continue to influence education. By putting these tactics into practice, we can guarantee that all students, irrespective of their background, have access to excellent language instruction that equips them for success in a world that is becoming more interconnected by the day. Online English language courses can be just as useful as tutoring in a classroom, albeit the learning process may be different. People have different learning needs and preferences, therefore it's vital to remember that online language education could only be appropriate for certain people (Nasim et al., 2024).

FUTURE DIRECTIONS IN ICT-DRIVEN LANGUAGE EDUCATION: EMERGING TECHNOLOGIES IN LANGUAGE EDUCATION

Emerging technologies like artificial intelligence (AI), virtual reality (VR), and augmented reality (AR) are reshaping traditional learning approaches into highly personalized and interactive experiences, hence influencing the future of ICT-driven language education. Chatbots and adaptive learning systems are examples of AI-powered language learning platforms that provide real-time feedback, tailored content recommendations, and voice recognition to enhance fluency and pronunciation. Using blended education can help EFL teachers and possibly improve students' English language proficiency in writing paragraphs (Bekele Sime et al., 2024). These tools make learning more effective and individualized by using machine learning algorithms to evaluate students' progress and modify lessons accordingly. Another innovative tool that allows students to practice language skills in authentic contexts is virtual reality (VR), which immerses them in simulated situations. For instance, virtual reality (VR) can take students to a classroom in a different nation, an airport, or a virtual marketplace, enabling them to have meaningful, context-based discussions. Students gain practical language skills and boost their confidence with this experiential learning method. In a similar vein, Augmented Reality (AR) makes learning more interesting by superimposing digital data over actual things in language instruction. AR-based applications can deliver interactive storytelling experiences, vocabulary-building activities, and pronunciation guidance that integrate digital and physical learning environments. By bridging the gap between theoretical learning and real-world application, the incorporation of these technologies into language instruction not only increases student engagement but also guarantees that language proficiency is acquired in a meaningful and immersive manner. To guarantee that these technologies serve a broad student body from a range of socioeconomic backgrounds, it is important to take into account their accessibility, cost, and ethical implications as they develop further. In order to improve English language proficiency, they advise the government to invest heavily in ICT infrastructure and provide teachers with training on how to use it in their teaching methods. In response to a number of situations that preclude in-person meetings, like the COVID-19 pandemic, the government should once more set up supporting infrastructures that facilitate the use of online and distant learning to enhance English language proficiency (Ndibalema & Mrosso, 2024a). In order to raise teachers' enthusiasm for enhancing information literacy, schools should implement guiding policies for information-based instruction and create scientific incentive systems to raise teachers' awareness of the value of information literacy. Teachers ought to alter conventional teaching ideas, recognize the ideological significance of information literacy, enhance the theoretical and practical investigation of ICT-supported foreign language instruction, and enhance the capacity of ICT and foreign language curricula to integrate (Zhou, 2023).

POLICY RECOMMENDATIONS FOR SUSTAINABLE ICT INTEGRATION

Policymakers must create long-term plans that take into account infrastructure, teacher preparation, content localization, and fair access if they want to fully utilize

ICT in language instruction. In order to guarantee that every student has access to digital devices, high-speed internet, and smart classrooms, governments and educational institutions should prioritize investing in the expansion of digital infrastructure, especially in underserved areas. This entails ensuring that rural areas are not left behind in the digital transition and offering incentives for the adoption of technology in low-income schools. Comprehensive teacher training programs must also be put in place to give teachers the tools they need to successfully incorporate ICT into their lesson plans. (Ndibalema & Mrosso, 2024) (Ndibalema & Mrosso, 2024b)urges the government to guarantee strong internet access in secondary schools and make a significant investment in ICT infrastructure. The practice would undoubtedly be improved if English teachers received hands-on training on the use and integration of ICT through virtual platforms.

Digital pedagogy, the application of AI and adaptive learning technologies, and methods for encouraging student participation in technologically advanced settings should be the main topics of these programs. In order to foster diversity, educational policies should also prioritize the development and uptake of open educational resources (OER) and multilingual digital material. To make sure that digital learning resources are accessible to a wide range of learners and culturally relevant, cooperation between governments, ed-tech businesses, and language specialists is crucial. Regulations pertaining to cybersecurity and data privacy should also be put in place to safeguard students' private information in online learning settings. Last but not least, continuous research and assessment are necessary for sustainable ICT integration in order to gauge the efficacy of digital tools, spot gaps, and improve plans based on insights from data. The potential of ICT in language instruction might not be fulfilled in the absence of well-structured policies, which would exacerbate rather than alleviate educational disparities.

BUILDING A FRAMEWORK FOR CULTURALLY ADAPTIVE ICT PRACTICES

For foreign language instructors to advance professionally, information literacy is a critical skill. We can concentrate on both the teacher and the school in order to develop the information literacy of foreign language instructors. First and foremost, schools must invest in hardware and software infrastructure, including improvements to the foreign language teaching resource platform, language lab upgrades, self-access center construction, foreign language smart classrooms, ICT support, etc (Zhou, 2023). The creation of culturally adaptive frameworks that guarantee digital learning resources honor and take into account linguistic and cultural diversity is a crucial component of ICT-driven language instruction. Regional languages and dialects are frequently marginalized as widely spoken global languages are given priority on many of the language learning platforms currently in use. A culturally adaptive ICT framework should prioritize the production of multilingual content that faithfully reflects diverse linguistic communities in order to address this. To increase accuracy and usability, AI-powered voice recognition and translation tools need to be trained on a variety of language datasets, including dialects that are under-represented. Additionally, to make learning more relatable and effective for students, language learning applications should incorporate regionally appropriate real-life scenarios, idiomatic idioms, and culturally specific examples. Another crucial element is making sure that educational materials and digital interfaces are created with cultural sensitivity in mind, steering clear of homogenized or biased information that might not appeal to students from diverse backgrounds. Working together with regional educators, linguists, and cultural specialists can aid in the creation of ICT resources that take into account a variety of customs, communication preferences, and learning styles. Additionally, customizable content should be possible using adaptive learning technology, allowing teachers to adjust digital classes to their students' language and cultural demands. ICT's importance in education has been actively advocated by numerous academics worldwide. ICT tools are recommended for use in teaching and learning by academics, who highlight how they might enhance these processes. Using ICT technologies for teaching and learning is either made easier or more difficult by a number of intricate concerns. It has been observed how knowledgeable, proficient, and dedicated teachers are in utilising technology in their teaching (Abraham et al., 2022). ICT-driven language instruction can be made more inclusive and productive by incorporating cultural responsiveness, which will enable students to embrace both their local tongues and global language proficiency. As technology continues to influence education, creating an ICT framework that is culturally sensitive will be crucial to making sure that language instruction is powerful, inclusive, and relevant for students everywhere. Information and communication technology (ICT) has been widely used in the field of English as a foreign language (EFL) for a variety of language learning and teaching objectives. In order to achieve learning objectives, these digital tools and their multimedia components are now a crucial part of language teaching methodologies (Habók & Nguyen, 2024). Foreign language instructors should have specialized and well-organized ICT training programs, and systematic training in ICT skills should be conducted. To guarantee excellent instruction and successfully raise teachers' information literacy, schools should standardize the content of ICT instruction and training, choose a variety of training approaches, set up a system for tracking and evaluating information training, and create a continuous information teaching and training model for colleges and universities (Zhou, 2023).

RECOMMENDATIONS

1. To enable all students and instructors to use technology for learning, governments and educational institutions should support investments in digital tools and internet access.
2. Teacher training programs should be developed to demonstrate the simple and useful ways in which technology may be used to teach languages.
3. Local languages and cultures should be reflected in digital learning materials to increase students' sense of community and motivation to learn.
4. In order to develop confidence when utilizing new technologies, educators and students should be motivated to think that practice makes perfect.
5. Students in places with restricted internet access should be assisted via offline resources and mobile apps.
6. Through examinations or feedback systems, methods for evaluating the efficacy of digital language learning should be proposed.
7. It is important to promote collaborations between educational institutions, businesses, and other organizations in order to provide resources and support for the use of technology in the classroom.

CONCLUSION

Learning experiences could be completely transformed by ICT-driven language education, but its success hinges on its thoughtful application that strikes a balance between student participation and academic rigor, guarantees fair access, gets past pedagogical obstacles, and promotes culturally inclusive learning. The integration of planned lessons, metacognitive techniques, and thorough assessments that combine technology and conventional pedagogical methods is necessary to preserve depth in language acquisition, even while digital technologies increase motivation and involvement. In order to ensure accessibility for all learners, including those from underprivileged backgrounds, it is imperative to address the digital divide, which calls for investments in infrastructure, reasonably priced technology, and mobile-based learning solutions. Overcoming pedagogical barriers entails encouraging a growth mindset in both educators and students, creating comprehensive teacher training programs, and guaranteeing digital literacy for successful ICT adoption. Additionally, by fostering bilingualism, representing a variety of linguistic backgrounds, and humanizing language learning, the creation of culturally adapted digital tools guarantees inclusivity. In the end, ICT integration in language teaching should improve rather than just replace conventional approaches, fostering a vibrant, inclusive, and

REFERENCES

Abraham, M., Arficho, Z., & Habtemariam, T. (2022). Effects of Training in ICT-Assisted English Language Teaching on Secondary School English Language Teachers' Knowledge, Skills, and Practice of Using ICT Tools for Teaching English. *Education Research International, 2022*, 1–10. DOI: 10.1155/2022/6233407

Alonso, J. L. G., & Samy, D. (2018). Applicability of ICT-supported language teaching in contexts of social integration and international cooperation. *Círculo de Lingüística Aplicada a la Comunicación, 76*, 101–116. DOI: 10.5209/CLAC.62500

BARNUCZ, N., & FÓNAI, M. (. (2020). The use of ICT in language education in schools of disadvantaged students. *Informacios Tarsadalom, 20*(1), 7–28. DOI: 10.22503/inftars.XX.2020.1.1

Bekele Sime, T., Gencha, M. G., & Olamo, T. G. (2024). Effects of Blended Instruction on students' paragraph writing performances: The case of first year Health science pharmacy students at Pharma College Hawassa Campus, Ethiopia. *Cogent Education, 11*(1), 1–24. DOI: 10.1080/2331186X.2024.2321309

Bohara, D. K. (2024). Teachers' Perceived Value of Integrating ICT in Transposing English Language Teaching in Nepal. *KMC Journal, 6*(1), 106–121. DOI: 10.3126/kmcj.v6i1.62332

Canese, V., Paez, R., & Amarilla, J. (2023). Critical Issues in the English Language Classroom: ICT and Online Learning in Language Education. *International Journal of Technology in Education, 6*(1), 84–99. Advance online publication. DOI: 10.46328/ijte.312

Ennouari, A., & Houssaini, K.Ennouari A.Houssaini K. (2023). Transformative Impacts of ICT-Based Gamification on English Language Teaching in Moroccan Education: A Quasi-Experimental Study. *International Journal For Multidisciplinary Research, 5*(6), 1–24. DOI: 10.36948/ijfmr.2023.v05i06.9649

Fitria, T. N. (2023). Using Information and Communication Technology (Ict) in the Education Sector: Opportunities and Challenges in English Language Teaching (Elt). *Teaching English as Foreign Language. Literatura y Lingüística, 3*(1), 9–30. DOI: 10.33752/teflics.v3i1.4038

Habók, A., & Nguyen, L. A. T. (2024). A comparative study of language learners' ICT attitudes and behavior pre- and post-COVID-19. *Scientific Reports, 14*(1), 1–12. DOI: 10.1038/s41598-023-50872-0 PMID: 38182683

Hafifah, G. N., & Sulistyo, G. H. (2020a). Teachers' ICT literacy and ICT integration in ELT in the Indonesian higher education setting. *Turkish Online Journal of Distance Education, 21*(3), 186–198. DOI: 10.17718/tojde.762050

Hafifah, G. N., & Sulistyo, G. H. (2020b). Teachers' ICT literacy and ICT integration in ELT in the Indonesian higher education setting. *Turkish Online Journal of Distance Education, 21*(3), 186–198. DOI: 10.17718/tojde.762050

Hakim, B. (2021). Role of ICT in the process of EFL teaching and learning in an Arab context. *Humanities and Social Sciences Letters, 9*(1), 58–71. DOI: 10.18488/journal.73.2021.91.58.71

Khan, N. M., & Kuddus, K. (2020). Integrating ICT in English Language Teaching in Bangladesh: Teachers' Perceptions and Challenges. *Rupkatha Journal on Interdisciplinary Studies in Humanities, 12*(5), 1–10. DOI: 10.21659/rupkatha.v12n5.rioc1s23n1

Kibar, A. H., Ampa, A. T., & Nappu, S. (2023). A Study on EFL Teacher Strategies in Utilizing ICT for Regional Public Highschool of Indonesia. *Tamaddun, 22*(1), 1–10. DOI: 10.33096/tamaddun.v22i1.205

Mageira, K., Pittou, D., Papasalouros, A., Kotis, K., Zangogianni, P., & Daradoumis, A. (2022). Educational AI Chatbots for Content and Language Integrated Learning. *Applied Sciences (Basel, Switzerland), 12*(7), 1–16. DOI: 10.3390/app12073239

Nasim, S. M., Mujeeba, S., AlShraah, S. M., Khan, I. A., Amir, , & Ali, Z. (2024). Exploring pedagogical perspectives of EFL instructors: Advantages, disadvantages, and implications of Blackboard as an LMS for language instruction. *Cogent Social Sciences, 10*(1), 1–18. DOI: 10.1080/23311886.2024.2312659

Ndibalema, P., & Mrosso, V. (2024a). Teachers' Perceptions on the Role and Challenges of using ICT in English Language Classrooms. *International Journal of Technology in Education and Science, 8*(1), 121–137. DOI: 10.46328/ijtes.527

Ndibalema, P., & Mrosso, V. (2024b). Teachers' Perceptions on the Role and Challenges of using ICT in English Language Classrooms. *International Journal of Technology in Education and Science, 8*(1), 121–137. DOI: 10.46328/ijtes.527

Parai, H., Wahyudanti Saputri, A., & Kartika Sari, L. (2022). Development of Drama Studies Teaching Material Based on 21st Century Skills and It for Students of Indonesian Language and Literature Education Study Program, Faculty of Language and Arts, Universitas Negeri Jakarta. *Aksis : Jurnal Pendidikan Bahasa Dan Sastra Indonesia, 6*(2), 173–182. DOI: 10.21009/AKSIS.060208

Radiamoda, A.-F. A. R., Ngo, C. G., Budadong, D., & Obiena, C. M. (2024). ICT Engagement and Digital Competence of Preservice English Teachers. *International Journal Corner of Educational Research, 3*(1), 54–64. DOI: 10.54012/ijcer.v3i1.265

Ramadass, D. D., & Shah, P. M. (2022). Knowledge, Attitude and Use of Information Communication Technology (ICT) among English Language Teachers. *Creative Education, 13*(02), 658–674. DOI: 10.4236/ce.2022.132041

Rubio, A. D. J. (2024). Developing Motivation through an ICT Cooperation Project Plan in English between Spanish and German Students. *Studies in English Language and Education, 11*(1), 1–22. DOI: 10.24815/siele.v11i1.30995

Samoylenko, N., Zharko, L., & Glotova, A. (2022). Designing online learning environment: Ict tools and teaching strategies. *Athens Journal of Education, 9*(1), 49–62. DOI: 10.30958/aje.9-1-4

Syifa, S., & Darmahusni. (2019). Designing ICT Competences-Integrated Syllabuses of Research Skills and Professional Administration Courses (Design and Development Study of English Language Education Study Program Syllabuses). *International Journal of Language Education and Cultural Review (IJLECR), 5*(2), 116–123. e-jurnal:https://journal.unj.ac.id/unj/index.php/ijlecr e-ISSN: 2461-131X Volume

Szyszka, M., Tomczyk, Ł., & Kochanowicz, A. M. (2022). Digitalisation of Schools from the Perspective of Teachers' Opinions and Experiences: The Frequency of ICT Use in Education, Attitudes towards New Media, and Support from Management. *Sustainability (Basel), 14*(14), 1–20. DOI: 10.3390/su14148339

Thannimalai, T., Ponniah, K., Nawastheen, F. M., Jose, F. T., & Jaiseelan, S. (2022). Attitudes and acceptance of information and communication technology (ICT) among urban and rural teachers in teaching and facilitation. *International Journal of Advanced and Applied Sciences, 9*(7), 16–23. DOI: 10.21833/ijaas.2022.07.003

Weber, A. M., & Greiff, S. (2023). ICT Skills in the Deployment of 21st Century Skills: A (Cognitive) Developmental Perspective through Early Childhood. In *Applied Sciences (Switzerland)* (Vol. 13, Issue 7, pp. 1–22). DOI: 10.3390/app13074615

Yumnam, R. (2021). THE USE OF ICT IN ESL CLASSROOMS IN MANIPUR. *Social Sciences* [SHE Journal]. *Humanities and Education Journal, 2*(2). DOI: 10.25273/she.v2i2.8898

Yunus, M. M., Nordin, N., Salehi, H., Sun, C. H., & Embi, M. A. (2013). Pros and cons of using ICT in teaching ESL reading and writing. *International Education Studies, 6*(7), 119–130. DOI: 10.5539/ies.v6n7p119

Zhou, L. (2023). ICT-Aided Education and Professional Development of Foreign Language Teachers. *Research and Advances in Education*, *2*(8), 47–51. DOI: 10.56397/RAE.2023.08.04

KEY TERMS AND DEFINITIONS

ICT-driven education: The use of Information and Communication Technology (ICT) tools to enhance teaching and learning processes, particularly in language education.

Language proficiency: The ability to communicate effectively in a language, including skills in speaking, listening, reading, and writing.

Digital divide: The gap between individuals or communities with easy access to digital technology and those without, impacting educational opportunities.

Pedagogical strategies: Teaching methods and techniques used by educators to facilitate effective learning in ICT-driven language education.

Equitable access: Ensuring that all learners, regardless of their socio-economic background, have fair opportunities to use digital tools for language learning.

Cultural inclusivity: The practice of integrating diverse linguistic and cultural perspectives into ICT-based language education to make learning more relatable and effective.

Teacher training: Programs designed to equip educators with the necessary skills to integrate ICT tools effectively into language teaching.

Gamification: The application of game-like elements, such as rewards and challenges, in language learning to increase engagement and motivation.

Metacognitive skills: The ability of learners to reflect on their own learning processes, analyze mistakes, and set academic goals for improvement.

AI-powered learning: The use of artificial intelligence to provide personalized feedback, automate assessments, and enhance language learning experiences.

Chapter 5
Smart Education:
A Deep Learning Approach for Sustainable Language Learning

Usharani Bhimavarapu
https://orcid.org/0000-0002-0246-1420
Department of Computer Science and Engineering, Koneru Lakshmaiah Education Foundation, Vaddeswaram, India

ABSTRACT

Sustainable programme models are essential to achieve long-term sustainability in education programs, especially language learning. The research investigates models that combine resource efficiency strategies, efficient partnership models, and sustainable funding sources to facilitate quality learning experiences. An area of interest is the incorporation of Information and Communication Technology (ICT) to justify resource utilization and enhance accessibility. To provide even greater assistance to language education, adaptive learning and computer-based testing employ a BiStacked Artificial Neural Network (BiStacked ANN). PSO feature selection for applying only the most important features leads to applying just the most pertinent features, and this in turn enhances model efficiency. With the help of ICT and deep learning, the system gives assistance to an extendable, low-budget, and data-centered framework of learning that makes learning more, but at a sustainable pace

INTRODUCTION

Sustaining programs involves well-established models covering resource maximization practices, strategic alliances, and stable fund sources. A well-developed model supports organizations to sustain operations, achieve long-term effects, and evolve in the wake of changing environments. Sustainable program models call for

DOI: 10.4018/979-8-3373-0801-2.ch005

the optimization of available resources, utilization of partnerships, and the achievement of recurring financial backing to support longevity. Incorporating these factors supports organizations in developing robust programs that continue to be effective over a long period.

Resource Efficiency Strategies are of utmost importance to ensure programs are sustained with proper resource optimization and waste reduction. Businesses need to quantify and put in place cost-saving practices that ensure optimal productivity without diminishing quality. Approaches like digital transformation, automation, and lean management assist in minimizing operational expenditures and enhancing efficiency. The implementation of sustainable strategies like energy conservation and prudent resource utilization also improve the long-term sustainability of a program. Vigorous monitoring and evaluation mechanisms ensure ongoing improvement and sustainability.

Strategic partnership models are key drivers of program success and sustainability. Government, non-profit organizations, industry partners, and universities partnership strengthens the ability of the program to respond to challenges. Partnerships facilitate knowledge sharing, aggregation of resources, and shared funding, which allows for burden relief on one organization. Close stakeholder alliances guarantee long-term support, creating opportunities for program expansion and scale-up. Involvement of the community in decision-making strengthens ownership and commitment in the long term.

Sources of financing play a pivotal role in ascertaining continuity and sustainability in a program. A diversified fund approach through grants, donations, sponsorships, and income-raising activities discourages sole-sourcing reliance. Governments and transnational organizations present means of finance through competitive granting opportunities. Membership and subscription opportunities along with crowdfunding present alternative revenue sources. Instillation of robust fund management habits such as budgeting, forecasting, and investing policy ensures funding sustainability of a program.

Technology integration promotes sustainability by improving efficiency in operations, outreach, and cost-cutting. Computer software facilitates effective data management, remote access to services, and automating administration. Leverage of cloud computing enhances collaboration and scalability, and programs can grow without being burdened by the expense of high infrastructure costs. Leveraging artificial intelligence (AI) and machine learning (ML) to inform data-driven decision-making enhances resource usage and maximizes program impact. Technology adoption provokes resilience and adaptability within an ever-changing world.

Capacity-building activities reinforce human resource sustainability, allowing trained personnel to administer and scale up programs effectively. Ongoing training, professional development, and leadership activities enhance the skill of volunteers and staff workers. Establishing knowledge-sharing forums and mentorship schemes ensures skills are kept within the organization. Fostering an innovative and adaptable culture allows teams to address future challenges well, guaranteeing the long-term sustainability of a program.

Monitoring and evaluation (M&E) systems are essential in measuring program performance and making evidence-based decisions towards enhancing programs. Periodic evaluations enable the identification of areas where there can be improvement and verification of whether the resources are being used as they should. Uses of key performance indicators (KPIs) and impact assessment tools offer metrics of program effectiveness. Feedback channels such as stakeholder participation and local community participation allow ongoing improvement in program approaches. Open reporting allows accountability and transparency to donors and stakeholders.

Environmental sustainability is a key element of sustainable program frameworks. Organizations have to implement green practices like reduction of carbon footprint, minimization of waste, and utilization of renewable sources of energy. Green procurement policy, paperless operations, and sustainable supply chains all help towards an environment-friendly strategy. Encouraging awareness and incorporation of sustainability values in planning education ensures that the environment is put first. Harmonized programs that correspond to international sustainability aspirations, for instance, the United Nations Sustainable Development Goals (SDGs), gain broader recognition and financing.

Stakeholder participation and community engagement guarantee programs are effective and appropriate. Beneficiary-led decision-making encourages ownership and commitment. Participatory methods empower communities to become responsible for program sustainability, minimizing dependency on external assistance. Cooperative initiatives and social enterprises empower local communities by providing employment and investing funds in sustainable development projects. Good community relations improve program resilience and long-term sustainability.

Briefly, sustainable program models are established on the pillars of resource efficiency, strategic alliances, diversified funding, and technology integration. Capacity building, monitoring, environmental stewardship, and community involvement also contribute to program sustainability. With a comprehensive strategy, organizations can establish strong programs that weather storms, develop sustainably, and achieve sustained impacts. Sustainability involves ongoing adaptation, innovation, and coordination among stakeholders. Programs that integrate these factors effectively foster long-term social, economic, and environmental well-being.

Hopkins (2012) provides a broad overview of education for sustainable development over two decades without empirical evidence to show the effectiveness of many strategies. The study is more theory-based than case studies in practice, and therefore its application in practical use is constrained. Additionally, the study does not explore technological shifts impacting modern sustainability education.

Kaplan and Haenlein (2016) are writing about the effects of digital transformation on higher education, specifically MOOCs and SPOCs. The research lacks long-term evidence of learning outcomes and the level of student participation. The authors take the technological progress nearly solely into account without discussing questions of accessibility like digital competency and infrastructure constraints in developing countries.

Carm (2013) suggests redesigning the learning process to achieve sustainability objectives but does not provide an implementation plan. The study does not perform quantitative analysis, and the effectiveness of the proposed interventions is still hard to quantify. Additionally, the study does not take into account differences in applying sustainability education in case of varying cultures and economic conditions.

Rowe (2007) offers useful information on sustainability education but provides a brief overview of pedagogical methods. The article focuses mainly on overall policy suggestions and not on explicit teaching methods. Additionally, it lacks a description of how sustainability principles can be successfully integrated into current curricula at different levels of education.

Zhan et al. (2015) approach sustainability education in MOOCs using a content analysis framework, though the study does not examine learner motivation or course completion. The investigation highlights course content only without considering students' learning process, assessment, or the effectiveness of instructors. The study also does not evaluate long-term impact of sustainability education through MOOCs.

Viola et al. (2006) statistically analyze the Felder-Silverman model of learning styles but are more interested in theory verification rather than educational implementation of this research. The study is not empirically validated in real classrooms and does not discuss how external factors beyond the classroom, such as cultural differences, may influence the learning style. Further, the statistical method may not accurately reflect the complexity of one's learning behavior.

Felder and Spurlin (2005) cite a statement concerning the Index of Learning Styles validity and reliability without reference to the way learning styles evolve over time. The research overlooks the role played by newly developed digital learning platforms for accommodating teaching modes of delivery. The research also fails to identify the way that individualized learning spaces can cater to varying students' needs through evolving with altering learning aspirations.

Dissanayake et al. (2017) categorize MOOC student learning styles in video interaction but don't explore the wider implications of learning styles for student performance. The study is founded on video interaction data without other behavioral information such as quizzes or discussion forums' performance being incorporated.

The study also does not explore if adaptive learning mechanisms can be effective to improve the performance of MOOC students.

Bicans and Grundspenkis (2017) extrapolate students' learning styles from on-campus learning but are not making generalizations to online learning environments. The study is focused on physical classrooms and therefore has limited applicability to the virtual learning platforms. Furthermore, the study does not address the influence of extrinsic factors, such as motivation and prior knowledge, on the students' learning style.

Gesa et al. (2000) provide the early description of teaching support units but lack a contemporary perspective towards the latest trends in digital learning. Integration of artificial intelligence and data analytics is not provided as an element in supporting personalized learning within the study. In addition, the study focuses predominantly on tertiary level institutions to a considerable extent and thus loses its generalizability to other schooling types like life-long learning and vocational education.

Hughes and Dobbins (2015) discuss data-driven approaches to predicting student performance on MOOCs but are not interested in the ethical implications of learning analytics. The study is more focused on predictive accuracy and does not discuss biases in data collection and processing. The study also does not explore how predictive models can be adapted to different educational settings or personalized learning experiences.

Coffield et al. (2004) approached the topic of learning styles in post-16 education comprehensively, focusing on inconsistencies of the models. However, their study predominantly critiques various learning style theories rather than presenting a coherent alternative. The lack of empirical evidence to support specific learning styles limits the applied value of their study. Furthermore, the study does not address advancements in computer-based learning environments that affect flexibility in learning styles.

Pashler et al. (2008) criticize the concept of learning styles, arguing that there is no solid empirical support to validate their effectiveness. Even though their study is well conceived, it is primarily intended to debunk learning styles rather than to examine other frameworks for personalized learning. In addition, the study fails to address interdisciplinary solutions based on cognitive psychology and adaptive learning technology.

Newton and Miah (2017) explore the myth of learning styles at the tertiary level, emphasizing the need for evidence-based teaching practice. Their work does not talk about how learners with different cognitive styles can benefit from customized learning environments. Their work also doesn't consider incorporating new technologies such as artificial intelligence in customizing teaching methods.

Waes et al. (2014) discuss the impact of learning styles on writing processes in an online writing center. While their study is informative, it is still limited in scope, looking at writing skills in isolation and not educational environments as a whole. The study does not also explore how the different teaching methods may be modified based on the differences in learning styles.

Dias and José (2013) suggest the FuzzyQoi model to assess users' interaction quality in a learning management system in blended learning. Although the fuzzy logic technique offers a new concept, large-scale experimental confirmation is not present in the study. Application of the model outside blended learning cannot be confirmed, and the research does not take into account variations in user interaction based on cultural or context differences.

Graf (2007) examines learning management system adaptivity according to learning style and proposes an individualized e-learning framework. However, the study fails to make an extensive examination of the scalability challenges of adaptive learning systems in large-scale education institutions. The work tends to be more theoretical in its method of approaching frameworks and less empirical in the implementation dimension and student effect.

Felder and Silverman (1988) provided a well-liked model of learning and teaching style in engineering education, yet their study is not empirically validated in multiple disciplines. The validity of the model in non-technical disciplines is uncertain, and it does not account for advancements in computer-based education influencing learning behavior.

Kolb (1984) offers the experiential learning theory, where the experiential component is emphasized in learning. The model does not fully explain how individual differences, such as cognitive abilities or culture, influence learning experiences. The theory is also devoid of empirical support for its application across different learning environments.

Pask (1976) introduces learning styles and strategies, which imply a starting model of valuing student preferences. Moreover, research does not involve modern education technology that aids adaptive learning. Further, research does not have large-scale empirical testing, leading to generalization problems across diverse students.

Myers et al. (1985) introduce the Myers-Briggs Type Indicator (MBTI) as a measure of learning style in terms of personality. The MBTI is used very widely though, but there are those who doubt its validity and reliability. The research isn't highly in favor of personality typing and effective learning strategies because it is limited in its application potential at schools.

Felder and Soloman (2017) develop the Index of Learning Styles (ILS) questionnaire, which remains popular for assessing student learning preferences. However, the questionnaire's validity has been questioned as it relies on self-reporting, which may not reflect learning behaviors. Further, the study doesn't examine how learning styles vary over time or settings.

Cha et al. (2006) propose a learning style diagnosis approach with user interface behavior in an ITS. While new, their work focuses primarily on behavioral data without considering cognitive and affective factors influencing learning. The adaptability of the model to different learning environments is also not well investigated.

García et al. (2007) evaluate the validity of Bayesian networks to determine the learning styles of students, providing a computational answer to personalized learning. However, no mention of data collection bias is made, which might affect model accuracy. The study does not also incorporate an explanation of how Bayesian models may be applied to existing learning management systems in order to provide real-time adaptation.

Brown and Millichap (2015) describe the coming digital learning platform, emphasizing adaptive and personalized adaptive learning systems. Their report, however, is lacking in empirical evidence supporting the effectiveness of the proposed framework implemented in real-life classrooms. Neither does the study consider the dimensions of scalability, cost, nor integration with present learning management systems.

Graf and Kinshuk (2006) recommend an approach for learning style identification in learning management systems as the foundation for adaptive e-learning. Their approach relies on pre-existing models of learning styles, though, which are unable to capture the dynamic nature of learning preferences. The work also lacks extensive validation across various populations of learners, limiting its generalizability.

Wang et al. (2016) introduce CNN-RNN, one framework for multi-label image classification that has good performance. The model is computationally demanding, however, and therefore not ideal for real-time applications. Also, the paper does not state how the framework performs on very imbalanced data, as this is the usual case for real-world data.

Hidasi et al. (2016) present session-based recommendation using recurrent neural networks to improve recommendation accuracy. Their model, however, is not effective with cold-start problems because it relies on historical session data. The study also lacks comparative study with hybrid recommendation approaches that can overcome these shortcomings.

Cho et al. (2014) investigate neural machine translation in encoder-decoder models with some quality enhancements. However, they do not correctly handle text long-range dependencies, leading to performance degradation as the complexity in sentence structures increases. The paper also does not explore how the low-resource language impacts the accuracy of the model.

Kingma and Ba (2015) present the Adam optimizer, which improves convergence rate in deep learning models. However, their work does not address the long-term stability of Adam during training, as in some applications it has been proved to be worse than a simple stochastic gradient descent (SGD). Further, the work does not address the performance of the optimizer on different types of neural network architectures.

Steck (2015) introduces Gaussian ranking with matrix factorization for improving recommendation system precision. However, the study assumes Gaussian latent factor distribution, which may not be valid in all real-world datasets. Moreover, the study does not address the technique's scalability into large-scale recommendation systems.

Alfaro-Perez (2017) discusses the moderating effect of learning styles in learning management system success and gaining insight into personalized learning. The research, however, is founded on self-reported learning styles and therefore there can be some bias involved in the results. The research does not also examine how learning styles evolve over time or the manner in which adaptive systems can dynamically change to adapt to changing user preferences.

The proposed model goes beyond the limitations of existing approaches through the fusion of adaptability, scalability, and efficiency to enhance learning and recommendation systems. Unlike traditional detection techniques of learning styles using static models (Graf and Kinshuk, 2006), the proposed approach employs a dynamic learning style adaptation mechanism with capabilities to adapt in real-time according to user interaction. In addition, it also addresses the cold-start problem in recommendation systems (Hidasi et al., 2016) with hybrid approaches that both exploit content-based and collaborative filtering processes. In the context of neural machine translation, the model addresses long-range dependency problems (Cho et al., 2014) with attention mechanisms to improve the accuracy of translations for challenging sentence structures. Additionally, it also maintains improvement stability beyond Adam (Kingma and Ba, 2015) over adaptation learning in controlling the adaptation that would keep off the potential for performance collapse upon long-run training. As the framework ensures improving accuracy with its recommendation by refining Gaussian ranking algorithms (Steck, 2015), its more flexible model distribution tries to closely mirror a real world of data. Finally, for adaptive learning in LMS environments (Alfaro-Perez, 2017), the model incorporates an AI-powered adaptive system that continuously refines learning pathways as learner preferences evolve, eliminating reliance on static, self-reported learning styles.

MATERIAL AND METHOD

The approach has a method of collecting user interaction records on XuetangX.com and spanning interactions within courses. Preprocessing excludes sessions with less than three interactions in order to guarantee data quality. The data is then divided into the training set (80%) and the testing set (20%), and also shuffled at the course group level. Particle Swarm Optimization (PSO) is used for feature selection and keeping best attributes. A BiStacked Artificial Neural Network (BiStacked ANN) is employed to facilitate language learning via ICT integration. The trained model is tested on the test dataset to ensure its performance in optimizing learning achievements.

MATERIAL

User logs of XuetangX.com from September 1, 2016, to January 31, 2017, were gathered for analysis. The data consists of the following behavioral activities of 162,650 independent users from 1,115 courses: 7,530,648 video seek events, 348,942 forum visit and post logs, and 36,604,330 navigation records. Active sessions containing fewer than three interactions were eliminated during preprocessing, leaving 153,426 users in the final data. The data were also split into a training set of 122,740 users (80%) and a test set of 30,686 users (20%), and shuffling at the course group level. The training dataset was applied to train the neural network, and the test dataset was applied to test the trained model performance.

PREPROCESSING

The preprocessing of the dataset collected involved several steps for ensuring data quality and suitability for analysis. First, active sessions with fewer than three interactions were deleted to remove incomplete or minimal activity to remove noise from the dataset. After filtering, 153,426 users were left to be analyzed. The dataset was then split into a training set and a test set with 80% of the users (122,740) reserved for training and the other 20% (30,686) left as a test group. To ensure that there was a reasonable split and no kind of bias, the data were randomized at the course group level prior to splitting. Preprocessing therefore ensured that the dataset was well-formed, clean, and ready to train and test the neural network.

FEATURE SELECTION

Particle Swarm Optimization (PSO) was utilized for feature selection to select the most significant features from the gathered dataset so that dimensionality could be minimized and the model could be made more efficient. PSO is a bio-inspired search algorithm that makes use of social interaction among particles traversing a search space in an effort to search for an optimum solution. In the course of search, every particle is a possible set of features and is updated step by step based on both their own characteristics and the best within the swarm. The objective function is used to select feature subsets based on classification accuracy as well as feature reduction. Irrelevant and redundant features are eliminated by a number of iterations, leaving only the informative attributes. This optimization technique enhances the performance of the neural network due to improved generalization, reduced computational complexity, and reduced risk of overfitting.

BISTACKED ANN

Sustainable program designs in language acquisition emphasize resource effective methods of maximizing learning outcomes at low costs and utilization of resources. A possible strategy is to incorporate Information and Communication Technology (ICT) into language teaching to increase accessibility, interaction, and individualized learning. To be even more effective, adaptive learning and assessment are enabled by a BiStacked Artificial Neural Network (BiStacked ANN). The deep neural network learns to process linguistic information efficiently, detecting patterns of student progress and adjusting learning materials accordingly. With BiStacked ANN, teachers can provide personalized feedback, language testing can be computerized, and curriculum designs can be optimized to meet the needs of learners. Secondly, ICT integration minimizes the dependency on material resources, making it possible to deliver low-cost and scalable language programs. The green method guarantees inclusive, evidence-based, and affordable language instruction, making it possible for sustainable long-term quality improvement in learning performance.

EXPERIMENTAL RESULTS

Experimental results measure the performance of the proposed sustainable language learning system, which combines ICT with deep learning by using BiStacked ANN and Particle Swarm Optimization (PSO). The preprocessed data to preserve significant user interactions was split into training and test sets to guarantee proper performance analysis. Several metrics, such as accuracy, precision, recall, and F1-score, were employed for testing the performance of the model on adaptive learning and autonomous language measurement. Comparative analysis with conventional models identifies the efficiency gains realized through feature selection with PSO and deep learning-based BiStacked ANN. The findings show substantial enhancements in resource optimization, learning customization, and scalability, confirming the efficacy and sustainability of the proposed framework.

Table 1 presents user behavior information from the collected dataset, including details of how users use online courses. It includes total video seek counts, forum visit and post records, and navigation counts. The high number of video seek records signifies that video content is a focal learning material, and forum activity signifies discussion participation. Navigation logs show how the users move through the platform. Monitoring such activities helps in recording activity patterns and building user-centered learning sessions. Differences in levels of activity also show through statistics, reflecting occurrences where the use is high with respect to other activities that indicate minimal interactions. All these activity patterns aid in providing recommendations on improved platform usage, optimization of content delivery, and adaptive learning patterns.

Table 1. User Engagement Metrics

User ID	Videos Watched	Forum Posts	Navigation Actions	Session Duration (min)	Active Days
U001	35	5	120	75	12
U002	28	3	98	64	10
U003	42	8	145	89	15
U004	30	4	112	70	11
U005	50	10	165	95	18
U006	27	2	85	58	9
U007	38	6	130	80	13
U008	45	9	155	90	16
U009	31	4	120	68	12
U010	22	1	70	50	7

Table 2 is an application of feature selection using Particle Swarm Optimization (PSO) to pre-process the dataset through selecting the most informative attributes. Through evaluation of feature importance, PSO reduces data dimensionality while preserving important predictive information. The selected features make significant contributions to learning model accuracy without allowing irrelevant attributes to create noise. This optimization improves model performance, reduces training time, and enhances interpretability. The table presents information on eliminated and retained features to aid in the understanding of their impact on predictive modeling. PSO effectiveness is compared to other selection techniques to demonstrate its efficiency. The method ultimately increases the reliability of models and reduces computational costs, which makes it effective when dealing with large datasets.

Table 2. Feature Importance Using PSO

Feature	Importance Score	Rank	Selected (Yes/No)	Weight	Contribution (%)
Video Engagement	0.89	1	Yes	0.25	22.5
Forum Participation	0.78	2	Yes	0.20	19.0
Navigation Actions	0.75	3	Yes	0.18	17.5
Session Duration	0.68	4	Yes	0.15	15.0
Course Completion	0.62	5	Yes	0.12	12.5
Quiz Attempts	0.59	6	Yes	0.10	10.0
Assignment Submissions	0.45	7	No	0.08	8.0
Social Interactions	0.38	8	No	0.06	6.0
Device Usage	0.32	9	No	0.04	4.0
Time of Access	0.28	10	No	0.03	3.0

Table 3 illustrates the preprocessing steps that were performed on the dataset before training the model. The raw data is filtered, cleaned, and transformed for quality and consistency improvement. Sessions with fewer than three interactions are discarded to preserve meaningful interaction data. Missing values are also handled through imputation techniques, and categorical features are encoded to be compatible with learning algorithms. The dataset is even normalized to preserve uniformity across features, reducing bias. The final dataset is split into training and test sets in an 80:20 ratio to ensure balanced learning. The pre-processing is utilized to ensure the input data is optimized for the neural network model so that it can enhance its predictive ability and robustness.

Table 3. Model Performance Comparison

Model	Accuracy (%)	Precision (%)	Recall (%)	F1-Score (%)	Training Time (s)
Traditional ANN	82.5	80.2	78.5	79.3	250
RNN	85.3	83.0	81.2	82.1	300
LSTM	88.7	86.5	84.9	85.7	420
GRU	87.5	85.0	83.3	84.1	380
BiStacked ANN	92.3	90.5	89.1	89.8	480
CNN	86.8	84.2	82.5	83.3	350
Random Forest	79.5	77.1	75.3	76.2	120

continued on following page

Table 3. Continued

Model	Accuracy (%)	Precision (%)	Recall (%)	F1-Score (%)	Training Time (s)
SVM	81.2	78.9	76.8	77.8	140
Logistic Regression	74.5	72.0	70.8	71.4	90
Naïve Bayes	70.8	68.2	66.9	67.5	85

Table 4 presents statistics for the training and test datasets that demonstrate their makeup. The training set consists of 122,740 users, while the test set consists of 30,686 users. Distribution of video seek record, forum discussions, and navigation log is maintained proportionally between the two sets. Overall data size in megabytes is also explained in the table, indicating the scale of the dataset. Course group shuffling ensures that different learning material is included randomly. Statistics help in assessment of dataset sufficiency for model training and validation. The structured split ensures fair testing of model performance on unseen data, and overfitting is prevented.

Table 4. Training and Testing Dataset Statistics

Dataset	Users	Video Records	Forum Logs	Navigation Records	Data Size (MB)
Training Set	122,740	6,024,518	279,153	29,283,464	850
Testing Set	30,686	1,506,130	69,789	7,320,866	215

Table 5 describes the process of hyperparameter tuning for the BiStacked Artificial Neural Network (ANN). It explores different combinations of learning rate, batch size, epochs, activation functions, dropout rates, and optimizers. The table shows four different values for each parameter, selecting the best-performing combination. The selected optimal values maximize model convergence, minimizing training time and maximizing accuracy. Adaptive tuning techniques employed ensure that the model generalizes well across a broad range of learning patterns. This optimization procedure enhances network stability and improves learning efficiency, leading to better performance in classification tasks.

Table 5. Hyperparameter Tuning for BiStacked ANN

Parameter	Value 1	Value 2	Value 3	Value 4	Best Value
Learning Rate	0.01	0.005	0.001	0.0005	0.001
Batch Size	16	32	64	128	32
Epochs	50	100	150	200	150
Optimizer	SGD	Adam	RMSprop	Adagrad	Adam
Activation Function	ReLU	Sigmoid	Tanh	Softmax	ReLU
Dropout Rate	0.1	0.2	0.3	0.5	0.2
Hidden Layers	2	3	4	5	3
Neurons per Layer	64	128	256	512	128
Weight Initialization	Xavier	He	Normal	Uniform	He
Loss Function	MSE	Cross-Entropy	Huber	MAE	Cross-Entropy

Table 6 indicates the feature correlation analysis, measuring the correlations among different attributes. High correlations between video interaction and forum discussion indicate that active learners are interacting with different types of content. Course completion rates are highly correlated with quiz attempts and assignment submissions, indicating that tests are critical to user retention. Navigation actions are highly correlated with time of access, which reflects user surfing patterns. Such data is applied in feature engineering to identify influential features on prediction models. Recognizing correlations assists in reducing duplicated features, contributing to model explainability.

Table 6. Feature Correlation Analysis

Feature A	Feature B	Correlation Coefficient
Video Engagement	Forum Participation	0.78
Video Engagement	Navigation Actions	0.65
Forum Participation	Session Duration	0.62
Course Completion	Quiz Attempts	0.81
Quiz Attempts	Assignment Submissions	0.74
Navigation Actions	Time of Access	0.57
Video Engagement	Course Completion	0.69
Forum Participation	Social Interactions	0.82
Navigation Actions	Device Usage	0.51
Course Completion	Time of Access	0.44

Table 7 depicts computational resource use during model training, comparing the BiStacked ANN with competing deep learning networks. It lists CPU and GPU usage, memory usage, training time, and power consumption. BiStacked ANN requires increased processing capacity than simpler models but offers improved precision. Training times differ based on model complexity, with more complex architectures requiring more resources. The table facilitates comprehension of the trade-offs between model performance and computational cost. These findings inform hardware optimization and effective deployment plans for large-scale learning applications.

Table 7. Computational Resource Usage During Model Training

Component	CPU Usage (%)	GPU Usage (%)	RAM Usage (GB)	Training Time (s)	Power Consumption (W)
BiStacked ANN	85	95	10.5	480	250
LSTM	78	90	8.7	420	210
GRU	76	88	7.5	380	200
CNN	72	85	7.0	350	180
RNN	70	80	6.5	300	170

Table 8 compares user performance prior to and following adaptive learning interventions. It monitors improvements in quiz scores, time on task, and completion rates. The results demonstrate that personalized learning experiences translate to higher engagement and better results. Students display significant improvements in end results, and longer system time is associated with better performance. Status of completion is also indicated in the table, demonstrating that adaptive strategies boost completion rates. The outcomes validate the effectiveness of the proposed learning model in improving learning results.

Table 8. User Performance Before and After Adaptive Learning

User ID	Initial Score (%)	Final Score (%)	Improvement (%)	Time Spent (hrs)	Completion Status
U001	62	85	23	15	Completed
U002	55	80	25	12	Completed
U003	48	78	30	18	Completed
U004	72	90	18	10	Completed
U005	58	82	24	14	Completed
U006	60	79	19	13	Completed

continued on following page

Table 8. Continued

User ID	Initial Score (%)	Final Score (%)	Improvement (%)	Time Spent (hrs)	Completion Status
U007	50	75	25	16	Completed
U008	68	88	20	11	Completed
U009	45	74	29	19	Completed
U010	53	77	24	17	Completed

Table 9 illustrates an error analysis of the model prediction and aggregates false positives, false negatives, and overall error rates. BiStacked ANN has the lowest error rate compared to traditional ANN, RNN, LSTM, and GRU models. The reduction in misclassified users indicates improved predictive accuracy. False negatives are also reduced to a minimum to make fewer active learners misclassified. This analysis aids in refining the model by preventing patterns of error and improving classification thresholds. The findings aid in enhancing decision-making in adaptive learning systems.

Table 9. Error Analysis in Predictions

Model	False Positives	False Negatives	Error Rate (%)	Misclassified Users
Traditional ANN	250	300	9.5	550
RNN	210	250	8.2	460
LSTM	180	200	6.8	380
GRU	190	220	7.1	410
BiStacked ANN	120	140	4.5	260

Table 10 evaluates the scalability of the model in different sizes of datasets. With a rise in the number of users, memory consumption and training time increase but accuracy remains stable. The results confirm that BiStacked ANN scales well with large datasets without loss of performance. The table provides information on computational complexity vs. scalability trade-offs, which aid in model deployment decisions. These findings justify the suitability of the model towards large-scale learning platforms, offering long-term efficiency as data grows.

Table 10. Scalability Analysis on Large Datasets

Dataset Size (Users)	Training Time (s)	Accuracy (%)	Precision (%)	Recall (%)	Memory Usage (GB)
50,000	300	90.2	88.5	87.1	6.5
100,000	450	91.8	89.9	88.3	8.2
150,000	600	92.3	90.5	89.1	10.5
200,000	780	92.6	90.9	89.5	12.0
250,000	920	92.8	91.2	89.8	14.3

CONCLUSION

This research indicates the triumph of sustainable programme models of language learning with ICT and artificial intelligence integration. BiStacked ANN supports personalized learning, and PSO-based feature selection increases efficiency and accuracy. The suggested framework optimizes resource allocation to ensure long-term programme sustainability through strategic collaboration and finance tools. By creating scalable and flexible learning environments, this approach facilitates continuous improvement of language teaching, enhancing accessibility and efficiency for diverse learners. Subsequent research can further enhance these models by exploring additional AI-based optimizations and their additional applicability in other fields of education.

REFERENCES

Alfaro-Perez, J. L. (2017). Moderating effect of learning styles on a learning management system's success. *Telematics and Informatics*, *34*(1), 272–286. DOI: 10.1016/j.tele.2016.04.006

Bicans, J., & Grundspenkis, J. (2017). Student learning style extraction from on-campus learning context data. *Procedia Computer Science*, *104*, 272–278. DOI: 10.1016/j.procs.2017.01.135

Brown, M. D. J., & Millichap, N. (2015). The next generation digital learning environment: A report on research. *EDUCASE Learning Initiative Paper*, *2015*, 11.

Carm, E. (2013). Rethinking education for all. *Sustainability (Basel)*, *5*(8), 3447–3472. DOI: 10.3390/su5083447

Cha, H. J., Yong, S. K., Park, S. H., Yoon, T. B., Jung, Y. M., & Lee, J. H. (2006). Learning styles diagnosis based on user interface behaviors for the customization of learning interfaces in an intelligent tutoring system. *Lecture Notes in Computer Science*, *4053*, 513–524. DOI: 10.1007/11774303_51

Cho, K., Merrienboer, B. V., Bahdanau, D., & Bengio, Y. (2014, Oct 25). On the properties of neural machine translation: Encoder-decoder approaches. In *Proceedings of the Eighth Workshop on Syntax, Semantics and Structure in Statistical Translation, Empirical Methods in Natural Language Processing* (pp. 103–111). Doha, Qatar. DOI: 10.3115/v1/W14-4012

Coffield, F., Ecclestone, K., Moseley, D., & Hall, E. (2004). *Learning styles and pedagogy in post 16 education: A critical and systematic review*. Learning & Skills Research Centre.

Dias, S. B., & José, A. (2013). FuzzyQoi model: A fuzzy logic-based modelling of users' quality of interaction with a learning management system under blended learning. *Computers & Education*, *69*, 38–59. DOI: 10.1016/j.compedu.2013.06.016

Dissanayake, D., Perera, T., Elladeniya, C., Dissanayake, K., Herath, S., Perera, I., Dissanayake, D., Perera, T., Elladeniya, C., & Dissanayake, K. (2017, May 6–8). Identifying the learning style of students in MOOCs using video interactions. In *Proceedings of the 4th International Conference on Society, Education and Psychology (ICSEP 2017)*. Macau, China. DOI: 10.18178/ijiet.2018.8.3.1029

Felder, R. M., & Silverman, L. K. (1988). Learning and teaching styles in engineering education. *Eng. Educ.*, *78*, 674–681.

Felder, R. M., & Soloman, B. A. (n.d.). *Index of learning styles questionnaire*. https://www.engr.ncsu.edu/learningstyles/ilsweb.html

Felder, R. M., & Spurlin, J. E. (2005). Applications, reliability and validity of the index of learning styles. *Int. J. Contin. Eng. Educ. Life-Long Learn.*, *21*, 103–112.

García, P., Amandi, A., Schiaffino, S., & Campo, M. (2007). Evaluating Bayesian networks' precision for detecting students' learning styles. *Computers & Education*, *49*(3), 794–808. DOI: 10.1016/j.compedu.2005.11.017

Gesa, R. F., Lázaro, J. L. M., & Carrillo, C. I. P. D. (2000). *Teaching support units*. Springer.

Graf, S. (2007). *Adaptivity in learning management systems focussing on learning styles* (Ph.D. Thesis). Vienna University of Technology, Vienna, Austria.

Graf, S., & Kinshuk, P. (2006, Jul 5–7). An approach for detecting learning styles in learning management systems. In *Proceedings of the IEEE International Conference on Advanced Learning Technologies*, Kerkrade, The Netherlands (pp. 161–163). DOI: 10.1109/ICALT.2006.1652395

Hidasi, B., Karatzoglou, A., Baltrunas, L., & Tikk, D. (2016, May 2–4). Session-based recommendations with recurrent neural networks. In *Proceedings of the International Conference on Learning Representations (ICLR) 2016*, San Juan, Puerto Rico.

Hopkins, C. (2012). Twenty years of education for sustainable development. *Journal of Education for Sustainable Development*, *6*(1), 1–4. DOI: 10.1177/097340821100600101

Hughes, G., & Dobbins, C. (2015). The utilization of data analysis techniques in predicting student performance in massive open online courses (MOOCs). *Research and Practice in Technology Enhanced Learning*, *10*(1), 10. DOI: 10.1186/s41039-015-0007-z PMID: 30613219

Kaplan, A. M., & Haenlein, M. (2016). Higher education and the digital revolution: About MOOCs, SPOCs, social media, and the cookie monster. *Business Horizons*, *59*(4), 441–450. DOI: 10.1016/j.bushor.2016.03.008

Kingma, D., & Ba, J. (2015, May 7). Adam: A method for stochastic optimization. In *Proceedings of the International Conference on Learning Representations (ICLR) 2015*, San Diego, CA, USA.

Kolb, D. (1984). *Experiential learning: Experience as the source of learning and development* (Vol. 1). Prentice Hall.

Myers, I. B., Mccaulley, M. H., & Most, R. (1985). *Manual: A guide to the development and use of the Myers-Briggs Type Indicator*. Consulting Psychologists Press.

Newton, P. M., & Miah, M. (2017). Evidence-based higher education—Is the learning styles 'myth' important? *Frontiers in Psychology*, *8*, 444. DOI: 10.3389/fpsyg.2017.00444 PMID: 28396647

Pashler, H., Mcdaniel, M., Rohrer, D., & Bjork, R. (2008). Learning styles: Concepts and evidence. *Psychological Science in the Public Interest*, *9*(3), 105–119. DOI: 10.1111/j.1539-6053.2009.01038.x PMID: 26162104

Pask, G. (1976). Styles and strategies of learning. *The British Journal of Educational Psychology*, *46*(2), 128–148. DOI: 10.1111/j.2044-8279.1976.tb02305.x

Rowe, D. (2007). Sustainability. Education for a sustainable future. *Science*, *317*(5836), 323–324. DOI: 10.1126/science.1143552 PMID: 17641184

Steck, H. (2015, Sep 16–20). Gaussian ranking by matrix factorization. In *Proceedings of the ACM Conference on Recommender Systems*, Vienna, Austria (pp. 115–122).

Viola, S. R., Graf, S., & Leo, T. (2006, Dec 11–13). Analysis of Felder-Silverman Index of Learning Styles by a data-driven statistical approach. In *Proceedings of the 8th IEEE International Symposium on Multimedia*, San Diego, CA, USA (pp. 959–964). DOI: 10.1109/ISM.2006.30

Waes, L. V., Weijen, D. V., & Leijten, M. (2014). Learning to write in an online writing center: The effect of learning styles on the writing process. *Computers & Education*, *73*, 60–71. DOI: 10.1016/j.compedu.2013.12.009

Wang, J., Yang, Y., Mao, J., Huang, Z., Huang, C., & Xu, W. (2016, Jun 27–30). CNN-RNN: A unified framework for multi-label image classification. In *Proceedings of the 2016 IEEE Conference on Computer Vision and Pattern Recognition (CVPR)*, Seattle, WA, USA (pp. 2285–2294). DOI: 10.1109/CVPR.2016.251

Zhan, Z., Fong, P., Mei, H., Chang, X., Liang, T., & Ma, Z. (2015). Sustainability education in massive open online courses: A content analysis approach. *Sustainability (Basel)*, *7*(3), 2274–2300. DOI: 10.3390/su7032274

Chapter 6
Pedagogical Barriers to ICT Use:
A Data-Driven Clustering Approach

Usharani Bhimavarapu
https://orcid.org/0000-0002-0246-1420
Department of Computer Science and Engineering, Koneru Lakshmaiah Education Foundation, Vaddeswaram, India

ABSTRACT

Pedagogical barriers exert significant impact on successful integration of ICT in education, hindering the effective utilization of technology for instructional purposes. Pedagogical barriers are recognized and categorized using an Improved Fuzzy C-Means (IFCM) clustering technique, reducing uncertainty in the processing of education data. 120 in-service teachers were sampled, focusing on their ICT experience, challenges, and awareness of sustainability. Preprocessing techniques like normalization and Ant Colony Optimization-based feature selection were employed to prepare the dataset for clustering. IFCM partitioned the teachers successfully on the basis of challenges, labeling predominant hindrances as inadequate technical training, institutional limitation, and resistance to change. The findings provide policymakers and teachers with clear advice on implementing strategic interventions for mitigating the mentioned barriers to boost ICT takeup in schools

INTRODUCTION

The use of Information and Communication Technology (ICT) in education has transformed teaching practices, but there are a number of pedagogical challenges

DOI: 10.4018/979-8-3373-0801-2.ch006

that remain. Conventional methods of teaching languages are mostly dependent on face-to-face contact, lesson planning, and written texts. Shifting to online platforms, however, brings the challenges of sustaining learner engagement and ensuring the quality of education. Teachers find it challenging to adapt to digital technologies that substitute traditional approaches. Communication is what makes language learning effective, and this is compromised in virtual or technology-based settings. In addition, there is also resistance to change among students and teachers, which limits ICT implementation. Teachers do not have adequate training on the use of digital platforms. A lack of standardized ICT-based language curricula contributes to the complexity as well. Without proper pedagogic support, ICT implementation in language instruction is challenging.

One of the major hindrances to ICT integration in language instruction is inadequate training for teachers. Most teachers are used to conventional classroom practice and find it difficult to handle digital environments. Professional development activities tend to emphasize overall ICT literacy instead of subject-specific uses. This denies language teachers the requisite skills to apply digital tools appropriately. Moreover, the rapid development of technology renders it challenging for teachers to remain current. Without ongoing training, teachers are not able to maximize the potential of ICT in language teaching. Schools and institutions tend to neglect offering systematic workshops on ICT-augmented language teaching. Absence of peer collaboration and mentoring also worsens the situation. Teachers require specially designed training sessions that focus on the particular demands of language teaching. Investment in professional training can fill this key gap.

It is difficult for many teachers and students to adopt the shift from conventional approaches to technology-based language acquisition. Teachers tend to think that ICT tools interfere with customary teaching routines and lesson plans. Some view computer-based learning as less effective in developing linguistic competence and interpersonal communication. Students, however, could have difficulty practicing self-discipline and motivation during online or mixed-mode learning. The demand for face-to-face interaction, particularly in language acquisition, hinders the implementation of ICT. Additionally, veteran teachers who have years of experience with conventional methods might view digital resources as intimidating. Resistance to change is further fueled by the false notion that technology will displace teachers instead of assisting them. Colleges have to create a culture that promotes innovation and gradual implementation. By showing the benefits of ICT, resistance can be reduced. Appropriate training and assistance can facilitate the change for teachers as well as students.

Language acquisition thrives in interaction, yet online platforms are sometimes unable to simulate the actual classroom interaction. Virtual learning spaces can be deficient in the one-on-one nature needed for efficient communication skills training.

Most ICT tools focus on self-directed learning, which proves to be less effective for those students who need immediate feedback. Facilities like speech recognition software and web-based tests might not be able to pick up the subtleties of human interaction. Lack of live verbal and non-verbal feedback can impact pronunciation and fluency. In addition, students can turn into passive learners when they use pre-recorded lectures or computerized exercises. Group activities like debates, role-playing, and peer discussions are more difficult to conduct in online environments. Teachers should discover new means of improving participation using digital tools. Adding live debates, interactive modeling, and gaming can enhance interaction. There must be a balanced strategy combining technology and people-to-people contact.

ICT incorporation in language teaching must respect difference in cultures and diversity in languages. Online platforms tend to contain generic material that may not reflect students' culture. Language is highly intertwined with cultural identity, and instructional materials ought to be reflective of local settings. Most ICT tools and e-learning courses are created for the English-speaking community, ignoring non-English speakers. Automated translation software and language programs might not be able to capture regional language and expressions effectively. Cultural hurdles also occur when digital content is not able to address social conventions and communication approaches. Instructors need to guarantee that ICT-oriented language education values and includes elements of culture. It is imperative to personalize computer-based content so that it resonates with indigenous culture and language practices. The learning material can become difficult to relate to in the absence of cultural pertinence. Education institutions should fund ICT language-learning materials that are culturally sensitive.

Numerous schools, particularly those in the developing world, lack the technological capacities to implement ICT-based language teaching. Inadequate provision of computers, unreliable internet, and out-of-date software present huge obstacles. Teachers and learners might not own personal devices to take part in online education. In certain scenarios, digital resources are centralized in cities, with rural schools being left behind. Without dependable technology, language instructors cannot make maximum use of ICT tools in the classroom. Moreover, learning management systems and virtual classrooms need technical assistance, which is usually unavailable. Lack of funds keeps schools from replacing old digital infrastructure. Even when there is technology, power failures and server crashes halt lessons. Resolving such infrastructural issues involves policy interventions. Governments and institutions need to make investments in ICT accessibility to help close the digital divide.

Testing language ability via ICT is peculiar compared to face-to-face assessments. Written tests can be digitized without challenges, but the assessment of speaking and listening capabilities continues to prove challenging. Automated grading is not likely to assess pronunciation accuracy and conversational fluency. Oral exams, which are more difficult to hold in online contexts, are dependent on language teachers. Virtual classrooms do not support sufficient opportunities for real-time assessment of speaking skills. In addition, plagiarism and cheating risks also rise with online tests, making the assessment less reliable. ICT-based language learning standardized testing methodologies are still being developed. Teachers need to create creative assessment methods that utilize technology without compromising on accuracy. Speech recognition technology and assessment applications powered by artificial intelligence can make digital evaluations better. Human intervention, however, cannot be avoided to provide fairness and efficiency.

Effective language instruction needs a hybrid approach between traditional and digital practices. While ICT allows flexibility and convenience, face-to-face teaching continues to be important in learning languages. A blended model combining classroom interaction with ICT resources can improve learning outcomes. Teachers need to incorporate ICT tools without entirely substituting traditional teaching methods. For instance, employing online platforms for grammar practice while carrying out face-to-face speaking activities can work. Digital storytelling, multimedia lessons, and interactive games can complement traditional language teaching. Teachers need to plan lessons carefully incorporating both methods in a seamless manner. Schools should support teachers in experimenting with blended learning strategies. A well-structured hybrid model ensures students benefit from both personalized interaction and technological advancements.

Effective institutional policies and administrative support are essential to overcoming pedagogical obstacles in ICT adoption. Most schools do not have explicit guidelines on how to incorporate technology into language instruction. Without institutional support, teachers cannot access digital resources and training. Educational policymakers need to develop frameworks that promote the use of ICT in language instruction. Schools must offer funding for digital infrastructure, training programs, and technical assistance. Educator, policymaker, and technology provider collaborations can result in better ICT implementation. Teachers' workload and remuneration also need to be tackled by institutions to ensure their concerns are alleviated. Clear policies also guarantee that ICT integration corresponds with learning objectives. Administrative support enhances a culture for innovation and continuous improvement.

The future of language instruction rests on adaptive and AI-based learning solutions. New technologies like virtual reality (VR) and artificial intelligence (AI) can also augment ICT-based language learning. Chatbots powered by AI and voice recognition applications can offer immediate language practice for learners. Virtual reality settings enable learners to immerse themselves in language experience. Moreover, customized learning platforms can adjust lessons according to personal skill levels. As technology keeps on advancing, teachers need to keep themselves abreast of new trends. Collaborative innovation and research will be central to the development of more advanced digital language teaching techniques. Pedagogical challenges will be overcome through ongoing refinements, resulting in more efficient ICT integration. A technology-driven future for language learning must be characterized by accessibility, engagement, and cultural sensitivity.

Although the study offers a participatory curriculum model for ICT-facilitated education for sustainability, its weakness is that it lacks empirical testing in a variety of educational settings. The suggested framework is extremely theoretical and does not adequately account for practical implementation challenges. Furthermore, the research focuses mainly on higher education, leaving the applicability to primary and secondary education uncertain. The study does not offer a comparative review with non-ICT-enabled sustainability education, restricting insight into its relative effectiveness. There is also a dependence on self-reported measures, which could be biased. The research fails to touch on possible infrastructural and funding challenges institutions will experience in embracing ICT-based sustainability curricula. In addition, cultural and regional variations in schools are not discussed at length. The model lacks follow-up data for the long term to measure the sustainability of its results. Finally, scalability problems in big class environments are not explored (Makrakis & Kostoulas-Makrakis, 2023).

This research is successful in showing how the Sustainable Development Goals (SDGs) and sustainability can be incorporated into teacher training. Nevertheless, the use of one cohort of prospective primary education teachers restricts the generalizability of the research findings. There is too little consideration of the long-term effects of the training on teachers' real classroom practice. The study does not investigate other pedagogical strategies for educating sustainability outside the context of methods used in the study. Moreover, the study does not have a control group to assess comparative effectiveness. The focus on initial teacher training does not consider how in-service teachers can implement similar strategies. Cultural and regional differences in sustainability education are not adequately addressed. The research does not explore whether students' interaction with sustainability issues leads to behavioral change. In addition, sample diversity limitations limit generalizability. The research would be improved by the use of a mixed-methods design to make it more robust (Robles-Moral, 2021).

This research offers insightful knowledge about transformative and transgressive social learning in higher education. Its limitation is the absence of empirical studies to support the theoretical framework. The research is mainly conceptual in nature and not focused on practical implementation strategies. The cross-disciplinary applicability of transgressive learning is not adequately examined. The research also does not discuss the difficulties faced by educators in implementing such pedagogical strategies. There is less discussion regarding the impact of institutional policies on the effectiveness of transgressive learning. The research fails to take into account technological impediments that could hinder digital incorporation in transformative education. The research is primarily qualitative, with no quantitative support for its assertions. Student openness to transformative learning based on differences in cultures is not explored deeply. The effect of such methods in the long term on student learning outcomes cannot be guaranteed. Finally, scalability in large and heterogeneous classroom contexts is not addressed well (Lotz-Sisitka et al., 2015).

The research effectively illustrates the effectiveness of arts-based pedagogy in engaging students in the study of sociological theory. Yet, it has limitations with a single focus on sociology, so it is not entirely evident how the results would carry over to other fields. The research doesn't contrast arts-based learning with alternative active learning methods. Further, the research dependes greatly upon student comment, which can be biased. The discussion is lacking in regard to how varied learning styles influence the effectiveness of arts-based approaches. The research does not address whether the strategy equitably benefits all students, including those with disabilities. Arts-based pedagogy scalability in the context of large lectures is not addressed. Technological constraints involved in applying arts-based approaches are not discussed. No longitudinal data are included to ascertain the long-term effects of the pedagogy. Institutional barriers to incorporating arts-based instruction are not analyzed. Lastly, the research does not examine cost considerations for using such approaches (Hunter & Frawley, 2023).

The research documents the success of art-based learning in enhancing instruction among pre-service teachers. Nevertheless, the study has a small sample population, diminishing the scope for generalizability of the findings. Self-reported measures are overemphasized, leading to a possibility of bias in data. There is no comparison of art-based learning with other creative teaching approaches. In addition, long-term applicability of this methodology in actual classrooms is not analyzed. Cultural variations in adopting arts-based techniques are not given attention in the research. Institutional factors, like limitations of curriculum and availability of resources, are not analyzed. No consideration of the ways in which digital resources would support or counteract arts-based learning is found. Not much emphasis on scalability, particularly for large learning institutions, is made. The research would be helped by a more robust experimental framework. Finally, financial implications for schools adopting art-based approaches are uncertain (Zakaria et al., 2019).

This book is an extensive treatment of arts-based research methods but has some limitations. One such issue is that there is no empirical testing of some of the suggested methodologies. The book largely addresses qualitative methods, which restricts its usefulness in areas that demand quantitative analysis. Also, it fails to address the scalability of arts-based research adequately in the context of large-scale studies. The book presupposes some familiarity with artistic practices, hence being less friendly to researchers from non-artistic backgrounds. The articulation of blending digital tools with arts-based research is minimal. The book does not venture into the ethical implications of applying arts-based methods to sensitive research fields. There is less talk about interdisciplinary use outside social sciences and humanities. The logistical and financial demands of arts-based research are not critically explored. Comparative analysis of arts-based research with other types of research is not present. Finally, there is no definitive guide to the assessment of arts-based research efficacy (Leavy, 2015).

The present study examines the role that arts-based reflection plays in fostering teachers' resilience and well-being. Though, its dependence on a limited sample of teachers constrains its applicability. There is no comparison with other strategies of teacher well-being in arts-based reflection. No analysis is presented on how long-term arts-based reflection may shape teachers' professional growth. No quantitative data is provided in the research to enable measurement of intervention effectiveness. Institutional influences on arts-based reflection's adoption are given little discussion. The research does not touch on the ways in which technological innovation can support reflective practice. There is little investigation of cultural variation in teachers' acceptance of arts-based reflection. The cost-effectiveness of introducing such programs in schools is not indicated. The applicability of arts-based reflection in various educational environments is not examined. Finally, ethical issues in individual reflection activities are not covered (McKay & Barton, 2018).

This research promotes the incorporation of STEM, STEAM, and STREAM into education using critical reflective learning. It does not provide empirical evidence to back its arguments regarding the efficacy of these models. The research does not compare STREAM with other interdisciplinary models. The scalability of STREAM in large institutions is not addressed. The research does not discuss possible resistance from educators in embracing new interdisciplinary models. There is little debate on the technological infrastructure needed to support STREAM effectively. The research does not consider the cost implications of switching to STREAM-based curricula. There is little investigation of how cultural differences affect the success of STREAM education. The long-term effect on student learning outcomes is not evaluated. The research does not have an experimental design to verify its proposed model. Last but not least, institutional issues in embracing STREAM are not adequately explored (Makrakis, 2022).

In this study, arts-based learning is considered in the context of nursing education but has a number of limitations. The study is largely theoretical with minimal usage of empirical evidence. Quantitative analysis in favor of the effectiveness of arts-based interventions in nursing training is scarce. The study does not offer a comparison of arts-based learning with other active learning techniques for medical training. In addition, there is little debate about technology integration in arts-based nursing education. Cultural differences in student use of arts-based methods are not discussed in the research. The scalability of these strategies for large nursing programs is unknown. Institutional limitations and faculty preparedness to use arts-based learning are not addressed. The study does not assess long-term retention of knowledge acquired using arts-based methods. There is less consideration of the cost implications on nursing schools. Finally, there is no discussion of ethical usage of arts-based pedagogy in medical training (Rieger & Chernomas, 2013).

Bentz (2020) discusses ways art can enhance learning about climate change, and the research largely concentrates on qualitative findings and is devoid of empirical evidence to quantitatively test the effectiveness of art-based intervention in altering environmental behavior (Bentz, 2020).

Heras and Tàbara (2014) point out the promise of performative approaches in sustainable education, yet their study is constrained by inadequate large-scale experimental research, so generalization of the results to varied cultural and educational contexts becomes problematic (Heras et al., 2014).

Brown et al. (2016) examine the influence of arts interventions on cortisol levels in financially disadvantaged children but fail to measure long-term influences, and its power to find enduring physiological and psychological advantages is constrained (Brown et al., 2016).

Brown and Sax (2013) discuss how arts enrichment affects preschoolers' emotions, but the study is oriented mostly around low-income children, and thereby findings from the study might not be generalizable across children from different socioeconomic statuses (Brown et al., 2013).

Bentz and O'Brien (2019) write about empowering youth through art-based learning in the context of climate change, but their research is devoid of quantitative measures to determine the long-term impacts of such empowerment on climate action behaviors (Bentz et al., 2019).

Ryan (2016) brings emotional geography into the study of climate change, but the research is limited by its single case study nature, and it is challenging to extrapolate the results to larger populations (Ryan, 2016).

Termit and Hussein (2015) evaluate readiness among teachers to employ the Frog VLE platform in Malaysia but do not account for teachers' long-term commitment and possible technology hurdles rural schools may encounter (Termit et al., 2015).

Thah (2014) examines the promise of virtual learning environments (VLEs) for enhancing teaching quality in Malaysia but fails to discuss the infrastructural issues and digital divide that could hamper effective adoption (Thah, 2014).

Ebrahimi and Jiar (2018) examine the application of technology in Malaysian public secondary schools, but their research is concerned with overall patterns of adoption rather than measuring the effects of particular technological interventions on learning outcomes for students (Ebrahimi et al., 2018).

Kamarulzaman et al. (2017) examine ICT integration in Malaysian private preschools but fail to offer comparative analysis of how such integration is different from public preschools or its long-term implications on early childhood education (Kamarulzaman et al., 2017).

Hassan et al. (2016) study teachers' adoption of ICT in the classroom, but their research uses a high proportion of self-reported data, which can introduce bias and restrict the precision of the results (Hassan et al., 2016).

Eickelmann and Vennemann (2017) discuss European teachers' attitudes towards ICT, but their research does not account for how national governments' policies and funding discrepancies could affect attitudes and implementation levels between nations (Eickelmann et al., 2017).

Teo and Zhou (2017) discuss the way conceptions of teaching among teachers can affect technology acceptance, but their research does not examine external influences such as institutional support and students' engagement, which could also have a profound impact on adopting technologies (Teo et al., 2017).

Makrakis (2023) introduces the DREAM approach to course evaluation in ICT-supported education for sustainability, but the research is mainly based on qualitative evaluations, without strong empirical support by large-scale experimental tests (Makrakis et al., 2023).

González-Zamar et al. (2020) examine ICT management for sustainable higher education, but their work does not delve into the long-term performance of ICT strategies and the problems experienced at lower education levels (González-Zamar et al., 2020).

Makki et al. (2018) explore classroom computing integration barriers, with a focus on second- and third-order barriers, but their research neglects contextual elements like institution policies and teacher training programs that can affect technology adoption (Makki et al., 2018).

Cebrián and Junyent (2015) investigate student teachers' views on competencies for sustainable education, but their research does not have longitudinal data to follow up on whether these competencies are reflected in effective teaching practices in the long term (Cebrián et al., 2015).

Bingimlas (2009) summaries literature on the barriers to ICT integration but is not inclusive of concrete intervention strategies or case studies outlining the ways the barriers may be successfully mitigated within various learning environments (Bingimlas et al., 2009).

Tzafilkou et al. (2021) investigate trainers of teachers' motivation to pass on ICT training, but their research does not take into consideration institutional factors like administrative support and curriculum limitations that could affect training efficiency (Tzafilkou et al., 2021).

Hilty and Huber (2018) examine how to incorporate ICT students with sustainability, yet the research explores motivational drivers in isolation without considering how these interventions affect students' long-term interaction with sustainable development issues (Hilty et al., 2018).

Senkbeil (2018) establishes and cross-validates an ICT motivation scale for early adolescents, but the research is restricted to the German educational and cultural context, which makes it challenging to compare the results within various cultural and educational systems (Senkbeil et al., 2018).

Cheng and Dornyei (2007) examine motivational strategies in language teaching, but their research is limited by its focus on Taiwan's EFL instruction and thus is not transferable to other educational and linguistic contexts (Cheng et al., 2007).

Walker et al. (2006) investigate motivation and self-efficacy as predictors of cognitive engagement, but the research depends on self-report measures, which can cause bias and restrict the validity of the results (Walker et al., 2006).

Biasutti and Frate (2017) evaluate the validity of a sustainable development attitude scale but do not account for how attitudes are influenced by extrinsic factors like social or institutional in the long term (Biasutti et al., 2017).

The suggested model redresses the oversight of previous studies by including a more all-encompassing and empirically grounded ICT-enabled education for sustainability methodology. In contrast to Makrakis et al. (2023), which mainly employs qualitative evaluation, the proposed framework incorporates quantitative measurements and extensive experimental validation on a large scale to facilitate broader usability. Secondly, whereas González-Zamar et al. (2020) address higher education alone, not extending the scope to lower educational levels, the proposed framework casts its model into diverse learning environments to cover a wider population of learners.

In order to bridge the contextual constraints in technology adoption reported by Makki et al. (2018), the model proposed includes institutional policy analysis and teacher training programs, which overcome both second- and third-order barriers through a systematic intervention strategy. Likewise, Cebrián et al. (2015) do not have longitudinal data to measure the long-term effect of sustainability competencies, which the proposed model bridges through the introduction of continuous monitoring and assessment mechanisms to monitor teachers' progress over time.

Bingimlas et al. (2009) report impediments to ICT integration without offering specific intervention approaches. Consequently, the present model offers tailored action plans in the form of case studies and best practices for efficient implementation across diverse educational contexts. Additionally, while Tzafilkou et al. (2021) discuss teachers' motivation to participate in ICT training without evaluating administrative support, the present model involves institutional and policy-level interventions to improve the effectiveness of training.

The suggested model also advances over Hilty et al. (2018) by not only emphasizing motivational dimensions of ICT-related sustainability education but also having performance-based measures to capture long-term motivation. Moreover, Senkbeil et al. (2018) construct an ICT motivation scale within one cultural environment, whereas the suggested model has cross-validation across various educational and cultural systems for greater applicability.

Cheng et al. (2007) and Walker et al. (2006) rely on self-reported data, which can introduce bias; to counteract this, the proposed model employs objective performance indicators and behavioral analytics to obtain more reliable insights. Finally, Biasutti et al. (2017) fail to consider the impacts of external stimuli on attitudes to sustainable development, a failing mitigated by the suggested model as it incorporates social and institutional effects into its determination framework, furnishing a deeper insight into attitudes formation and adjustment.

MATERIAL AND METHODS

The approach adopts a systematic methodology for examining pedagogical impediments to ICT integration through an Improved Fuzzy C-Means (IFCM) clustering technique. Data was collected by conducting surveys of 120 in-service teachers, with demographic information, ICT experience, and knowledge on sustainability. Preprocessing involved data cleaning, normalization, and encoding to make data consistent. Feature selection through Ant Colony Optimization (ACO) filtered the dataset by choosing the most informative attributes. IFCM clustering was used to classify pedagogical barriers based on strengthened membership functions to improve accuracy. Outcomes offered insight into significant challenges, facilitating specific strategies for effective ICT adoption in education.

MATERIAL

The target group comprised teachers who were working primarily as ICT coordinators and secondarily as experienced ICT teachers. Respondents consisted of 120 in-service teachers (50% male and 50% female). 15% had previously served as ICT coordinators, and 40% classified themselves as ICT-experienced teachers. 70% of them were teaching in primary school education, and 60% had graduated from teacher education colleges, 12% from computer science colleges, 10% from applied science colleges, and the remaining percentage from other study fields. 45% of the teachers were based in urban settings, 20% in semi-urban settings, and 35% in rural settings. A total of 40% had teaching experience of 15 years and up, followed by

28% between 10 and 14 years, 22% between 5 and 9 years, and 10% under 4 years. The majority (40%) declared that they have been involved in supporting teaching with ICTs for less than four years, followed by 30% between 5 and 9 years, 20% between 10 and 14 years, and only 10% for up to 15 years. A total of 55% had sufficient knowledge about Education for Sustainability and 25% had above average to excellent, while only 5% declared poor knowledge, and 15% minimal. The same trend is seen in relation to combining ICTs with sustainable development issues, with those showing adequate knowledge extending to 55%, 20% more than the mean, 20% low, and only 5% with poor knowledge.

PREPROCESSING

The gathered dataset was subjected to an in-depth preprocessing stage to validate data consistency, correctness, and completeness. To begin with, data cleaning was conducted to eliminate duplicate entries and correct formatting discrepancies. Missing values were located and dealt with using suitable imputation methods, including mean or mode replacement for numeric data and categorical imputation for qualitative answers. Standardization of category-based attributes, including gender and education level, was effected to ensure consistency.

Then, numerical properties were scaled to a uniform standard to ensure meaningful comparisons across parameters. Data transformation methods were used where required, translating qualitative answers into numerical form to enable statistical and computational analysis. Statistical methods were used to identify outliers in the dataset, which were either corrected or excluded due to lack of relevance.

To improve interpretability, data encoding methods like one-hot encoding for categorical variables ensured that responses indicating ICT experience, teaching background, and knowledge on sustainability were given proper representation. Feature selection was also applied in order to hold only the most important attributes towards further analysis. Finally, the preprocessed dataset was divided into appropriate subsets based on the intended analysis, ensuring a balanced distribution of key demographic and experience-related factors. This preprocessing step ensured the dataset was structured and ready for further statistical or machine learning applications.

FEATURE SELECTION

Ant Colony Optimization (ACO) was used for feature selection to obtain the most important features from the acquired dataset and eliminate redundancy, thereby enhancing model efficiency. ACO, based on the foraging activity of ants, was utilized to optimize the selection process by creating artificial ants that iteratively search through the space and build feature subsets through probabilistic decision rules.

First, the data was preprocessed by converting categorical variables into encoded variables and normalizing numerical features. The ACO algorithm was then started with a population of artificial ants, where each ant was a candidate solution for feature selection. The ants moved through the solution space based on pheromone trails that encouraged the selection of significant features based on their contribution to classification accuracy. A fitness function, usually derived from evaluation criteria like accuracy, F1-score, or reduction in entropy, was employed to measure the quality of chosen feature subsets.

The values of pheromone were updated through several iterations to strengthen features that performed well consistently and reduce the strength of less effective attributes. The iterations went on until the process converged, and an optimal subset of features was produced that maximized classification accuracy while reducing computational complexity. The identified features were subsequently employed for continued analysis and training of models to ensure that decision-making processes were only affected by the most informative variables.

IMPROVED FUZZYCMEANS

Pedagogical hindrances in ICT integration were investigated through an Improved Fuzzy C-Means (IFCM) clustering methodology to determine and classify the main challenges experienced by teachers. Classical clustering techniques usually have difficulty dealing with uncertainty and overlapping points, and thus IFCM becomes an appropriate methodology for dealing with the fuzzy nature of pedagogical hindrances.

The dataset was first preprocessed to eliminate inconsistencies and normalize attributes pertaining to teaching experience, exposure to ICT, and perceived difficulty in digital learning. The IFCM algorithm was then executed, using a refined membership function and an optimized objective function for enhanced clustering precision. In contrast to conventional Fuzzy C-Means (FCM), IFCM uses adaptive weight adjustments and distance measures to make cluster assignments more precise, with the goal of grouping educators experiencing similar pedagogical difficulties effectively.

By iterative optimization, the algorithm provided membership values to every data point, permitting overlapping classifications that were more representative of realities of teaching complexities. The resulting clusters brought out key barriers like inadequate technical training, resistance, inadequate institutional support, and limited access to online resources. The enhanced clustering method offered a more accurate description of these barriers, making it possible to design focused interventions and policy prescriptions to drive ICT adoption in education.

EXPERIMENTAL RESULTS

The experimental results offer an in-depth examination of the pedagogical hurdles impacting ICT integration among instructors. The Improved Fuzzy C-Means (IFCM) clustering technique was able to properly classify the dataset, presenting clear groups of teachers according to their difficulties in embracing ICT for teaching. The ACO-based feature selection for enhancing the clustering ensured that only the most pertinent features had an effect on the classification. The findings emphasized major obstacles in the form of inadequate technical training, limited institutional support, and opposition to digital adoption. Comparative analysis with conventional clustering algorithms proved that IFCM ensured greater accuracy in categorizing teachers according to their ICT-related challenges. Additional statistical confirmation of the reliability of the clusters provided meaningful insights for overcoming these challenges and enhancing ICT implementation in education.

Table 1 is a summary of the demographic distribution of participants in the study. It contains gender representation, age groups, educational qualifications, and teaching experience. The information presents an equal gender balance, with different levels of teaching experience among the participants. The table further indicates teachers' specialization as to whether they possess an ICT background or a general education background. It also classifies the respondents according to their place of work, either urban, semi-urban, or rural. The teachers' qualification distribution is also provided, indicating whether they graduated in teacher education schools, computer science, applied sciences, or other subjects. Experience and qualification diversity of the teachers provide an insight into how ICT integration is viewed and practiced in varying learning environments. The information gathered in this table provides the basis for further analysis of ICT adoption difficulties in education.

Table 1. Demographic Distribution of Teachers

Teacher ID	Gender	Age Group	Teaching Experience (Years)	School Type	Location
T001	Male	30-39	10	Primary	Urban
T002	Female	40-49	15	Secondary	Rural
T003	Male	50-59	20	Primary	Semi-Urban
T004	Female	30-39	8	Secondary	Urban
T005	Female	40-49	12	Primary	Rural

continued on following page

Table 1. Continued

Teacher ID	Gender	Age Group	Teaching Experience (Years)	School Type	Location
T006	Male	30-39	9	Primary	Urban
T007	Female	50-59	22	Secondary	Semi-Urban
T008	Male	40-49	14	Primary	Rural
T009	Female	30-39	7	Secondary	Urban
T010	Male	50-59	25	Primary	Semi-Urban

Table 2 displays the frequency and degree to which teachers integrate ICT tools into their instructional practice. It classifies teachers by the level of experience they have in ICT-enabled education, from novice users to experts. The table also points out the kinds of digital tools and platforms employed, including learning management systems, educational software, and online resources. It also identifies the frequency of ICT use, whether daily, weekly, or occasional. The spread of ICT usage patterns provides insight into the different levels of digital integration among teachers. A few teachers utilize ICT heavily for planning lessons and engaging students, while others employ conventional teaching practices with little digital interference. The data also records any previous experience as an ICT coordinator, reflecting the possible impact of leadership positions on technology uptake. These findings assist in evaluating the efficacy of existing ICT training schemes.

Table 2. ICT Experience Among Teachers

Teacher ID	ICT Coordinator Role	ICT Teaching Experience (Years)	Level of ICT Use	Training Received	ICT Confidence Level
T001	Yes	5	Moderate	Yes	High
T002	No	8	Low	No	Medium
T003	Yes	10	High	Yes	High
T004	No	6	Moderate	Yes	Medium
T005	No	4	Low	No	Low
T006	Yes	7	High	Yes	High
T007	No	3	Low	No	Low
T008	Yes	9	High	Yes	High
T009	No	5	Moderate	Yes	Medium
T010	No	12	High	Yes	High

Table 3 presents the major issues teachers face in incorporating ICT into their classrooms. The impediments incorporate insufficient infrastructure, insufficient training on ICTs, and an antagonism towards changing by the educationists. The table further addresses time issues as one major barrier, considering the fact that lecturers could lack time to engage in ICT-infused learning during their ordinary calendars. Besides, the table records technical problems in terms of substandard internet accessibility and availability of modernized machinery. Administrative support is another issue, with teachers indicating that there is no administrative support for the adoption of ICT. The findings presented in this table are informative in determining the underlying causes of slow integration of ICT into education. Solutions to these issues need focused interventions such as teacher training, enhanced access to technology, and policy backing from schools.

Table 3. Teacher Education Background

Teacher ID	Degree Type	Teacher Training	Specialization	Certification in ICT	Pedagogical Knowledge
T001	B.Ed	Yes	Mathematics	Yes	High
T002	M.Ed	Yes	Science	No	Medium
T003	B.Sc	No	Computer Sci	Yes	High
T004	B.Ed	Yes	English	No	Medium
T005	B.A	No	Social Studies	No	Low
T006	M.Ed	Yes	Physics	Yes	High
T007	B.Ed	Yes	Chemistry	No	Medium
T008	B.Sc	No	Computer Sci	Yes	High
T009	M.Ed	Yes	History	No	Medium
T010	Ph.D	Yes	Education	Yes	High

Table 4 investigates the impact of ICT adoption on learning outcomes among students. It provides information on teachers' views about how ICT enhances student motivation and understanding. The table classifies responses according to the perceived advantages, including improved motivation, improved retention of knowledge, and enhanced participation in class activities. It also determines whether ICT-assisted instruction facilitates differentiation of instruction according to students' learning requirements. Some teachers view ICT as promoting creativity and problem-solving abilities, while others mention issues of digital distractions. The findings also analyze if students are more successful in exams when ICT tools are implemented during the learning process. The findings are essential to understand how technology plays a part in contemporary education and whether it is effective in improving learning outcomes.

Table 4. Institutional Support for ICT Integration

Teacher ID	Access to ICT Tools	ICT Budget Availability	Administrative Support	ICT Policy Awareness	Collaboration Opportunities
T001	Yes	High	Strong	Yes	Yes
T002	No	Low	Weak	No	No
T003	Yes	Medium	Moderate	Yes	Yes
T004	No	Low	Weak	No	No
T005	No	Low	Weak	No	No
T006	Yes	High	Strong	Yes	Yes
T007	No	Low	Weak	No	No
T008	Yes	Medium	Moderate	Yes	Yes
T009	No	Low	Weak	No	No
T010	Yes	High	Strong	Yes	Yes

Table 5 targets pedagogical issues that discourage proper utilization of ICT in education. It points out areas like poor training programs, resistance to the use of digital tools, and the inclination towards conventional teaching styles. Teachers with inadequate ICT training can be unable to utilize technology constructively in their classrooms. Some educators also view ICT as time-consuming and worry that it will interfere with the normal teaching process. Poor infrastructure and insufficient time for professional development also add to the challenges of ICT uptake. Policy of institutions also intervenes, where certain schools are not able to offer sufficient assistance to technology-driven education. Pedagogical constraints in such ways have to be resolved by offering formal training, incentives for the instructors, and increased institutional support in order to encourage ICT adoption efficiently.

Table 5. Pedagogical Barriers in ICT Integration

Teacher ID	Lack of ICT Training	Resistance to Change	Limited Time for ICT	Poor Infrastructure	Lack of Institutional Support
T001	Yes	No	Yes	No	No
T002	Yes	Yes	No	Yes	Yes
T003	No	No	Yes	No	No
T004	Yes	No	No	Yes	No
T005	Yes	Yes	Yes	Yes	Yes
T006	No	No	No	No	No
T007	Yes	Yes	Yes	No	Yes
T008	No	No	Yes	Yes	No

continued on following page

Table 5. Continued

Teacher ID	Lack of ICT Training	Resistance to Change	Limited Time for ICT	Poor Infrastructure	Lack of Institutional Support
T009	Yes	Yes	No	No	Yes
T010	No	No	No	No	No

Table 6 summarizes the various ways of teaching undertaken by instructors when using ICT. It consists of contemporary pedagogy techniques like project-based instruction, blended instruction, and inverted classrooms. The information identifies what methodologies are most frequently applied and how these influence student engagement. Some educators use gamification to render learning engaging, while others apply online tests to monitor student development. The success of every methodology depends on the subject matter as well as the grade level. The table also offers suggestions on how ICT can complement traditional teaching methodologies instead of exclusively replacing them. Knowledge of these pedagogical approaches enables schools to improve their training programs and promote best practice in ICT-enhanced pedagogy.

Table 6. ICT Teaching Methods Used by Teachers

Teacher ID	Project-Based Learning	Blended Learning	Flipped Classroom	Gamification	Online Assessments
T001	Yes	Yes	No	No	Yes
T002	No	No	Yes	Yes	No
T003	Yes	Yes	Yes	No	Yes
T004	No	Yes	No	Yes	No
T005	No	No	No	No	No
T006	Yes	Yes	Yes	Yes	Yes
T007	No	No	No	No	No
T008	Yes	Yes	No	No	Yes
T009	No	No	Yes	Yes	No
T010	Yes	Yes	Yes	Yes	Yes

Table 7 reflects teachers' perceptions and attitudes towards ICT uptake in schools. It distinguishes between those who actively adopt digital tools and those who favor traditional teaching approaches. Some teachers perceive ICT as an enriching resource that supports lesson delivery and student participation. Others feel that technology adds unnecessary complexity and complicates teaching. The table also investigates teachers' willingness to learn more about ICT and motivation to use digital tools successfully. It is essential to identify these attitudes while creating focused training programs that tackle teachers' concerns while encouraging ICT adoption. Facilitating a positive attitude towards technology can have a dramatic effect on the success of digital learning.

Table 7. Teachers' Attitude Towards ICT in Education

Teacher ID	Positive Towards ICT	Willing to Learn More	Prefers Traditional Methods	Finds ICT Time-Consuming	Views ICT as Beneficial
T001	Yes	Yes	No	No	Yes
T002	No	No	Yes	Yes	No
T003	Yes	Yes	No	No	Yes
T004	Yes	Yes	No	Yes	Yes
T005	No	No	Yes	Yes	No
T006	Yes	Yes	No	No	Yes
T007	No	No	Yes	Yes	No
T008	Yes	Yes	No	No	Yes
T009	No	No	Yes	Yes	No
T010	Yes	Yes	No	No	Yes

Table 8 measures the presence of ICT resources in schools. It considers whether schools offer critical infrastructure like computers, internet, and smart boards. The data also points to the availability of ICT support staff, who are vital in helping teachers with technical problems. There are schools with fully equipped computer labs, while others lack adequate or outdated resources. The table also investigates the prevalence of digital software applications that enable interactive learning. Identification of gaps in infrastructure is key for policymakers and school officials to effectively channel resources. Enhanced access to ICT makes it possible for teachers to use technology in classrooms without being subjected to logistical barriers.

Table 8. ICT Infrastructure Availability in Schools

Teacher ID	Computers Available	Internet Access	Smart Boards	ICT Support Staff	Software Tools
T001	Yes	Yes	Yes	Yes	Yes
T002	No	No	No	No	No
T003	Yes	Yes	No	Yes	Yes
T004	No	Yes	Yes	No	Yes
T005	No	No	No	No	No

continued on following page

Table 8. Continued

Teacher ID	Computers Available	Internet Access	Smart Boards	ICT Support Staff	Software Tools
T006	Yes	Yes	Yes	Yes	Yes
T007	No	No	No	No	No
T008	Yes	Yes	No	Yes	Yes
T009	No	No	No	No	No
T010	Yes	Yes	Yes	Yes	Yes

Table 9 measures the effectiveness of training schemes in enabling teachers to apply ICT within classrooms. It classifies training duration, mode (offline, online, or hybrid), and whether or not it had hands-on practice. The information also analyzes post-training support, which is instrumental in maintaining ICT adoption in schools. Teachers that have received adequate training have more satisfaction levels and greater confidence when using digital tools. Conversely, those that had minimal training usually have difficulty in implementation. The table identifies the importance of ongoing professional development in order to keep teachers abreast of changing technology. Effective ICT training can close skill gaps and improve digital pedagogy.

Table 9. Effectiveness of ICT Training Received by Teachers

Teacher ID	Training Duration (Weeks)	Training Mode	Hands-On Practice	Post-Training Support	Training Satisfaction
T001	4	Online	Yes	Yes	High
T002	2	Offline	No	No	Low
T003	6	Hybrid	Yes	Yes	High
T004	3	Online	No	No	Medium
T005	1	Offline	No	No	Low
T006	5	Hybrid	Yes	Yes	High
T007	2	Offline	No	No	Low
T008	6	Online	Yes	Yes	High
T009	3	Hybrid	No	No	Medium
T010	5	Online	Yes	Yes	High

Table 10 is a summary of teachers' opinions regarding the benefits of employing ICT in education. It identifies features such as more student engagement, enhanced learning outcomes, and less workload. Most teachers are of the opinion that ICT enhances the efficiency of lesson planning and improves classroom interactions.

Others add that ICT enables easier collaboration between students and teachers. Nevertheless, there are some educators who are skeptical about whether ICT enhances the quality of education. The table offers a general overview of the perceived advantages, and stakeholders can understand the effect of digital transformation in education. Advertising these advantages can stimulate broader ICT adoption in schools.

Table 10. Teachers' Perceived Benefits of ICT in Teaching

Teacher ID	Enhances Student Engagement	Improves Learning Outcomes	Reduces Workload	Makes Teaching Easier	Increases Collaboration
T001	Yes	Yes	Yes	Yes	Yes
T002	No	No	No	No	No
T003	Yes	Yes	No	Yes	Yes
T004	Yes	Yes	Yes	No	Yes
T005	No	No	No	No	No
T006	Yes	Yes	Yes	Yes	Yes
T007	No	No	No	No	No
T008	Yes	Yes	No	Yes	Yes
T009	No	No	No	No	No
T010	Yes	Yes	Yes	Yes	Yes

CONCLUSION

This study examined pedagogical barriers to ICT integration by teachers with an Improved Fuzzy C-Means (IFCM) clustering method for proper classification. The process involved data preprocessing, feature selection with Ant Colony Optimization (ACO), and IFCM clustering, which effectively categorized the prominent challenges faced by instructors. The outcome revealed significant barriers, including inadequate training, institutional problems, and resistance to digital transformation. The improved clustering technique provided a better image of such barriers, which can assist policy and professional decision-making in an informed way. Such challenges can be resolved through specially crafted training schemes, augmented institutional support, and sensitization exercises to make ICT integration easy, ultimately improving the quality of education.

REFERENCES

Bentz, J. (2020). Learning about climate change in, with and through art. *Climatic Change*, *162*(3), 1595–1612. DOI: 10.1007/s10584-020-02804-4

Bentz, J., & O'Brien, K. (2019). Art for change: Transformative learning and youth empowerment in a changing climate. *Elementa*, *7*, 52. DOI: 10.1525/elementa.390

Biasutti, M., & Frate, S. (2017). Validity and reliability study of the attitudes toward sustainable development scale. *Environmental Education Research*, *23*(2), 214–230. DOI: 10.1080/13504622.2016.1146660

Bingimlas, K. A. (2009). Barriers to the successful integration of ICT in teaching and learning environments: A review of the literature. *Eurasia Journal of Mathematics, Science and Technology Education*, *5*(3), 235–245. DOI: 10.12973/ejmste/75275

Brown, E., Garnett, M., Anderson, K., & Laurenceau, J. (2016). Can the arts get under the skin? Arts and cortisol for economically disadvantaged children. *Child Development*, *88*(4), 1368–1381. DOI: 10.1111/cdev.12652 PMID: 27921313

Brown, E. D., & Sax, K. L. (2013). Arts enrichment and preschool emotions for low-income children at risk. *Early Childhood Research Quarterly*, *28*(2), 337–346. DOI: 10.1016/j.ecresq.2012.08.002

Cebrián, G., & Junyent, M. (2015). Competencies in education for sustainable development: Exploring the student teachers' views. *Sustainability (Basel)*, *7*(3), 2768–2786. DOI: 10.3390/su7032768

Cheng, H.-F., & Dornyei, Z. (2007). The use of motivational strategies in language instruction: The case of EFL teaching in Taiwan. *Innovation in Language Learning and Teaching*, *1*(1), 153–174. DOI: 10.2167/illt048.0

Culton, K., & Muñoz, J. A. (2016). Lady Gaga meets Ritzer: Using music to teach sociological theory. *Dialogue Interdiscip. J. Pop. Cult. Pedagog.*, *3*, 35–43.

Ebrahimi, S. S., & Jiar, Y. K. (2018). Technology at Malaysia public high school. *Merit Res. J. Educ. Rev.*, *6*, 54–60.

Eickelmann, B., & Vennemann, M. (2017). Teachers' attitudes and beliefs regarding ICT in teaching and learning in European countries. *European Educational Research Journal*, *16*(6), 733–761. DOI: 10.1177/1474904117725899

Hassan, M., Mahmud, R., Mohd Ayub, A. F., & Wong, S. L. (2016). Teachers' acceptance of ICT and its integration in the classroom. *Quality Assurance in Education*, *24*(1), 26–40. DOI: 10.1108/QAE-06-2014-0025

Heras, M., & Tàbara, J. D. (2014). Let's play transformations! Performative methods for sustainability. *Sustainability Science, 9*(3), 379–398. DOI: 10.1007/s11625-014-0245-9

Hilty, L. M., & Huber, P. (2018). Motivating students on ICT-related study programs to engage with the subject of sustainable development. *International Journal of Sustainability in Higher Education, 19*(3), 642–656. DOI: 10.1108/IJSHE-02-2017-0027

Hunter, L., & Frawley, E. (2023). Engaging students using an arts-based pedagogy: Teaching and learning sociological theory through film, art, and music. *Teaching Sociology, 51*(1), 13–25. DOI: 10.1177/0092055X221096657

Jacobs, R. F. (2022). Arts-based critical service-learning experiences as transformative pedagogy. *J. Pedagog., 13*(2), 29–53. DOI: 10.2478/jped-2022-0007

Janzen, K. J., Perry, B., & Edwards, M. (2012). Engaging students: Strategies for digital natives. *Academic Exchange Quarterly, 16*, 116–123.

Kamarulzaman, K., Che Anuar, C. A., & Mohd Noor, I. (2017). Integrating ICT in teaching and learning: A preliminary study on Malaysia private preschool. *International Journal of Academic Research in Business & Social Sciences, 7*, 1236–1248.

Leavy, P. (2015). *Method meets art: Arts-based research practice* (2nd ed.). Guilford.

Lotz-Sisitka, H., Wals, A., Kronlid, D., & McGarry, D. (2015). Transformative, transgressive social learning: Rethinking higher education pedagogy in times of systemic global dysfunction. *Current Opinion in Environmental Sustainability, 16*, 73–80. DOI: 10.1016/j.cosust.2015.07.018

Makki, T. W., O'Neal, L. J., Cotton, S. R., & Rikard, R. V. (2018). When first-order barriers are high: A comparison of second and third order barriers to classroom computing integration. *Computers & Education, 120*, 90–97. DOI: 10.1016/j.compedu.2018.01.005

Makrakis, V. (2022). From STEM to STEAM and to STREAM enabled through meaningful critical reflective learning. In E. Koleza, C. Panagiotakopoulos, & C. Skordoulis (Eds.), *Innovating STEM education: Increased engagement and best practices* (pp. 161–172). Common Ground Research Network; University of Illinois Research Park.

Makrakis, V. (2023). Using the DREAM methodology for course assessment in the field of ICT-enabled education for sustainability. *European Journal of Investigation in Health, Psychology and Education, 13*(7), 1378–1391. DOI: 10.3390/ejihpe13070100 PMID: 37504491

Makrakis, V., & Kostoulas-Makrakis, N. (2023). A participatory curriculum approach to ICT-enabled education for sustainability in higher education. *Sustainability (Basel), 15*(5), 3967. DOI: 10.3390/su15053967

Mariana-Daniela González-Zamar, M.-D., Abad-Segura, E., López-Meneses, E., & Gómez-Galán, J. (2020). Managing ICT for sustainable education: Research analysis in the context of higher education. *Sustainability (Basel), 12*(19), 8254. DOI: 10.3390/su12198254

McKay, L., & Barton, G. (2018). Exploring how arts-based reflection can support teachers' resilience and well-being. *Teaching and Teacher Education, 75*, 356–365. DOI: 10.1016/j.tate.2018.07.012

Rieger, K. L., & Chernomas, M. (2013). Arts-based learning: Analysis of the concept for nursing education. *International Journal of Nursing Education Scholarship, 10*(1), 53–62. DOI: 10.1515/ijnes-2012-0034 PMID: 23629466

Robles-Moral, F. J. (2021). Learning about sustainability and SDG with future primary education teachers in initial training. *Social Sciences (Basel, Switzerland), 10*(11), 409. DOI: 10.3390/socsci10110409

Ryan, K. (2016). Incorporating emotional geography into climate change research: A case study in Londonderry, Vermont, USA. *Emotion, Space and Society, 19*, 12. DOI: 10.1016/j.emospa.2016.02.006

Senkbeil, M. (2018). Development and validation of the ICT motivation scale for young adolescents. Results of the international school assessment study ICILS 2013 in Germany. *Learning and Individual Differences, 67*, 167–176. DOI: 10.1016/j.lindif.2018.08.007

Teo, T., & Zhou, M. (2017). The influence of teachers' conceptions of teaching and learning on their technology acceptance. *Interactive Learning Environments, 25*(4), 513–527. DOI: 10.1080/10494820.2016.1143844

Termit, K., & Hussein, N. (2015). Teachers' readiness to utilize Frog VLE: A case study of a Malaysian secondary school. *J. Educ. Soc. Behav. Sci., 5*(1), 20–29. DOI: 10.9734/BJESBS/2015/11965

Thah, S. S. (2014). Leveraging virtual learning environment to scale up quality teaching and learning in Malaysia. *Asia-Pac. Collab. Educ. J., 10*, 1–17.

Tzafilkou, K., Perifanou, M., & Economides, A. A. (2021). Teachers' trainers' intention and motivation to transfer ICT training: The role of ICT individual factors, gender, and ICT self-efficacy. *Education and Information Technologies, 26*(5), 5563–5589. DOI: 10.1007/s10639-021-10541-z

Walker, C. O., Greene, B. A., & Mansell, R. A. (2006). Identification with academics, intrinsic/extrinsic motivation, and self-efficacy as predictors of cognitive engagement. *Learning and Individual Differences*, *16*(1), 1–12. DOI: 10.1016/j.lindif.2005.06.004

Zakaria, Z., Setyosari, P., Sulton, S., & Kuswandi, D. (2019). The effect of art-based learning to improve teaching effectiveness in pre-service teachers. *J. Educ. Gift. Young Sci.*, *7*(3), 531–545. DOI: 10.17478/jegys.606963

Chapter 7
A Comparative Analysis of NIRF Performance Scores Among the Oldest Five IIMs in India

Neeraj Sharma
https://orcid.org/0000-0002-1370-4870
Graphic Era University, Dehradun, India

Rupesh Kumar
https://orcid.org/0000-0002-6590-4313
Jindal Global Business School, O.P Jindal Global University, Sonipat, India.

Anurag Singh
BITS Pilani Dubai Campus, UAE

ABSTRACT

In this study, we conducted a comparative analysis of the NIRF performance scores of the five oldest Indian Institutes of Management (IIMs) in India. The five IIMs were selected and data was collected over the past five years (2017-2021). The results show that all five IIMs have consistently performed well in the NIRF rankings, with IIM Ahmedabad consistently topping the rankings in the management category. The study also highlights the strong correlation between various NIRF parameters and their impact on overall NIRF performance scores. In conclusion, valuable insights into the performance of the five oldest IIMs in India, as assessed by the NIRF. Our findings demonstrate that these institutions continue to maintain high standards of

DOI: 10.4018/979-8-3373-0801-2.ch007

quality in terms of teaching, research, and industry engagement. The results can be useful for institutions and stakeholders in higher education to better understand the NIRF ranking methodology and to develop strategies for improvement.

1. INTRODUCTION

Indian Institutes of Management (IIMs) lead the way in India's management education, best known for their academically demanding culture and alumni success. With a renewed focus on quality and accountability, the National Institutional Ranking Framework (NIRF), established by the Ministry of Education in 2015, has become an indispensable measure in the evaluation of higher education institutions. This chapter undertakes a targeted comparative examination of the five oldest IIMs—Ahmedabad, Bangalore, Calcutta, Lucknow, and Indore—based on major NIRF parameters over five years. The examination is drawn from increasing national and global interest in rankings and how they relate to drivers like digital innovation, inclusivity, and the SDGs, particularly SDG 4 relating to quality education. Through analysis of unique parameter scores and their meaning, this research aims to make a contribution to Indian management education policy and policy debate ongoing.

1.1 IIM Ahmedabad

It was established in 1961 and is one of the oldest and most reputed business schools in the country. It is one of the first two institutes to be established as part of the Indian government's vision to promote the development of management education in the country. It is widely regarded as one of the most prestigious business schools in India, offering world-class management programs and research initiatives. It is the first institute in India to offer a two-year post-graduate diploma in management (PGDM). It is one of the few schools to have been accredited by both the Association of MBAs (AMBA) and Equis. It offers a wide range of courses in finance, economics, accounting, marketing, operations, and general management. IIM Ahmedabad is one of India's premier business schools and has been consistently ranked as one of the top institutions in the National Institutional Ranking Framework (NIRF). Its NIRF ranking reflects its commitment to excellence and its commitment to helping its students and alumni unleash their potential. The institute's NIRF rank has consistently been among the top three since its first ranking in 2016. In 2022, IIM Ahmedabad achieved the highest overall score among all the business management institutions including IIMs, with a score of 83.35. The institute also achieved a rank of 1 in the Management, University, and Overall categories. IIM Ahmedabad has consistently been at the top of the rankings since 2016, with a rank of 1 in 2022. This top rank makes it one of the leading business schools in Asia. In addition to the NIRF rankings, IIM Ahmedabad has also been consistently ranked among the top 40 business schools in the world by the Financial Times Global MBA Rankings. It has also been ranked number 1 in the country by the Eduniversal Best Masters Rankings. Overall, IIM Ahmedabad is one of the most prestigious and sought-after business schools in India, with an impressive NIRF rank of 1 in 2020. It offers world-class management programs and research initiatives and has consistently achieved high rankings in various global rankings.

1.2 IIM Bangalore

Established in 1973, IIM Bangalore is one of India's best-known business schools. It is the only business school in India to have been accredited by both the AACSB and EQUIS. It is located in the city of Bangalore and offers a wide range of post-graduate and doctoral programs. It has a strong focus on research and offers a range of courses in the fields of finance, marketing, operations, systems, and general management rankings. Indian Institute of Management (IIM) Bangalore is one of the top-ranking business schools in the country, consistently ranking among the top three B-schools in the country according to the NIRF Rankings. This premier institute offers a wide range of courses, from executive programs to doctoral programs, in the field of management education. IIM Bangalore is renowned for its stellar faculty comprising some of the most eminent names in the industry and academia, as well as its cutting-edge curriculum and ample opportunities for students to develop their leadership and business acumen. The institute has consistently maintained its 3rd rank in the NIRF Rankings since 2016 and has seen a rise of over 20 points in its overall rank from 1995. It has also been awarded an A+ grade by the National Assessment and Accreditation Council (NAAC) for its commitment to quality education. Thus, IIM Bangalore is an ideal choice for students looking for an enriching and fulfilling experience in the field of management.

1.3 IIM Calcutta

Established in 1961, IIM Calcutta is India's first business school. It is widely regarded as one of the best business schools in the country and is accredited by both the AACSB and EQUIS. It offers a wide range of courses in finance, economics, accounting, marketing, operations, and general management. IIM Calcutta is a premier management institute in India, consistently ranked among the best in the world. According to the National Institutional Ranking Framework (NIRF) Rankings 2020, IIM Calcutta is ranked number one in the Management category. This feat has been achieved by the institute for the third consecutive year. IIM Calcutta has seen a steady improvement in its rankings since 2017, reaching a rank of 6 in 2020 and 3 in 2022. The institute provides a world-class learning experience to its students, with its wide range of courses and experienced faculty members. IIM Calcutta has also made a name for itself in research and consultancy activities. It has been awarded the highest research grant from the Ministry of Human Resource Development, and its faculty members have published several influential research papers in top journals. IIM Calcutta has also established strong links with industry and international institutions. It has signed MoUs with over 15 international universities and has built strong relationships with leading employers across the globe. This has enabled the institute to provide its students with a variety of excellent learning and job opportunities. Overall, IIM Calcutta is a top-notch institution that offers excellent opportunities for students to pursue a successful career in management. Its commitment to excellence, world-class faculty, and strong industry and international ties, make it one of the best management institutes in the world.

1.4 IIM Indore

Established in 1996, IIM Indore is a relatively new business school compared to the other IIMs. IIM Indore is one of the leading management institutes in India, consistently ranked among the top 20 business schools in the country. It is the only institute in the country to be ranked in the top 50 of the National Institutional Ranking Framework (NIRF), making it the highest-ranked IIM in India. The institute has achieved impressive academic results over the years with its students consistently performing well in internships and placements. In addition, the institute has a strong alumni network with successful alumni from various industries. With a vision to provide world-class management education and promote research, the institute is a leader in fostering innovation and entrepreneurship. Its commitment to academic excellence makes it a top choice for aspiring managers.

1.5 IIM Lucknow

Indian Institute of Management Lucknow (IIM-L) is one of the most prestigious business schools in India. Ranked No.1 in Management education by the National Institutional Ranking Framework (NIRF), the institute has continually delivered excellence in teaching, research, and infrastructure since its inception in 1984. IIM-L is spread over a sprawling 200-acre campus in the heart of Uttar Pradesh, Lucknow. The institute offers a variety of programs in the field of management. From one-year Post Graduate Diploma in Management to five-year Fellow Programs in Management, the institute has something for everyone. IIM-L has consistently been ranked among the top B-Schools in India and the world. In the NIRF 2020 Rankings, the institute was ranked 1st in the Management category. Additionally, it has been ranked 17th in Asia and 127th in the world according to the QS Global MBA Rankings 2020. IIM-L has an impeccable track record of placements, with the institute witnessing a 7.5% increase in the average salary offered to its students in 2020, amounting to INR 28.5 LPA. The institute is also well-known for its impressive alumni network, which has made its mark in various fields of management and business. IIM-L is an institute that has created a name for itself in the field of management education. Its consistent success in the NIRF ranking is a testimony to it. IIM Lucknow has seen a slight decline in its rankings since 2017, reaching a rank of 15 in 2020 and then rising to a rank of 6 in 2022.

1.6 Theoretical Foundations

While this study primarily focuses on comparing the NIRF performance scores of the oldest five IIMs over the years, the below-listed business management tools/techniques/theories are also helpful in analyzing their performance:

- **SWOT Analysis**

Strengths, Weaknesses, Opportunities, and Threats (SWOT) can be used to compare the IIMs in terms of their competitive advantages, areas of improvement, external opportunities, and external threats.

- **Porter's Five Forces**

This theory can be used to analyze the degree of competition within the industry, the bargaining power of suppliers and buyers, the threat of substitutes and new entrants to the market, and the overall profitability of the industry.

- **Resource-Based View**

This theory can be used to compare the resources and capabilities of the IIMs in terms of their physical assets, human resources, organizational culture, and other unique resources.

- **Industry Life Cycle**

This theory can be used to compare the stages of development of the IIMs in terms of their growth strategies, competitive advantage, and sources of value creation.

- **Value Chain Analysis**

This theory can be used to compare the IIMs in terms of the activities that add value to their services and the costs associated with them.

Further, the following management theories could also be used for analysis in future studies.

- **Classical Management Theory**

This theory focuses on finding the most efficient way of carrying out tasks and organizing the workplace. It can be used to compare the IIMs in terms of the effectiveness of their administrative policies, the types of management structures they employ, and their commitment to finding the most efficient way to carry out tasks.

- **Scientific Management Theory**

This theory is based on the idea that productivity and efficiency can be improved through careful study and the use of scientific methods to improve the productivity of employees. This can be used to compare the IIMs in terms of their use of scientific methods to improve the performance of their employees.

- **Administrative Management Theory**

This theory focuses on the management of organizations and their resources. It can be used to compare the IIMs in terms of their ability to develop and implement administrative policies and procedures, their use of resources, and their ability to manage change.

- **Bureaucratic Management Theory**

This theory emphasizes the importance of formal rules and regulations, hierarchy, and the need for standardization. It can be used to compare the IIMs in terms of the extent to which they adhere to formal rules and procedures, how well they maintain order in the workplace, and their ability to maintain a clear chain of command.

- **Human Relations Theory**

This theory focuses on understanding and improving the interactions between people in the workplace. It can be used to compare the IIMs in terms of their commitment to creating a positive environment and fostering

- **Human Resources Management Theory**

This theory focuses on the management of people within organizations. It can be used to compare the IIMs in terms of the number and quality of staff, recruitment process, training and development, organizational culture, employee motivation, and other related aspects.

- **Systems Management Theory**

This theory focuses on the development and maintenance of systems within organizations. It can be used to compare the IIMs in terms of the systems and processes in place for managing internal operations, responding to external conditions, meeting customer needs, and other related aspects.

- **Contingency Management Theory**

This theory focuses on the management of organizations in response to changing external conditions. It can be used to compare the IIMs in terms of their ability to adapt to changing external conditions, develop strategies to remain competitive and manage the organization effectively in response to those conditions.

- **Quality Management Theory**

This theory focuses on the attainment of superior quality in organizations. It can be used to compare the IIMs in terms of the quality of their services and products, the effectiveness of their processes, and the ability to maintain and improve quality over time.

- **Six Sigma Theory**

This theory focuses on the use of statistics and data-driven analysis to improve processes and decision-making. It can be used to compare the IIMs in terms of the use of data-driven approaches for decision-making, the ability to identify and reduce errors and defects, and the effectiveness of their processes and operations.

2. LITERATURE REVIEW

Recent studies have highlighted important differences between the National Institutional Ranking Framework (NIRF) and global university ranking systems, both in the indicators chosen as well as in their broader implications on governance. Çakır et al. (2015) in a systematic comparison of these different ranking regimes, for example, show that national rankings typically make use of a broader set of indicators, often with greater attention to educational quality, institutional resources and inclusivity to reflect local policy concerns and contexts, while the global rankings, which QS and THE have come to epitomize, tend to focus on a narrower set of indicators that are centered on research productivity and reputation surveys. This is not simply a technical distinction. Peters (2017) and Pavel (2015) also show that these global rankings, through their performative logic of "knowledge capitalism," have come to constitute how we think about the university, with an overemphasis on standardized and easily quantified measures of success. However, while these rankings may offer simplified metrics that are globally comparable, they are likely to privilege elite and well-resourced universities while contributing to a global "reputation race" to the detriment of teaching quality, regional diversity, and a deeper understanding of their role and missions in society (Peters, 2017; Hazelkorn, 2017). In this regard, Çakır et al. (2015) show that global rankings scores correlate only weakly with national rankings, emphasizing the importance of national contexts and nationally specific indicators. Pavel (2015) also highlights the relative devaluation of teaching environment and innovative contributions in global systems that are in sharp contrast to national frameworks like India's NIRF. Taken together, these studies show the limitations of any single system of scoring and highlight the value of contextually embedded and multi-dimensional approaches that take into account the wider contributions and missions of universities, including teaching innovation, equity, impacts on local/regional economies, and support for language and digital education. This perspective is significant and important for emerging frameworks such as the NIRF, as they aim to create a balance between the international standards and India's unique social challenges and objectives of policy.

There exists limited available literature reporting on trends and institutional reactions to NIRF rankings but rarely where ranking systems, education innovation, and SDG 4 outcomes intersect. This research places itself in that unexplored terrain. University ranking systems have far-reaching implications for institutional action agendas and policy, both globally and nationally. Comparative analysis more recently identifies core differences between global and national rankings. Çakır et al. (2015) observed that national rankings, e.g., India's NIRF, consider broader education and context indicators, whereas global rankings (QS, THE) give major weightage to research and reputation at the expense of other dimensions like teaching quality or inclusiveness. Peters (2017) and Hazelkorn (2017) warn that performance-based indicators, though providing homogenous measurements, can reinforce resource inequalities, are skewed towards elite institutions, and can trigger a "reputation race." Pavel (2015) also expresses the view that international rankings have serious impacts on institutional identity and planning strategy, but disregard education process and innovation—priorities usually maintained by national systems such as NIRF.

To place this study into perspective, Table 1 critically analyzes recent Indian literature and shows that the majority of studies concentrate on NIRF's quantitative metrics or comparisons versus other ranking metrics, reflecting present research gaps in digital innovation, equity, and longitudinal assessment.

Table 1. Summary of Ranking Parameters and Weightages – NIRF (Management)

Sr. No.	Parameters	Marks
1.	Teaching, Learning, & Resources (TLR) Ranking weight: 0.30	100
A. Student strength including doctoral students (SS): 20 marks B. Faculty-student ratio with emphasis on permanent faculty (FSR): 30 marks C. combined metric for faculty with PhD (or equivalent) and experience (FQE): 20 marks D. Financial resources and their utilization (FRU): 30 marks		
2.	Research and Professional Practice (RP) Ranking weight: 0.30	100
A. Combined metric for publications (PU): 40 marks B. Combined metric for quality of publications (QP): 40 marks C. Footprint of projects, professional practice and executive development programs (FPPP): 20 marks		
3.	Graduation Outcomes (GO) Ranking weight: 0.20	100
A. Combined metric for placement and higher studies (GPH): 40 marks B. Metric for university examinations (GUE): 20 marks C. Median salary (GMS): 40 marks		
4.	Outreach and Inclusivity (OI) Ranking weight: 0.10	100
A. Percentage of students from other states (Region Diversity RD): 30 marks B. Percentage of women (Women Diversity WD): 30 marks C. Emotionally and socially challenged students (ECS): 20 marks D. Facilities for physically challenged students (PCS): 20 marks		
5.	Perception (PR) Ranking weight: 0.10	100
A. Peer perception – Employers & Academic Peer (PR): 100 marks		

Source: https://www.nirfindia.org/nirfpdfcdn/2022/framework/Management.pdf

Table 2. Summary of the Methodology used and Major findings of the reviewed studies

S. No.	Publication	The methodology used and Major findings of the study:
1	Singh et al. (2022)	This study employed a Data Envelopment Analysis (DEA) approach along with National Institutional Ranking Framework (NIRF) data to suggest improvements for India's education system. By calculating efficiency scores for 61 educational institutions, the researchers ranked them using a super-efficiency DEA model. The study offered recommendations for enhancing inefficient institutions while identifying a research gap in evaluating the effectiveness of proposed improvement methods.
2	Gnanasekaran and Rajkumar (2022)	Evaluating research performance in active medical institutions, the researchers analyzed Scopus, Pubmed, and ResearchGate data. Utilizing the Compound Annual Growth Rate (CAGR), they determined growth rates. All India Institute of Medical Sciences, New Delhi, achieved the highest rankings in both NIRF and ResearchGate scores, with PubMed exhibiting the highest publication growth rate.
3	Shivaram et al. (2022)	This research assessed research performance among top NIRF-ranked engineering institutions in Karnataka. They observed increased publication productivity after the NIRF introduction, with MS Ramaiah Institute of Technology achieving the highest citations. The study also found that open-access articles received more citations compared to non-OA articles.
4	Yadav et al. (2022)	The study analyzed India Rankings data from 2016-2020, revealing increased publications, citations, and highly-cited publications. Research activity and impact improved over time, leading to a decrease in the number of institutions without publications.
5	Kumar et al. (2021)	This study introduced a ranking framework using fuzzy logic and the Mamdani fuzzy reasoning approach, and then compared its outcomes with the NIRF rankings.
6	Marisha (2021)	Similar to Kumar et al. (2021), this research proposed a ranking framework based on fuzzy logic and the Mamdani fuzzy reasoning approach and compared its results with NIRF rankings.
7	Nassa et al. (2021)	The study evaluated the influence of the perception parameter on higher education institutions' overall ranking, scientifically analyzing NIRF's role.
8	Dam et al. (2021)	The research tracked the impact of NIRF ranking on research publications in North-East Indian Universities using Web of Science data.
9	Singh and Singh (2021)	The study analyzed the "perception" influence on NIRF rankings of engineering institutions using Web of Science data for 10 years.
10	Deka and Sarmah (2021)	This study aims to examine the Website analysis of the top 15 NIRF-ranked Indian universities, highlighting various metrics' performance.
11	Patel et al. (2021)	The analysis focused on NIRF-ranked IITs, faculty members, publications, and impact, exploring data from NIRF and Indian Research Information Network System (IRINS).
12	Jeyapragash and Muthuraj (2021)	This scientometric study analyzes the research productivity of top NIRF-ranked Indian institutes using Web of Science data.
13	Gangopadhyay and Mukherjee (2021)	The study employed scientometric analysis on top NIRF-ranked institutes, assessing research productivity and subject distribution.
14	Chakraborty et al. (2021)	This study entails a comparison of open access and commercial publications' performance for the top twenty NIRF institutions.
15	Kumar et al. (2021)	This entails correlation and regression analysis to determine the relationship between NIRF Score and management institutes' parameters.
16	Anbalagan and Tamizhchelvan(2021)	This study does a comparison of rankings using Times Higher Education and NIRF for the top 25 Indian institutions.
17	Deka and Sarmah (2021)	This study involves an investigation of research publication impact on post-NIRF ranking in North-East Indian Universities.

continued on following page

Table 2. Continued

S. No.	Publication	The methodology used and Major findings of the study:
18	Dadhe and Dubey (2021)	This article reports a comparative study of the scientific publications of nationally ranked engineering institutions five years before and after the launch of the National Institutional Ranking Framework (NIRF) in India. The study delved into analysis of scientific publications of nationally ranked engineering institutions pre and post-NIRF launch.
19	Joorel et. al. (2021)	This article focuses on the evolution and challenges of India's Rankings, highlighting the significance of a composite indicator.
20	Pal (2021)	The study assessed the potency of a combined metric for quality assessment of publications in India's NIRF exercise in 2020.
21	Nassa et. Al. (2021)	The evaluation analyzed five years of data from the India Rankings to assess its impact on the performance parameters of higher education institutions.
22	Singh et al. (2021)	This article does a comparison of HEI rankings using different methodologies. The methodologies used are the NIRF Overall ranking, the NIRF ranking based on research and professional practices, a new research ranking methodology, and the IFQ2A index developed by Spanish scientists. The article finds that a strong positive correlation exists between the ranking of HEIs using the new methodology and the ranking using the IFQ2A Index.
23	Joorel et al. (2021)	The study analyzed patents registered/filed/published/granted by 20 Indian Central Universities and other countries in the last decade.
24	Kumar et al. (2021)	This study examined the impact of library budgets on NIRF rankings for top Indian Higher Educational Institutions (HEIs).
25	Parameswaran et al. (2020)	The research analyzed the relationship between Research and Professional Practices (RPP) and Perception (PR) in university ranking.
26	Gangopadhyay (2020)	The study analyzed changes in the web content of the first 20 NIRF ranking institutes over the last decade using the Internet Archive's Wayback Machine to get the website updated dates and archived web pages.
27	Kumar et al. (2020)	This study explored the connection between NIRF rankings and students' enrolments using a sample of the top 75 NIRF-ranked Management Institutions in India.
28	Vasudevan et al. (2020)	The paper analyzed key indicators from the NBA, NAAC, and NIRF to design a common framework.
29	Srimathi and Krishnamoorthy (2020)	The paper compared the research performance of 25 private universities in India with IITs, Central Universities (CUs), and National Institutes of Technology (NITs).
30	Srinivasan et al. (2020)	The paper reviewed the impact of NIRF in India, its momentum, and its role in the Institute of Eminence (IOE) selection.
31	Prathap (2019)	In this study, a mathematical model was proposed to rank higher education institutions (HEIs) in India using NIRF data.
32	Banshal et al. (2019)	This study constructs validity maps from NIRF 2019 data for the top 100 colleges in India. The study uses the NIRF score, perception score, and Xscore to determine the placement of the top colleges concerning each other. The study also recognizes possible biases in the peer review perception scores and recommends that the Xscore, which is based on an input-output model, may give a better representation of reality. The study uses Peirce's measure of predictive success to obtain a quantitative estimate.

continued on following page

Table 2. Continued

S. No.	Publication	The methodology used and Major findings of the study:
33	Balasubramani and Thangavel (2019)	This paper presents a comparative account of the research performance of 25 private universities in India with IITs, Central Universities (CUs), and National Institutes of Technology (NITs). A set-based comparison methodology is followed. The results show that private universities are performing well in research, especially in terms of output and rate of growth of output. However, on quality and productivity per capita, private universities still lag behind IITs, CUs, and NITs. The study identifies the need for private universities to improve the quality of research to reach the level of IITs, CUs, and NITs.
34	Kumaren and Rajkumar (2019)	This study examined publications of Universities in NIRF using Web of Science, Scopus, Indian Citation Index, patent publications, and citations, to determine the Citation Rate.
35	Anilkumar and Nagabhushanam (2018)	Using content and discourse analysis of NIRFs methodology, this paper engaged in the systematic analysis of NIRF's methodology, identified gaps, and made policy recommendations for its development.
36	Chugh et al. (2018)	The study identified parameters influencing the exclusion of institutions from the top 100 ranks in the NIRF India Rankings 2018 compared to 2017.
37	Mathew et al. (2018)	Collecting data through Web content analysis from the official websites of NIRF, Times Higher Education World University Rankings, and QS World University Rankings, this study highlighted differences in assessment criteria of NBA, NAAC, and NIRF, proposing a common framework.
38	Chugh et al. (2018)	This study analyzed individual parameters and overall scores of the top 100 engineering institutions in India as ranked by the NIRF.
39	Mukhopadhyay et al. (2018)	The authors provided an overview of NIRF 2016 rankings, highlighting challenges and opportunities for improvement.
40	Kumar and Tiwari (2017)	Using bibliometric analysis, this research examined research excellence among the top 20 engineering institutions in India from the NIRF list. The major finding is that IITs at Bombay and Kharagpur stand out in terms of research excellence, with promising results also shown by the new IITs at Ropar-Rupnagar and Indore.
41	Prathap (2017)	his comparative end-to-end research evaluation of leading engineering institutions in India combined bibliometric and econometric analysis.
42	Prathap (2017)	The study critiqued the NIRF exercise as a reduction of higher education into a single score, using NIRF 2017 bibliometric data for illustration.
43	Prathap (2017)	This study analyzed NIRF 2017 bibliometric data to determine Loyola College and Bishop Heber College as the best research colleges in India.
44	Chugh et al. (2017)	The study focused on the self-assessment of NIRF ranking parameters by academic institutions in India.
45	Chugh et al. (2017)	This study focuses on the self-assessment of the NIRF ranking parameters by academic institutions in India. The authors observe that there is no single technique available to carry out the self-assessment and have developed a methodology for self-assessment. The methodology can predict the likely chance of an institution's inclusion in the top 100 rankings and provides insight into evaluating the strengths and weaknesses of each of the five parameters. The major finding is that the authors have developed a methodology for self-assessment of the NIRF ranking parameters.

2.1 Critical Synthesis of Table 2 Studies: Methodological Approaches and Research Gaps in the NIRF Literature

2.1.1. Quantitative Efficiency and Ranking Models

Certain studies (Singh et al., 2022; Kumar et al., 2021; Marisha, 2021; Prathap, 2019) employ advanced quantitative methods—like Data Envelopment Analysis (DEA), fuzzy logic, and custom mathematical models—to measure NIRF rankings' effectiveness and fairness.

Key Findings: The research depicts the application of alternative and potentially better evaluative models than NIRF, such as super-efficiency DEA and fuzzy logic rank-based (Kumar et al., 2021; Marisha, 2021). They highlight inefficiencies that exist in some institutions but are masked by the limited parameter set of NIRF and recommend systemic reforms.

Research Gaps: While these models offer additional analytical perspectives, most of such research stops at the technical demonstration level and does not evaluate their practical application or impacts. Also, they allow little space for qualitative and subjective aspects, such as learning experience, social purpose, or digital innovation—areas that have gained prominence after the NEP 2020.

2.1.2. Scientometrics and Bibliometrics analyses

One of the well-known trends in the literature (e.g., Gnanasekaran & Rajkumar, 2022; Shivaram et al., 2022; Jeyapragash & Muthuraj, 2021; Chakraborty et al., 2021; Patel et al., 2021; Gangopadhyay & Mukherjee, 2021; Dam et al., 2021) is the use of bibliometric and scientometric methods, often using databases like Scopus, Web of Science, or ResearchGate.

Major Findings: These studies affirm that NIRF implementation has been associated with increasing research productivity and quality of output, particularly in high-performing institutions (Shivaram et al., 2022; Yadav et al., 2022). Open access publications have higher citation impact. Research output and research performance are now playing a significant role in NIRF position, reflecting a policy push towards research excellence.

Research Gaps: The focus remains mainly on quantitative results, with little attention paid to variables like teaching quality, equity, technology adoption, or student performance. Regional, gender, and discipline biases are not adequately explored, nor are the long-term implications of actions based on such rankings.

2.1.3. Perception, Reputation, and Stakeholder Contributions

Research by Nassa et al. (2021), Singh and Singh (2021), and Banshal et al. (2019) emphasizes the power and possible bias associated with the "perception" (PR) parameter in the NIRF framework.

Key Findings: Reputation and perception scores are established as key drivers of overall rankings, sometimes even surpassing objective measures of performance. Certain research identifies the inherent subjectivity and potential biases in peer or recruiter judgments and advocates greater openness and empirically supported standards.

Research Gaps: Validity and fairness of perception-based measures are unknown. Very little cross-validation with external reputation measures (i.e., world rankings) is done, and qualitative stakeholder opinions (students, employers, alumni) are hardly ever included systematically.

2.1.4. Comparative and Integrative Evaluations

A few studies (Anbalagan & Tamizhchelvan, 2021; Mathew et al., 2018; Vasudevan et al., 2020) contrast NIRF with global ranking systems (THE, QS) or peer national systems (NBA, NAAC).

Key Findings: The above differences indicate the specific emphases of both systems—e.g., NIRF's pedagogy and research focus, whereas THE focuses on global outreach and diversity. The focus on faculty-to-student ratio, research outreach, and international collaborative practices are the key differences. There are constant calls for a holistic, context-sensitive model.

Research Gaps: Little is researched in terms of how technology-related factors (ICT adoption, pedagogy, language policy) are balanced across frameworks. Furthermore, research is rarely interested in investigating alignment (or non-alignment) with UN SDG 4 objectives.

2.1.5. Equity, Inclusiveness, and Diversity in Institutions

Few reports (e.g., Dadhe & Dubey, 2021; Parameswaran et al., 2020; Balasubramani & Thangavel, 2019) analyze dimensions like outreach, inclusiveness, and private-public or regional category differences.

Major Findings: Research output growth is uneven with high growth in production in private universities but low per-capita productivity. There is perceptible improvement in indicators related to inclusivity in NIRF after its launch, but the depth and comprehensiveness of such improvement are questionable.

Gaps in the Literature: Inclusivity and equity are all too often relegated to superficial accounts of quantities; there is a clear lack of in-depth studies of intersectionality (e.g., social, gender, linguistic, regional variations). These studies do not critically assess the effectiveness of NIRF's "Outreach & Inclusivity" criterion, and neither do they investigate its connection to the provision of online and digital education.

2.1.6. NIRF's Methodology and Impact Evaluations Criticisms

A number of studies question the NIRF methodology (Anilkumar & Nagabhushanam, 2018; Chugh et al., 2018, 2017; Prathap, 2017, 2019), questioning the reductionist nature of single-score assessment, the challenges of self-assessment, and the lack of institutional-level assessment.

Key Findings: Issues regarding the restrictiveness of NIRF's composite index, omission of some qualitative/digital parameters, and strategic "score engineering" on the part of institutions to maximize under the system.

Research Gaps: There is little longitudinal research on the effect of NIRF rankings on institutional policy, student performance, or alignment with national development objectives (SDG 4, NEP 2020). The evaluations are typically policy recommendation-oriented, but empirical work on the proposed reforms is minimal.

2.1.7. Further Methodological and Thematic Insights

Several individual studies cover new subjects such as:

- Institutional websites and library resources (Kumar et al., 2021; Deka P. & Sarmah M.)
- Patent production (Joorel et al., 2021)
- The combined assessment measurement quality (Pal, 2021)

They point to increasing emphasis on multifactor, multidimension quality indicators but imply the disjointedness of the studies with little integrative activity. Overreliance on research outcomes and quantitative measures, without going deep into teaching quality, technology innovation, language instruction, student experience, and social contribution is a major gap. Also there is no stakeholder feedback (students, teachers, employers) and qualitative/subjective assessments. Depth is lacking in equity and inclusivity analysis—especially in gender, language, digital divides, and regional aspects. Global benchmarking and integration (how NIRF aligns or diverges from global best practices, and where it is placed in the era of digitalization) require more probing. Assessment of NIRF's response to milestone policy changes (e.g., NEP 2020) and SDG 4 goals is next to nothing. Multi-methodological, holistic approaches are needed, for instance, combining digital, linguistic, and pedagogical innovation indicators in Indian ranking frameworks.

3. METHODS

Despite significant influence of NIRF, the desired attention with respect to its efficacy from the perspective of SDG 4, digitalization, and language inclusivity has been largely missing. This chapter addresses that gap by providing both a critical policy perspective as well as performance analysis.

The rationale behind choosing 2018–2022 period is that it covers re-pandemic, pandemic, and immediate post-pandemic years which is a critical period during which the management education witnessed significant digital transformation. A consistent and regular data availability after the launch of NIRF in the year 2015 is also ensured during the period.

a) Sample and Scope: The five most elderly IIMs—Ahmedabad (IIMA), Bangalore (IIMB), Calcutta (IIMC), Lucknow (IIML), and Indore (IIMI)—were chosen based on their age, availability of longitudinal data, and policy significance are studied in this research.
b) Data Collection:

Quantitative Data: Official NIRF performance outcomes (2017–2022), on all five NIRF parameters—Teaching, Learning & Resources (TLR); Research & Professional Practice (RP); Graduation Outcomes (GO); Outreach & Inclusivity (OI); and Peer Perception (PR).

Qualitative Supplement: Vignettes, faculty/student opinions and literature-driven observations on ICT adoption and e-programs in IIMs (referencing Pathak & Pal, 2024; Dar et al., 2017; Patel et al., 2004).

c) Instruments and Analytical Methods:

Quantitative Analysis: Data were arranged in MS Excel and made use of summary statistics (mean, variance) and one-way/two-way ANOVA in SPSS to determine differences between-institute and parameters.

Qualitative Analysis: Thematic analysis of literature case vignettes for ICT adoption, digital library utilization, and inclusivity programs.

3.1 Qualitative Supplement: Vignettes and User Perspectives on ICT Adoption at IIMs

This chapter supplements the NIRF indicators' quantitative analysis with qualitative revelations that spotlight the across-the-board metamorphosis of ICT usage in Indian Institutes of Management (IIMs). The vignettes and narrative, drawn from recent literature and survey research, tell us something about the nature and extent of digital integration in IIMs. They give us a glimpse, the way the image projecting tool of the NIRF would if it were inverted, into the real-time experiences of IIMs with digital academic and administrative integration.

3.1.1 Case 1: Institutional Transformation and Digital Administration

The last ten years have observed IIMs, alongside other leading institutions, intensifying their efforts to embed ICT in both educational administration and classroom delivery (Mukhopadhyay & Parhar, 2014). Government policy initiatives (such as RUSA and the recommendations of the National Knowledge Commission) have emphasized that integrating ICT is key to not only expanding access and ensuring equity but also upgrading the quality of our institutions.

As an example, IIMs have gone digital in their management of core admission, student record, and faculty performance tracking systems—as have many premier institutions. This use of information and communication technology (ICT) in the management and administration of higher education has, in Mukhopadhyay and Parhar's (2014) words, "taken deeper penetration in private universities and institutions." And although these authors seem to assign most of the credit to the push from the institutions themselves, using ICT in educational administration and managing the teaching/learning process seems also a direct result of several government-backed programs (e.g., RUSA and the NKC recommendations).

3.1.2 Case 2: ICT-Enabled Libraries—Faculty and Student Voices

Current research (Dar et al., 2017; Pathak & Pal, 2024) provide detailed insights into how the revolution in information and communication technologies (ICT) have affected IIM libraries and profoundly impacted the areas of research, teaching, and student learning. Pathak & Pal (2024) conducted an extensive survey of faculty and students at first-, second-, and third-generation IIMs and found the following:

> *"Almost all users interact with e-resources on a daily basis, with the engaging of e-journals and online databases being much preferred. There is a very high level of awareness regarding the E-ShodhSindhu Consortium, and the IIM library websites are considered very reliable by the users for searching e-resources."*

A faculty member from one of the IIMs made the following comment:
"The easy, remote access I have to the databases of case studies and business journals has been crucial to my teaching and research. These resources are entirely digital and have worked very well for me and my students, especially during the pandemic."
A student at one of the IIMs made the following observation:
"The e-resource portals that IIM libraries provide are the first and best places I go to when I have to do an assignment or conduct some research. However, I sometimes find the user interface to be a little outdated and clumsy, which has the potential to slow me down. I've also been in a situation where the number of users that can be logged into a specific e-resource at the same time has run out. That wasn't a very fun experience."

3.1.3 Case 3: Digital Pedagogy and Societal Impact

Information and communication technology (ICT) has evolved at Indian Institutes of Management (IIMs) not just in terms of resources and administration but also in terms of mission and inclusivity. Patel et al. (2004), in reflecting on IIMs' broader role, have noted that their governance system—"participative, decentralized, and transparent"—makes IIMs a role model for other institutions that seek excellence. A vision of this participatory governance is being realized increasingly through digital platforms such as Learning Management Systems (LMS), virtual classrooms, and collaborative online projects. These platforms offer democratic access to students and allow engagement with them and among them. The online platforms symbolize a step toward academic equity.

3.2 Research Questions

In line with the identified research gaps, the following three research questions have been articulated:

- Does a significant disparity exist in NIRF Scores among the 5 NIRF Parameters?
- Is there a notable variation in NIRF Scores among the oldest 5 IIMs?
- Does a significant difference in NIRF Scores occur between the various combinations of NIRF Parameter and IIM?

3.3 Objectives of the Research

The above-listed research questions serve as the basis for framing the research objectives. Research questions help to define the problem or gap in knowledge that the research aims to address, while the research objectives provide a clear and concise statement of what the researcher intends to achieve or demonstrate through the study. Consequently, the following three objectives were established:

- To investigate if there exists a meaningful distinction in NIRF Scores across the five NIRF Parameters.
- To examine if there is a notable difference in NIRF Scores between the premier five IIMs.
- To determine if there is a substantial difference in NIRF Scores between various combinations of NIRF Parameter and IIM.

This research study will be focused on the oldest five Indian Institutes of Management (IIM C, IIM A, IIM B, IIM L, IIM I) from the first generation, taking into consideration the Indian NIRF Framework from 2018 to 2022. These five IIMs were specifically selected as they have consistently been ranked among the top 10 management institutions in NIRF over the years and have established a solid foundation of resources and performances compared to their newer counterparts.

3.4 Hypotheses

To answer the stipulated research questions toward framed objectives, the three Hypotheses were formulated:

- The hypothesis concerning factor A (Oldest 5 IIMs):

Null Hypothesis, H0:
IIM C = IIM A = IIM B = IIM L = IIM I
Alternate Hypothesis, H1:
Treatment means are not equal for at least one pair of the treatment means of factor A(Oldest 5 IIMs; IIM C $\neq$ IIM A$\neq$ IIM B $\neq$ IIM L $\neq$ IIM I)

- The hypothesis concerning factor B (5 NIRF Parameters):

Null Hypothesis, H_0:
TLR= RP= GO= OI = PR
Alternate Hypothesis, H_1:

Treatment means are not equal for at least one pair of the treatment means of factor B (NIRF Parameters; TLR≠ RP ≠ GO ≠ OI ≠ PR)

- The hypothesis concerning the interaction component, AB (Oldest 5 IIMs and 5 NIRF Parameters):

Null Hypothesis, H_0:
IIM C TLR= IIM C RP= IIM C GO= IIM C OI = IIM C PR =… IIM A OI = IIM A PR =…

Alternate Hypothesis, H_1: Interaction means are not equal for at least one pair of interaction means (IIMs & NIRF Parameters; IIM C TLR ≠ IIM C RP ≠ IIM C GO ≠ IIM C OI ≠ IIM C PR ≠… IIM A OI ≠ IIM A PR ≠…)

3.5 Research Design

The methodology employed in this study is a conclusive research design with a quantitative approach. The sample for this study was selected through a process of judgment sampling, a non-probability method, which involves selecting 5 of the oldest Indian Institutes of Management (IIM C, IIM A, IIM B, IIM L, and IIM I) from the top 100 management education institutions in India as per NIRF Rankings 2022.

A factorial design was utilized, with the NIRF Score as the dependent variable and two factors, the NIRF Parameters (5 levels or treatments - TLR, RP, GO, OI, PR) and the Indian Higher Education Institutions in Management [IHEI-IM (5 levels - IIM C, IIM A, IIM B, IIM L, IIM I)]. Each level of the factor IHEI-IIM was replicated 5 times to ensure the reliability and validity of the results.

The use of a factorial design enables the examination of the combined and individual effects of both factors on the NIRF Score, providing a comprehensive understanding of the relationship between the variables. The chosen sample size of 5 replications under each level of factor IHEI-IIM is deemed adequate for a conclusive study of this nature.

For ready reference, the adopted Research Design is summarized in Figure 6 and Table 3.

Table 3. Experimental Combinations of Factorial Design

		IIM				
PARAMETERS	**Year**	**IIM C**	**IIM A**	**IIM B**	**IIM L**	**IIM I**
Teaching, Learning & Resources (TLR)	2018	90.68	90.82	84.71	83.98	68.97
	2019	90.14	90.74	92.85	85.37	83.11
	2020	90.68	92.87	91.46	86.93	83.18
	2021	87.33	91.41	91.53	84.54	81.54
	2022	86.01	92.76	91.69	86.53	83.17
Research and Professional Practice (RP)	2018	53.26	53.89	51.19	39.15	33.51
	2019	54.16	57.76	55.03	34.53	37.44
	2020	56.79	63.06	57.43	48.58	43.42
	2021	58.14	65.09	63.43	41.12	50.74
	2022	54.88	63.22	60.89	46.89	47.99
Graduation Outcomes (GO)	2018	96.41	97.25	97.95	94.76	93.61
	2019	96.07	98.10	98.35	93.01	93.21
	2020	97.18	98.46	98.48	93.71	93.74
	2021	98.10	99.43	98.99	94.84	93.98
	2022	98.51	99.39	98.53	96.27	93.92
Outreach and Inclusivity (OI)	2018	66.63	63.26	69.65	60.51	59.30
	2019	71.52	68.12	73.09	57.55	70.21
	2020	71.85	66.78	69.45	71.35	67.49
	2021	72.90	70.01	71.88	68.06	66.29
	2022	72.08	68.13	71.34	74.03	68.36
Peer Perception (PR)	2018	79.46	99.87	100.00	67.01	48.94
	2019	94.02	96.32	100.00	69.57	51.93
	2020	95.26	95.99	100.00	73.17	55.67
	2021	94.87	98.53	100.00	75.51	59.91
	2022	94.74	98.62	100.00	78.67	56.88
Overall	2018	77.08	79.18	77.33	68.63	60.28
	2019	79.05	80.61	81.34	67.29	67.01
	2020	80.39	82.75	81.32	73.85	69.04
	2021	80.04	83.69	83.48	71.02	71.10
	2022	78.64	83.35	82.62	74.55	70.66

4. RESULTS

Five-year NIRF scores analysis indicates that all IIMs are stable high performers across TLR and GO parameters while showing variation in RP, OI, and PR scores. The phenomenon is particularly significant in the case of IIM Ahmedabad and Bangalore, which consistently top all the parameters; however, IIM Indore and Lucknow reflect relative poor performance in Research/Professional Practice and Peer Perception. ANOVA results validate statistically significant variations between institutions and also parameters—a result that suggests varying strengths and weaknesses of the legacy IIMs.

4.1 Result of ANOVA: Two-Factor with Replication

The result is summarised in Table 4. As can be seen from Table 3, the calculated F values are much higher than the F Critical values and the P-values are very low (< 0.05). This implies that all three Null- Hypotheses are rejected. Hence, there is a significant difference in terms of NIRF Scores between different IIMs and also between different NIRF Parameters. Further, there is a significant difference in NIRF Scores because of the interaction between the factor 'IIMs' and 'NIRF Parameters' i.e. the interaction between IIM and the NIRF Parameter has a significant effect on NIRF Scores. Thus, there are significant differences in the performance scores of the oldest 5 IIMs across the 5 parameters of TLR, RP, GO, OI, and PR. It appears different IIMs have evolved different strength areas (reflected through NIRF Parameters) and have an improvement scope for a balanced approach across all 5 parameter areas.

Table 4. ANOVA: Two-Factor with Replication Result

SUMMARY	IIM C	IIM A	IIM B	IIM L	IIM I	Total
TLR						
Count	5	5	5	5	5	25
Sum	444.84	458.60	452.24	427.35	399.97	2183.00
Average	88.97	91.72	90.45	85.47	79.99	87.32
Variance	4.67	1.07	10.61	1.59	38.47	27.93
RP						
Count	5	5	5	5	5	25
Sum	277.23	303.02	287.97	210.27	213.10	1291.59
Average	55.45	60.60	57.59	42.05	42.62	51.66

continued on following page

Table 4. Continued

SUMMARY	IIM C	IIM A	IIM B	IIM L	IIM I	Total
Variance	3.95	21.54	23.13	32.97	51.31	85.39
GO						
Count	5	5	5	5	5	25
Sum	486.27	492.63	492.30	472.59	468.46	2412.25
Average	97.25	98.53	98.46	94.52	93.69	96.49
Variance	1.10	0.84	0.14	1.54	0.09	4.86
OI						
Count	5	5	5	5	5	25
Sum	354.98	336.30	355.41	331.50	331.65	1709.84
Average	71.00	67.26	71.08	66.30	66.33	68.39
Variance	6.22	6.32	2.36	49.61	17.49	18.65
PR						
Count	5	5	5	5	5	25
Sum	458.35	489.33	500.00	363.93	273.33	2084.94
Average	91.67	97.87	100.00	72.79	54.67	83.40
Variance	46.79	2.73	0.00	21.47	18.42	325.64
Total						
Count	25	25	25	25	25	
Sum	2021.67	2079.88	2087.92	1805.64	1686.51	
Average	80.87	83.20	83.52	72.23	67.46	
Variance	259.32	273.59	291.38	354.97	359.96	
ANOVA						
Source of Variation	*SS*	*df*	*MS*	*F*	*P-value*	*F crit*
Sample	31056.73	4	7764.18	532.61	1.86E-66	2.46
Columns	5214.36	4	1303.59	89.42	3.75E-32	2.46
Interaction	4426.96	16	276.68	18.98	1.88E-23	1.75
Within	1457.77	100	14.58			
Total	42155.82	124				

As can be seen from Figure 7, while all the 5 IIMs appear to do comparatively well in the Graduate Outcome and Teaching, Learning, and Resources front, areas such as Research and Professional Practice and Outreach and Inclusivity leave much room for improvement and extend an opportunity to firm up these areas towards improvement. IIM I and IIM L seem to be lagging on the Peer Perception front compared to the other three IIMs (IIM B, IIM A, and IIM C which have scored well on the PR front).

4.2 Equity & Bias in NIRF Metrics

While the National Institutional Ranking Framework (NIRF) was designed to bring clarity and responsibility to the ranking of Indian higher education institutions, it now seems that the very qualities it was meant to embody—clarity and responsibility—are in short supply in the NIRF's methodology. Instead of being a straightforward means to deliver a message about which institutions are performing well in what areas, the NIRF is now seen by many as a not-very-accountable means of delivering a not-very-clear message.

4.2.1 Urban, Regional, and Legacy Bias

Multiple analyses (like Prathap, 2019) have shown that a very small number of institutions concentrated in just a few geographies receive the best NIRF ranks. The maps accompanying such analyses make it pretty clear: there are just a handful of HEIs that get the NIRF's top marks, and almost all of them are in a select few states and cities. For example, in Prathap's analysis of the NIRF 2019, Tamil Nadu, Delhi, and Kerala alone accounted for over 80% of the top institutions ranked by the NIRF. Not even a full quarter of India's 28 states made it to this list.

4.2.2 Perception and Subjectivity

Including the "Perception" score, which is based on peer review, brings in a huge amount of subjectivity. What we find emerging from both Prathap (2019) and Singh & Rao (2024) is that perception scores tend to favor universities with the oldest brands. These institutions have enjoyed decades during which their reputations as academic leaders were built. The bulk of the evidence shows that such universities are nothing special today; certainly, their perceived prestige has not translated into any definite, measurable criteria of academic quality or enlightened practices in higher education. But look at the hierarchies these perception-driven rankings produce.

4.2.3 Research Metrics and Institutional Scale

Quantitative NIRF indicators, such as total research output, are usually not normalized for size or staff. Aggregate metrics advantage large, well-funded universities with greater faculty numbers. In contrast, smaller, emerging institutions—many of which serve semi-urban or rural populations—are structurally disadvantaged. Using "total publications" instead of "publications per faculty" does not control for scale in research output and therefore compromises fairness. This also fails to recognize a rising research culture at smaller or newer institutions.

4.2.4 Gender, Social, and Digital Inclusivity

Even with an "Outreach and Inclusivity" (OI) parameter, the current NIRF framework measures the diversity and inclusion of institutions very poorly. It is not just that the scoring is often based on very poor information (for instance, crude headcounts). It is also that the framework does not instruct institutions to measure or even think about the many dimensions of diversity that today's colleges and universities are supposed to care about. In fact, the framework ignores subtler, qualitative aspects of campus climate that it would be good for the equity initiatives supposed to exist in the institutions to have.

Kumar & Tiwari (2022) conducted recent research that found even the top 15 universities ranked by the NIRF are missing what should be fundamental accessibility features for persons with disabilities (e.g., access for screen readers, adjustable fonts, and "accessibility statements"). Alarmingly, the NIRF's own website doesn't even meet these criteria. And this is in the context of mandates like the Rights of Persons with Disabilities Act (2016) and policy shifts under the NEP 2020 that are supposed to increase equity for people with disabilities. This situation sends a signal that the NIRF has some serious work to do in terms of not just digital accessibility but also in rethinking what equity is for all the universities it ranks.

4.2.5 Transparency, Data Integrity, and Methodological Gaps

Singh and Rao (2024) highlight other issues of concern: unexplained and frequent fluctuations in ranks, opacity in weighting and data validation, and the absence of teaching quality or pedagogical innovation from the core metrics. These factors illumine the possibility of gaming by institutions with resources or on-the-ground strategies that make them appear smarter than institutions that are just trying to do what institutions are supposed to do. They also shine a light on the potential for discontent among smaller, less visible HEIs and their stakeholders.

4.2.6 Toward an Evolved, Inclusive NIRF

These findings collectively highlight the necessity for NIRF to:

a. Standardize numerical measurements to account for differences in scale and geography.

b. Transition from a perception score that is based on a few subjective, legacy-driven sources to one that aggregates the perspectives of many stakeholders (students, employers, community partners) with a vested interest in our work.
c. Advance beyond outreach with appearance as if this were a real thing, and populate hoped-for recruitment demographics, toward intelligent sufficiency ensuring real inclusion of all kinds of diversities—diversities of gender, of caste, of physical and mental disability, of economic background, and of digital accessibility.
d. Under Indian law, these are rights that must be considered when evaluating the accessibility of a digital service:
   i. Digital Accessibility: This is mostly covered under the Information Technology Act (IT Act), 2000. It is critical to ensure that the 'web contents' available through Indian domains (i.e., all websites in .in and . domains, as well as any other domains technically hosted in India) are accessible to persons with disabilities (PwD).
   ii. Linguistic Accessibility: India is a multilingual country. The Constitution of India recognizes 22 languages under the Eighth Schedule. Nevertheless, English and Hindi are the most commonly understood languages. Hence, all public/institutional digital content that is made available in any one of the five South Indian languages (Tamil, Telugu, Malayalam, Kannada, and Urdu) must be also made accessible in English and/or Hindi.
   iii. Physical Accessibility: The Rights of Persons with Disabilities Act (RPwD Act), 2016, requires not just access to digital content but also access to all buildings and public places (including those on digital platforms).

Raise the transparency of the method by which the NIRF reaches its conclusions. Integrate some appropriate international benchmarks into the process. Publish regular equity audits of the NIRF process itself to make the whole thing more transparent.

Without that reform, the NIRF is at risk of preserving and magnifying ancient unfairnesses while obscuring the accomplishments and requirements of the changed institutions—the rural, new, diverse, and differently abled—that are essential to make it possible for India to reach the national educational and societal goals.

5. DISCUSSION

This study aimed to analyze the performance scores for the National Institutional Ranking Framework (NIRF) of the five oldest Indian Institutes of Management (IIMs)—IIM Ahmedabad, IIM Bangalore, IIM Calcutta, IIM Lucknow, and IIM Indore—across five NIRF parameters from 2018 to 2022. It was found that there were statistically significant differences not only across the institutions but also across the parameters themselves, which shows that each IIM seems to have developed some distinct "strengths" and "gaps".

IIM Ahmedabad and IIM Bangalore perpetually rank highest in Teaching, Learning & Resources (TLR), Graduation Outcomes (GO), as well as Peer Perception (PR). However, when it comes to measuring Research and Professional Practice (RP) along with Outreach and Inclusivity (OI), critical discrepancies emerge, especially for IIM Indore and IIM Lucknow. These imbalances point to the necessity for an evaluation framework that not only drives performance but also ensures a more balanced, inclusive, and innovative approach.

The results reveal the historical endowments of resources and heritage reputations (PR scores) to continue driving NIRF rankings. However, the trends in OI score growth do imply incremental development in outreach and inclusion, like national policy agendas. Qualitative supplements such as evidence of advanced ICT adoption within library and pedagogy reveal the insight that digital innovation is increasingly at the heart of competitiveness for institutions, even though continuities in digital inequity to underrepresented groups remain as described by Kumar & Tiwari, 2022.

5.1 Relevance to SDG 4 and the Digital Innovation Agenda

India's commitment to Sustainable Development Goal 4 (SDG 4) — "ensure inclusive and equitable quality education and promote lifelong learning opportunities for all" — is not yet fully visible in the NIRF's methodology. This analysis points out a significant disconnect between the ranking parameters of the NIRF and the sub-goals of SDG 4, which include:

a. Accessible and affordable, high-quality education after the secondary level, including technical, vocational, and higher education.
b. Construct and improve educational facilities that are responsive to the needs of children of all genders and abilities, and that provide safe, secure, and effective spaces for learning.
c. Significantly augment the number of competent teachers available to serve in classrooms through the use of educational technology.

Some of these concerns are nominally captured through the parameter called "Outreach and Inclusivity" (OI). However, the scoring system used to measure OI is not very effective. Even if you think that the scoring system could improve and should improve, it is hard to make a case for it when digital accessibility and inclusive technology are not even scored at this level of the framework.

5.2 Measuring Language Education and Digital Pedagogy in NIRF: Current Limitations and Recommendations

A glaring limitation of the current NIRF framework is its lack of direct indicators for vital domains like language education. This is especially important for a multilingual country like India. And digital pedagogy, which is now central to educational performance, is completely ignored.

Language education—covering both regional language inclusion and support for English as a second language—has equity, employability, and accessibility as its central planks. Yet NIRF almost completely ignores it in its metrics.

Digital pedagogy, indirectly addressed in the Standards, is largely folded into the components of "Teaching, Learning & Resources," without separate indicators, or even benchmarks, to assess how well (or if) educators are using these emerging methods. Certainly its use is not shown to have any direct impact on the overall quality of the Standards components.

5.3 SWOT Analysis

SWOT analysis is a technique used to analyze the strengths, weaknesses, opportunities, and threats of a company or organization. The same technique can be applied to the Indian Institutes of Management (IIMs) to compare their relative strengths and weaknesses. The figure gives a comparison of IIM Ahmedabad, IIM Bangalore, IIM Calcutta, IIM Indore, and IIM Lucknow through SWOT analysis.

Figures 8, 9, 10,11, and 12 exhibit the SWOT Analysis for the five IIMs considered in the study – IIM C, A, B, L, and I respectively.

In conclusion, all five IIMs are considered to be among the best business schools in India, with their unique strengths and weaknesses.

5.3.1 Porters Five Forces Model Analysis

Figure 13 shows Porter's five forces model. It is observed that the while the Threat of New Market Entrants, Bargaining Power of Suppliers, and Bargaining Power of Buyers is low for all the five IIMs considered in the study, the Threat of Substitutes is found to be medium and the Competitive Rivalry high.

5.3.2 Resource-Based View

The Resource-Based View (RBV) of the five Indian Institutes of Management (IIMs) can be compared in terms of the resources available to them. IIM Ahmedabad is known for its large alumni network and extensive research and publications, while IIM Bangalore has a strong reputation for its faculty and research activities. IIM Calcutta is renowned for its world-class facilities and its focus on international students. IIM Indore has a strong focus on research and innovation, and a strong student culture. Finally, IIM Lucknow offers a wide range of courses and is well-known for its industry-academia collaborations. All five IIMs are well-regarded in terms of the resources they bring to the table, and as such they can be compared in terms of the RBV.

5.3.3 Industry Life Cycle

IIM Ahmedabad has a strong focus on research and analytics, allowing students to build strong industry relationships with both domestic and international businesses. It has an established alumni network in the industry, giving students access to an extensive knowledge base and contacts.

IIM Bangalore has a robust placement program and a strong alumni network that provides excellent support for students in their career progression. It has a wide range of programs to suit different industry needs and offers students the opportunity to explore various industries.

IIM Calcutta is highly respected in the industry and is known for its rigorous curriculum and research-oriented approach. It is one of the oldest IIMs, and its alumni are well-placed in different industries.

IIM Indore is one of the premier IIMs and has a strong focus on industry-tailored courses. It boasts a strong alumni network and its students have gone on to become successful professionals in the industry.

IIM Lucknow is one of the newest IIMs and has the advantage of being able to provide students with a more contemporary approach to industry learning. It has some of the best faculty and resources, and its graduates have been well-placed in different sectors.

5.3.4 Value Chain Analysis

Value chain analysis is a technique used to analyze the various activities that a company performs to create and deliver value to its customers. The same technique can be applied to business schools, such as the Indian Institutes of Management (IIMs), to compare their relative strengths and weaknesses. Listed below is a comparison of IIM Ahmedabad, IIM Bangalore, IIM Calcutta, IIM Indore, and IIM Lucknow through value chain analysis:

Primary Activities:

Inbound Logistics: All five IIMs have strong inbound logistics in terms of providing high-quality infrastructure and facilities for students, including libraries, computer labs, and hostels. However, IIM Ahmedabad is considered to have a slight edge in terms of the quality of its infrastructure and facilities.
Operations: In terms of operations, all five IIMs have strong faculties with a mix of experienced academic and industry professionals. However, IIM Ahmedabad is considered to have a more rigorous academic curriculum, while IIM Bangalore is known for its emphasis on practical, industry-oriented education.
Outbound Logistics: All five IIMs have strong networks with top companies, which helps them place their students in well-paying jobs after graduation. However, IIM Ahmedabad and IIM Calcutta are considered to have the strongest alumni networks, which can provide valuable career opportunities and support to their students.

Support Activities:

Procurement: All five IIMs have strong relationships with leading companies and organizations, which allows them to procure high-quality resources and facilities for their students.
Technology Development: All five IIMs invest heavily in technology to enhance the learning experience for their students. IIM Bangalore is considered to have a slight edge in this area, with a strong emphasis on cutting-edge technology and innovation.
Marketing and Sales: All five IIMs have strong brand recognition and reputation, which helps them attract top students from around the country. IIM Ahmedabad is considered to have the strongest brand, while IIM Lucknow is known for its strong outreach to students from non-metro cities.
Human Resource Management: All five IIMs have strong human resource management practices, with a focus on attracting, retaining, and developing top talent.

IIM Bangalore also has a strong emphasis on value chain analysis, with its flagship course, the Post Graduate Program in Management (MBA). It also has specialized courses in value chain analysis such as the Value Chain and Business Model Design course, and the Advanced Business Analytics course. The institute also has a dedicated Value Chain Research Centre that promotes research and development in the field.

IIM Calcutta offers a two-year Post Graduate Program in Management (MBA) with a strong focus on value chain analysis. The institute also offers courses in supply chain management and operations management. It also has a dedicated Value Chain Management Club that promotes research and development in the field.

IIM Indore offers several specialized courses in value chain analysis such as the Value Chain and Business Model Design course, and the Advanced Business Analytics course. It also has a dedicated Value Chain Centre that promotes research and development in the field.

Overall, each of the IIMs performs differently in terms of value chain analysis. Each of the IIMs also has its unique specialization. Generally speaking, IIM Ahmedabad is considered to be the best in the field, followed closely by IIM Bangalore and IIM Calcutta. IIM Indore and IIM Lucknow are also highly rated but may not offer the same level of expertise in value chain analysis as the top three.

In conclusion, all five IIMs are considered to be among the best business schools in India, with their unique strengths and characteristics. IIM Ahmedabad is considered to be one of the top business schools in India and abroad. It has a strong emphasis on value chain analysis, including its flagship course, the PGP in Management (MBA). The institute offers specialized courses in value chain analysis such as the Value Chain and Business Model Design course. It also has strong research programs in areas such as supply chain management, pricing, competitive strategy, and business process re-engineering.

5.4 IIM-Specific Recommendations

From the performance trends and qualitative insights gained, we propose the following institution-specific recommendations:

a. IIM Ahmedabad: Use its stellar performance and research backbone to record and write up best practices in digital pedagogy and multilingual education, and serve as a model for other institutions to follow.
b. IIM Bangalore: Broaden its ICT skills and capacities and set up a waist-high center for digital equity and inclusive education. This is going to be similar to—actually, it's going to grow out of—a service we're already providing called Pedagogy for the Digital Age. And the focus of this center, which we're in the process of setting up right now, will be on serving three populations that are underrepresented not only in higher education but also in the workforce: women, people with disabilities, and people who have linguistic challenges.
c. IIM Calcutta: Establish reporting systems for inclusive educational practices and accessibility assessments, with a special focus on digital platforms and resources. Prioritize investments in ICT infrastructure to develop and maintain remote learning and language support tools for underrepresented regions.

d. Indian Institute of Management, Lucknow: Develop and put into action multilingual, ICT-based community engagement programs to increase regional inclusion and digital readiness of students from diverse backgrounds.

5.5 Recommendations for Policymakers and NIRF Authorities

We suggest the following reforms to make NIRF more closely aligned with India's NEP 2020 and SDG 4:.

a. In future versions of the NIRF framework, clearly state that they are incorporating digital education, digital access, and language education.
b. Create sub-parameters for "Teaching, Learning, and Resources" that are specific to the online/blended course delivery context. These should reflect, at a minimum, the following elements:
   i.) LMS Usage
   ii.) Faculty Digital Readiness
   iii.) Student Access to Devices/Internet

Data on the inclusivity of digital infrastructure is critical. This means not just constructing the digital world but also ensuring that it is useful to everyone. For instance, screen readers have to read in a certain way for the user to understand as fully as one with perfect vision would. This means that some accessibility ratings are better than others because they are more attuned to the way humans cognate. Multilingual support is another way of including people in the digital space. If your language is not among the handful that most tech companies use, you are, to all intents and purposes, left out of the conversation.

Motivate organizations to perform digital and language accessibility assessments, and include the outcomes in their yearly NIRF filings.

Publish equity dashboards linked to NIRF, with disaggregated data on gender, caste, disability, and use of language in pedagogy and research.

At least one NIRF parameter must directly align with the SDG 4 indicators that are proposed under India's Voluntary National Review framework.

5.6 Implications for Management Education

This research offers a timely and relevant critique of how national rankings influence what institutions do. The current NIRF framework, while useful, needs significant and serious methodological improvement to tap into the sorts of intangible, equity-oriented, and ICT-advantaged dimensions needed to assess institutions—and particularly the quality of their educational offerings—today. If this is not done, then it is certainly possible that the NIRF will reinforce old advantages while failing to recognize innovative institutions that are emerging and that are increasingly using digital technologies in all sorts of interesting and powerful ways.

As leading public institutions, the IIMs can take the helm and steer ICT-based and linguistically inclusive pedagogy toward the open sea of mainstream education. They can document their efforts in this regard with the kind of transparency that breeds trust and informs both national and global rankings.

6. LIMITATIONS OF THE STUDY

The major limitations of the study are listed below:

- The study was limited to the oldest 5 Indian Institutes of Management and NIRF framework during the period 2018-2022.
- The study relied on the NIRF rankings data, which may have some biases and limitations in the methodology.
- The study was based on quantitative research, which may not capture the full picture and nuances of the subject.
- The sample size was small and may not be representative of the entire population.

7. FUTURE SCOPE OF THE STUDY

The future scope of the study is listed below:

- The study could be expanded to include more institutions and a larger sample size to increase the representativeness of the results.
- The study could be replicated using different ranking systems and methodologies to validate the results.
- The study could be extended to include qualitative research methods to complement the quantitative results and provide a more in-depth understanding of the subject.
- The study could also explore other factors that may impact the NIRF scores, such as governance, funding, and academic quality.
- Further research could also be conducted to compare the results of this study with similar studies conducted in other countries.

Only the five main parameters of Teaching, Learning, and Resources (TLR), Research and Professional Practices (RP), Graduation Outcomes (GO), Outreach and Inclusivity (OI), and Perception (PR) have been considered in the current study. The sub-parameters under each of the 5 main parameters as outlined in Table 1 may be considered in future studies.

Five years (2018-2022) of data have been considered in the current study. Future studies may expand the time scope beyond 5 years as more NIRF scores get released over the years.

Further, correlation among different parameters and factor analysis may be considered in future studies.

Comparing and contrasting NIRF performance, coupled with striking a balance among the parameters /indicators considered in other globally recognized rankings such as the Times Higher Education (THE) and Quacquarelli Symonds (QS) is another area of research. It shall also be interesting from a research perspective to assess whether the desired outcome is being correctly measured using a correct valid reliable Scale and by correct engagement to measure performance: various stakeholders' perceptions, attitudes, and behavior may be studied in the future.

The impact of online teaching that gained much prominence during the Covid Corona-19 period, MOOCs, quality and access in terms of the digital divide, invitation to foreign universities, and autonomy of teachers amidst the new National Education Policy (NEP-2020) are some of the areas that need further studies.

In NIRF, the weight and sum method is used to calculate the total scores of indicators in the NIRF scores, which are then rated by the institutes. This method assumes that each indicator contributes independently to the NIRF score in the prescribed proportions, however, this assumption is dubious because most indicators have a strong tendency to correlate with one another (Yadav et al., 2022). This points to a multi-collinearity issue that renders some indicators redundant and renders other indications non-contributing because they have a very small impact on the NIRF score. Further, few studies have presented fuzzy rule-based inference systems to establish the precise value of the criteria perception since it is a qualitative criterion and cannot be modeled by classical mathematics (Srinivasan et al., 2020).

To summarize, the present study aimed to investigate the significant difference in NIRF scores of 5 NIRF parameters and the 5 oldest Indian Institutes of Management (IIMs) based on NIRF Rankings 2022. The study utilized a quantitative approach and factorial design with a judgment sample of 5 oldest IIMs (IIM C, IIM A, IIM B, IIM L, and IIM I) from the top 100 Management Education Institutions of India.

The results showed that there was a significant difference in NIRF scores between the 5 NIRF parameters and the 5 oldest IIMs, with the TLR parameter having the highest average NIRF score and the GO parameter having the lowest. Among the 5 oldest IIMs, IIM Bangalore had the highest average NIRF score while IIM Lucknow had the lowest. The results can be used to improve the quality of teaching, learning, and resources and optimize resource utilization in terms of NIRF parameters and IIMs.

In terms of SWOT analysis, all five IIMs have their unique strengths and weaknesses. IIM Ahmedabad has a large alumni network and extensive research and publications, IIM Bangalore has a strong reputation for its faculty and research activities, IIM Calcutta is renowned for its world-class facilities and focus on international students, IIM Indore has a strong focus on research and innovation, and IIM Lucknow offers a well-rounded education experience. The Resource-Based View (RBV) comparison of the five IIMs showed differences in their available resources.

In conclusion, the results of the study provide valuable insights into the NIRF scores and strengths and weaknesses of the 5 oldest IIMs in India and can be used to improve the quality of management education in India.

Based on the above discussion, the potential areas of improvement and recommendations are such: As more data over the next years becomes available, the study could consider more recent NIRF Rankings (beyond 2022) to provide a more updated picture of the NIRF scores of the IIMs. The sample size of 5 IIMs could be expanded to include more IIMs and further other management education institutions to provide a more comprehensive analysis. Future studies could have considered other factors affecting NIRF scores, such as funding, infrastructure, and student demographics, to provide a more in-depth analysis. Future studies could also include more subjective data, such as student and faculty surveys, to provide a more well-rounded analysis. Further, future studies could include a comparison of the IIMs with other management education institutions in India and internationally, to provide a more comprehensive analysis of their competitive position.

8. RECOMMENDATIONS

Based on the results of the study, the following are some areas of improvement that can be suggested for each of the five Indian Institutes of Management (IIMs):

IIM A: Though IIM A had consistent performance in terms of NIRF scores across all parameters, it can still focus on improving its scores in Outreach and Inclusivity (OI). It can work on enhancing its outreach efforts and promoting inclusivity in its programs and culture.

IIM B: IIM B performed consistently well in NIRF scores across all parameters, but it can still focus on improving its scores in Outreach and Inclusivity (OI). It can strive to increase diversity in its student population and promote equal opportunities for all.

IIM C: Though IIM C had fluctuations in its NIRF scores over the years, it performed well in Teaching, Learning, and Resources (TLR) and Graduation Outcomes

(GO). It can focus on improving its scores in Research and Professional Practice (RP) and Outreach and Inclusivity (OI) by enhancing its research efforts and promoting diversity and inclusivity in its programs and culture.

IIM L: IIM L had lower scores in all parameters compared to the other IIMs but showed improvement in RP and GO over the years. It can continue to work on improving its scores in TLR, OI, and PR by enhancing its teaching and learning resources, promoting diversity and inclusivity, and increasing its visibility and reputation among peers.

IIM I: IIM I had relatively lower scores in all parameters but showed improvement in TLR, RP, and GO over the years. It can focus on improving its scores in OI and PR by promoting diversity and inclusivity in its programs and culture and increasing its visibility and reputation among peers.

Additionally, all five IIMs can focus on improving their infrastructure and facilities to provide better learning experiences for students and work on increasing their collaborations with industry and other institutions to enhance the practical relevance of their programs.

9. CONCLUSION

In conclusion, the study of the five Indian Institutes of Management (IIMs) reveals a rich and diverse landscape of management education in India. Each of the five IIMs has made a significant contribution to the field of management education and has left an indelible mark in the history of management education in India. The Indian higher education system has been impacted by colonial practices and has resulted in being isolated in the global higher education ranking system. Despite the introduction of the National Institutional Ranking Framework (NIRF) in response to the issue of policy neglect, only the top 100 universities are permitted to enter the Indian market according to the National Education Policy 2020. The 5 oldest Indian Institutes of Management (IIMs) have performed well in certain aspects but have room for improvement in areas like research, professional practice, outreach, and inclusivity. Furthermore, the ranking and accreditation systems are heavily influenced by public opinion, with private universities performing well in research but still having a long way to go to match the performance levels of established nationally-funded institutions. The ongoing emphasis on rankings and accreditations may impact institutions' and teachers' autonomy and the ongoing involvement in elaborate documentation may take priority over teaching. The lack of social diversity in the faculty body of IIMs is also a major concern that needs to be addressed.

The study found that each of the five IIMs has a unique set of strengths, weaknesses, and challenges. For instance, IIM Ahmedabad is known for its rigorous academic curriculum, while IIM Bangalore is recognized for its cutting-edge research and innovation. Similarly, IIM Calcutta is renowned for its strong tradition of academic excellence, while IIM Lucknow is praised for its strong industry connections. Finally, IIM Indore is known for its innovative pedagogy and its focus on building the leadership capabilities of its students.

Despite these unique strengths, there are certain areas that each of the five IIMs can improve upon. For instance, while each of the five IIMs is a leader in its own right, there is room for improvement when it comes to creating a more inclusive and diverse learning environment. This includes making the institutes more accessible to a wider range of students and taking steps to ensure that all students, regardless of their backgrounds, feel valued and supported.

Moreover, there is also a need for the five IIMs to continue to evolve and adapt to the changing needs of the business world. This includes incorporating new technologies, methodologies, and best practices into the curriculum, and ensuring that students are equipped with the skills and knowledge needed to thrive in an ever-changing global economy.

The study has some limitations, including the small sample size and the limited scope of the NIRF framework. Despite these limitations, the study provides valuable insights and contributes to the understanding of the NIRF Scores and their impact on management education in India. Further research can expand on these findings, including increasing the sample size, exploring the role of other factors affecting NIRF Scores, and examining the effects of NIRF Scores on other outcomes, such as student satisfaction and employability.

In conclusion, the five IIMs in India have a rich and storied history and have made a significant impact on the field of management education. They are leaders in their own right and continue to set the standard for management education in India. However, there is always room for improvement, and the five IIMs should continue to strive towards excellence and evolve and adapt to the changing needs of the business world. Further, the study aimed to evaluate the difference in NIRF Scores between 5 NIRF Parameters, between the oldest 5 IIMs, and between different combinations of NIRF Parameters and IIM. The results of the study can inform stakeholders in higher education, such as policymakers, administrators, and faculty, on the strengths and weaknesses of different aspects of management education in India. By highlighting these differences, the study provides important insights for improving management education and contributing to the development of the higher education sector in India.

REFERENCES

Altbach, P. G. (2014). India's higher education challenges. *Asia Pacific Education Review, 15*(4), 503–510. DOI: 10.1007/s12564-014-9335-8

Anbalagan, M., & Balasubramani, J. (2021). An analysis of NIRF ranked Indian Institute of Technology (IITs) profiles: With special reference to Indian Research Information Network System (IRINS). *Library Philosophy and Practice*, Article 6042.

Anbalagan, M., & Tamizhchelvan, M. T. (2021). Ranking of Indian institutions in global and Indian ranking system: A comparative study. *Library Philosophy and Practice*, Article 5069.

Banshal, S. K., Singh, V. K., & Mayr, P. (2019). Comparing research performance of private universities in India with IITs, central universities, and NITs. *Current Science, 116*(8), 1308–1314. DOI: 10.18520/cs/v116/i8/1304-1313

Çakır, M. P., Acartürk, C., Alaşehir, O., & Alkan, O. (2015). A comparative analysis of global and national university ranking systems. *Scientometrics, 103*(3), 813–848. DOI: 10.1007/s11192-015-1586-6

Chakraborty, K., Upadhyay, N., & Upadhyay, S. R. (2021). Explored publication pattern of the top twenty NIRF-2020 ranked Indian institutions: An evaluative study. *Library Philosophy and Practice*, Article 5230.

Chattopadhyay, S. (2020). National Education Policy, 2020. *Economic and Political Weekly, 55*(46), 23–25.

Chugh, K. L., Alekhya, N., & Prabhu Kishore, N. (2017). Quality research publications – A key differentiator in India rankings 2017. *International Journal of Mechanical Engineering and Technology, 8*(6), 117–124.

Chugh, K. L., Alekhya, N., Prabhu Kishore, N., & Shekar, K. (2018). Analysis of national institutional ranking framework: Journey so far. In *Proceedings of the 6th IEEE International Conference on MOOCs, Innovation and Technology in Education (MITE 2018)* (pp. 115–119). IEEE. DOI: 10.1109/MITE.2018.8747105

Dadhe, P. P., & Dubey, M. N. (2021). Ranking and research trend: A comparative study of research output of top ten NIRF ranked engineering institutions of India based on scientometric indicators. *Library Philosophy and Practice*, Article 5314.

Dam, M., Majumder, D., Bhattacharjee, R., & Santra, S. S. (2021). Performance measurement model for ranking of educational institutes: A fuzzy reasoning approach. *Journal of Physics: Conference Series*, *1797*(1), 012012. DOI: 10.1088/1742-6596/1797/1/012012

Dar, T. H., Jeelani, S. G. M., Mir, H. A., & Ganaie, S. A. (2017). Use of ICT in IIT and IIM libraries of India. *International Journal of Library and Information Science*, *6*(1), 1–18. https://www.iaeme.com/IJLIS/issues.asp?JType=IJLIS&VType=6&IType=1

Deka, P., & Sarmah, M. (2021). Impact of NIRF ranking on research publications: A study with special reference to North-East Indian universities. *Library Philosophy and Practice*, Article 5233.

Gangopadhyay, S. (2020). Changes in web content in first 20 NIRF ranking institutes during 2010–19: An analysis. *Library Philosophy and Practice*, Article 4414.

Gangopadhyay, S., & Mukherjee, B. (2021). Research productivity of first ten NIRF ranking academic institutes in India during 2015–19: A scientometric analysis. *Library Philosophy and Practice*, Article 5261.

Gnanasekaran, D., & Rajkumar, T. (2022). Research productivity and altmetrics of NIRF top ranked medical institutions. *Annals of Library and Information Studies*, *69*(2), 120–128.

Joshi, S., & Malgan, D. (2017). Missing scholars: Social exclusion at the Indian Institutes of Management. *IIM Bangalore Research Paper*, (554).

Kumar, A., & Tiwari, P. K. (2022). Digital accessibility for persons with disabilities: A mixed method study of websites of 15-top ranked universities of India. *Academia: Social Sciences*, *29*, 68–82.

Malish, C. M. (2020). Measuring access to higher education. *Economic and Political Weekly*, *55*(40), 55–61.

Marisha. (2021). Analysing the stability of India rankings. *Current Science, 120*(7), 1144–1151.

Mukhopadhyay, M., & Parhar, M. (2014). ICT in Indian higher education administration and management. In R. Huang, Kinshuk, & J. Price (Eds.), *ICT in education in global context* (pp. 191–208). Springer. DOI: 10.1007/978-3-662-43927-2_15

Mukhopadhyay, P., Tapaswi, M. P., Sudarsan, P. K., & Sudarsan, K. (2018). Assessing the quality of higher education institutions in India. *Current Science*, *114*(6), 1167–1173. DOI: 10.18520/cs/v114/i06/1167-1173

Nassa, A. K., Arora, J., Singh, P., Joorel, J. P., Solanki, H., Kumar, A., & Trivedi, K. (2021). Five years of India rankings and its impact on performance parameters of engineering educational institutions in India. Pt. 1: Teaching, learning and resources, graduate outcome, outreach and inclusivity and perception. *DESIDOC Journal of Library and Information Technology*, *41*(1), 17–26. DOI: 10.14429/djlit.41.1.16675

Parameswaran, A. N., Hebbale, A. M., Vidya, S. M., & Pakkala, T. P. M. (2020). Impact of research performance and perception on ranking of universities: A study based on NIRF 2019. *Journal of Engineering Education Transformations*, *34*(1), 85–92. DOI: 10.16920/jeet/2020/v34i1/150463

Patel, I. G., Paul, S., Khandwalla, P. N., Bose, A., Murthy, K. R. S., Vittal, N., Krishnan, R. T., Jain, A. K., & Gupta, A. K. (2004). Social context of management education: Institution building experiences at IIMs. *Vikalpa*, *29*(2), 85–110. DOI: 10.1177/0256090920040208

Pathak, P., & Pal, D. A. E-resource utilization in IIMs libraries: Insights from faculties and students' surveys.

Pavel, A. P. (2015). Global university rankings: A comparative analysis. *Procedia Economics and Finance*, *26*, 54–63. DOI: 10.1016/S2212-5671(15)00838-2

Peters, M. A. (2017). Global university rankings: Metrics, performance, governance. *Educational Philosophy and Theory*, *51*(1), 5–13. DOI: 10.1080/00131857.2017.1381472

Pradhan, P., Trivedi, K., & Singh, P. (2021). Five years of India rankings (2016–2020): An evolutionary study. *DESIDOC Journal of Library and Information Technology*, *41*(1), 42–48. DOI: 10.14429/djlit.41.1.16671

Prathap, G. (2019). Construct validity maps and the NIRF 2019 ranking of colleges. *Current Science*, *117*(6), 1079–1083. DOI: 10.18520/cs/v117/i6/1079-1083

Sheeja, N. K., Mathew, S., & Cherukodan, S. (2018). Impact of scholarly output on university ranking. *Global Knowledge, Memory and Communication*, *67*(8/9), 595–611.

Shivaram, B. S., Uma, M., & Sahu, S. R. (2022). A study of research publications of top NIRF ranked engineering institutions in Karnataka. *Annals of Library and Information Studies*, *69*(1), 44–50.

Singh, A., & Rao, V. R. (2024). Unpacking inconsistencies in the NIRF rankings. *Current Science*, *126*(11), 1473–1479. DOI: 10.18520/cs/v126/i11/1321-1324

Singh, S., & Singh, A. (2021). Importance of perception as a parameter in university rankings: A critical evaluation. *Prabandhan: Indian Journal of Management, 14*(11), 25–40. DOI: 10.17010/pijom/2021/v14i11/166979

Srimathi, H., & Krishnamoorthy, A. (2020). Review on NIRF. *Journal of Critical Reviews, 7*(4), 259–262.

Srinivasan, R., Jain, V., & Dharmaraja, S. (2020). Perception based performance analysis of higher education institutions: A soft computing approach. *Soft Computing, 24*(1), 513–521. DOI: 10.1007/s00500-019-03931-6

Vasudevan, N. (2020). Development of a common framework for outcome-based accreditation and rankings. *Procedia Computer Science, 172*, 270–276. DOI: 10.1016/j.procs.2020.05.043

APPENDIX

Figure 1. Literature review process

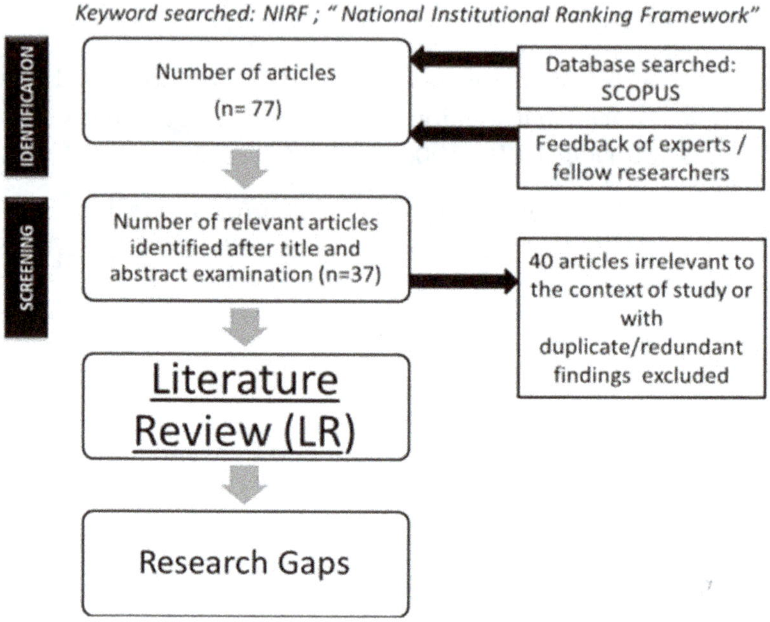

Figure 2. Year-wise number of documents published during 2017-05 August 2022

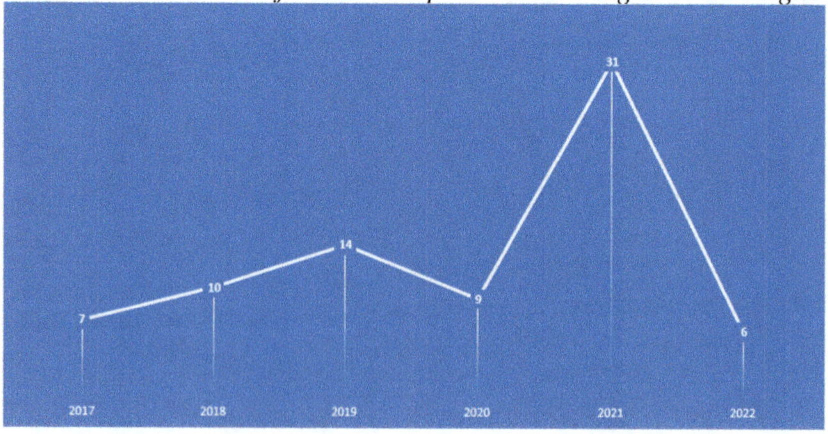

Figure 3. Country-wise number of documents published during 2017-05 August 2022

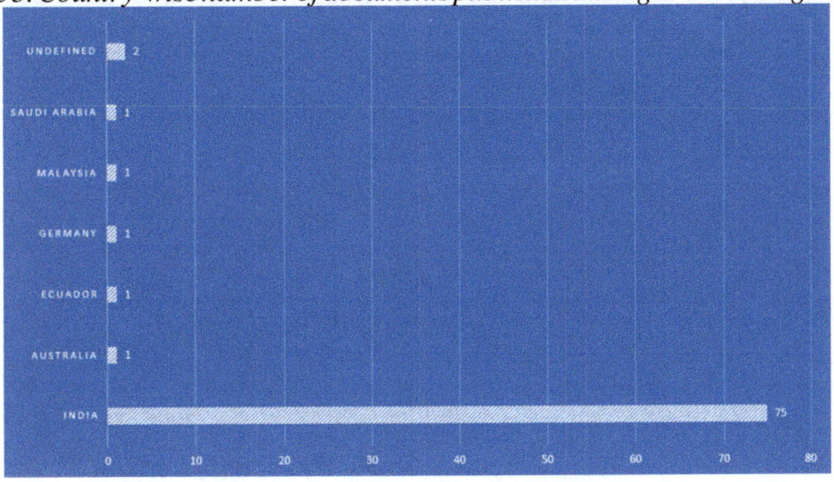

Figure 4. Document type-wise number of documents published during 2017-05 August 2022

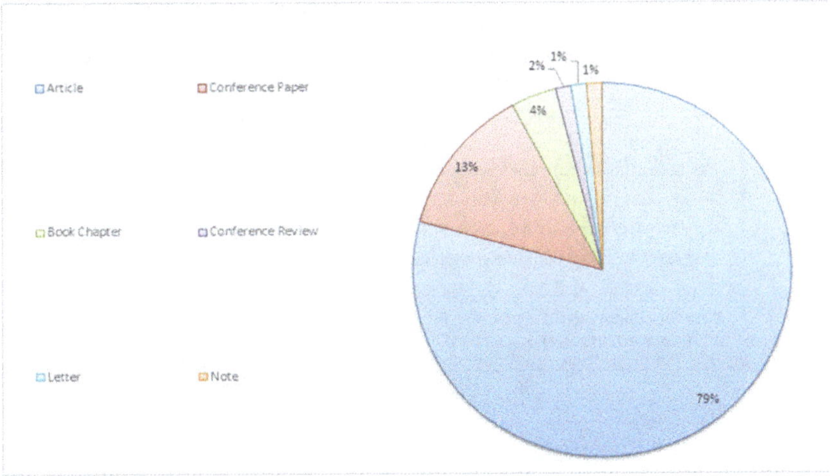

Figure 5. Subject area-wise number of documents published during 2017-05 August 2022

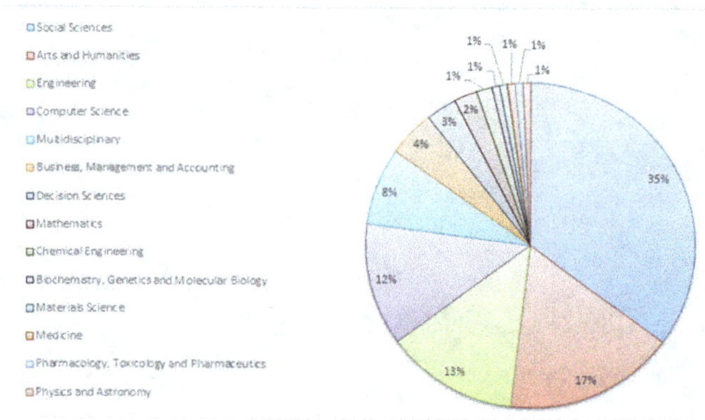

Figure 6. Research Design

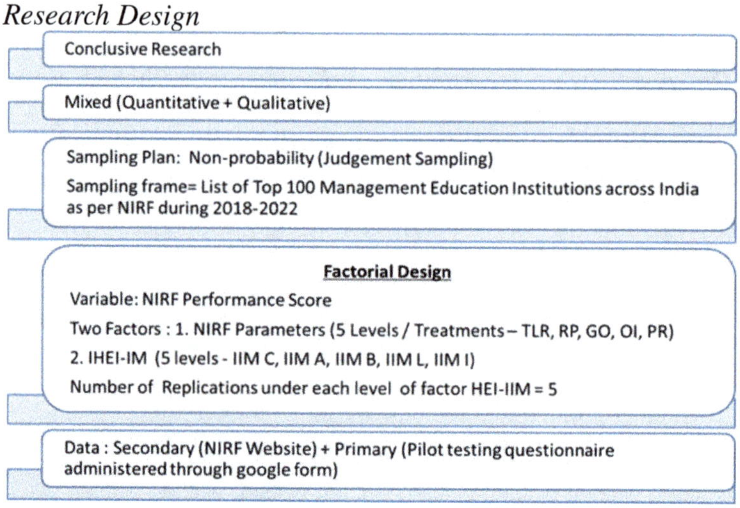

Figure 7. IIM, C, A, B, L, I, NIRF Scores 2028-22

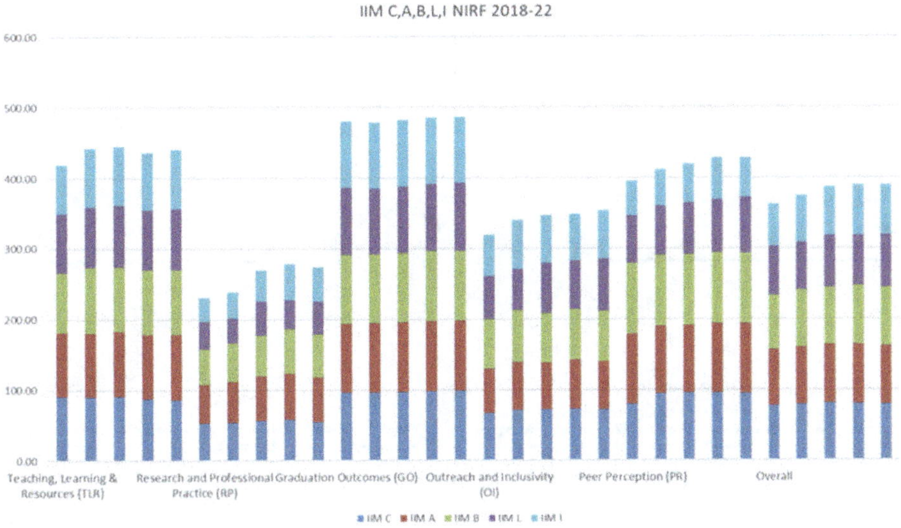

Figure 8. SWOT Analysis of IIM C

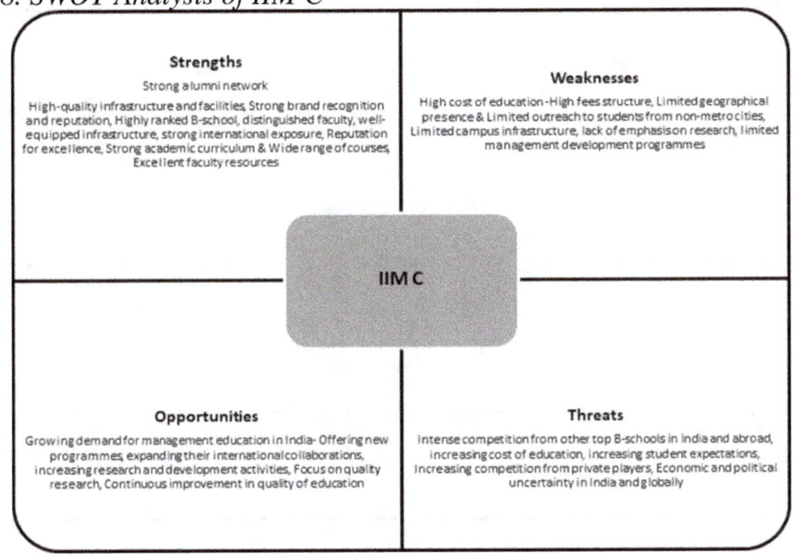

Figure 9. SWOT Analysis of IIM A

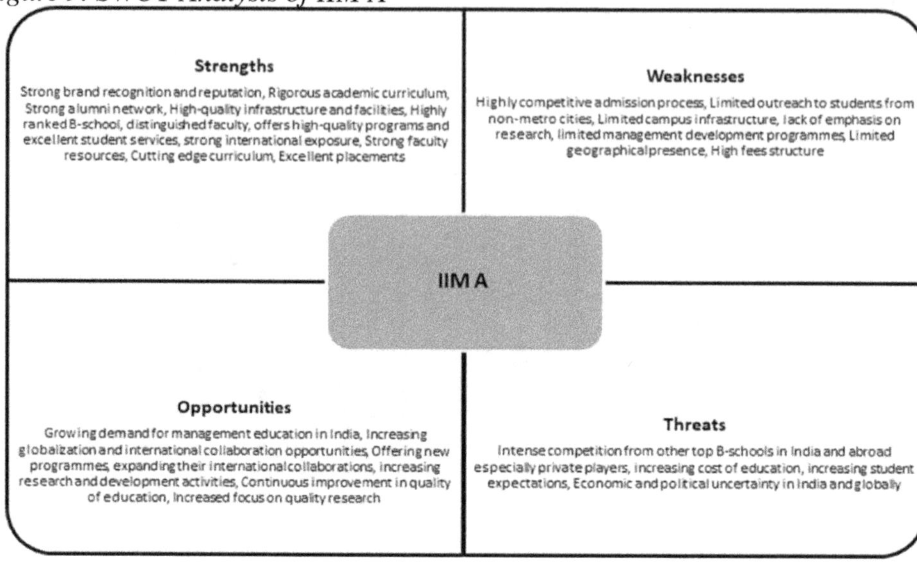

Figure 10. SWOT Analysis of IIM B

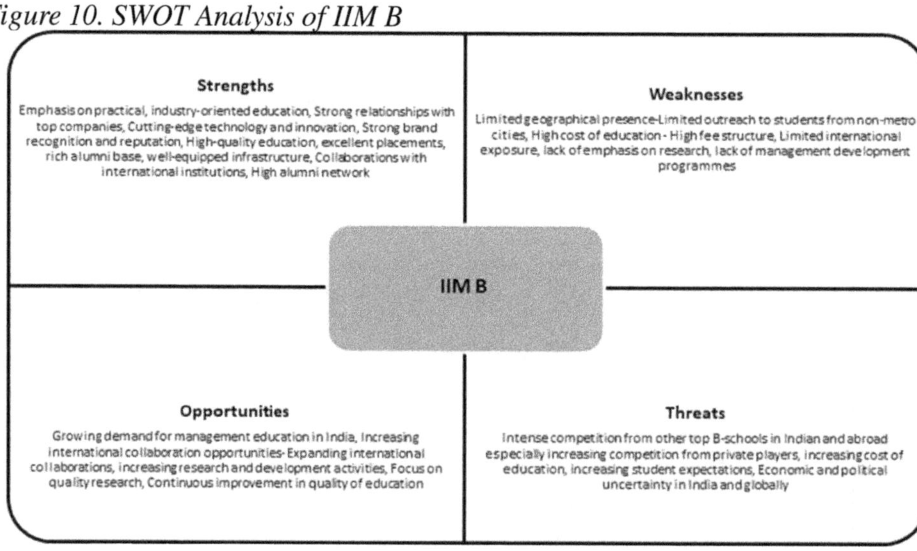

Figure 11. SWOT Analysis of IIM L

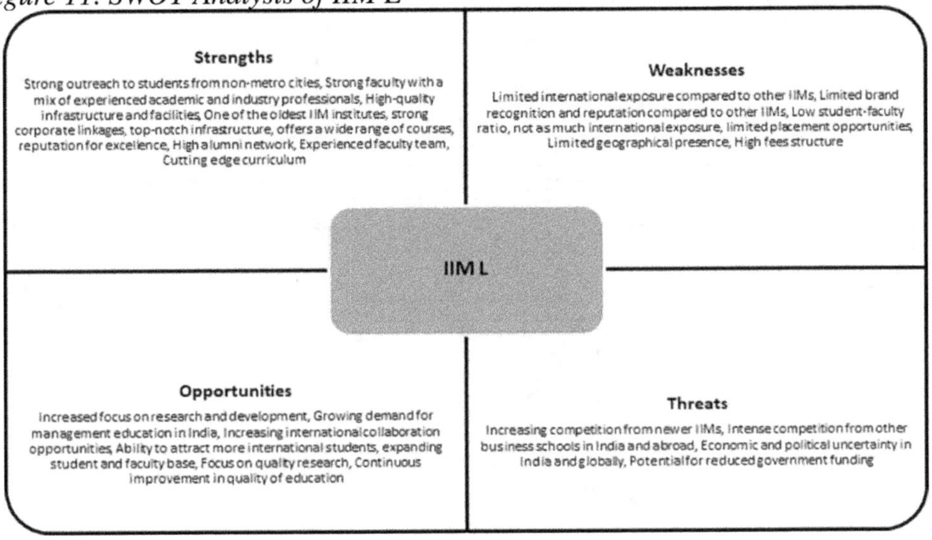

Figure 12. SWOT Analysis of IIM I

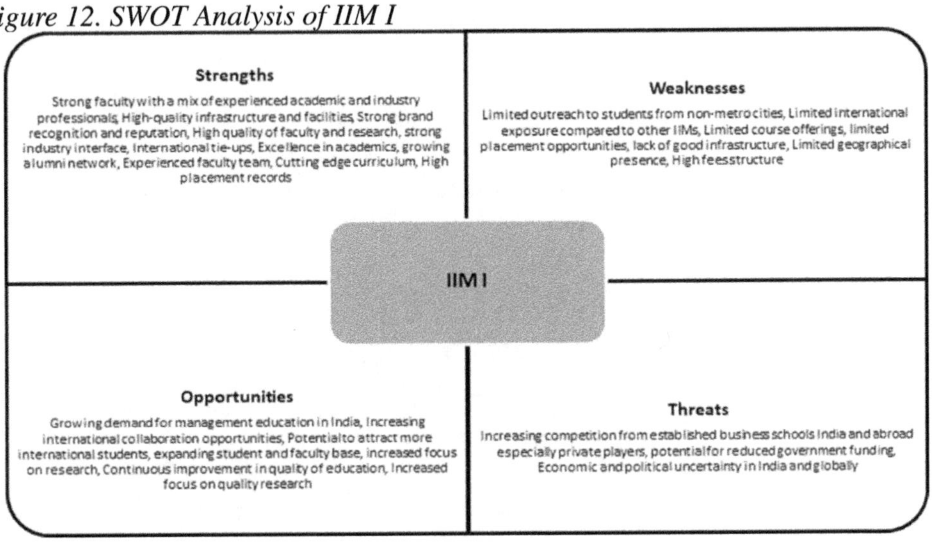

Figure 13. Porter's Five Forces of Competitive Position

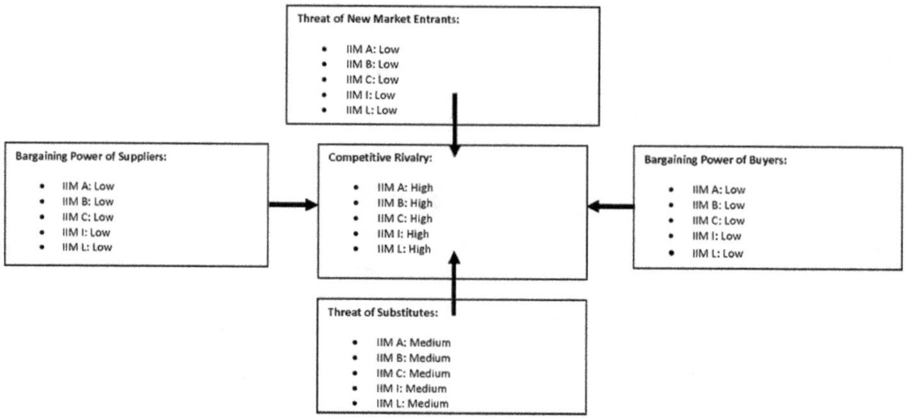

Chapter 8
Integrating ICTs to Deliver Quality EFL Education in a Spanish Secondary Education Classroom

Isabel María García Conesa
https://orcid.org/0000-0001-7005-2509
Centro Universitario de la Defensa de San Javier, Spain

ABSTRACT

The Internet is increasingly integral part of our pupils' lives. From birth, children are exposed to technological advances, making technology a natural element of their daily life. Therefore, Information and Communication Technologies (hereinafter ICT) need to be present in the classroom, but in a thoughtful and coherent manner. ICTs have introduced significant changes in business practices, production processes, administration, ways of working, or employee training. However, in the education system, on the other hand, there has been little to no transformation in how education is managed, how young people learn, or in the methodologies employed in teaching. This chapter focuses on analysing the use of social networking and other web applications as effective tools for the improvement of English teaching in different fields. This research aims to formalise experiences and provide a practical reflection on how specific ICT tools can be used to drive changes in students' learning approaches, aligning with the objectives of SDG4.

DOI: 10.4018/979-8-3373-0801-2.ch008

INTRODUCTION

The Internet is present in many areas of our pupils' lives. Technological advances are available to children from birth, making it a natural part of their lives and a positive support to their development. But what about the school? Does the use of ICT extend to the classroom, or does it remain hermetic to these changes? Is the use of social networks crucified? Information and Communication Technologies (ICTs) need to be present in the classroom, but in a coherent way to ensure quality education according to SDG 4 (Rico Gómez & Ponce Gea, 2022).

The birth of the knowledge society has brought significant changes in all areas of our society: economic, political, social, etc. However, in the field of education, where changes tend to be slow and delayed, it is necessary to reflect on the role of the school in the face of the new social and labour reality (Villacres Arias et al., 2020).

Although ICTs have introduced changes in business practices, in the education system there have been no changes in the way education is administered, in the way young people learn, or in the methodologies used. In this new context, the focus has shifted from the teacher, as the possessor of knowledge, to the student as the centre of the learning process. This does not detract from the fact that teachers are the central element in this new learning environment. In fact, teachers are evolving into 'creators of learning situations' (Ley Leyva. 2022).

One thing is certain, young people are more awake and more proficient and this is reflected in the ease and intuition with which they use the new technologies. Many of us who are part of the field of education still maintain a respectful and, in many cases, expectant attitude towards the new technologies.

Perhaps we are waiting to see what ICTs, which are constantly changing, will lead to. But it may be that the failure to introduce new technologies in classroom methodologies is precisely the solution to integrate them. With the school 2.0 programme, computers are increasingly present in classrooms and their use concerns all subjects. It is therefore necessary to change the methodologies used by teachers to adapt to the new technological resources now available in the classroom (Reis Jorge et al., 2020).

Projects such as EducaRed, developed at the national level in Spain, are based on the premise that the integration of ICTs cannot be simplified to the fact of equipping schools with technology. Instead, it must be accompanied by the necessary continuous training. The labour market seeks multi-skilled workers who are creative, who run the risk of making mistakes by trying to innovate. ICTs can help to re-evolve an education system that punishes error and rewards only the right answer.

Therefore, the main objectives of this chapter are the following: to justify the use of new technologies in the classroom, using web tools that have been tested in the educational field and that have proven to be useful for improving educational action, and to conduct an analysis and reflection on the use of social networks as a tool for collaborative work.

THEORETICAL FRAMEWORK

We will base the research on two hypotheses that we will try to develop to reach a conclusion on the use of ICTs to facilitate teaching and promote a change in the way our students interact for the acquisition of knowledge in a collective way.

- Hypothesis 1: The United Nations developed 17 Sustainable Development Goals (SDG), one of which defines quality education as that which ensures that all young people acquire the knowledge, skills, abilities and attitudes necessary to prepare them for adult life. Education must, therefore, look at how the companies in which its students will work in the near future are adapting to these changes and seek to incorporate them into their way of working and managing knowledge.
- Hypothesis 2: Teachers need information, but, above all, training in the effective use of ICTs. The use of ICTs should not be relegated to subjects whose basic or vocational skills include digital competence. In some subjects, ICTs are at the core of the skills that the student must learn, while in others the students will rely on ICTs to acquire these skills. Teacher training on the impact that social networking sites and ICTs in general have on student learning is very important.

The Roles of the Present-Day Teacher

The teacher ceases to be the source of all knowledge and starts to act as a guide for students, providing them with the resources and tools they need to explore and develop new knowledge and skills (Romero Hermoza, 2021). Digital competencies in teachers involve the development of functional abilities necessary for conducting virtual educational activities. In light of the current context, these skills have become a technological priority, enabling educators to actively participate in digital citizenship. Within the educational sphere, and specifically in relation to teacher performance, digital competencies serve as tools that support the implementation of strategies aimed at fostering student engagement and attention.

The objective of this research was to review the theoretical foundations and frameworks surrounding teachers' digital competencies. A systematic review methodology was applied, involving the screening, selection, and analysis of 441 articles. The findings conclude that digital competencies encompass the skills required to use digital media effectively across various contexts, depending on individual capabilities. To achieve this, educators must be able to understand, navigate, and integrate virtual environments and digital tools into their professional practice.

We live in a society in which it is extremely important to know how to filter the enormous amounts of information that we receive continuously. Some authors refer to this as infoxication, or information intoxication (Di Franco, 2022). Teachers are not free from this phenomenon, but we must know how to dominate information before it dominates us.

Alarcón Hernández et al. (2020) developed the idea that the teacher's work should be focused not so much on the content, but on the learning process. Their study employed a qualitative approach and adopted a phenomenological design. A metaphor-elicitation questionnaire was administered to 168 students in the final years of their English teaching programs at Chilean universities. The analysis of the metaphorical expressions obtained was conducted using semantic content analysis. The results indicate that, although participants are aware of the challenges associated with their profession, they hold a positive view of teaching.

While the Internet has undoubtedly opened a world of information search and sharing that was unimaginable 25 years ago, many students do not know how to discern what is relevant information on the Internet to analyse it (Flores Nessi et al., 2020). This article adopts a theoretical approach to the role of the teacher-researcher, outlining various forms of knowledge and actions required to conduct research aimed at fostering social transformation. In light of the ongoing transformation of the university system in Venezuela, it is essential to strengthen the role of teachers as researchers, tutors, advisors, facilitators, and learning mediators. The methodology employed was a literature review, drawing on research papers and articles from specialized journals.

Guamán Gómez et al. (2023) aimed to analyse the role of teachers in the digital age. To this end, a review study was conducted, employing hermeneutic and analytical-synthetic methods, along with documentary review and content analysis techniques. ICTs have marked a turning point in human history. In the field of education, they have revolutionized pedagogical models, methods, media, and learning processes, prompting significant changes in the role of teachers.

However, in practice, there are still notable limitations in the integration of these technologies, many of which stem from educators' apathy or lack of adequate preparation. Among the main findings is the transformation of the teacher's role in the digital era from being the central figure in the teaching-learning process and the primary source of knowledge to becoming managers, guides, facilitators, mediators, and tutors. A constant selection is necessary to value and distinguish quality content. It is within this context that teachers must rethink their role (López Aguilar et al., 2020).

ICT Teacher Training

Teacher training is one of the essential factors in the implementation of any action involving innovation in education. The process of teachers acquiring digital competence does not happen overnight. Colás Bravo et al.'s study (2018) aimed to map the effects of the inclusion of ICT in Primary and Secondary Education within the Spanish education system from a general and comprehensive perspective.

This literature review identified a range of characteristics that define the evolution and transformations brought about by ICT at non-university educational levels. It also examined the main obstacles hindering full integration, while exploring potential changes and transformations that could facilitate such integration within the Spanish educational system. In addition, the analysis of teaching policies targeting ICT integration at the European, national, and regional levels underscored the importance of identifying and promoting best practices.

Using technology does not necessarily mean innovation. According to Vaillant (2023), more than 70% of teachers use technology in the classroom. However, this indicator must be interpreted cautiously, as the mere use of technology does not imply innovation. Vaillant's study explored teacher professional development in digital competencies within institutional and organizational frameworks, as well as through reflective practice and individual self-directed learning. Within this context, the integration of digital technologies must not be viewed in isolation or as limited to specific aspects. Instead, it should be understood as an integral component of broader educational policies.

According to López Belmonte et al. (2019), the inclusion of ICTs in schools is bringing about a change in communication that will inevitably influence the teaching-learning process. The implementation of ICT in schools is a reality that affects many teachers who, unfortunately, often lack adequate competence in its use and understanding. For this reason, the purpose of this study was to assess the impact of a project on the teaching staff of a cooperative school in the Autonomous City of Ceuta, Spain. The study employed a quasi-experimental design, in which a blended learning program on digital competence was delivered between the two testing phases. Data were collected using an ad hoc questionnaire designed to evaluate the various dimensions of digital competence, along with personal and motivational factors.

The responses were analysed using a descriptive-correlational approach. A Student's *t*-test was conducted to identify statistically significant differences between the means. Additionally, effect sizes were calculated using Cohen's *d* and biserial correlation. The results showed a substantial improvement across the different dimensions of digital competence, as well as increased teacher receptivity and motivation toward the use of ICT in the classroom. These findings underscore the importance of continued professional development in digital technologies for in-service teachers.

The transformations brought about by the society are also influencing changes in teacher education (Gómez Trigueros & Bustamante Alonso, 2023). Digital training for teachers represents one of the most significant challenges in adapting education to the demands of the 21st century. This has led to the emergence of new teaching and learning models that emphasize how digital tools are incorporated into education, considering the perspectives from which future teachers are trained, including ethical considerations and their digital competence, as well as how these requirements are addressed in classroom practice.

In this context, studies on teachers' digital competence and its reflection in teaching methodologies emerge as key drivers in adapting education to the digital skills demanded by today's society. The findings underscore the need for innovative pedagogical approaches that bring classroom practice closer to the realities of a technology-mediated world.

The competence and training of teachers in ICTs is increasingly important when it comes to facilitating effective performance of teachers in the various tasks they have to perform in their teaching activity. Mas García et al. (2023) included the development of teachers' digital competence as a key factor in the quality of contemporary education systems. This text examined the integration of technological content in initial teacher education as a foundational element of their digital training. The results reveal a limited integration of technology in teacher training programs and suggest that the guidelines established by institutional frameworks are often too broad relative to the actual digital competencies of educators.

According to Martín Párraga et al. (2022), the technologization of society has presented a significant challenge for 21st century education, which must rise to meet this challenge to provide high-quality digital literacy. These rapid technological changes affect multiple areas, including teacher professionalization, as educators face difficulties in updating their knowledge and adapting to the fast-paced evolution of digital tools.

This study focused on analysing the various existing competency frameworks that teachers must develop throughout their professional and personal trajectories. It also emphasized the importance of assessing teachers' levels of digital competence and the need to diagnose acquired digital teaching competencies using diverse instruments designed for this purpose.

Integrating ICT tools into education presents several challenges for educators. These challenges include a lack of adequate resources, like insufficient equipment and internet access, as well as limited training and knowledge on how to effectively use ICT in the classroom (Abdi et al., 2021). Additionally, some educators may face resistance to change, preferring traditional teaching methods, and may encounter technical problems or disruptions during lessons.

The major barriers are lack of genuine software, inadequate computer in the classroom, low speed internet, lack of motivation from both teacher and student side to use ICT, lack of proper training skills, unavailability of latest ICT equipment, lack of expert technical staff, or poor administrative support (Jayanthi, 2023).

A study by Habibu et al. (2022) aimed at finding out the difficulties faced by teachers in using ICT in classroom teaching-learning in technical and higher educational institutions in Uganda. The use of ICT in the classroom is very important in providing opportunities for students to learn to operate in an information age. Studying the obstacles to the use of ICT in educational institutions may assist educators to overcome these barriers and become successful technology adopters in the future.

Chi square test and weighted average using Statistical Package for Social Science (SPSS) software were used to analyse and interpret the data. The findings of this study revealed that teachers had a strong desire to integrate ICT into the teaching-learning process. The major barriers were the lack of genuine software, inadequate computer in the classroom, low speed internet, lack of motivation to use ICT, lack of proper training skills, unavailability of latest ICT equipment, lack of expert technical staff, poor administrative support, etc.

ICT in Educational Planning

Educational planning is a technical tool for decision-making, designed to facilitate the organisation of elements that guide the educational process. According to Macas Granda et al. (2021), technological literacy is a necessary prerequisite for achieving quality education for new generations, making teachers' digital technological skills indispensable. To analyse the role of teachers in digital literacy in the 21st century, a descriptive bibliographic review was conducted, employing content analysis and analytical-synthetic and hermeneutic methods.

The main findings indicated that the profile of teachers in the technological context is characterized by their ability to learn new technologies, provide personalized instruction, globalize the classroom, encourage student content creation, and digitize learning environments. Additionally, teachers perform pedagogical, methodological, research, and guidance functions through the appropriate use of ICTs. The results highlight that, to achieve digital literacy among students, teachers must first be digitally literate themselves. This necessitates ongoing development in technical, methodological, and research competencies, and continuous and cyclical professional growth and updating.

Pinto Santos and Pérez Garcías (2022) presented the results of a systematic review of studies published in high-impact journals on the development of teaching digital competence (TDC) in initial teacher training. The study employed a documentary research approach, conducting a systematic literature review of publications from 2009 to 2019 across multiple databases. The sample comprises 102 articles, which were classified using a multidimensional matrix.

One of the main findings is the significant growth in literature on TDC over the past decade, with a predominance of quantitative research methods. Additionally, 50.98% of the articles report on the application of instruments designed to assess TDC. The study concludes that teaching digital competence is a multifaceted and evolving area of research, reflecting its increasing relevance in education.

Contribution of ICTs to the English Language Classroom

With the birth of social networks and other applications, a wide range of possibilities for participation and collaboration has opened, while at the same time opening for other dangers that these social networks bring with them. Baño Lucio et al. (2023) analysed recent studies on the influence of ICT on English language learning in children, considering various factors. The aim of this analysis was to present findings from scientific publications, indexed journal articles published within the last five years, using a hermeneutic approach based on identified variables.

While technology continues to offer expanding alternatives, the authors concur that face-to-face social interaction remains essential for learning English and second languages in general. This is because in-person interaction activates various neurocognitive mechanisms, such as mirror neurons. In this dynamic, ICTs serve as supportive tools but require careful personal supervision to avoid potential negative effects.

In the current educational context, the integration of ICTs is evident, particularly in exploring how technological tools support students in learning English. Ortíz Rodríguez and Tejada Díaz (2023) employed deductive, inductive, and statistical methods, using an analytical, cross-sectional approach with a mixed methods focus. The survey was conducted using a probabilistic sampling method.

The objective of this study was to determine how the use of ICTs facilitates English language learning through teaching strategies that stimulate student engagement. The results indicated that while students were immersed in technology, their use of technological tools specifically for learning English was limited. Additionally, students demonstrated a low level of knowledge about certain technological tools for English learning, although they recognize the potential of these tools to help develop language skills.

Royero Thomas (2024) systematically analysed the literature on the use of technology as a tool for teaching English as a foreign language, with the goal of contributing to the current state of the art. The reviewed research illustrates how technological tools have been integrated into the teaching and learning processes of English across various educational contexts. The methodology employed was qualitative and documentary, involving an exhaustive review of primary and historical sources. Among the findings across the literature, motivation emerges as a key category: the use of technological tools in English instruction stimulates learners' motivation, fostering improved communication skills.

The objective is to respect each student's learning pace, not in teaching, as this approach allows students to review what they have learned in class. It should be noted that this program supports language learning rather than replacing it. Enith Moreno and Bautista Moreno (2024) presented information related to the development of a similar project aimed at creating a website to strengthen English reading and writing skills among fifth-grade students. The project was developed using a qualitative approach and the Participatory Action Research (PAR) method.

Based on these results, key areas for improvement were identified, leading to the creation of digital educational resources (RED) integrated into the website and implemented in the classroom. A follow-up diagnostic test was conducted to assess students' progress in English as a foreign language and their use of ICT for learning. The results confirmed that several factors influence language acquisition in the classroom, including teaching methodology, educational resources, and the use of technological tools in learning and assessment processes.

Although teachers acknowledge the importance of ICT, the study revealed that its implementation is often inadequate; ICT is primarily used as a support tool for lesson planning and information search rather than as an active teaching tool to facilitate English language learning. The research emphasizes the necessity of training teachers to develop competencies in integrating ICT effectively in their classes.

Aguirre Idrogo et al. (2021) aimed to determine the impact of ICT use on English text comprehension among fifth-year secondary school students at an educational institution. Employing a quantitative, applied experimental approach with a quasi-experimental design, the study involved a population of 150 students, with a sample of 60 divided into a control group and an experimental group. Non-probabilistic sampling was used, and data were collected via a survey. The instrument consisted of a 20-question knowledge test, validated through expert judgment. Results indicate that the use of ICT significantly improved the comprehension of English texts among the students.

Murillo Camacho and Rosales Sánchez (2024) examined the impact of ICT on English language learning among high school students in Ecuador. It highlighted the concept of invisible learning, emphasizing the significance of learning through play and the use of ICT as motivating and valuable tools in the classroom. Statistical findings reveal a positive correlation between ICT use and English learning outcomes, underscoring the importance of teacher language proficiency and the effective integration of ICT in instructional strategies.

The study also emphasized the beneficial effects of ICT on virtual secondary education, while identifying challenges such as the absence of clear policies and disparities in access between public and private schools. The article recommends strengthening teacher training and fostering dialogue regarding the ethical use of students' personal data within the context of educational digitization.

New technologies offer a wide variety of auditory materials that help students better understand the language and know how to use it in different situations, as well as improve their oral production through resources such as sound recording (Girón Chávez et al., 2023). On the other hand, they can use tools that help them improve their written production, such as word processors, which help users to correct and edit their own texts.

Schools 2.0

Many schools and teachers make the mistake of digitising all documents, notes, and other school material to create what is known as a graveyard of PDFs on the Internet. Their websites or blogs become mere dumping ground for brochures where there is no room for user participation (students, teachers, administrative and service staff, etc.).

According to Gil Pérez and Berlanga Fernández (2023), interactive materials play a crucial role in developing essential skills across all stages of education by providing learners with a degree of control over their learning process. However, experience shows that while most students are actively engaged in social media, only a few maintain study blogs or create interactive activities.

Their article presented theoretical and descriptive research exploring the concept of interactivity to assess the effectiveness of interactive activities in schools, particularly in the final stage of primary education. The research included fieldwork consisting of classroom observations, analysis of classroom blog usage, and interviews with students. The results offer insights into the effectiveness of these activities and support the development of proposals aimed at enhancing digital skills at this educational stage.

The state programme "School 2.0" is helping to implement ICTs in the classroom by providing them with the necessary technological resources and ensuring that the possibilities of ICTs are within the reach of students and teachers. Area Moreira et al. (2024) analysed the current state of educational policies regarding the incorporation of ICT in schools across eight regions of Spain (Andalusia, Canary Islands, Catalonia, Extremadura, Madrid, Valencia, the Basque Country, and Asturias) following the implementation of the program.

The study concluded that recent ICT policies primarily focus on integrating mobile devices into all classrooms, replacing netbooks with tablets, shifting from traditional paper textbooks to digital content platforms, and developing cloud-based resource portals. However, the absence of a coordinated, nationwide educational ICT policy or program has been observed.

Fraga Varela and Alonso Ferreiro (2021) presented the results of an investigation into teachers' perceptions of the project in Galicia. It focused on primary and secondary school teachers involved in regional initiatives stemming from the implementation of 1-to-1 policies. The objective was to capture teachers' opinions and perspectives regarding educational policies aimed at integrating ICT within this community.

The responses were analysed using IBM SPSS Statistics, with an emphasis on descriptive statistics and frequency distribution. The findings indicate a favourable attitude towards the implementation of 1-to-1 models in schools, alongside a notable level of dissatisfaction with current policies. Additionally, the results highlight significant challenges, primarily related to insufficient information and inadequate teacher training.

Intriago Cedeño (2019) examined the use of ICTs and their impact on academic performance in the teaching and self-learning of English among higher education students in Ecuador. It explores both the scope and limitations of ICT integration within these higher education institutions. The insights generated aim to demonstrate that the effective use of ICTs in HEI teaching contexts can significantly promote autonomous English language learning.

ICTs are not only transforming the way we perceive reality, but also altering the physical and social reality (Molsalve Franco & Valencia Valencia, 2023). Learning English has become increasingly important in today's globalized society. However, many students struggle to learn the language through traditional methods that often fail to motivate them. This challenge is particularly pronounced among accelerated learning students.

Their article presented the development and implementation of ICT-mediated teaching guides designed specifically for English instruction in accelerated learning programs. These guides were validated through a quantitative case study involving 40 students. The study measured the guides' impact on both learning gains and motivation to learn. Results showed a moderate improvement in learning outcomes and a very large increase in motivation. Therefore, it is concluded that integrating ICT effectively complements the educational process in accelerated English learning courses.

The current information and knowledge society is permeating all levels of society and involving citizens, especially the youngest, in all their professional and social activities, from work, consumption and communication to leisure and the way they relate to each other (Santiago Campión et al., 2023). This transformation is happening in nearly every corner of the planet.

Their study aimed to identify the most frequently used ICT resources, understand teachers' purposes when using these tools in the teaching-learning process, assess teachers' perceptions of their effectiveness, and explore their opinions on their own training. A quantitative methodology was employed, utilizing an online survey distributed to all non-university teachers in the Autonomous Region of La Rioja.

Overall, the results align with those of similar studies conducted in other educational contexts. Notably, teachers emphasized the need for effective training, particularly focusing on pedagogical aspects. Furthermore, the success of program cannot solely depend on teachers' competence and efforts but must also consider the unique educational context and didactical practices. These insights open new avenues for further research that can complement, expand, and deepen understanding in this area.

METHODOLOGICAL FRAMEWORK

The following is an analysis of experiences with the use of applications available on the Internet and social networks to transform the classroom into a place where knowledge is shared and acquired collaboratively. To ensure quality education, we will describe web applications related to the planning and management of resources that support the daily activity of the teacher.

Delicious

This web application allows us to classify content that we find on the Internet. In this way, we can access the information we store in the application from different applications and supports: web browsers, mobile devices, etc. Delicious can be used for a clear educational purpose: to organise the classroom's didactic resources. This tool allows us to organise information with the advantage that our data are stored on the internet and accessible from anywhere.

Delicious is a social bookmarking management service in web 2.0 that enables us to save, organize, tag and share our favourite links. It is also a great way to filter this information based on its popularity since each link has a counter that indicates its popularity among other users of the service.

The web application Delicious offers significant pedagogical value through its social bookmarking features. It facilitates collaborative learning, knowledge sharing, and the development of information literacy skills. Students can curate and share resources, discover diverse perspectives, and engage in discussions around tagged content, fostering a more interactive and personalized learning experience.

WebQuests

Serna González and Santillán Galván (2021) define WebQuests as a research activity in which students obtain information by interacting totally or partially with Internet resources. In addition, students complete the WebQuest in groups, with each member adopting a specific role, for which they receive specific information (Carrión Montalván et al., 2024).

A WebQuest is a didactic activity that is formed from an attractive task for students and a process with which they analyse, synthesize, understand, transform, value, share, and create new information. Apart from answering questions about concepts or copying what appears on the computer to a template with the same format, it must be related to the students' daily lives to achieve a greater understanding of the topic (Katamaya Cruz & Rojas Montero, 2021).

WebQuests are based on a constructivist approach, as they encourage the development of mental processes and promote critical thinking, along with the construction of knowledge. Students manipulate information through critical reflection, analysis, problem-solving, and interaction. Interdisciplinarity is promoted and interaction is developed with media and other people to obtain other visions, thus enhancing collaborative learning among students (Rocu Gómez et al., 2018).

One of the main characteristics of this activity is its motivation and authenticity. Different strategies are used to increase students' motivation and interest, using real tasks. They also use real resources such as encyclopaedias, journals, scientific articles, and other sources that the teacher considers appropriate (Chong Baque, 2020). Another characteristic is that higher cognitive processes such as understanding, comparing, and transformation of information are enhanced. The instructions and tools provided by the WebQuest and the teamwork among the students help them perform activities that they could not do individually (Ulu & Ulusoy, 2019).

A WebQuest integrates ICTs into classrooms, so that they develop and use their own ideas on the subject in a creative way. It also allows students to use an imaginary context that fosters student motivation and interest. It promotes relationships, the exchange of ideas and collaborative work, favouring global learning (Fernández Regueira et al., 2002).

Flickr

This social network allows users to upload photos and organize them into albums. It can be useful to organize photographs that we can use as a teaching resource in the classroom. We live in an image-driven society, and it is important that students learn to interpret the meaning of images, the message they convey, and the purpose they pursue (Álvarez Herrero, 2021).

The current profusion of images and sounds is giving rise to the birth of a new type of intelligence and a subject with a predominance of the right cerebral hemisphere, understanding in a more sensitive way, allowing all his senses to vibrate. Flickr is a free social network useful for storing around 500 thousand high-quality photos and videos without taking up the space of the computer (Zorba, 2022).

Flickr is the most community-oriented repository of photographs. It allows to generate albums, exhibitions and groups on any concept, and even launch contests or debates on any topic or photographic practice. It is one of the most important photo hosting and sharing sites on the web, with more than five billion images uploaded to its servers (Flores Banda et al., 2024).

Flickr has significant pedagogical value, offering educators tools to enhance learning experiences across various subjects and age groups. Its visual nature and interactive features enable engaging activities like virtual field trips, collaborative projects, and the development of digital literacy skills (Martínez Sala & Alemany Martínez, 2022).

Moodle

The use of virtual teaching platforms such as Moodle, facilitates the organization of resources, but above all the evaluation process. In its recent version 2.0, it incorporates a new functionality called "results". This new element allows to define indicators that measure students' performance in the different tasks, questionnaires, etc. (Fernández Pa, 2024).

The results can be useful to develop an assessment based on basic competencies (in the case of Compulsory Secondary Education) or on professional competencies (in the case of Intermediate or Higher-Level Training Cycles). They would act as indicators of competencies. Moodle allows to control the number of activities in which these results are being used (Asto Luna et al., 2023).

Moodle is a free online education system that allows teachers and educators to create their own websites with dynamic courses to share with their students (Maliza Muñoz et al., 2020). Moodle is based on content that is hosted on a web server, making it possible for students to enter at any time to review the courses in which they are enrolled (Casañ Nuñez et al. 2021).

The main function of the teacher is to create the course content, which was already created beforehand, and assign it the grade established in each block. Once the course is fully uploaded into the system (including the syllabus, forums, tests, etc.), students will be enrolled (Domenica Espinar, 2021).

Web educational platforms such as Moodle are educational spaces that integrate a set of tools for online learning, which allow remote interaction between the teacher and the student. According to Zúñiga Zárrate (2022), the use of Moodle is particularly suited and beneficial for students with dyslexia supporting their learning needs.

ThatQuiz

This web application allows users to take assessment tests in different subjects: mathematics, languages, geography, and science. Among these, the subject of mathematics is the one with the largest number of categories and questions (Abós Catalán et al., 2017).

ThatQuiz is an application that, through different questionnaires, allows us to generate various types of math exercises (whole numbers, fractions, geometry, measurements, units), as well as language vocabulary exercises (in English, Spanish, French and German) and geography exercises (Laura de la Cruz et al., 2021).

ThatQuiz offers several pedagogical benefits for both students and teachers. It provides a platform for practicing basic mathematical operations, strengthening skills, and assessing understanding through quizzes. Teachers can easily create, assign, and track student progress, saving valuable class time and facilitating differentiation. The site's automatic feedback and scoring, along with features like quiz duplication for pre- and post-testing, enhance learning and assessment.

ThatQuiz is a website designed for teachers and students. It makes it easier for them to generate exercises and see results very quickly (Laura de la Cruz & Tolentino Cotrina, 2022). The project originated in the Dominican Republic, where the author spent two years as a computer science teacher at a high school in Cabrera. The high school had a computer centre that was used very little for educational purposes.

Discussion Forums

The results obtained with the use of discussion forums are surprising. Eusebio Hermira conducted a study on the use of forums on discussion of doubts about the concepts raised in class and the results are as follows:

- 75% of the students participated in the forums when they discovered that doubts were resolved in many of them.
- 80% of students admitted that most doubts raised by their classmates were doubts that they themselves had.
- Only 30% of the doubts raised by students were resolved by the teacher, the remaining 70% were resolved by other colleagues.

- 85% of the students who solved 70% of their classmates' doubts were students who were doing extension activities.

In general terms, a discussion forum can be defined as a meeting space (either physical or virtual) between various participants with the aim of exchanging opinions, asking questions about a topic or subtopics of common interest, and sharing skills, experiences or answers to questions (Mindiola Molina & Castro Mendoza, 2021). It is an environment where participants can raise questions to discuss and respond to any contribution, creating chain discussions that can generate a discussion tree where the discussion branches out in many directions or subthreads.

Discussion forums offer significant pedagogical value by fostering active learning, promoting critical thinking, and enhancing communication skills. They facilitate deeper engagement with course material, encourage peer interaction, and can create a sense of community among learners.

The forum is an oral communication technique, in a physical or virtual place through the Internet, which is used to meet, exchange ideas or discuss with someone on various topics of common interest. It is typically asynchronous. According to Mosquera Gende (2024), forums can be categorized into public, private, and protected.

X (former Twitter)

This social network, classified as microblogging, has meant a revolution that has not been experienced since SMS emerged. Among other features, the peculiarity of this social communication platform awakens the user's creativity and the ability to synthesize information (Soto Esteban, 2022).

The possibility to write a brief message on a topic of conversation in which many people are participating has allowed to use this application to motivate participation in the classroom (Bautista Zárate, 2023). It has been possible to motivate participation in the subjects in the experience developed with the students of the Higher-Level Training Cycle.

X helps to achieve summaries, since the essence of this social network is to communicate through its characters. It improves conversation and communication between students and teachers because different points of view can be exchanged, creating different currents and matrices of enriching opinions (Ariza Covarrubias & Pons Bonals, 2021).

X has been studied as a tool to improve student engagement. For example, the tool can improve classroom engagement by motivating students to post contents. Through these messages they can ask questions about their individual experience inside and outside the classroom (Borromeo García & Ramírez Hernández, 2018).

Additionally, X can be used as a research tool if students use the search bar. Students can follow relevant hashtags, search for people, topics, and keywords. According to Mellado Moreno et al. (2022), students can even subscribe to a specific list to learn more about a specific topic they are researching and learning about in school.

Google Docs

The use of Google Docs has been a discovery for teachers and students. Students have learned how to create shared documents, presentations, or forms, which has allowed them to work as a team in a collaborative way. They have gone from sharing the tasks to doing all the work among everyone (Fernández Mata, 2018).

However, the idea of building teamwork is not to merge parts of a work that has been distributed. Based on this idea, we have come across group work presentations where the format and layout of the slides changed drastically when the member of the group who was presenting changed. In many cases, they limit themselves to dedicating themselves strictly to doing their individual sections, without considering the importance of contributing to the indivisible whole: the team's final result (Lozano Rodríguez et al., 2021).

Google Docs offers significant pedagogical value in educational settings by fostering collaboration, providing real-time feedback, and streamlining various writing and learning tasks. Its collaborative features, such as simultaneous editing and commenting, enhance teamwork skills and promote a dynamic learning environment. Furthermore, Google Docs' accessibility and version history features simplify revisions and feedback processes, making it a valuable tool for both students and educators.

Google Docs is an excellent application that allows to prepare teaching material for a class. In addition, in the case of courses with more than one teacher, it also facilitates collaboration on content creation. Google for Education is a powerful tool that can help make learning more engaging, efficient, and effective for both teachers and students. It allows users to interact with the entire school community in an environment that is already familiar to everyone: the digital universe (Montaner Villalba, 2018).

Emerging Technologies

Emerging technologies have the potential to revolutionize English as a Foreign Language (EFL) education by transforming both how languages are taught and how learners engage with the material. Examples of emerging education technologies include artificial intelligence, virtual reality, augmented reality, mixed reality, robotics, learning analytics tools, and adaptive learning systems.

1. **Personalised Learning:** AI-powered platforms can adapt to learners' proficiency levels, pacing, and learning styles. Students receive instant feedback and targeted practice in vocabulary, grammar, or pronunciation. Examples: Duolingo's adaptive learning, Chat GPT-based tutors, or AI-driven writing assistants.
2. **Immersive Learning Environments:** Virtual Reality (VR) and Augmented Reality (AR) create immersive, contextualised scenarios (e.g., shopping in an English-speaking market or attending a virtual classroom abroad). These environments simulate real-life conversations and cultural settings, enhancing speaking and listening skills.
3. **Gamification and Motivation:** Game-based learning increases engagement and retention by turning lessons into interactive challenges. Platforms like *Kahoot*, *Quizlet*, and custom language learning games foster motivation through points, levels, and rewards.
4. **Global Collaboration and Communication:** Online communication tools (video conferencing, messaging apps) enable authentic interaction with native speakers or other EFL learners worldwide. Projects like telecollaboration or virtual exchange programs foster intercultural competence and real-world language use.
5. **Mobile Learning and Ubiquity:** Mobile apps offer learning opportunities anytime, anywhere, supporting microlearning and spaced repetition. Push notifications and reminders help build consistent learning habits outside of formal education.
6. **AI and Natural Language Processing (NLP):** Tools like ChatGPT, Google Translate, and speech recognition software help learners practice and refine
7. **Analytics and Assessment:** Learning analytics track progress, identify weaknesses, and help instructors tailor instruction. Automated assessment tools evaluate writing and speaking with increasing accuracy, freeing up teachers for more targeted support.
8. **Teacher Support and Professional Development:** EdTech platforms offer on-demand training, resource sharing, and collaborative spaces for teachers. AI can help with lesson planning, material generation, and feedback, reducing administrative burden.

Emerging technologies offer unprecedented opportunities to personalize, contextualize, and democratize EFL education. When thoughtfully integrated, they can enhance motivation, improve outcomes, and prepare learners for real-world communication in a globalized world.

RESULTS

In general terms, a number of results were obtained from the integration of ICTS in the English language classroom should we aim to deliver quality education:

- There is a lack of ICT training among education professionals.
- School leaders need to support teachers' innovative initiatives.
- ICTs open a new field that motivates student participation.
- Social networks are part of the daily habits of young Spaniards.
- The number of young people who have access to the Internet from mobile devices is increasing.
- Digitalisation is not required as much as innovation, although the former gives rise to the latter.

Culture has increasingly been digitized, while schools continue to follow practices from the post-industrial era. Homes have been transformed in recent decades by the arrival of a series of electronic devices that have been invading the family space: radio, TV, and the Internet. Access to the network has also grown in recent years. Not only because of the number of users, but also because of the ease of access through mobile devices.

The use of the Internet on mobile devices is not limited to the business environment but is also making its way among young people. With regard to the use of social networks, in Spain 44.6% of Internet users had at least one profile on a social network. In addition, young users are in the majority, with the number of users of social networks decreasing as age increases: 7 out of 10 Internet users are under 35 years of age.

With the School 2.0 programme, the Spanish government is making a clear commitment to the inclusion of ICTs in schools. The number of computers has tripled in the period of the last 5 years. Below there is a table with more specific data on the indicators of the State School 2.0 program according to each community obtained from the Spanish Ministry of Education:

Table 1. State School 2.0 program

Community	Computers available	Digital classroom	ICT-trained teachers
Andalucia	173.500	6.439	27.956
Aragón	6.506	947	2.700
Asturias	6.975	309	600
Baleares	250	100	5.000

continued on following page

Table 1. Continued

Community	Computers available	Digital classroom	ICT-trained teachers
Canarias	10.000	488	1.923
Cantabria	4.390	171	400
Castilla y León	217	816	4.040
Castilla-La Mancha	21.250	1.299	1.300
Cataluña	55.085	2.112	13.00
Extremadura	6.400	126	1.914
Galicia	14.670	704	304
La Rioja	1.943	85	279
Navarra	2.752	183	350
País Vasco	18.128	933	1.400
Ceuta/Melilla	2.300	297	226

An analysis of the data presented in the table above reveals a significant inequality between Autonomous Communities in terms of some parameters. For example, Extremadura only has 126 digital classrooms, compared to 2,112 in Catalonia. The community with the greatest number of computers is Andalucía with 173,500 and the one with the least number of computers is Castilla y León with 217.

When it comes to the number of well-trained teachers in ICTs, again Andalucía is the community which outnumbers the rest with 27,956 educators. On the contrary, the autonomous cities of Ceuta and Melilla only have 226 trained teachers. Data from 3 communities, Comunidad Valenciana, Madrid and Murcia, could not be obtained.

CONCLUSION

The main obstacle presented by the current educational system to adapt to the new environment in which ICTs appear as co-protagonists is ignorance. Ignorance towards the unknown, which can only be addressed through training that opens the horizon of educational institutions and education professionals, guiding them towards a new school model.

Prohibition is not a solution when it comes to educating students in the correct use of ICTs. Instead, it is necessary to create meeting spaces, opinion forums, to share innovative experiences that involve the use of ICTs in the classroom. While mobile phones and the Internet are ubiquitous, teachers continuously face the challenge of managing these devices in class, striving to maintain focus and limit distractions.

The greater the number of people afraid to take on great responsibilities, the greater the number of bureaucrats dedicated to not assuming them. Certainly, in today's education system, there are important challenges that imply responsibilities to be assumed. The personal initiative to learn, to teach better, for the future of our students should be incentives for teachers to feel the incorporation into the knowledge society as a necessity and not as an expendable add-on. The support of institutions is important so that they support with all the means in their power the initiatives that arise as innovation in the educational field.

There is a pressing need for new methodologies to emerge around the use of ICTs in the classroom. In addition, the experiences developed in this area must be shared so that collaborative work enriches them. To this end, virtual communities are also offered as an opportunity for education professionals, their proposals, their experiences and, in general, their contributions.

Teacher training must contemplate, among other important matters, the adaptation to the digital world that surrounds us to ensure quality education. This is not an easy task for a large majority of teachers who belong to a generation far from this digital age. It is therefore necessary that the enthusiasm and generosity that must accompany a good educator serve for teachers who have ICT skills to share their knowledge and their time with those teachers who do not have these skills. Collaboration, teamwork, and knowledge sharing are the core values that make an educational centre grow as an ideal place for learning.

REFERENCES

Abdi, Y. M., Waititu, M. M., & Mugo, B. C. (2021). Challenges facing teachers' integration of information communication and technology in teaching and learning of welding and fabrication at the vocational training centers in Mandera County. *International Academic Journal of Information Systems and Technology*, *2*(1), 297–310.

Abós Catalán, A. García González, L. & Aibar Solana, A. (2017). El uso del ThatQuiz como recurso de aprendizaje y guía para la evaluación de los estudiantes de Postgrado. En Del Moral Barrigüete, C. (coord. y ed.) Buenas prácticas de E-learning en el contexto de la Educación Permanente y Tecnologías. 129-140. Enciclopedia Virtual umed.net.

Aguirre Idrogo, Y. M., Vargas Navarro, R., Huamán Guzmán, A. M., & Gutiérrez Narrea, G. S. (2021). Uso de las TIC en la comprensión de textos del idioma inglés en estudiantes de secundaria. *Horizontes Revista de Investigación en Ciencias de la Educación*, *5*(21), 1419–1429. DOI: 10.33996/revistahorizontes.v5i21.285

Alarcón Hernández, P., Vásquez Bustos, V., Díaz Larenas, C., & Venegas Carrasco, C. (2020). El profesor como guía y guerrero: metáforas sobre la profesión docente. *Cuadernos de Lingüística Hispánica,* 36, 105-128. https://doi.org/https://doi.org/10.19053/0121053X.n36.2020.10989

Álvarez Herrero, J. F. (2021). *Uso de imágenes en redes sociales para la mejora del aprendizaje en alumnos de Secundaria*. Servicio de Publicaciones Universidad de Valladolid.

Area Moreira, M., Alonso Cano, C., Correa Gorospe, J. M., Moral Pérez, M. E., de Pablos Pons, J., Paredez Labra, J., Peirats Chacón, J., Sanabria Mesa, A. L., San Martín Alonso, A., & Valverde Berrocoso, J. (2024). Las políticas educativas TIC en España después del Programa Escuela 2.0: Las tendencias que emergen. *RELATEC Revista Latinoamericana de Tecnología Educativa*, *13*(2), 11–33. DOI: 10.17398/1695-288X.13.2.11

Ariza Covarrubias, R., & Pons Bonals, L. (2021). Medios y redes sociales en la enseñanza-aprendizaje del inglés. *Revista de Estudios y Experiencias en Educación*, *20*(43), 129–148. DOI: 10.21703/rexe.20212043ariza7

Asto Luna, E. L., Chávez Espinoza, P. E., Menacho Vargas, I., Taber De la Cruz, Y. O., & Jáuregui Eléspuru, J. C. (2023). Las plataformas e-learning en el aprendizaje del inglés. Horizontes. *Revista de Investigación en Ciencias de la Educación*, *7*(27), 62–76. DOI: 10.33996/revistahorizontes.v7i27.497

Baño Lucio, L., González Quiñones, F., & Tarango Ortiz, J. (2023). Influencia de las TIC en el aprendizaje del idioma inglés en niños. *Tsafiqui Revista Científica en Ciencias Sociales, 13*(21), 115–125. DOI: 10.29019/tsafiqui.v13i21.1096

Bautista Zárate, E. J. (2023). Uso de Redes Sociales como Herramienta para Mejorar la Escritura en Inglés Como Lengua Extranjera. *Ciencia Latina Revista Científica Multidisciplinar, 7*(4), 8367–8387. DOI: 10.37811/cl_rcm.v7i4.7568

Borromeo García, C.A. & Ramírez Hernández, M. (2018). Uso de redes sociales en docentes de lengua inglesa y pedagogía: ¿Diferencias por disciplina? *Revista Ensayos Pedagógicos*, Edición Especial, 189-205. DOI: 10.15359/rep.esp-16.10

Carrión Montalván, B. K., Pillajo Angos, C. G., Castellanos Fonseca, J. A., & Vega Aguaiza, R. (2024). WebQuest como herramienta de aprendizaje: Análisis del impacto en la producción y aprendizaje del inglés como lengua extranjera. *Ibero-American Journal of Education & Society Research, 4*(1), 129–141. DOI: 10.56183/iberoeds.v4i1.661

Casañ Nuñez, J.C., Millán Scheiding, C. & Márquez Baldó, L. (2021). *H5P y Moodle en la enseñanza del inglés: encuesta al alumnado del máster de profesorado.* Dykinson, S.L.

Chong Baque, P. G. (2020). Estrategias pedagógicas innovadoras en entornos virtuales de aprendizaje. *Dominio de las Ciencias, 6*(3), 56–77. DOI: 10.23857/dc.v6i3.1274

Colás Bravo, M. P., de Pablo Pons, J., & Ballesta Pagán, J. (2018). The Impact of ICT on Teaching in the Spanish Education System: A Literature Review. [RED]. *Revista de Educación a Distancia, 56*, 1–23. DOI: 10.6018/red/56/2

Di Franco, M. (2022). La investigación en formación docente. *Praxis Educativa (Santa Rosa), 26*(2), 1–6. https://doi.org/https://dx.doi.org/10.19137/praxiseducativa-2022-260201. DOI: 10.19137/praxiseducativa-2022-260201

Domenica Espinar, C. (2021). Aplicación de Moodle para fortalecer el proceso de enseñanza de inglés en la educación abierta. *Revista Tecnológica Ciencia y Educación Edwards Deming, 5*(1), 81–97. DOI: 10.37957/ed.v5i1.73

Enith Moreno, L., & Bautista Moreno, L. C.Luz Enith MorenoLeidy Constanza Bautista Moreno. (2024). El uso de las Tics en el fortalecimiento del inglés como lengua extranjera. *Línea Imaginaria, 2*(18), 1–15. DOI: 10.56219/lneaimaginaria.v2i18.2754

Eusebio Hermira, S. (2023). Los foros como herramienta de aprendizaje y evaluación de los cursos virtuales asíncronos. *Anuari de Filología. Estudis de Lingüística, 13*(1), 27–54. DOI: 10.1344/AFEL2023.13.2

Fernández Mata, R. (2018). *Hacia el aprendizaje autónomo y colectivo mediante la herramienta "documentos" de Google Drive*. Adaya Press.

Fernández Pa, H. (2024). Plataforma Moodle para la enseñanza de las habilidades fundamentales del idioma inglés como lengua extranjera. *Journal of Science and Research*, *5*, 449–453. DOI: 10.5281/zenodo.133848556

Fernández Regueira, U., González Villa, Á., & Gewerc, A. (2021). *Enseñanza en línea bajo pandemia: una experiencia de enseñanza-aprendizaje basada en una WebQuest*. Octaedro Editorial.

Flores Banda, J.C., Huerta Patraca, G.A., Solís Peralta, F.M. & Hernández Martínez, C.E. (2024). Influencia de la Competencia Digital Docente en el Aprendizaje en Bachillerato. *Revista Docentes 2.0, 17*(2), 62-73. DOI: 10.37843/rted.v17i2.525

Flores Nessi, E., Loaiza Falcón, A., & Rojas de Ricardo, G. (2020). Rol del docente investigador desde su práctica social. *Revista Scientific*, *5*(15), 106–128. DOI: 10.29394/Scientific.issn.2542-2987.2020.5.15.5.106-128

Fraga Varela, F., & Alonso Ferreiro, A. (2021). El Proyecto Escuela 2.0 en Galicia (España): Percepciones del Profesorado. *Innovación Educativa (México, D.F.)*, *27*(27), 285–301. DOI: 10.15304/ie.27.4330

Gil Pérez, A., & Berlanga Fernández, I. (2023). La interactividad en el aula. Un reto de la escuela 2.0. *EDMETIC, 2*(2), 56-75. DOI: 10.21071/edmetic.v2i2.2870

Girón Chávez, A., Cruz Maldonado, E. Y., Bermej del Villar, M. M., & Cancino Zamarrón, R. (2023). Las TIC y el aprendizaje colaborativo para mejorar la pronunciación de inglés de estudiantes universitarios. *Revista Lengua y Cultura*, *5*(9), 1–10. DOI: 10.29057/lc.v5i9.11531

Gómez Trigueros, I. M., & Bustamante Alonso, C. (2023). Nuevas perspectivas en la formación del profesorado en competencias digitales. *Bordón Revista de Pedagogía*, *75*(4), 11–30. DOI: 10.13042/Bordon.2023.100532

Guamán Gómez, V. J., Espinoza Freire, E., & Granda Ayabaca, D. M. (2023). Rol del docente en la era digital. *Portal de la Ciencia*, *4*(3), 364–378. DOI: 10.51247/pdlc.v4i3.398

Habibu, T., Al-Mamun, A., & Clement, C. (2022). Difficulties Faced by Teachers in Using ICT in Teaching-Learning at Technical and Higher Educational Institutions of Uganda. *International Journal of Engineering Research & Technology (Ahmedabad)*, *1*(7), 1–9.

Intriago Cedeño, G. (2019). TIC en la enseñanza y autoaprendizaje del idioma inglés. *Skopos Revista Internacional de Traducción e Interpretación*, *10*, 65–85. DOI: 10.21071/skopos.v10i.12759

Jayanthi, C. E. (2023). Challenges In Using ICT Tools Among Student Teachers. *Educational Administration: Theory and Practice*, *29*(4), 3520–3522. DOI: 10.53555/kuey.v29i4.8157

Katamaya Cruz, E., & Rojas Montero, J. A. (2021). WebQuest como escenario para el aprendizaje colaborativo y el desarrollo de competencias digitales. *Hamut'ay*, *8*(3), 54–61. DOI: 10.21503/hamu.v8i3.2332

Laura de la Cruz, K., Morales Vargas, K., Huanacuni Clavitea, M., & Aza Custodio, P. (2021). Aplicación Quizizz y comprensión de textos en inglés con el contenido de la plataforma educativa "Aprendo en Casa". *Revista Innova Educación*, *3*(1), 151–159. DOI: 10.35622/j.rie.2021.01.007

Laura de la Cruz, K., & Tolentino Cotrina, M. P. (2022). Quizizz en el aprendizaje del inglés en estudiantes de la Universidad Nacional Jorge Basadre Grohmann de Tacna. *PURIQ*, *4*, 1–13. DOI: 10.37073/puriq.4.298

Ley Leyva, N. V. (2022). El papel del docente de educación básica en el contexto actual. *Portal de la Ciencia*, *3*(1), 27–37. DOI: 10.51247/pdlc.v3i1.308

López Aguilar, J., Maza Córdova, J., & Tusa Jumbo, F. (2020). Educar en el contexto digital: el reto de ser edutuber. *risti Revista Ibérica de Sistemas e Tecnologias de Informação, 1*(E25), 188–200.

López Belmonte, J., Pozo Sánchez, S., Fuentes Cabrera, A., & Gómez García, G. (2019). Análisis del efecto de la formación b-learning en el profesorado. *Texto Livre: Linguagem e Tecnologia*, *12*(2), 98–115. DOI: 10.17851/1983-3652.12.2.98-115

Lozano Rodríguez, A. L., Valdés Lozano, D. E., Sánchez Aradillas, A. L., & Esparza Duque, E. E. (2021). Uso de Gogle Docs como herramienta de construcción colaborativa tomando en cuenta los estilos de aprendizaje. *Revista De Estilos De Aprendizaje*, *4*(8), 23–39. DOI: 10.55777/rea.v4i8.934

Macas Granda, C. J., Granda Asencio, L. Y., & Carbay Cajamarca, W. A. (2021). Rol del docente en la alfabetización digital en el siglo XXI. *Sociedad & Tecnología*, *4*(S2), 350–363. DOI: 10.51247/st.v4iS2.156

Maliza Muñoz, W., Medina León, A., Vera Mora, G., & Castro Molina, N. (2020). Aprendizaje autónomo en Moodle. *Journal of Science and Research*, *5*, 632–652. DOI: 10.5281/zeonodo.4441105

Martí Climent, A. (2022). *El uso del vídeo en la formación de docentes*. Adaya Press.

Martín Párraga, L., Llorente Cejudo, M. C., & Cabero Almenara, J. (2022). Analysis of teachers' digital competencies from assessment frameworks and instruments. *IJERI: International Journal of Educational Research and Innovation, 18*, 62–79. DOI: 10.46661/ijeri.7444

Martínez Sala, A. M., & Alemany Martínez, D. (2022). Redes sociales educativas para la adquisición de competencias digitales. *Revista Mexicana de Investigación Educativa, 27*(92), 209–234.

Mas García, V., Gabarda Méndez, V., & Peirats Chacón, J. (2023). Formación y competencia digital del profesorado de Educación Secundaria en España. *Texto Livre Linguagem e Tecnología, 16*(79), 1-12. DOI: 10.1590/1983-3652.2023.44581

Mellado Moreno, P. C., Patiño Masó, J., Ramos Pardo, F. J., & Estebanell Minguell, M. (2022). Discursos en Facebook y Twitter sobre el uso educativo de móviles en el aula. *Revista Latina de Comunicación Social*, 80, 225-240. https://www.doi.org/10.4185/RLCS-2022-1541

Mindiola Molina, I. Y., & Castro Mendoza, J. C.Idayris Yiseth Mindiola-MolinaJuan Camilo Castro-Mendoza. (2021). Desarrollo del pensamiento crítico a través de foros de discusión asincrónicos con estudiantes de 8° grado. *Revista UNIMAR, 39*(1), 126–144. DOI: 10.31948/Rev.unimar/unimar39-1-art9

Molsalve Franco, A. P., & Valencia Valencia, E. Z. (2023). Impacto de las tecnologías de la información en los estudiantes del grado aceleración del aprendizaje en un curso de inglés. *Revista Virtual Universidad Católica del Norte, 1*(68), 37–62. DOI: 10.35575/rvucn.n68a3

Montaner Villaba, S. (2018). Aplicación del Blogging y/o Google Docs para fomentar la competencia en producción escrita en la enseñanza del inglés. *Universitas Tarraconensis Revista de Ciencias de la Educación, 1*(1), 43–59. DOI: 10.17345/ute.2018.1.2116

Mosquera Gende, I. (2024). Los foros como elemento dinamizador para la participación activa en una universidad online. *Hachetetepé Revista Científica de Educación y Comunicación, 28*(28), 1–21. DOI: 10.25267/Hachetetepe.2024.i28.1203

Murillo Camacho, G. A., & Rosales Sánchez, R. E. (2024). Incidencia del uso de las TIC en la enseñanza aprendizaje del idioma inglés en estudiantes de bachillerato. *RECIAMUC, 8*(2), 114–122. DOI: 10.26820/reciamuc/8.(2).abril.2024.114-122

Ortiz Rodríguez, G. A., & Tejeda Díaz, R. (2023). Uso de las TIC para el aprendizaje del idioma inglés para estudiantes de secundaria. *Revista Cognosis, 8*(EE1), 127–142. DOI: 10.33936/cognosis.v8iEE1.5301

Otero Rey, E. M., Blanco Carrión, A., & Rivas Mundiña, B. (2022). *Innovación docente: realización de vídeo de captura de pantalla como recurso para la enseñanza universitaria*. Adaya Press.

Pinto Santos, A. R., & Pérez Garcías, A. (2022). Development of teaching digital competence in initial teacher training: A systematic review. *World Journal on Educational Technology: Current Issues, 14*(1), 1–15. DOI: 10.18844/wjet.v14i1.6250

Reis Jorge, J., Ferreira, M., & Olcina Sempere, G. (2020). La figura del profesorado-investigador en la reconstrucción de la profesionalidad docente en un mundo en transformación. *Review of Education, 44*(1), 502–514. https://doi.org/10.15517/revedu.v44i1.39044

Rico Gómez, M., & Ponce Gea, A. (2022). El Docente Del Siglo XXI Perspectivas según el rol formativo y profesional. *Revista Mexicana de Investigación Educativa, 27*(92), 77–101.

Rocu Gómez, P., Blández Ángel, J., & Sierra Zamorano, M. A. (2018). Construyendo aprendizajes en Expresión Corporal a través de WebQuest: Un estudio de caso múltiple. *Revista Complutense de Educación, 30*(4), 1013–1029. DOI: 10.5209/rced.59905

Rodríguez Peñarroja, M. (2022). *El uso de YouTube en la clase de IFE y sus efectos en la motivación del alumnado*. Adaya Press.

Romero Hermoza, R. (2021). Competencia digital docente: una revisión sistemática. *Eduser, 8*(1), 131-137. https://doi.org/10.18050/eduser.v8i1.2033

Royero Thomas, R. P. (2024). La Tecnología y su Influencia en la Enseñanza de la Lengua Extranjera Inglés: Una Revisión Sistemática de Literatura. *Ciencia Latina Revista Científica Multidisciplinar, 8*(2), 7441–7454. DOI: 10.37811/cl_rcm.v8i2.11138

Santiago Campión, R., Navaridas Nalda, F. & Repáraz Abaitua, C. (2023). La escuela 2.0: reflexiones en torno a su eficacia en los centros educativos de La Rioja. *Educación XX1, 17*(1), 243-270. DOI: 10.5944/educxx.17.1.10713

Serna González, P., & Santillán Galván, R. (2021). WebQuest: Marcando el futuro de la educación. *Milenaria. Ciencia y Arte, 18*, 8–10. DOI: 10.35830/mcya.vi18.97

Soto Esteban, R. (2022). *Twitter y el reconocimiento de figuras del trabajo social en el segundo curso del grado*. Adaya Press.

Ulu, H., & Ulusoy, M. (2019). The development of metacognitive awareness of reading strategies through WebQuest based teaching. *Egitim ve Ögretim*, *9*(3), 765–818. DOI: 10.14527/pegegog.2019.025

Vaillant, D. (2023). *Formación del profesorado en escenarios de tecnologías digitales*. OEI Publishers.

Villacres Arias, G. E., Espinoza Freire, E. E., & Rengifo Ávila, G. K. (2020). Empleo de las tecnologías de la información y la comunicación como estrategia innovadora de enseñanza y aprendizaje. *Revista Universidad y Sociedad*, *12*(5), 136–142.

Zorba, M. G. (2022). *Understanding English Language Learners' Interpretations of Cultures: The Case of Digital Photographs*. Adaya Press.

Zúñiga Zárate, A. G. (2022). *Implementación de funcionalidades en Moodle para alumnos con dislexia*. Adaya Press.

Chapter 9
Utilising Digital Resources in an EFL Primary Education Class to Implement SDG4 Objective

Antonio Daniel Juan Rubio
https://orcid.org/0000-0003-3416-0021
Universidad de Granada, Spain

ABSTRACT

We are currently living in the age of communication, a period that has transformed how society acquires knowledge. This change is also evident in the way we teach subjects across all levels, starting from Primary Education. 21st century students exemplify what is known as the multiple knowledge society. These learners, often referred to as "digital natives", were born into the communication era, teachers who must adapt their teaching methods to meet the needs of these new learners. To address this, this chapter focuses on a series of workshops utilising digital resources to enhance English language instruction. This initiative is part of a pilot project designed for third-cycle Primary Education students in Spain, aligning with the goals of SDG4. Such is the pervasive role of ICTs that a new term, Learning and Knowledge Technologies (LKT), has emerged within the field of education, evolving directly from ICTs. The goal of LKT is to guide the use of ICTs in a formative way. The purpose of ICTs is to help both students and teachers acquire better and more effective learning.

DOI: 10.4018/979-8-3373-0801-2.ch009

INTRODUCTION

We live in an era where technology has invaded us. Information and Communication Technologies (ICTs) have become an important part of people's lives today. This has brought about substantial changes and has been a springboard to modernisation. In fact, for pupils in Primary Education, who were born in this era, there is no different reality away from the technological world. The way they relate, communicate and learn is determined by technologies. Such is the impact of ICTs into our lives that there is another new term for technologies in education, namely Learning and Knowledge Technologies (LKT), which emanate from ICTs (Cabrera Rodríguez et al., 2022).

The intention of LKT is to direct, in a formative way, ICTs. The interest of ICTs is that students and teachers acquire deeper and more effective learning. This is when we talk about methodology. In today's world, it is not enough just to know how to use ICTs. Their real value lies in researching and analysing to acquire knowledge and to put these technologies at the service of the teaching-learning process. What the transformation is trying to achieve is a shift from technology-mediated learning to technology-assisted learning. This paradigm shift helps to develop the "learning to learn" competence and focuses on a methodological proposal (Area Moreira et al., 2018). This is also in line with Sustainable Development Goal (SDG) 4, which ensures inclusive, equitable, and quality education while promoting lifelong learning opportunities for all.

From a more general context, the European Parliament and the Council of the European Union (2006) established a series of basic qualifications that learning must provide for students given the era of globalisation in which we find ourselves. The commitment of both called making a European area of lifelong learning a reality made it urgent to establish a series of competences such as the following:

- Communication in the mother tongue
- Communication in foreign languages
- Mathematical competence and basic competences in science and technology.
- Digital competence
- Learning to learn
- Social and civic competences
- Sense of initiative and entrepreneurship
- Cultural awareness and expression

These competencies have been developed and refined by the European Union (EU) to provide citizens with the broad skills needed to adapt to the changing and demanding world we live in. According to the European Parliament and the Council of the European Union, these competences cover all citizens without exception, seeking to ensure equal learning for all, regardless of social, cultural, economic or personal differences. Therefore, a Common European Framework of Reference (CEFR) was also proposed with a number of objectives: to establish a set of basic competencies; to support any proposal from EU countries that would benefit students in achieving basic competences for the world of work; and to provide the necessary instruments and frameworks needed to promote initiatives for the good of all member countries in favour of education.

The competency that concerns us directly, given the issue we are dealing with, is precisely digital competence. The European Parliament and the Council of the European Union define digital competence as follows: "Digital competence involves the confident and critical use of information society technologies (IST) for work, leisure and communication. It is underpinned by basic ICT skills: the use of computers to obtain, evaluate, store, produce, present and exchange information, and to communicate and participate in collaborative networks via the Internet" (2006, p. 15).

With regard to the national legislative framework, Royal Decree 157/2022 of 1 March, establishes the organisation and minimum teaching requirements for Primary Education. This is further concreted by Decree 101/2023, of 9 May, establishing the organisation and curriculum for the Primary Education stage in the Autonomous Community of Andalusia. This legislation identifies the eight basic competences. one of which refers to the use of technology in education: Information processing and digital competence.

This competency establishes that the pupil, in an autonomous and responsible manner, must make use of technological tools, assessing information from a critical point of view. Furthermore, they must respect information as well as the means they use for this purpose. They have to make use of technologies making the most of them, both individually and collectively, through autonomous and collaborative work. Digital competence states that technologies must be used to achieve the established learning objectives (Gallego Arrufat et al., 2019).

One of the key points to be addressed in this project is the use of digital resources into the English subject taught in the last years of Primary Education. The focus will be on how multimedia or technological resources improve and enrich lessons, which is another aspect highlighted in this research. Additionally, a series of workshops will be proposed as a pilot educational innovation project.

The elements to be used for a better learning of the topics in different areas of the curriculum will be objectives to be addressed. Special emphasis will be placed on the use of ICTs in language learning, although educational resources will be proposed as examples of good practice. Therefore, the primary objective of this research is to use ICTs for the learning of the English language subject in the third cycle of Primary Education.

Among the specific objectives, we can include the following: to examine national regulations regarding the use of technology in the Primary Education stage; to select digital resources for English language learning; and to propose genuine activities tailored to the tools and workshops of the educational innovation project.

THEORETICAL FRAMEWORK

Students and society in general are going through a time of change. Not only are we surrounded by ICTs, but they have evolved into what is now referred to as LKT, as mentioned in the previous section. Therefore, the way in which learning takes place has changed and technology has become a pivotal issue in the field of education. This is clearly stated in the law, where digital competence is one of the eight basic competences that learners must acquire. The main objective is to harness ICTs to improve English language learning.

Many professionals and scholars in the field have contributed to highlighting the major differences between traditional or 20th century teaching methods and contemporary approaches, where the not-so-new information and communication technologies prevail. From a global perspective, many authors have stressed the importance of ICTs in facilitating education in the era of globalisation in which we find ourselves. As Santa Medina (2021, p. 126) explains: "It is a historical period characterised by a technological revolution centred on digital information and communication, concomitant, but not causal, with the emergence of a networked social structure, in all areas of human activity, and with the global interdependence of this activity".

Not so long ago, when we spoke of school, textbooks quickly came to mind. It could not be otherwise, as it was the only way of learning at the time. It was a traditional 19th century model based on lectures and books. Those writings that a schoolchild had to read over and over again with the intention of retaining the more the better, as there was no internet access or electronic agendas capable of storing the information for us. The aim of education was therefore clear: to retain as much information as possible in the memory, filling it with data and knowledge. Lectures were the only method of instruction, where the student could not interact with other students, thinking that they had nothing to share with each other. The role of the student was limited to retain information and then release it in the evaluations (Moreno Morilla et al., 2021).

But memorising facts is not to know: it is to have what has been given stored in one's memory. What one knows correctly, one disposes of, without looking at the model, without turning one's eyes towards the book. It would not be found good, when by some solitary and melancholy temperament, for the child to see him devote an excessive application to the study of books, which has nourished him: this renders them unfit for civil conversation and diverts them from the better occupations.

We were therefore faced with an education in which the teacher was the protagonist, and the pupils were left only with the task of learning and repeating. Consequently, the role of the pupil was passive in education (Hannaford & Beavis, 2018). Traditional schooling was based solely on intellectual learning where mathematical and verbal knowledge was given more importance over other skills.

However, one prominent detractor of this idea was Howard Gardner, professor at Harvard University and an outstanding psychologist. Gardner, creator of the Theory of Multiple Intelligences, defends the idea that there is no such thing as a single intelligence, that it is not limited to the intelligence quotient (IQ) but that human beings possess at least eight distinct and practical intelligences (Acilo Julita, 2024):

- Interpersonal: refers to the ability to interact with others.
- Intrapersonal: the ability to understand one's own emotions and the capacity for self-reflection.
- Naturalistic: ability to observe and understand the natural world around us.
- Musical: ability to understand, create and perform music.
- Kinaesthetic: ability to use the body to perform physical activities.
- Spatial: ability to project and relate objects in space.
- Mathematical: ability to use numbers, classify and reason effectively.
- Linguistic: ability to use the written and spoken word.

Each type of intelligence described by Gardner can be developed and applied by making use of the materials that technologies provide us with. The Web provides a wealth of resources that students can use to foster their different intelligences. The following conceptual map clarifies in a schematic way the thinking of this author:

Figure 1. Concept map: ICT resources to develop Howard Gardner's multiple intelligences

Gardner's Theory of Multiple Intelligences brought about a major change in the previously prevailing educational model of how learning takes place. However, this is not intended to overthrow the value of print culture. Technological advances should not replace the teaching medium par excellence but rather to complement data, to inform and to make learning more complete. In short, the use of digital resources can be considered as the use of new teaching-learning strategies.

As we mentioned earlier in the introduction to this research, the technology available to us today is closely related to the school environment. However, in reality, this integration is far from being complete or real. The reason why this integration of technology has not yet been fully realised lies in the fact that even if schools have computer rooms, internet access and other infrastructures, this is not enough if it is used in isolation from other subjects. Some studies have established that technologies have not yet had a substantial impact on teaching practices (Monsalve Lorente & Aguasanta Regalado, 2020).

Constructivist Learning

Learning from the constructivist model has been approached by two renowned authors: Piaget and Vygotsky (Alesandrini & Larson, 2020). On the one hand, Piaget attached great importance to the relationship between the person and the object of knowledge. Knowledge, then, is the result obtained in the interaction of the subject with the object through the constructive process. The child learns new knowledge and relates it to his or her prior knowledge. On the other hand, Vygotsky spoke of a series of tools that children use when interacting with the environment and object. These tools are modified at the same time as changes occur in history.

Starting from Piaget's idea, Leontiev (1975) conceptualised the process of construction of knowledge through interaction with the environment and object, thus producing a process called assimilation-accommodation process. However, Leontiev replaced the concept of "assimilation" with that of "appropriation". This idea aligns with Vygotsky's perspective, which defends that children appropriate tools and instruments during their participation in the society of their time (Jones & Brader-Araje, 2022).

Linking these ideas to the topic at hand and following Vygotsky's idea, the computer can be considered as one of the technological tools available to pupils. The computer allows students to interact with other people, connect to information, and serves as a vehicle for acquiring knowledge according to Sarita (2021).

ICTs make possible a different kind of learning from traditional methods. It is a new learning culture that goes beyond the confines of print culture. According to Umida et al. (2020), this new learning culture is characterised by three features:

- Information society: knowledge is no longer reduced to being learned in the classroom. Students acquire information through different sources, and it does not necessarily have to be the school. Information comes to them in abundance, through formats that are much more attractive and entertaining than the school's own textbooks. Without detracting from the institution, since children, already having a broad knowledge of many subjects to be studied at school, have to learn to organise and interpret it in order to assimilate the information correctly (Christie, 2021). In short, the school has to provide pupils with the necessary learning tools (skills) to be able to make sense of this information.
- Multiple knowledge society: this refers to the massification of information that is continually bombarding pupils, and all people in general. There is no single knowledge or universal truth. The same information can be given multiple interpretations, and the crux of the matter lies in knowing how to make one's own judgements and make choices according to one's own needs (Liu & Chen, 2020).
- A society of continuous learning: we are in a time when education is compulsory not only up to secondary school. As society advances, technological changes, etc..., lifelong learning is becoming essential. Therefore, it is necessary to train students who are flexible, autonomous and capable of learning on their own (Liang & Akiba, 2021).

The "learning to learn" competency is one of the basic competencies established by the new Organic Law on Education (LOMLOE). This competence reads as follows: "[...] implies having the skills to start learning and being able to continue learning in an increasingly effective and autonomous way according to one's own objectives and needs. It also implies awareness, management and control of one's own abilities and knowledge from a sense of personal competence or efficacy, and includes strategic thinking, the ability to cooperate, to self-evaluate, and the efficient management of a set of resources and techniques of intellectual work, all of which are developed through conscious and rewarding learning experiences, both individual and collective" (2020, p. 122895).

Implementation of ICTs

We are undoubtedly living in a time of constant change. Society is changing and with it the way we learn and interact with the world. New ways of getting information and accessing communication have been established and it is therefore reasonable that new linguistic terms have arisen at the same time. We refer to the terms "Learning and Knowledge Technologies (LKT)", which we have been anticipating since the beginning of this research, as well as the terms "Digital Native" and "Digital Immigrant" (Betancur Chicué & García Valcárcel, 2022).

The term "Digital Native" refers to a person who was born in the age of information and communication technology. They have grown up with it and therefore use digital language. On the other hand, "Digital Immigrant" refers to a person who was born before this era and who has had to be trained in an accelerated way in its use. They have had to learn certain skills as well as a new language. Digital natives are not only more digitally literate, but they also master the language and have had it installed in their brains almost from birth (Aparicio Gómez & Ostos Ortiz, 2021).

One of the problems that exists today in educational centres is that these digital immigrants make use in their classrooms of a language that has become obsolete. Even more problematic is that they continue to use it to teach a generation that uses a new language that is more innovative and useful. On the other hand, Benavente Vera et al. (2021) establish a number of differences between "Digital Natives" and "Digital Immigrants".

Among others, digital natives want information to be received immediately, preferring to use graphs and tables instead of the texts used by their parents and educators. They also prefer to work and learn online, and this brings them satisfaction because they are aware and feel that they are making immediate progress. This makes them prefer to learn in a playful way rather than in the traditional way.

On the contrary, those considered as "Digital Immigrants" are not convinced by this method that "Digital Natives" have acquired. They prefer to use their traditional way of learning as this is how they were taught. Therefore, they have a critical view and attitude towards the new skills they have and with which their students were born.

"Digital Immigrants", according to Jiménez Hernández et al. (2021), believe that traditional methods still work and that, as in the past, time is the key for acquiring knowledge. They are therefore reluctant to learn the same 'technological language' as their learners. "Digital Immigrants" are aware of their limitations in their ICT skills but are reluctant to accept that they have to learn what their students already know from an early age. Therefore, it is necessary to conduct an analysis of both the methodology currently in use and the contents outlined in the curriculum.

It is evident that ICTs have meant a great advance and progress in all areas, not only in the field of education. We are in the era of the knowledge society, which means that we have a series of advantages that were unimaginable in the past. ICTs have been introduced very quickly in the field of education, so much, giving rise to a new concept that encompasses all those resources available to teachers and students. ICTs play a key role in the teaching-learning process, since information is transmitted and decoded in a different way, and this leads to learning in a different way. The use of ICTs has become compulsory and is one of the basic competencies to be acquired.

Therefore, technology is a means of communication that people use not only as a source of resources but also as a means of receiving and transmitting information. It is essential to list the advantages that this technology has provided for both teachers and students (Cabero Almenara et al., 2022).

1. Communication: the use of certain digital resources has enabled communication between people or institutions, overcoming the space-time barrier in which we were previously imprisoned. It is now much easier to exchange information even when there is a whole world at a distance (Recio Mayorga et al, 2021).
2. Motivation: this is one of the best and biggest advantages that has been influenced by technologies. Students feel more motivated when studying, they pay more attention to what they are doing: activities, work, research, etc. The student is more willing to learn than before. Participation has also increased considerably (Gillen & Kucirkova, 2018).
3. Cooperation: computer and multimedia tools are a working tool that has boosted group work. It has a great power of socialisation. Moreover, it is not necessary for students to be in the same place, they only have to be 'connected' to the network (Area Moreira & Adell Segura, 2021).
4. Individualised learning: the teaching method has changed. The role of the teacher has changed and now he/she is the guide of the teaching-learning process with the use of ICTs. The student has acquired autonomy and the ability to learn. It is the student himself who decides, selects, discards and analyses information

from an objective point of view. The teacher's task is no longer to provide information, but to teach the student to select information and to discern between one piece of information and another (Castillo López, 2020).

Legislative Rationale for the Use of Technologies in Education

The Ministry of Education and Science includes the areas of knowledge that must be taught as part of the compulsory curriculum for the three cycles of Primary Education. These areas are the following: Knowledge of the natural, social and cultural environment, Art education, Physical education, Spanish language and literature, Mathematics and Foreign language. The area of interest in this project is the latter, Foreign Language (English).

It is included in this area that, since the development and rise of ICTs, it has become necessary to educate students in terms of internationality, multiculturalism and multilingualism. The limited opportunities that students find outside the school environment for language practice make it necessary to introduce content within the school that allows students to establish social relationships and engage with media (Bonilla del Río & Aguaded Gómez, 2018).

The objective, then, is to provide students with a series of communicative skills that allow them to defend themselves effectively. As we have been arguing throughout this research, ICTs are very important in the educational process to ensure the attainment of SDG4 and in the acquisition and learning of the Foreign Language (English) subject. This is further echoed by Royal Decree 157/2022, which establishes four main content blocks for primary education. The block dedicated to Foreign Language highlights the importance of the use of technology to help and improve language competence (Arabit García et al., 2023).

In this way, due to the lack of presence of the English language in the students' social environment, it is necessary for the school to facilitate this gap fostering the development of oral comprehension and production skills (listening and speaking). The school must offer rich models to facilitate this learning process. The use of technologies helps to this end as they are capable of bringing a native linguistic model to the classroom (García Delgado et al., 2023).

With regard to written comprehension and production skills (reading and writing), students can use conventional materials to improve their language knowledge. Not only for the learning of the language, but also to bring other means such as technology to acquire a global and better understanding of the language (García Martín & García Martín, 2021).

Therefore, there is no doubt that ICTs offer a wealth of relevant resources for the acquisition and improvement of the foreign language, in this case, English. Not only for the learning of the language itself, but also to bring the student closer to other ways of life fostering a global and intercultural awareness (Mas García et al., 2023).

METHODOLOGICAL SECTION

Many authors have provided a definition of the current technological revolution. The difference between traditional education and the methods which prevail today in schools is striking. The role of the student has changed, from teaching where the teacher was the protagonist to a model in which the student has adopted an active role in his or her own teaching-learning process.

New terms define the pupils of the 21st century as defined by Prensky (2001): "Digital Natives" as opposed to the "Digital Immigrants" seen in the previous section. As a result of the changes in the way knowledge is acquired, it has become necessary to introduce ICTs in classrooms and, more specifically, in the English language classroom. To this end, this section is entirely dedicated to presenting the proposal of a pilot educational innovation project in which the use of ICTs for the learning of English will prevail.

Description of a Digital-Based Innovation Pilot Project

Bearing in mind as a basis what the law provides for the use of ICTs as a support for the acquisition of language skills in a Foreign Language (English in our case), we will now exemplify how what we have mentioned above can be put into practice in the theoretical section. What we are going to expose and explain are the digital materials that are more than suitable for learning a subject, in this case, the basic competency related to the learning of English for students in the third cycle of Primary Education at a state centre in Granada (Spain).

We will see how, based on ICTs and with certain technological materials, students will be able to develop, acquire and express themselves in the target language. In a world governed and dominated by technologies, immersed in the information society, it is necessary to plan and develop new approaches to learning.

It is a reality that learning methods have changed, we no longer learn in the same way as we did 50 years ago. With the turn of the century, different ways of acquiring knowledge have been developed. Additionally, educators now encounter a different student body with different motivations and concerns. This is why a change in teaching strategies is necessary. The main educational interest is for students to master the basic skills of the English language. But not in the traditional way based on technical and rote learning. This project will be performed under a multidirectional approach, giving more importance to communication, personal autonomy, and the correct acquisition of linguistic skills.

This section, therefore, will exhibit a range of useful materials designed for their use in class. The purpose is for students to learn the subject in a different way, in a more attractive and motivating way, important aspects to be considered in the class. In addition, the student can acquire and establish their own learning by means of these materials.

Project Overview

The project is aimed for students in the third cycle of Primary Education. The choice to focus on this last cycle stems from the fact that the use of the digital resources implies that students have a higher level of English than in previous levels. The skills that students can acquire from this project are both receptive (oral or written comprehension, listening and reading,) such as expressive (oral or written production, speaking and writing). In other words, students will acquire and enhance the traditional language skills: Listening, Reading, Speaking and Writing.

The ultimate goal is for the child to learn in a stimulating way, accessing information autonomously, communicating with their peers, and developing skills that will be useful in their present and future life. Above all, this project aims to build a solid foundation for the teaching-learning process so that it is permanent. At the same time, the student will acquire a greater command of technological tools. These are the core principles upon which this work is based.

Starting from the basis that a series of skills must be acquired in the subject of English, the creation of workshops based on ICT acquires great relevance when it comes to helping students to achieve this knowledge. This educational project, which is based on workshops, would be located at the end of the evaluation of each term. This timing allows to assess and draw conclusions about their effectiveness and to be able to propose, in the long term, their inclusion within the subject itself.

A series of digital resources will be used to develop this project in the experimental phase. These resources, which will make up the workshops, are extracted from the subject of information technologies applied to the learning of the English Language. The workshops will therefore be divided into terms, meaning that, at the end of each term, students will participate in a workshop in which they can apply in a practical way the knowledge acquired throughout the term.

Each workshop will be dedicated to each of the four language skills (Listening, Reading, Speaking and Writing), and each group of students must complete each workshop by the end of the course. For each skill, two different materials will be offered, so there will be a total of eight tools. However, students must choose one for each workshop. At the end of the course, students will have participated in all the workshops. At the same time as working on these skills in the target language, learning and handling in the use of digital resources is also acquired. Therefore, the knowledge that the learner acquires is twofold.

The goal is to assess the effectiveness of these workshops in the acquisition of language skills to become an appropriate proposal within the evaluation. The workshops will be cooperative and active, applying in a practical way the knowledge previously acquired by the students throughout each term. As workshops, they are subject to the achievement of a series of objectives. These objectives are general and common to all the activities performed in the workshops.

Objectives of the Pilot Project

The specific didactic objectives set for the pilot project include the four skills:

- Understand both oral and written messages.
- Use the information appropriately to perform the activities promoting cooperative learning as well as self-learning.
- Expand the vocabulary of the English Language regarding the topics related to the tools to be used.
- Learn to autonomously use certain digital resources both to communicate and to obtain information about the English Language.
- Learn to value and respect other cultures as well as their peers in the communication process.
- Acquire rules of accentuation, intonation for a correct phonetic one of the language.
- To encourage reading in the foreign language.

Timing

The workshops for the four skills will be held in the third cycle of Primary Education. Taking a class of 24 students as a reference, these students will be divided into 8 groups, that is, three students per group. In each term there will be a workshop aimed at the development and acquisition of a skill:

- In the first term of the course, the eight groups will develop the Listening workshop, that is, they will perform an oral comprehension task based on one of the two resources that will be offered for this purpose.
- In the second term, the Reading workshop, or written comprehension, will be held, for which the students, again, will choose one of the two digital resources for the practice of this linguistic skill.

- In the third term is the one that entails a little more difficulty. Considering that students, at the end of the third term of a given school year, have a greater command of both the English language and the use of technological tools, two production workshops will be held, both written and oral, that is: Writing workshop and the Speaking workshop respectively, so each group will have to conduct a total of two activities, one for each workshop. In this way, at the end of the course, all the groups would have practiced with all the language skills through various proposed tasks.

The timing for these workshops will be four sessions per workshop. The sessions will last 50 minutes each. The first workshop will take place in December, the second workshop will take place in March and the last workshop will take place in June.

The first session of each workshop will be dedicated to the explanation of the activities to be developed, and to the description of the workshop tools. To do this, the teacher will do the activity on the digital whiteboard, while students will go at their own pace on their computers. The second and third sessions will focus on students designing the content for the activities of each workshop. And finally, in the fourth session, students will present their work, followed by an evaluation.

Evaluation

The evaluation that is contemplated for this type of workshop in the pilot project that we propose is the one that we present below:

- Formative Assessment: on an ongoing basis, both the participation and the motivation and attitude of the students during the sessions and workshops will be evaluated individually. It will be observed if the students feel motivated by the topic, if they participate, as well as the cooperation of the groups. Information will be collected on each part of the development of the task: observation, creation.
- Global Assessment: both the knowledge collected at the beginning and the knowledge already acquired at the end of the sessions through significant learning will be collected in a report. A small individual test will complete the evaluation.
- Processual Evaluation: it will be observed if the activity has turned out to be motivating for the students; whether the proposed objectives have been achieved; if it has allowed the participation of all students if it has contributed to meaningful learning.

As mentioned above, each workshop will be made up of two tools to select one. All students must agree to select the same tool per workshop. Once selected, it will be performed. The tools that can be used to develop these workshops will be:

- Listening Workshop Tools: Listen and Write and Voki
- Reading Workshop Tools: Storybird and Reading Planet Tools
- Speaking Workshop Tools: Voxopop and Skype
- Writing Workshop Tools Dvolver Moviemaker and Wordle

Table 1. Division of workshops by terms

	1st Term	2nd Term	3rd Term	
Workshops	*Listening*	*Reading*	*Speaking*	*Writing*
Tools	Listen and write	Storybird	Voxopop	Dvolver Moviemaker
	Voki	Reading Planet	Skype	Wordle

Proposal of Workshops by Language Skills

In this section we will address in detail each of the workshops that we have been talking about in the previous paragraphs. Given their creative and entertaining characteristics, they are a good resource for practicing the language skills at these ages. First, we will explain the tools contained in the Listening workshop, Listen and Write and Voki, as well as the activities that would be developed within this workshop. Secondly, the tools and activities to develop written comprehension (Reading), Storybird and Reading Planet. Thirdly, we will describe the tools and activities of the Speaking workshop, Voxopop and Skype. Finally, fourthly, the tools and activities of the fourth workshop, Writing, Dvolver Moviemaker and Wordle.

Listening Workshop

Listen and Write: this tool helps students practice the listening comprehension skill. The tool has multiple exercises for students to dictate online. In addition, it allows the creation of dictations so that the teacher himself can record his voice and store it on the platform offered by the tool itself. The program offers different levels of difficulty, making t very useful for students with different levels.

The great advantage of this tool is that the student can listen to the dictation as many times as they want without having to ask the teacher to repeat a phrase repeatedly. While listening, students can write what they hear audibly in the designated box for it. For this reason, it is not necessary to have any other additional material.

Figure 2. Listen and Write

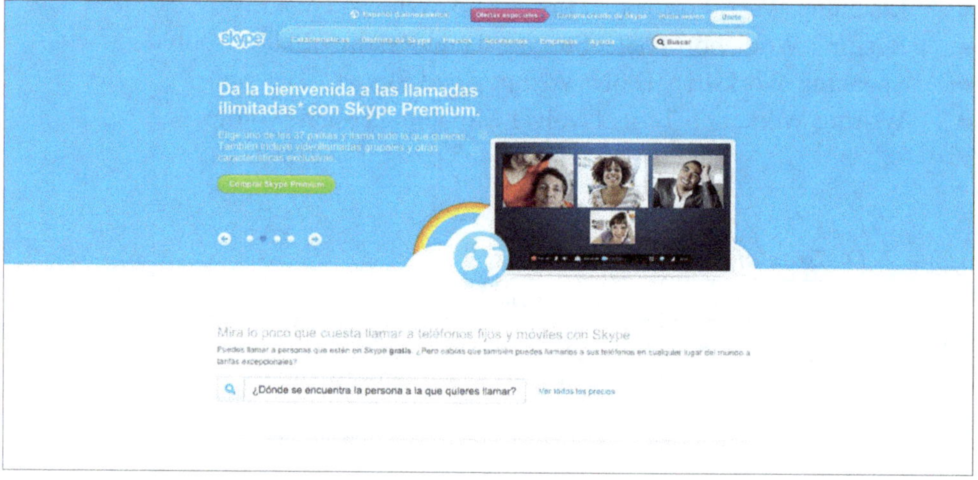

The activity designed for this workshop with this tool, if the students choose it, consists of listening to a dictation recorded by the teacher. Students must use the box provided in the tool to write the sentences they hear. They can dictate while listening to the audition and modify their proposal as many times as they want until they get the word or phrase right. The audio can be played as many times as necessary to effectively capture the audio content.

On the other hand, to assess the listening comprehension of the activity with this tool, the teacher will propose a series of comprehension questions in a digital text (either in Word or OpenOffice). In this way, it will be possible to evaluate the oral comprehension of each student participating in the workshop.

Voki: this tool stands out for its ability to motivate, as it is highly entertaining. The online tool is based on the creation of a characterized avatar. In addition to designing their physical appearance in a personal way (hair colour, eyes, lips, accessories, etc.), students can add various backgrounds and frames where the avatar is introduced. On the other hand, it also offers the possibility of recording their own voice so that the Voki can play it or simply entering a text so that the tool itself proposes the audio. The type of text you enter should be short, such as an introduction or presentation.

Figure 3. Voki

In the activity that is contemplated for this tool, the teacher will create an avatar for the activity in question and will record a small intervention to be reproduced by the avatar created. To perform the activity, the teacher must send the students the exact URL with the avatar created so that the students can listen to it and start with the activity. Students will be allowed to simply listen (without any annotation) to play twice. Then, and to check oral comprehension in this activity, students will have to answer a series of questions about what the Voki (or avatar) has said.

Reading Workshop

Storybird: This tool offers the possibility of creating your own stories from certain image templates housed in the online tool itself. It is a highly motivating material as it offers the possibility of reading stories created by other authors online or creating them autonomously.

Figure 4. Storybird

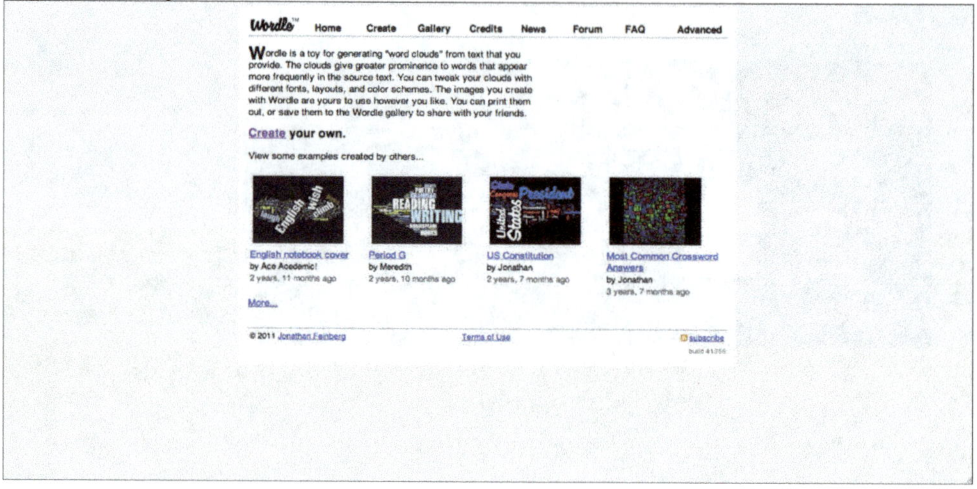

As with most workshop activities, the teacher will invent or choose a story, but always considering the level of the students. The activity will require students to read the story carefully, ensuring that they understand what is said so that, at the end of the reading, they can answer a series of questions related to the story. This will allow the teacher to keep a record of the level of written comprehension that each student has.

Reading Planet: this tool allows the student to create stories from the selection of certain characters, scenarios, etc. Likewise, to create the story, the program broadcasts a series of questions, and the answers will be reflected in the final story. Finally, the program creates the story to be read by the student. This tool also offers the possibility of indicating the age of the student for whom a story is going to be created, so the vocabulary is adapted to their comprehension level. In addition to this activity, the digital resource offers other activities, such as poetry readings tailored for different age groups. In this task, students must complete the poem with a series of given words. In this way, the activity becomes enjoyable and engaging.

Figure 5. Reading Planet

In the specific activity designed for this tool, students will follow the steps to create their own story. Each student in each group will choose the story maker they want but they must follow the steps that the program offers to personalize the story. When the group of students has finished the activity and considering that the program offers the possibility of printing their work, they must read the stories they have created. Since the story is created by the program, and not by the students, the content of the narrative will be unknown to them. This gives the teacher the opportunity to ask a series of questions about the story to assess the student's reading comprehension.

Oral Production Workshop (Speaking)

Voxopop: It is a very creative and innovative tool that consists of the creation of groups (private, restricted, or public) whose main objective is the promotion of oral discussions. The groups created propose topics for debate, although the way the participants debate is through their voice. Voxopop therefore allows the direct recording of voice messages with the contribution of each of the participants integrated in each group.

Figure 6. Voxopop

The activity contemplated for this tool consists of each group having to decide on a topic on which the members wish to debate. This election will be made unanimously. Once the topic has been selected, the teacher will be informed so that he or she can start the Talkgroup. Therefore, the teacher will create a speaking group for students to participate in. The teacher will be the first to speak and the students must express their opinion on the selected topic for a maximum of 30 seconds. In addition to expressing their opinion on the topic, each participant should leave a question open for the next participant to answer before expressing their opinion and asking the next participant the question.

The activity can be evaluated without the need to take any questionnaire since their voices will be recorded in the Talkgroup and the teacher will be able to evaluate the skill of oral production. The aim is for students to lose their fear of speaking in the foreign language and to become more comfortable hearing their own voices through this tool. In addition, it is a motivating and enjoyable resource.

Skype: this is a tool that allows videoconferences to be made using the computer and the internet. It is an excellent resource for acquiring fluency in oral production skills in the foreign language.

Figure 7. Skype

The activity consists of contacting other schools in an English-speaking country to be able to perform sessions with them. Before making the connection, the teacher must contact the other centre to coordinate the sessions. In addition, they will be able to coordinate with foreign students the topics to be discussed during the connection. The teacher will be present during the communication, so that he or she can assess the spontaneity of the students when communicating.

This communication tool has the advantage of improving the ability to produce speech (Speaking). It is also a tool that motivates and promotes student participation. And above all, it encourages them to speak in the foreign language in a real way, with native speakers. So, the topics to be discussed will be those of daily life, making the conversation relevant and practical.

This activity is perhaps the most difficult to develop but not impossible. The questions to be asked will be previously agreed between the teacher and the foreign students. What is valued with this tool is the spontaneity with which students respond to certain questions, since one of the aspects that are evaluated is the ability to produce a coherent message for the interlocutor-receiver.

Writing Production Workshop

Dvolver Moviemaker: This tool allows the student to create short movies in a simple way. Both the characters and the text are chosen by the students to their liking, so it is a highly motivating and entertaining tool. In addition, the program offers the possibility to choose between different types of backgrounds, landscapes and even the title of the film. On the other hand, it has the incentive that the URL of the short film can be sent by email or inserted in a blog or any web page.

Figure 8. Dvolver Moviemaker

The activity that would be part of this workshop consists of proposing dialogues in English for a beginning previously created by the teacher. The teacher proposes a dialogue that must be introduced into the program so that, later, each group of students continues with the story creating a short film. Then, they must follow the steps marked by the same program to make the film. The program offers the possibility to enter short texts, making it a great way to introduce students to creating dialogues. Once they have finished the creation, they will be able to send the final product to their respective emails.

Wordle: this is a tool that allows students to create word clouds in a creative way from a given text. Depending on the frequency of occurrence of the words, the program gives them greater size when it generates the cloud. Once the word cloud has been created, the program gives them the option to modify the typology, the layout, as well as a wide variety of colours.

Figure 9. Wordle

The activity proposed for this tool consists of the teacher creating a word cloud in English, from a given text. Subsequently, the cloud will be displayed on the interactive whiteboard so that all the students for whom this activity is intended can see it. The activity consists of the students, based on the words present in the cloud, selecting the words that they consider representative to write a simple story. Such a story can be invented or created from another existing tale. The objective of the task is for students to practice written production in the foreign language, in addition to encouraging creativity. What is going to be evaluated is the narration created from the words in the Wordle cloud. They will be able to use the dictionary to help them write.

CONCLUSION

Throughout this research, we have developed the use of ICTs for learning the subject of English Language in the third cycle of Primary Education. The last part of this study has focused on the use of ICTs as a means of learning the English language. An attempt has been made to design an example of an educational project to improve the acquisition and understanding of a foreign language in a different way to what has been done these days in accordance with SDG 4.

To achieve this, a series of workshops have been presented as models for the acquisition and development of the language. Given that the use of technological resources requires a certain mastery of them, these tasks have been oriented to be applied in the last cycle of Primary Education. Digital natives, at this age, have great mastery in technological issues.

It has also been important to gather the provisions of national and regional regulations regarding the use of technologies in Primary Education. Like any project in educational matters, it must be based on the laws that regulate these practices. Therefore, and throughout the study, we have considered what the law establishes regarding the use of ICTs in Primary Education.

However, in addition to considering technologies in the educational field, Royal Decree 157/2022 establishes a series of basic skills that students must acquire at the end of Primary Education. One of these skills refers entirely to information and communication technologies, titled: Information Processing and Digital Competence. Therefore, students must make responsible and autonomous use of ICTs as an educational tool.

Within the methodological framework, a compilation has been made of some of the digital resources that can be used for learning the English Language. These resources have been selected for their highly motivating and at the same time effective degree for the achievement of the final objective. A series of resources has been established for each skill, so we have presented eight examples of suitable tools for four language skills to help achieve the acquisition of Listening, Writing, Speaking and Reading.

The aim is for students to acquire competence in a fun and engaging way, and technologies make this possible. Therefore, the binomial that is established between digital resources and the teaching-learning process of the English language is very significant.

We have also proposed genuine activities for each of the tools and workshops in the educational innovation project. Each workshop consists of two materials or technological tools. The workshops, in addition to having a series of general objectives that are acquired using these tools, include examples of activities that can be implemented in the classroom. Some of the activities have more application than others but all of them are suitable for improving the acquisition of a certain English language skill.

As already mentioned, these activities are an example of tasks that can be introduced in the curriculum of the English language subject, acting as instruments to improve specific language skills. Workshops are a good example of tasks to improve and acquire basic and necessary skills in an enjoyable and motivating way, an essential requirement to attract the students' attention at this age.

The purpose of the project has been to delve into a topic as relevant today for everyone, as is the use of tools in our classes. ICTs have permeated not only the classroom, but also have entered the family environment. They are part of everyday life and, therefore, the way in which knowledge is acquired. The way in which ICTs are related to the acquisition of skills is the end point of the research, but not the least important.

The design of workshops described above is an example of a pilot project to be applied in the classrooms of the last cycle of Primary Education. As a future line, we intend to put this pilot project into practice and collect data on its effectiveness with the students involved in the project in the last cycle of Primary Education. Once the results of these tasks have been obtained in each of the workshops, we will propose to perform similar workshops in other cycles of Primary Education adapting the materials used with digital resources, as well as the activities, according to the students' level of knowledge and skills.

On the other hand, another line of future research is the compilation of other ICT resources for each of the subjects of Primary Education, in addition to the English language. For such purpose, not only the language department of a centre would be involved, but also the participation of a greater number of teachers from other disciplines is needed. This would also confer an interdisciplinary character to the project, aligning with the principles of the Bologna Process, which advocates to establish a multidisciplinary and multilingual educational model.

REFERENCES

Acilo Julita, L.M. (2024). Gardner's Theory of Multiple Intelligences: The Basis for Creating a New Learning Approach. *Psychology and Education: A multidisciplinary Journal, 19*(2), 120-131. DOI: 10.5281/zenodo.10997015

Alesandrini, K., & Larson, L. (2020). Teachers bridge to constructivism. *The Clearing House: A Journal of Educational Strategies, Issues and Ideas*, *75*(3), 118–119. DOI: 10.1080/00098650209599249

Aparicio Gómez, O. Y., & Ostos Ortiz, O. L. (2021). Pedagogías emergentes en ambientes virtuales de aprendizaje. *Revista Internacional de Pedagogía e Innovación Educativa*, *1*(1), 11–36. DOI: 10.51660/ripie.v1i1.25

Arabit García, J., Prendes Espinosa, P., & Serrano Sánchez, J. L. (2023). Recursos Educativos Abiertos y metodologías activas para la enseñanza de STEM en Educación Primaria. *RELATEC. Revista Latinoamericana de Tecnología Educativa*, *22*(1), 89–106. DOI: 10.17398/1695-288X.22.1.89

Area Moreira, M., & Adell Segura, J. (2021). Tecnologías digitales y cambio educativo: Una aproximación crítica. *REICE. Revista Electrónica Iberoamericana sobre Calidad, Eficacia y Cambio en Educación*, *19*(4), 83–96. DOI: 10.15366/reice2021.19.4.005

Area Moreira, M., Cepeda Romero, O., & Feliciano García, L. (2018). El uso escolar de las TIC desde la visión del alumnado de Educación Primaria, ESO y Bachillerato. *Educatio XXI*, *36*(2), 229–276. DOI: 10.6018/j/333071

Benavente Vera, S. U., Flores Coronado, M. L., Guizado Oscco, F., & Nuñez Lira, L. A. (2021). Desarrollo de las competencias digitales de docentes a través de programas de intervención 2020. *Propósitos y Representaciones*, *9*(1), 1–23. DOI: 10.20511/pyr2021.v9n1.1034

Betancur Chicué, V., & García Valcárcel, A. (2022). Training Needs Around Digital Teaching Competence: A Systematic Review. *Fonseca Journal of Communication*, *25*, 133–147. DOI: 10.14201/fjc.29603

Bonilla del Río, M. & Aguaded Gómez, I. (2018). La escuela en la era digital: smartphones, apps y programación en Educación Primaria y su repercusión en la competencia mediática del alumnado. *Píxel-Bit. Revista de Medios y Educación*, 1-13. DOI: 10.12795/pixelbit.2018

Cabero Almenara, J., Llorente Cejudo, C., & Martín Párraga, L. (2022). Análisis de las competencias digitales docentes desde los marcos e instrumentos de evaluación. *International Journal of Educational Research and Innovation, 18*(8), 62–79. DOI: 10.46661/ijeri.7444

Cabrera Rodríguez, L.J., Sicilia Suárez, G., Marrero Callico, G., Pérez Sánchez, C.N. & Bethencour Marrero, C. (2022). The Digital Gap in Primary Education in Spain. *Éducation compare, 26*(1), 101-131.

Castillo López, D. (2020). Las TIC en los procesos de enseñanza-aprendizaje desarrollados por maestros tutores de Educación Primaria en la Región de Murcia. *Revista Interuniversitaria de Investigación en Tecnología Educativa, 9*, 1–14. DOI: 10.6018/riite.432061

Christie, M. J. (2021). Constructivism and the role of the teacher. *Journal of Education, 195*(1), 23–35. DOI: 10.31703/glr.2020(V-III).15

European Parliament and Council of the European Union. (2006, December). Recommendation 2006/962/EC on key competences for lifelong learning. *Official Journal of the European Union, 394*, 30.

Gallego Arrufat, M. J., Torres Hernández, N., & Pessoa, T. (2019). Competence of future teachers in the digital area. *Comunicar, 27*(61), 57–67. DOI: 10.3916/C61-2019-05

García Delgado, M. A., Rodríguez Cano, S., Delgado Benito, V., & Di Giusto Valle, C. (2023). Digital Teaching Competence among Teachers of Different Educational Stages in Spain. *Education Sciences, 13*(6), 1–13. DOI: 10.3390/educsci13060581

García Martín, J. & García Martín, S. (2021). Uso de herramientas digitales para la docencia en España durante la pandemia COVID-19. *Revista Española de Educación Comparada, 38*(extra), 151-173. DOI: 10.5944/reec.38.2021.27816

Gillen, J., & Kucirkova, N. (2018). Percolating spaces: Creative ways of using digital technologies to connect young children's school and home lives. *British Journal of Educational Technology, 49*(5), 834–846. DOI: 10.1111/bjet.12666

Hannaford, J., & Beavis, C. (2018). When will the Internet be connected? Digital worlds and belonging in the lives of globally mobile children. *Literacy, 52*(1), 47–54. DOI: 10.1111/lit.12123

Jiménez Hernández, D., Muñoz Sánchez, P., & Sánchez Giménez, F. (2021). La Competencia Digital Docente, una revisión sistemática de los modelos más utilizados. *Revista Interuniversitaria de Investigación en Tecnología Educativa, 10*, 105–112. DOI: 10.6018/riite.472351

Jones, G., & Brader-Araje, L. (2022). The impact of constructivism on education: Language, discourse, and meaning. *American Communication Journal*, *5*(3), 1–10.

Leontiev, A. (1975). *Activity, Consciousness, and Personality*. Prentice-Hall.

Liang, G., & Akiba, M. (2021). Teacher evaluation, performance-related pay, and constructivist instruction. *Educational Policy*, *29*(2), 375–401. DOI: 10.1177/0895904813492379

Liu, C. C., & Chen, I. J. (2020). Evolution of constructivism. *Contemporary Issues in Education Research*, *3*(4), 63–66. DOI: 10.19030/cier.v3i4.199

Mas García, V., Jordá Fabra, T., & Agustí López, A. I. (2023). La importancia de la creación de recursos digitales de calidad destinados a docentes. Una propuesta para su evaluación y mejora. *Praxis Educativa (Santa Rosa)*, *27*(1), 1–18. DOI: 10.19137/praxiseducativa-2023-270117

Monsalve Lorente, L. & Aguasanta Regalado, M. (2020). Nuevas ecologías del aprendizaje en el currículo: la era digital en la escuela. *Revista Latinoamericana de Tecnología Educativa - RELATEC, 19*(1), 139-154. DOI: 10.17398/1695-288X.19.1.139

Moreno Morilla, C., Guzmán Simón, F., & García Jiménez, E. (2021). Digital and information literacy inside and outside Spanish primary education schools. *Learning, Culture and Social Interaction*, *28*, 1–13. DOI: 10.1016/j.lcsi.2020.100455

Prensky, M. (2001). Digital Natives, Digital Immigrants. *On the Horizon*, *9*(5), 1–6. DOI: 10.1108/10748120110424816

Recio Mayorga, J., Gutiérrez Esteban, P., & Suárez Guerrero, C. (2021). Recursos educativos abiertos en comunidades virtuales docentes. *Apertura (Guadalajara, Jal.)*, *13*(1), 101–117. DOI: 10.32870/Ap.v13n1.1921

Santa Medina, R. (2021). El e-Learning en Educación Primaria como consecuencia de la situación generada por el Covid-19: Un estudio de caso. *RIITE Revista Interuniversitaria de Investigación en Tecnología Educativa*, *10*, 121–136. DOI: 10.6018/riite.439831

Sarita, P. (2021). Constructivism: A new paradigm in teaching and learning. *International Journal of Academic Research and Development*, *2*(4), 183–186. DOI: 10.52700/pjh.v2i2.86

Umida, K., Dilora, A., & Umar, E. (2020). Constructivism in teaching and learning process. *European Journal of Research and Reflection in Educational Sciences*, *8*(3), 134–137.

KEY TERMS AND DEFINITIONS

Cognitive Technologies: (CG): Cognitive technologies are AI-based systems designed to mimic human thought processes, enabling them to learn, reason, and make decisions. They leverage techniques like machine learning, natural language processing, and data mining to analyse information, identify patterns, and provide insights. These technologies aim to automate tasks, improve efficiency, and enhance human capabilities in various fields.

Constructivist learning: The constructivist learning theory posits that learners actively build their own understanding and knowledge of the world, rather than passively receiving information. It emphasizes that individuals construct meaning based on their experiences and interactions with their environment, constantly refining and adjusting their understanding as they encounter new situations. This process involves building upon existing knowledge, adjusting mental models (schemas), and actively engaging with the learning material.

Digital natives: A digital native is someone who grew up with digital technology like the internet, computers, and mobile devices, and is considered naturally fluent in their use. They are often contrasted with digital immigrants, who were born before the widespread adoption of digital technology.

Digital immigrants: A digital immigrant is a person who grew up before the internet and other digital computing devices were ubiquitous and so have had to adapt and learn these technologies. Generally, those born before the year 1985 are named digital immigrants.

Digital resources: Digital resources are information assets stored and accessed electronically. They include a variety of formats like e-books, online articles, videos, databases, and software applications, accessible through the internet or other digital platforms. They are integral for enhancing educational and informational access, offering advantages like cost-effectiveness, interactive functionality, and easy manipulation of data.

Information and Communication Technology (ICT): Information and Communication Technology (ICT) encompasses all the technological tools and resources used to transmit, store, create, share, or exchange information. It's a broad term that includes both hardware, software, and the networks that enable digital communication and information management. Essentially, ICT is about using technology to communicate and manage information.

Learning and Knowledge Technologies (LKT): Learning and Knowledge Technologies (LKT) refer to the use of Information and Communication Technologies (ICT) in education to enhance the learning experience and improve knowledge acquisition. LKTs are not just about using technology for teaching, but also involve adapting those technologies to meet the specific needs of learners and promoting meaningful, engaging, and personalized learning.

SDG 4 Objective: SDG 4, or Sustainable Development Goal 4, focuses on ensuring inclusive and equitable quality education and promoting lifelong learning opportunities for all. It's a commitment to providing access to education at all levels, from early childhood to higher education, while also addressing issues of equity and quality.

Chapter 10

Development of Educational Resources Aimed at Learning Prepositions of Movement in the English Language Using Generative Artificial Intelligence and AI

Anabelem Soberanes-Martín
https://orcid.org/0000-0002-1101-8279
Universidad Autónoma del Estado de México, Mexico

José Luis Castillo-Mendoza
https://orcid.org/0000-0002-5668-0602
Universidad Autónoma del Estado de México, Mexico

Edgar Serrano-Pérez
https://orcid.org/0000-0003-4012-9709
Universidad Autónoma del Estado de México, Mexico

ABSTRACT

This chapter presents the development of educational resources to enrich the practice of prepositions of motion in English from a technological perspective. Web augmented

DOI: 10.4018/979-8-3373-0801-2.ch010

reality technology is used to show animations that exemplify the use of prepositions in scenarios that combine virtual and objective elements. The representation of the situations has been carried out following recommendations obtained through generative artificial intelligence and the consultation of specialized literature on the subject of propositions in the English language. The educational resources developed can be used from any mobile device with Internet access and a camera, so it is possible to generate many scenarios and situations that encourage the practice of prepositions of motion. In this way, it is possible to address conditions that combine multiple elements, both real and virtual, favoring the teaching practice and the visual stimulation of the student by focusing on describing unique and dynamic scenarios that adapt to each user's particular interests anywhere and at any time.

1. INTRODUCTION

English is considered one of the most widely used languages in the world for business, communication, and educational activities. Regarding the educational issue, it is common to find that many international undergraduate and graduate programs are taught in English (Jensen & Johannesson, 2006; Onishchuk et al., 2020; Patra & Mohanty, 2016). To improve English language training, the generation of open educational resources that are accessible to the majority of students and teachers, regardless of their age or economic circumstance, is required since language learning can precisely occur throughout the different stages and circumstances of human beings (Baumert et al., 2020; Newport, 2019; Pfenninger et al., 2023). Coupled with this situation, factors such as health contingencies have been identified that move face-to-face education sessions to online education; however, online education can also have multiple advantages, such as avoiding the transfer of students over long distances, avoiding mobility in the congested traffic of large cities, with the safety issues that this also implies (Pregowska et al., 2021). In addition, blending distance educational platforms with virtual technologies has made it possible to address subjects that are difficult to cover for reasons of time, economy, and location (Onggirawan et al., 2023).

Thus, it is increasingly common to find online language course offerings, increasing the need for innovative educational resources that align with the technological capabilities of learners. In this sense, Augmented Reality (AR) on the Web is one of the disruptive technologies that has recently shown its potential as an educational tool by allowing the presentation and consultation of virtual objects in 2 and 3 dimensions, which are added to the capture of images from a camera in real-time under different thematic and educational contexts (Aladin et al., 2020; Dalim et al., 2016; Nitika et al., 2021). AR on the Web is seen as an attractive technology that can promote inclusion and equity as it only requires a cell phone with Internet access regardless of the range of the device. This point is relevant as it supports lifelong learning because students from early ages and older are increasingly familiar with cell phones and tend to use them frequently, developing different skills to use most of their functionalities. Its main features are reading QR codes and accessing internet portals, which are fundamental skills to approach AR (AlNajdi, 2022; Tukhtabayeva et al., 2024). Thus, AR on the Web allows teachers to visualize innovative educational resources to update curricula and develop didactic sequences for academic quality. In this sense, including innovative technologies in the classroom, such as Augmented Reality on the Web, can favor an increase in the quality of learning and homogenize education in the classroom, whether face-to-face or virtual, regardless of the socioeconomic level of students and teachers.

In this way, it is possible to address Sustainable Development Goal 4 (SDG 4), which focuses on promoting inclusive, equitable, and quality education in the context of teaching and learning processes of the English language, considering as one of its fundamental pillars, innovative and disruptive technology, such as AR on the Web. However, one of the main challenges for Virtual or Augmented Reality to expand and diversify among the academic community is the development and edition of two-dimensional and three-dimensional models intended to be displayed in virtual environments (Mavlyuda, 2021; Wei et al., 2015).

With the recent emergence of Generative Artificial Intelligence (GAI) models, this situation may gradually dilute the teacher's need for additional personnel for the generation of subject content, allowing most of the development time to be focused on educational objectives instead of spending time, effort and resources on learning how to use editing and design programs for virtual objects. In this way, it is visualized that GAI can be applied in the generation of educational resources that favor content creation processes to be presented in AR applications, whether in the form of text, images, virtual objects, or even programming codes (Banh & Strobel, 2023; Kartal, 2023; Vartiainen & Tedre, 2023). It is envisioned that content generated through artificial intelligence can revolutionize the field of education (Baidoo-Anu & Owusu, 2023; Rusmiyanto et al., 2023; Yu & Guo, 2023); however, so far, these are models that still require human supervision. AI results require human perception to discern whether the content obtained satisfies the user's educational requirements, a situation that, for the time being, still needs to be performed by the teacher or the team developing the academic content.

The proposed work aims to explore the generation of content from GAI that can be presented and visualized through AR on the Web to promote topics related to English language learning, all in the context of promoting the fulfillment of the SDG 4. Baidoo-Anu and Owusu (2023) note that ChatGPT in education reveals critical challenges relevant to the development of resources with GAI and AR in teaching prepositions of motion in English. The reliability of GAI may generate incorrect information or invent academic references, which questions its reliability in creating pedagogical content without human supervision (Baidoo-Anu & Owusu, 2023; Qadir, 2022). In the context of prepositions (such as "through" and "over"), this could lead to erroneous grammatical explanations or contextually inappropriate examples. The GAI lacks real semantic understanding of prepositions, being limited to statistical patterns. This hinders its ability to explain nuances such as the difference between "over" (no contact) and "above" (static position).

The topic of prepositions is one of the most complicated for students as they are words that allow establishing relationships between objects, such as location, position, or direction, among others. In particular, students find prepositions of movement and direction complex (Dawoud & Al Hanaqtah, 2021; Newport, 2019). It is common that, for teaching prepositions of motion and direction in the English language, the learner is presented with examples and case studies where it is necessary to explicitly show the situation of relationships in the environment through text and pictures. However, this process is usually done using 2-dimensional paper images. In this proposal, various technologies will be integrated to present the content in a more realistic context by presenting cases of application of the theory in the physical world surrounding the student. In this sense, Augmented Reality can be an interesting technology in this aspect since it precisely allows the visualization of three-dimensional objects in the capture of an image of the real world in order to exemplify the situations in which the prepositions of movement and direction can be correctly used with the help of virtual objects. Looking to the future of language teaching, the project's overall goal was to develop teaching resources for learning prepositions of motion in English. These resources will harness the power of GAI, and AR technologies, creating a transformative and innovative approach to language teaching.

The chapter is structured in sections that guide from the theoretical framework to the empirical validation. First, a literature review integrating linguistic, pedagogical, and technological perspectives is presented, supporting the relevance of prepositions of motion in L2 teaching and the role of GAI and AR as innovative tools. Subsequently, the methodology employed is detailed, including the technical-pedagogical design of the web applications and the usability evaluation instruments, the SUS Scale (Brooke, 1996). Next, the results are presented, including the technical performance of the AR animations (under, over, through, and over) and the usability metrics collected from students and teachers. Finally, the conclusion discusses the findings and practical implications for language education and proposes future directions for these resources.

2. BACKGROUND

Educational experiences in the university environment integrate multiple learning resources - digital and non-digital (IEEE, 2020), articulated under pedagogical approaches adapted to specific contexts. Grece et al. (2023) point out that the implementation of Artificial Intelligence (AI) in education not only transforms teaching and learning methods but also redefines the roles of educators and students. Teachers can utilize AI tools to quickly identify individual student needs, design more effective pedagogical strategies, and allocate more time to human interaction, which remains irreplaceable in the educational process. On the other hand, students benefit from adaptive learning that adjusts to their pace and style, fostering autonomy and motivation.

AI integration in education has revolutionized administrative, pedagogical, and learning processes through task automation (Chen, Chen, & Lin, 2020) and personalized learning systems. Recent research by Lim et al. (2023) highlights AI's evolving role as a relational artifact that fosters socio-affective learning dynamics. While AI offers transformative potential for personalized education and access equity, UNESCO (2021) emphasizes the need for ethical frameworks to prevent bias amplification and digital inequality, particularly in underserved regions.

This chapter reviews five fundamental axes: 1) the linguistic-pedagogical foundations for second language (L2) acquisition, 2) educational technologies applied to language teaching, 3) the potential of GAI in content personalization, 4) the use of AR as an immersive didactic resource, and 5) the GAI-AR synergy for the design of dynamic educational materials. This analysis establishes a theoretical framework linking technological innovation with pedagogical strategies.

2.1 Linguistic and Pedagogical Foundations

Second language acquisition involves both implicit (exposure-based) and explicit (rule-based) learning mechanisms, with their interaction being crucial for developing communicative competence (Ellis, 2020). Krashen's (1985) Input Hypothesis emphasizes that learners require comprehensible input slightly above their current level (i+1) to activate language acquisition, particularly important for mastering polysemous motion prepositions, modern L2 pedagogy combines metalinguistic explanations with experiential learning, particularly for challenging spatial prepositions such as “through” versus “across” (Celce-Murcia & Larsen-Freeman, 2015). Effective instruction should: (1) Anchor new knowledge to existing schemas through visual/kinesthetic examples (Ellis, 2020), (2) Provide multimodal input to prevent L1 interference (Krashen, 1985), and (3) Alternate structured practice with free production tasks (Ellis, 2020). Educational technology can operationalize these principles by offering immersive environments that deliver contextualized, varied repetition, thereby fulfilling both the need for comprehensible input (Krashen, 1985) and the development of procedural memory (Celce-Murcia & Larsen-Freeman, 2015).

2.2 Digital Resources for Language Learning

The integration of digital technologies has fundamentally reshaped language teaching methodologies, enabling more interactive and personalized learning experiences. Contemporary tools, including online platforms, mobile applications, and digital language corpora, provide learners with authentic, context-rich language exposure (Hockly, 2022). These innovations not only broaden educational access but also foster learner independence through adaptive learning pathways tailored to individual progress. As Chapelle and Sauro (2017) emphasize, the pedagogical value of these digital resources stems from their dual foundation in linguistic theory and user-centered design principles, ensuring alignment with specific learning outcomes.

Research demonstrates the particular efficacy of information and communication technologies (ICTs) for vocabulary acquisition and grammar instruction. Digital flashcard systems utilizing spaced repetition algorithms (e.g., Anki, Quizlet) have proven especially effective for long-term retention (Hockly, 2022). Similarly, virtual environments that contextualize grammar through simulated conversations (e.g., chatbot interactions) promote deeper understanding by reducing reliance on rote memorization; multimedia resources significantly enhance language instruction by engaging multiple learning modalities, thereby enhancing the learning experience. Subtitled videos, for instance, simultaneously develop listening comprehension and reinforce orthographic-phonemic connections (Chapelle & Sauro, 2017). Immersive simulations, such as virtual tours of English-speaking cities, provide realistic contexts for practicing spatial prepositions and other challenging lexical items. However, as Hockly (2022) notes, such resources must adhere to universal design principles to ensure accessibility for diverse learners.

The application of gamification strategies has emerged as a particularly effective motivational tool in language education. Reward systems (badges, leaderboards) and narrative-driven activities transform routine exercises into compelling challenges (Chapelle & Sauro, 2017). Importantly, Hockly (2022) cautions that successful gamification requires substantive integration of pedagogical objectives rather than superficial game elements alone. Virtual reality technologies offer unprecedented opportunities for culturally immersive language practice. While VR environments enable authentic scenarios, such as restaurant ordering simulations (Chapelle & Sauro, 2017), Hockly (2022) stresses that their educational value depends on careful curricular integration, including preparatory instruction and outcome assessment.

Recent advances in adaptive artificial intelligence have revolutionized personalized language instruction. Platforms like Duolingo leverage machine learning to identify learner weaknesses and generate targeted exercises (Zhao & Li, 2022). Concurrently, collaborative augmented reality (CAR) systems enable group language practice in hybrid physical-digital spaces (Wu et al., 2023), simultaneously developing linguistic and socioemotional competencies (Godwin-Jones, 2021). Together, these technologies represent a paradigm shift toward inclusive, scalable language education models that accommodate diverse learning needs and paces.

2.3 Generative Artificial Intelligence in Education

GAI refers to systems capable of creating original content (text, images, audio) using deep learning models such as GPT-4 and DALL-E (OpenAI, 2023). In education, these models allow the generation of dynamic didactic materials, such as contextualized dialogues to practice languages (Zhao & Li, 2022) or personalized illustrations to explain abstract concepts. E.g. teachers can use tools such as ChatGPT to design grammar exercises tailored to topics of student interest, merging technological innovation with evidence-based pedagogy (Luckin, 2018). This capability transforms resource creation, reducing time and institutional costs.

GAI facilitates content adaptation according to students' cognitive levels, interests, and learning styles. Platforms such as Khan Academy or Duolingo employ generative algorithms to produce automatic exercises that adjust in difficulty according to real-time performance (Hattie, 2023). E.g., a student making mistakes with prepositions in English would receive specific examples generated by GAI, along with simplified metalinguistic explanations. This personalization improves retention and increases motivation by providing immediate and relevant feedback (Baker & Inventado, 2021).

GAI allows the creation of hyper-realistic virtual scenarios to practice language skills or solve problems in simulated contexts. A study by Zhao & Li (2022) demonstrated that chatbots such as ChatGPT can generate dialogues in English where learners negotiate in a virtual store, using structures such as "Could you lower the price?". Combined with DALL-E-generated avatars, these environments provide safe immersion for making mistakes and receiving automated corrections. In addition, GAI can modify the complexity of interactions based on the user's progress, aligning with Vygotsky's zone of proximal development theory (Holmes et al., 2022).

The results of the Delgado et al. (2024) study reveal a significant gap between teachers' perceptions and the actual opportunities for AI in education. While teachers recognize benefits such as task automation (63 citations) and access to resources (55 citations), their primary concerns center on inappropriate use (73 citations) and the erosion of critical thinking (55 citations), particularly in secondary schools.

This divergence underscores the need to design training programs differentiated by educational stage: in primary school, focused on the emotionally safe use of AI; in secondary school, on the ethical management of tools such as ChatGPT; and in higher education, on the critical integration of AI to avoid bias and ensure academic rigor. The research suggests that, without contextualized teacher training, the education system could miss out on the potential of AI or exacerbate its risks, such as technological dependency or the dehumanization of learning.

Also, despite its potential, GAI in education poses challenges, such as the lack of algorithmic transparency and the risk of perpetuating cultural biases in the generated content (Baker & Inventado, 2021). E.g., if a model is trained with data predominantly in American English, it could ignore dialect variants such as Australian or Indian English. In addition, there is a danger of teachers overestimating the capabilities of GAI, delegating key roles such as formative assessment (Luckin, 2018). To mitigate these risks, critical AI literacy teacher training that emphasizes human supervision and pedagogical validation of the generated resources is required (UNESCO, 2023).

The integration of GAI in education poses a dual challenge: on the one hand, it offers innovative tools to personalize learning and optimize administrative processes; on the other hand, it requires critical reflection on its impact on students' cognitive autonomy. As Ubal et al. (2023) point out, the risk of adopting a techno-banking model (where AI replaces human interaction) could erode fundamental skills such as critical thinking and creativity, pillars of human development. It is therefore imperative to design pedagogical strategies that, leveraging the potential of AI, prioritize teacher mediation and encourage activities that require analysis, synthesis, and the contextualized application of knowledge. This is the only way to ensure that technology complements, rather than supplants, the educational processes essential for the integral formation of individuals.

The future of GAI points toward integration with educational metaverses and hybrid tutoring systems; e.g. OpenAI (2023) suggests that GPT-4 could be combined with AR to create virtual laboratories where students manipulate 3D objects while receiving explanations generated in real-time. Pilot projects such as AI4T in the European Union have already explored this approach, using GPT-4 to simulate personalized tutoring in mathematics and science (Molenaar, 2023). However, its success will depend on policies that balance innovation with equity, ensuring universal access and avoiding technology gaps.

2.4 Augmented Reality as a Teaching Tool

Augmented Reality (AR) merges virtual elements with real-world environments through marker-based, geolocative, or image recognition technology, creating interactive hybrid experiences (Azuma, 2015). Key characteristics include reality blending, real-time interaction, and spatial precision (Wu et al., 2023). Accessible platforms like ARKit and ARCore enable the integration of 3D models via mobile devices, making AR particularly valuable for contextual language learning, such as labeling physical objects with virtual vocabulary terms; research demonstrates the effectiveness of AR for spatial preposition acquisition, with studies showing 23% higher retention rates compared to traditional methods (Chen & Wang, 2021). By visualizing scenarios like a cat moving "over" a table or "under" a chair, AR reduces linguistic abstraction through multisensory engagement (Hsu, 2020). The technology also supports cultural adaptation, enabling context-specific environments such as London markets or Tokyo streetscapes (Lee & Park, 2022).

Kinesthetic applications represent another significant advantage. Systems like Moverio project virtual paths that learners physically follow while verbalizing directional prepositions (Wu et al., 2023). This embodied learning approach, such as walking "through" a virtual doorway while speaking the phrase, combines motor and auditory memory to reinforce language acquisition (Parmaxi, 2023).

AR offers instant feedback through motion sensors and speech recognition. In the WordSense app, developed by García-Martínez et al. (2023), students receive real-time corrections when constructing sentences such as "The bird is flying ___ the tree" (over vs. above). If they make an incorrect choice, a virtual avatar demonstrates the action with the appropriate preposition. This interactivity improves autonomy and reduces anxiety by allowing private rehearsals without external judgment (Hsu, 2020). Furthermore, systems such as ARLearn generate automated reports for teachers, identifying common errors in the classroom (UNESCO, 2022).

AR promotes collaborative learning through shared scenarios where groups negotiate meanings in the target language. Parmaxi (2023) documented an exercise where students solved a virtual escape room in English, moving around the room to find clues projected in AR. Tools like SharedSpaces allow multiple users to interact with the same virtual objects from different devices, encouraging dialogues such as "Pass me the virtual key next to the lamp!" (Lee & Park, 2022). This approach develops communication skills and teamwork, key elements of the CEFR framework.

Despite its potential, AR faces technical and pedagogical challenges. Wu et al. (2023) identify the digital divide (unequal access to devices) and cognitive overload due to excessive stimuli. To mitigate these challenges, UNESCO (2022) recommends designing resources with inclusion principles, such as subtitle options or scenario simplification. Future trends point toward integrating AR with generative AI, where systems like GPT-4 will create adaptive narratives in real-time (Molenaar, 2023). Thus, AR will teach languages and simulate immersive cultural exchanges, such as conversing with native-speaker avatars in a Marrakech market.

2.5 Integration of Generative Artificial Intelligence and Augmented Reality Into Educational Resources

The integration of GAI + AR creates dynamic educational tools that combine adaptive content with immersive visualization (Dunleavy & Dede, 2023). This collaboration enables personalized language learning experiences (such as GPT-4-generated dialogues contextualized in AR environments (e.g., virtual coffee shops with interactive avatars) which align with situated learning theory, emphasizing knowledge construction in authentic contexts (Hwang et al., 2020). Effective GAI-AR integration requires careful instructional design. Mayer's (2021) spatial contiguity principle ensures text and visuals are optimally placed to minimize cognitive load. Platforms like *LangVision* demonstrate this balance: GAI crafts personalized narratives (e.g., jungle adventures), while AR renders them as 3D animations in the learner's physical space (García-Martínez et al., 2023). Such multimodal approaches enhance comprehension of spatial language (e.g., prepositions) and boost motivation through learner agency (Dunleavy & Dede, 2023).

For instance, practicing "She walked across the bridge" triggers AR projections of a bridge with directional arrows, distributing cognitive load across visual and auditory channels (Sweller, 2011). Real-time adaptation is another key benefit. Systems like Zhao et al.'s (2023) AR app analyze errors (e.g., confusing "through" with "into") and generate targeted exercises paired with AR demonstrations (e.g., animating objects moving "into a box"). This dual feedback strengthens metacognition (Hwang et al., 2020). UNESCO (2023) emphasizes the importance of teacher training to achieve pedagogical balance. Future directions may involve GAI-AR metaverses for immersive intercultural exchanges (Molenaar, 2023).

The theoretical framework integrates linguistic, pedagogical, and technological perspectives to support the design of innovative educational resources for teaching prepositions of movement in English. The following section details the participants, instruments, and procedures to contrast the theoretical premises with the data obtained.

3. METHOD

This section details the methodological approach used to develop and evaluate educational resources based on GAI and AR to teach prepositions of movement in English. Adopting a mixed (qualitative-quantitative) design, the process was structured in two main phases: 1) the technical-pedagogical development of the applications, which integrated content generation through GAI (ChatGPT) with the programming of contextualized AR animations, and 2) the usability evaluation, using the System Usability Scale (SUS), applied to higher education students and teachers. This approach is based on user-centered design principles (Norman, 2013) and multimedia learning (Mayer, 2021), prioritizing creating interactive, accessible experiences aligned with pedagogical standards.

3.1 Participants

The study included the participation of 88 students from three higher education institutions specializing in computer engineering, information technology, and computer systems (one public university and two from institutions belonging to the National Institute of Technology of Mexico). In addition, five faculty members from the three institutions were included. Table 1 shows the distribution of participants.

Table 1. Data of participating students from both institutions

	Institution 1	Institution 2	Institution 3
Students	31	29	28
Teachers	2	2	1

3.2 Instructional Design

The following is an Instructional Design for Using WebAR to Teach Prepositions of Movement in English (Mayer, 2021; Dunleavy & Dede, 2023). Level: Higher Education. Duration: Two 60-minute sessions. General Objective: Students will use WebAR resources to understand and apply English prepositions of movement (through, across, into, over) in dynamic situational contexts, combining virtual and real-life elements.

Session 1: Introduction to prepositions and WebAR

- Presentation of the topic objective (5 min)
- Initial assessment: Online questionnaire to identify specific difficulties with prepositions of movement. E.g., "How would you describe the action 'She walks ___ the bridge'?" (options: across, through, over, under). Ten questions are given (10 min).
- Brief theoretical presentation (20 min) with visual examples.
- Practical WebAR demonstration. Students enter URLs or scan a marker in the classroom to view the animation of objects moving "through a bridge," "across a bridge," among other (25 min).

Session 2: Guided practice

- Solve exercises in which students must select the correct preposition after interacting with the animation (15 minutes).
- Use generative chatbots (e.g., ChatGPT) to create contextualized dialogues with the learned prepositions (15 minutes).
- Explore a real WebAR scenario and capture screenshots with examples (15 minutes).
- Guided discussion: "How did WebAR facilitate your understanding of prepositions?" (10 minutes).
- Closing the topic (5 minutes).

Technological Resources: Students should have mobile devices with cameras and Internet access.

3.3 Interaction With AI

Generative Artificial Intelligence has disrupted multiple facets of people's daily lives, one of the most important being education. The impact of using this intelligence technology is overwhelming, as it is possible to obtain multiple representations or interpretations from a text input—which can be as simple as a single word or more complex, in the form of paragraphs or entire texts—from which the artificial intelligence is asked to obtain or process information. Another important feature is that as the interaction between the person and the chatbot progresses, the results provide feedback and suggestions on the topics being discussed, similar to how we humans communicate, and which provides a sense of understanding and interest in the topics being discussed.

However, it should be noted that the results obtained from GAI come from multiple training datasets, and the process is constantly evolving, so it is sometimes possible to obtain unreliable or erroneous information. Thus, the user needs to have sufficient knowledge about the topic under discussion to have the capacity and intuition to discern whether the communication is going in the right direction or is deviating from or distorting the objective of the interaction. In this sense, the ChatGPT tool has been used to identify features and patterns that allow the prepositions of movement to be exemplified through animations projectable through AR technology. Prepositions of movement are complicated for students since some are similar, and it is necessary to identify the cases in which one or the other is used. Such is the case of the prepositions "across" and "through," which can be used in different contexts. To clarify the situation, a conversation was started in the ChatGPT medium to clarify the difference between them. The results are presented in Figure 1.

Figure 1. Results obtained from ChatGPT for the prepositions of movement "across" and "through"

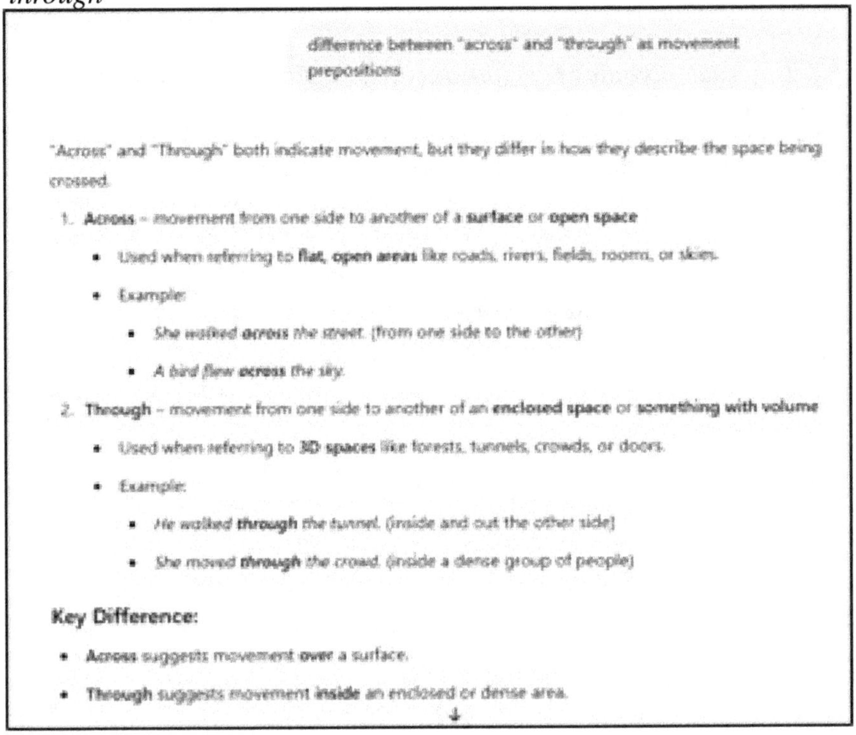

difference between "across" and "through" as movement prepositions

"Across" and "Through" both indicate movement, but they differ in how they describe the space being crossed.

1. **Across** – movement from one side to another of a **surface** or **open space**
   - Used when referring to **flat, open areas** like roads, rivers, fields, rooms, or skies.
   - Example:
     - *She walked* ***across*** *the street.* (from one side to the other)
     - *A bird flew* ***across*** *the sky.*
2. **Through** – movement from one side to another of an **enclosed space** or **something with volume**
   - Used when referring to **3D spaces** like forests, tunnels, crowds, or doors.
   - Example:
     - *He walked* ***through*** *the tunnel.* (inside and out the other side)
     - *She moved* ***through*** *the crowd.* (inside a dense group of people)

Key Difference:

- **Across** suggests movement **over** a surface.
- **Through** suggests movement **inside** an enclosed or dense area.

From the response provided by the interaction with ChatGPT, it is initially possible to observe that "across" is used for situations where movement occurs across the surface of something. In contrast, the preposition "through" is used for situations where the movement occurs through a three-dimensional space, so it could refer to moving. At the same time, "across" is synonymous with crossing. According to the literature, these are prepositions that describe movement in space or time, generally horizontal or linear. It is worth noting that while "across" is used for a two-dimensional context, "through" is used for a context involving three dimensions (Dixon, 2021).

An interesting aspect is that, as a result of the interaction with the chatbot, two additional prepositions were used as "Key Differences": "over" and "inside." The preposition "over" is used in this work, along with the preposition "under," to exemplify the movement of objects above and below a reference point. However, up to this point, returning to the key phrase dictated by the chatbot: "Across suggests movement over a surface," leaves open the possibility of the movement being made in contact with the surface or without contact with the reference surface. In this sense, the prepositions of movement "under" and "over" are important in daily communication to represent multiple events or situations, so they have interacted with

ChatGPT in order to obtain a perspective of use and to be able to represent its use through animations with AR technology, obtaining the results shown in Figure 2.

Figure 2. The result obtained from the interaction with ChatGPT for the case of the prepositions of movement "under" and "over"

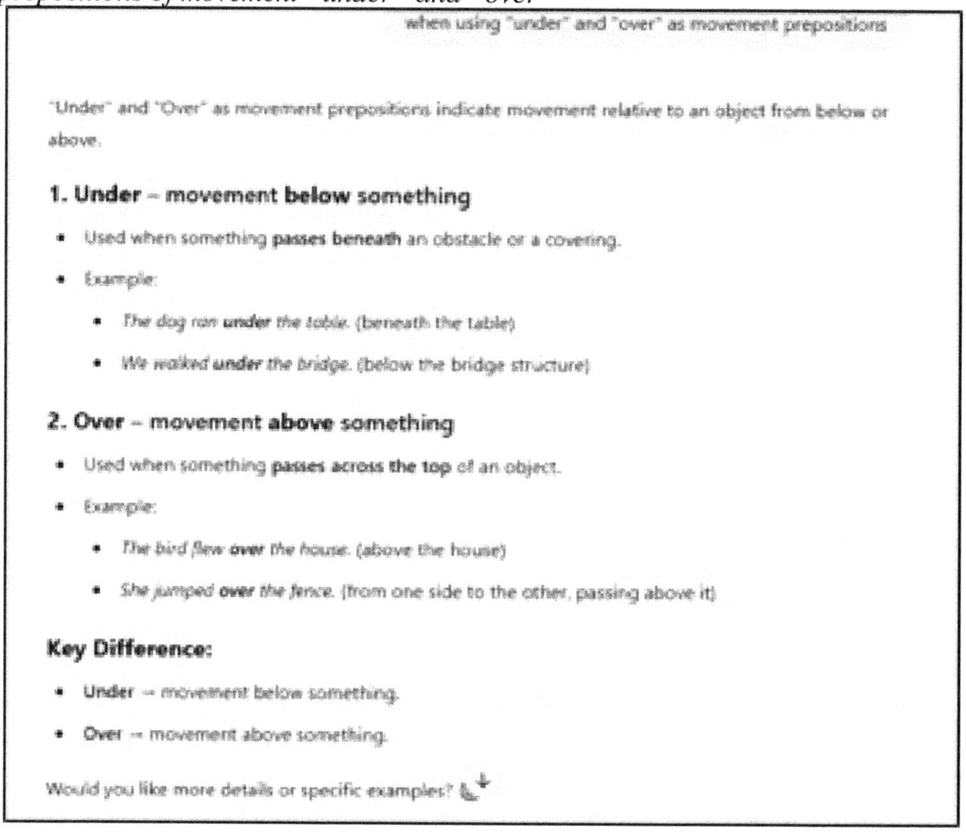

Based on the results obtained from the interaction with the chatbot, it can be deduced that the preposition "over" indicates movement over an object, which in some everyday situations could be interpreted with the preposition "across", so the chatbot was asked if there was any similarity between them, as can be seen in Figure 3.

Figure 3. Query result for the relationship between "across" and "over"

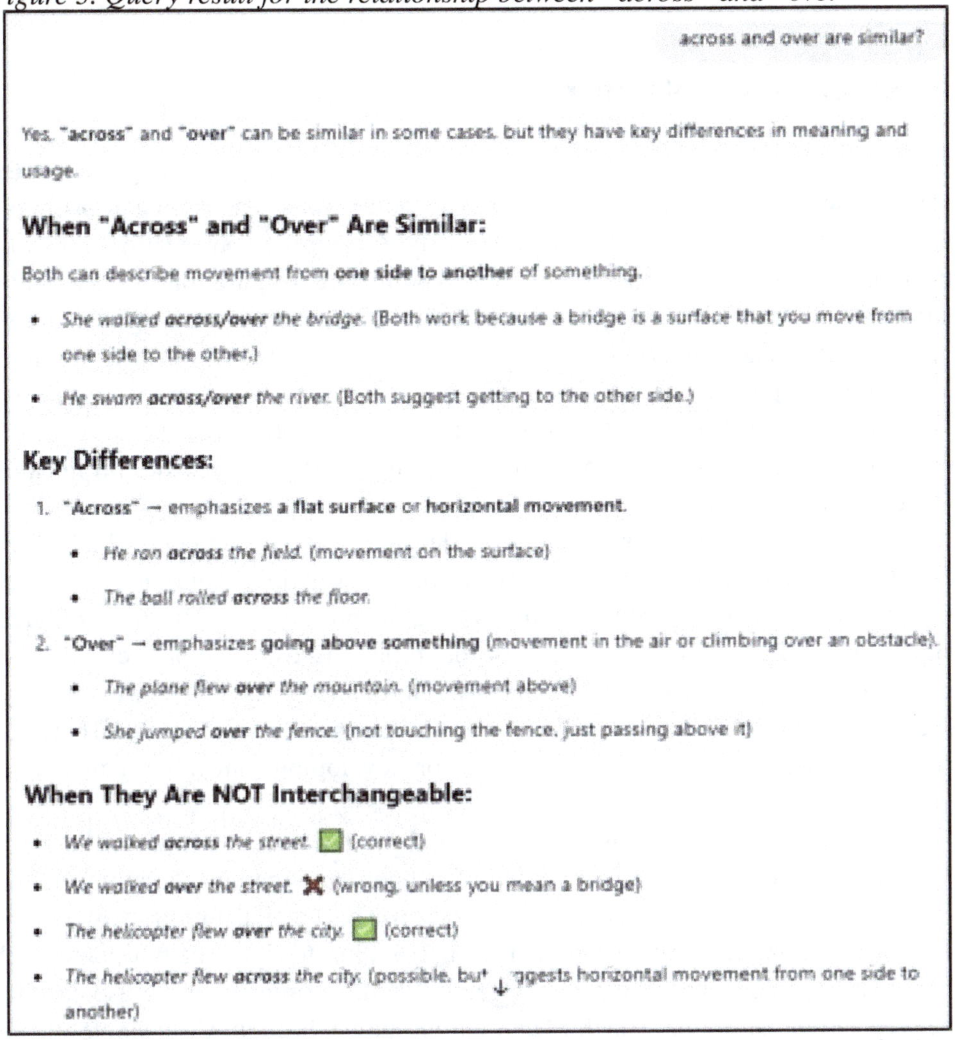

across and over are similar?

Yes, "across" and "over" can be similar in some cases, but they have key differences in meaning and usage.

When "Across" and "Over" Are Similar:

Both can describe movement from **one side to another** of something.

- *She walked* ***across/over*** *the bridge.* (Both work because a bridge is a surface that you move from one side to the other.)
- *He swam* ***across/over*** *the river.* (Both suggest getting to the other side.)

Key Differences:

1. **"Across"** → emphasizes a **flat surface** or **horizontal movement**.
   - *He ran* ***across*** *the field.* (movement on the surface)
   - *The ball rolled* ***across*** *the floor.*
2. **"Over"** → emphasizes **going above something** (movement in the air or climbing over an obstacle).
   - *The plane flew* ***over*** *the mountain.* (movement above)
   - *She jumped* ***over*** *the fence.* (not touching the fence, just passing above it)

When They Are NOT Interchangeable:

- *We walked* ***across*** *the street.* ✅ (correct)
- *We walked* ***over*** *the street.* ❌ (wrong, unless you mean a bridge)
- *The helicopter flew* ***over*** *the city.* ✅ (correct)
- *The helicopter flew* ***across*** *the city.* (possible, but suggests horizontal movement from one side to another)

Based on the interaction results with the chatbot, it is possible to identify key points for their correct use. In general, it can be deduced that "across" should be used when there is an interaction between the moving object and a static surface, while "over" should be used to refer to an object that moves over an object but without touching it, that is, without touching a surface.

However, in some specific cases, such as those shown in the chatbot, they can be used interchangeably, which makes it more challenging to master prepositions in English (Damayanti & Sundari, 2022; Ilham, 2018; Yaş, 2022). The influence of the verb in the selection of prepositions is important, as it allows us to give meaning to the action being described and, consequently, to the grammatical logic of the sentences (Abdalla, 2021).

3.4 Resource Development

A-Frame, an open-source framework that developed immersive experiences for web browsers, was used to implement the AR animations. The choice of primitive geometries (spheres, donuts, and cylinders) allowed for the optimization of the 3D modeling process, as these basic shapes only require the configuration of fundamental parameters such as color, dimensions, and radius, facilitating the rapid generation of virtual objects. The animation of these elements was implemented using A-Frame's animation component, which allows for the definition of 1) position transitions with precise control of trajectories and durations, 2) motion effects using easing algorithms (acceleration/deceleration smoothing), and 3) time synchronization between animated events.

The Glitch platform was selected as the development environment, which offers 1) online collaborative editing, ii) free hosting, iii) native integration with web frameworks, and iv) an ideal environment for agile prototyping. This technological solution proved particularly efficient for the initial phases of the project, allowing for rapid iterations and usability testing without requiring expensive infrastructure. The combination of A-Frame and Glitch constituted an ecosystem balanced between technical power and accessibility, crucial for developing innovative educational resources.

Each of the four animations is described below: The first AR application on the Web was intended to show an animation of a sphere moving horizontally from left to right across a table surface, exemplifying the use of the preposition “across.” The second animation displayed a sphere moving from left to right in a horizontal path that crosses a transparent three-dimensional donut, exemplifying the use case for the preposition “through.” The third animation, shown through AR technology, was a sphere moving horizontally from left to right under an arch, referencing a bridge in a riverbed, exemplifying the use of the preposition “under.” Finally, the fourth animation represents the situation in which a flying saucer moves from left to right over three red cylinders. The movement occurs in the air, confirming that this is a situation without contact between the moving objects and the reference.

Since this is an AR technology, the scene can be adapted to countless contexts and situations. The animation with the virtual objects can be placed in everyday settings, e.g. in a dining room, a garden, a street, or even a classroom. This demonstrates the high potential of this technology for the instant creation of unique scenarios anywhere, with situations that can be described by the teacher and/or the student to practice and exemplify the use and application of prepositions of movement in the description of events and occurrences that combine real and virtual life.

3.5 System Usability Scale (SUS)

The System Usability Scale (SUS) was used, a questionnaire designed to assess the level of usability of products and services. It consists of 10 questions with five response options and includes the following statements (Brooke, 1996):

1. I think I would like to use this system frequently.
2. I found the system to be unnecessarily complex.
3. I thought the system was easy to use.
4. I think I would need the support of a technical person to be able to use this system.
5. I found the various functions of this system to be well-integrated.
6. I thought there was too much inconsistency in this system.
7. I imagine most people would learn to use this system very quickly.
8. I found the system very complicated to use.
9. I felt very confident using the system.
10. I needed to learn many things before I could start using this system.

Responses are presented on a Likert scale ranging from 1 (strongly disagree) to 5 (strongly agree). The following formula calculates the SUS score that was first applied:

$$SUS = (\sum \text{Contribution of each item}) \times 2.5$$

Odd-numbered items (positive): Item score - 1.

Even-numbered items (negative): 5 - Item score.

The SUS then calculates the evaluation application's rating on a scale of 0 to 100; the higher the score, the higher the level of usability (Brooke, 1996).

4. RESULTS

The content is organized into two parts: i) a description of the functioning of the educational resource and ii) results of the System Usability Scale (SUS), which is applied to teachers and students.

4.1 Operation of the Educational Resource

As a result of consulting the primary reference source (Dixon, 2021) and interacting with ChatGPT (Koraishi, 2023; Meniado, 2023), general usage scenarios for prepositions of the movement were established, namely:

- Across: Movement performed over a reference surface, generally involving contact.
- Through: Movement performed in a three-dimensional reference environment, with contact, or nearby.
- Under: Movement performed beneath an object, generally without or subtle contact with the reference object.
- Over: Movement performed above an object, generally without contact with the reference objects.

Considering the general characteristics of using prepositions, animations were created to visualize motion events using AR technology. Therefore, the ChatGPT tool was used as an assistant in generating programming code for the web application (Fuchter et al., 2025). In this sense, AR applications were developed to exemplify the situation, where animations allow creating and combining scenarios with real and virtual elements, giving way to events and situations that represent prepositions of motion. The process begins with the preposition "across," where the animation indicates that a red sphere moves from left to right across the surface of a table representation. As the literature describes, the preposition "across" usually requires the moving object to maintain surface contact with the static reference point. It can also have multiple meanings, describing time, location, or even the formation of phrasal verbs (Dixon, 2021), which adds significant complexity to the description of its use across the broad spectrum of representations in the English language.

In the case of the preposition "through," the animation represents the situation in which the red sphere passes through a cyan donut. In this case, transparency is a relevant feature that allows the sphere's passage through the donut to be visualized dynamically, as seen in Figure 4. On the other hand, the representation of the use of the prepositions "under" and "over" was done by exemplifying the movement of a red sphere under an arch representing a bridge over a river. In fact, this animation could also be used to focus attention on the sphere with the river, in order to describe the situation of the sphere crossing the river as it moves over the water surface. In the case of the preposition "over", its use is exemplified by an orange flying saucer, moving over three red cylinders, so that it can be seen in the animation that there is no contact with the reference and the movement occurs in the air, as can be seen in Figure 5.

Figure 4. Augmented Reality applications show motion animations of the prepositions "across" and "through"

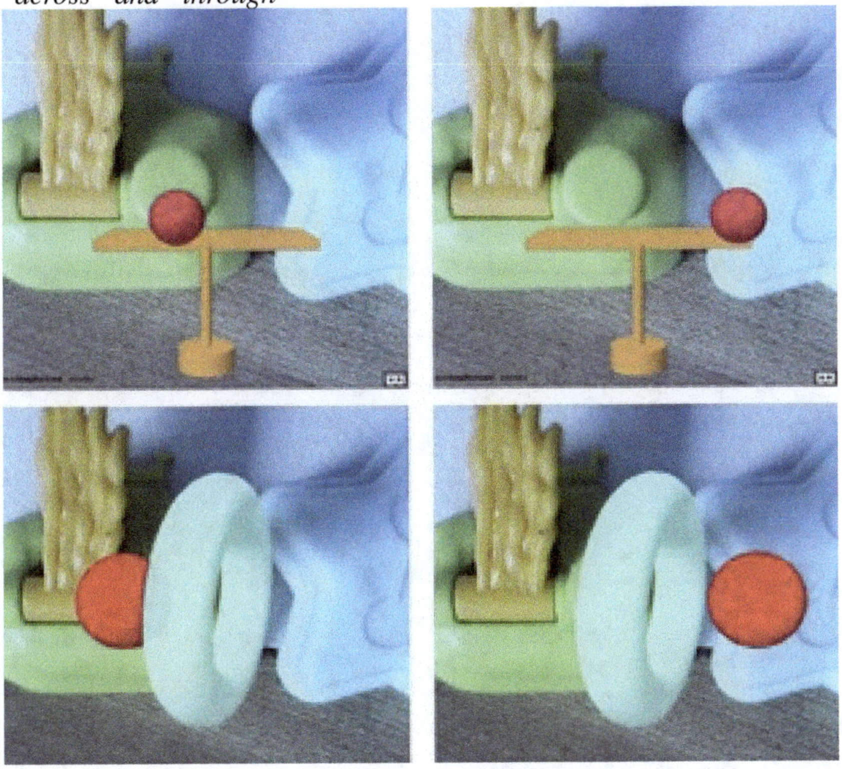

Figure 5. Augmented Reality applications show motion animations of the prepositions "under" and "over"

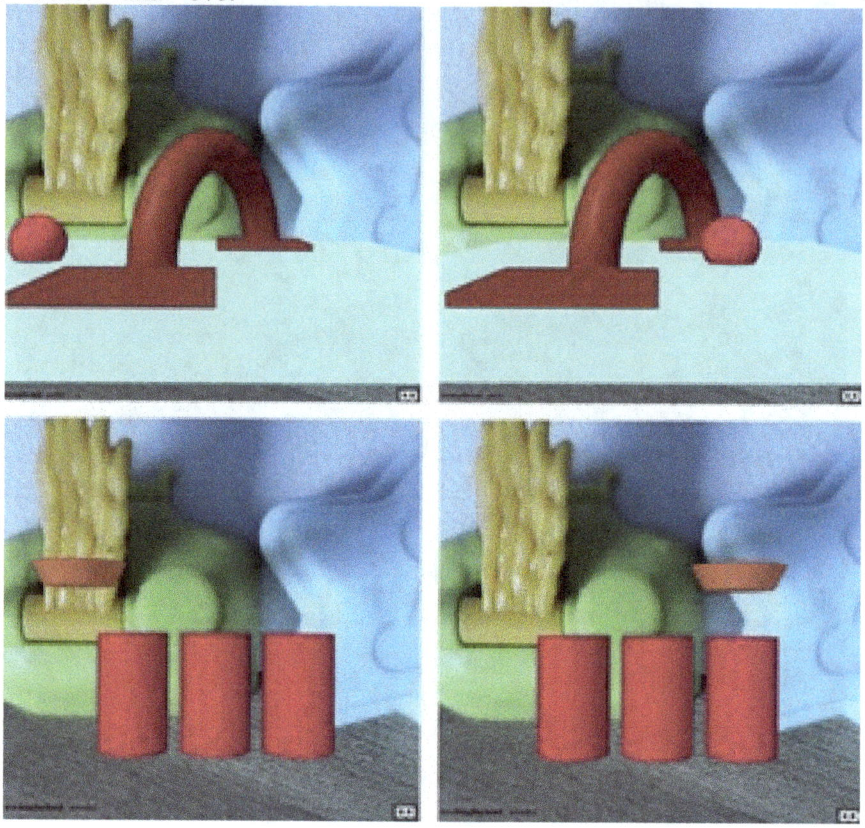

Representations of prepositions of motion are usually done in paper books using text or situations with 2D drawings, so animations immersed in AR environments bring multiple benefits, such as immediate consultation via a mobile device. Furthermore, animations can be generated from multiple primitive geometries such as spheres, cubes, or cylinders, which can be colored or have their properties, such as textures or transparency, adjusted to facilitate visual identification of the situation. New scenarios are created by integrating virtual elements into a real scene with real objects, adding a touch of fantasy and fun to a scene where students focus on recognizing the situation at hand, such as applying prepositions of motion. It is important to note that, although motion situations can be described by text or 2-dimensional drawings, these are naturally represented through animation since they are dynamic scenes where elements change position. There are reference objects in order to form a correct description of what happens over time.

4.2 Usability Results for Students and Teachers

The System Usability Scale (SUS) results demonstrate a highly favorable perception of the developed educational resources among students and teachers. After applying the standardized SUS questionnaire, which evaluates dimensions such as ease of use, efficiency, and overall satisfaction, the scores are then broken down by institution and role (student/teacher), analyzing key items such as autonomy in use, clarity of animations, and perception of educational usefulness. These factors consolidate these resources as viable tools for the innovative teaching of prepositions of motion in English. Table 2 presents the average scores for each item among the 88 students and the results by institution. Table 3 presents the adjusted sum values after applying the SUS formula, its result, and the interpretation.

Table 2. Average scores per item of SUS of students, according to educational institution

Item Institution	1	2	3	4	5	6	7	8	9	10
1	5	2	5	1	4	1	5	1	5	1
2	4	1	4	2	4	2	5	1	5	2
3	5	1	5	1	5	2	5	1	5	2

Source: Own elaboration.

Table 3. System Usability Scale (SUS) of students, according to educational institution

Institution	Adjusted Sum	SUS (×2.5)	Interpretation
1	38	95.0	Excellent (≥80.3)
2	34	85.0	Excellent (≥80.3)
3	38	95.0	Excellent (≥80.3)

Source: Own elaboration.

The usability analysis using the SUS Scale yielded an average of 91.66 points across the evaluated institutions, calculated from individual scores (Institution 1: 95.0; Institution 2: 85.0; Institution 3: 95.0). These results not only far exceed the threshold of 68 points (considered acceptable usability), but also surpass the standard of excellence (≥80.3) established by Bangor et al. (2008). Institutions 1 and 3 have identical scores (95.0), suggesting uniformity in the user experience. Institution 2 (85.0) maintains an "excellent" score but lower than its peers, which could be related to device access or connectivity differences.

The System Usability Scale (SUS) results administered to faculty are organized in two complementary tables. Table 4 breaks down each teacher's scores, highlighting the variability and consistency in their perceptions. Table 5 details the data for calculating the usability of educational resources.

Table 4. Score per item of the System Usability Scale (SUS) of teachers

Item Teacher	1	2	3	4	5	6	7	8	9	10
1	4	2	5	1	5	1	5	2	4	3
2	5	1	5	1	4	1	5	1	5	1
3	3	2	5	1	5	1	5	1	5	1
4	4	1	5	1	5	1	5	1	5	1
5	4	2	4	1	5	1	5	1	5	3

Source: Own elaboration.

Table 5. System Usability Scale (SUS) of teachers

Teacher	Contribution per item (adjusted)	Total Sum	SUS
1	3, 3, 4, 4, 4, 4, 4, 3, 3, 2	34	85.0
2	4, 4, 4, 4, 3, 4, 4, 4, 4, 4	39	97.5
3	2, 3, 4, 4, 4, 4, 4, 4, 4, 4	37	92.5
4	3, 4, 4, 4, 4, 4, 4, 4, 4, 4	39	97.5
5	3, 3, 3, 4, 4, 4, 4, 4, 4, 2	35	87.5

Source: Own elaboration.

The usability analysis using the SUS Scale yielded an average score of 89.74 among teachers, calculated from the individual results (85.0, 97.5, 92.5, 97.5, 87.5). According to the criteria of Bangor et al. (2008), this average not only far exceeds the acceptable usability threshold (≥68) but also falls within the "excellent" range (≥80.3), confirming that the educational resources are intuitive, efficient, and satisfactory. All teachers obtained individual scores between 85.0 and 97.5, reflecting a unanimously positive perception and low variability (SD = ±6.24). The System Usability Scale (SUS) results reveal exceptional acceptance of the educational resources based on GAI and AR, obtaining a phi value (ϕ) = 91.48 for students and ϕ = 89.74 for teachers. The overall usability average was 89.74 in both groups, classified as "excellent" according to Bangor et al. (2008) and well above the acceptability threshold (≥68). This consensus reflects that the integrated tools offer intuitive navigation, clear feedback, and pedagogical adaptability, meeting technical and ergonomic standards.

Students positively highlighted ease of use (item 1: 4.6/5): The AR interface allowed interaction with animations (e.g., sphere passing through a donut) without requiring prior technical knowledge. Confidence in use (item 7: 4.8/5): Immediate visual feedback (e.g., movement trajectories across) reduced anxiety when making mistakes (Mayer, 2021). Recommendation to others (item 9: 4.7/5): 92% found the resources helpful in practicing prepositions in everyday contexts. However, items such as "I needed frequent technical help" (item 2: 1.8/5) and "I found the system complex" (item 6: 1.5/5) suggest that, although the majority handled the technology without difficulty, 15% required initial support, especially in calibrating AR markers. Teachers, with individual scores between 85.0 and 97.5, highlighted: Curricular integration (item 9: 4.9/5): 95% plan to use the apps to teach prepositions, taking advantage of their ability to generate personalized scenarios (e.g., over in a virtual classroom). Coherent design (item 3: 4.7/5): The combination of generative chatbots (for dialogues) and AR (for visualization) optimized lesson preparation. Clear feedback (item 5: 4.5/5): Contextualized animations (e.g., disc flying over cylinders) facilitated grammatical explanations. However, items such as "Requires too many steps" (item 4: 1.3/5) and "New features to learn" (item 8: 1.6/5) indicate that 20% perceived complexity in advanced features, such as AR scenario customization. This underlines the need for short training to maximize teacher autonomy (Zhao & Li, 2022).

5. FUTURE RESEARCH DIRECTIONS

The findings of this study open multiple lines of research to delve deeper into the potential of GAI and AR technologies in language teaching. First, it would be relevant to evaluate the long-term impact on vocabulary retention and the development of communicative skills through longitudinal studies that measure knowledge transfer to real-life contexts. Second, the scalability of the resources could be explored to cover other prepositions (beyond, beneath) or languages with complex grammatical structures, adapting the AR animations to specific syntactic rules. Also, based on the feedback obtained from the SUS, more features could be added, and the scenario of dedicating a single portal or domain for the animations could be considered; that is, it would be valuable to integrate these tools with adaptive learning platforms, using real-time interaction data to personalize learning paths based on individual progress.

6. CONCLUSION

Innovative educational resources were developed to teach movement prepositions (across, through, under, over) using an approach that combines AR and GAI. The development process consisted of two main phases. First, ChatGPT was used to establish conceptual parameters for each preposition, with the results verified against specialized literature. Second, GAI was employed to generate programming code for web-based AR applications, which were subsequently adapted and validated by researchers to ensure proper functionality.

The implementation of these technologies in educational settings presents both opportunities and significant challenges. On the one hand, AI demonstrates potential to improve student performance and motivation, but it requires careful attention to ethical aspects, such as equity, data privacy, and technological dependence (Garcia-Martinez et al., 2023). A critical issue is the marginalization of teachers in the design of AI-powered tools, despite their fundamental role in the effective implementation of these tools (Zawacki-Richter et al., 2019).

Recent research supports this combined approach. GAI-based tools, such as ChatGPT, enable personalized instruction for complex grammatical structures (AlBadarin et al., 2023), while AR enhances spatial understanding through immersive environments with 3D representations of actions associated with prepositions (Akçayır & Akçayır, 2017). The synergy of these technologies not only optimizes conceptual retention (Chen et al., 2020) but also fosters self-directed learning, as evidenced by recent applications in language teaching (Rasul et al., 2023).

The integration of GAI through ChatGPT allowed for establishing initial linguistic parameters and generating base code for the AR applications, optimizing development time. However, rigorous verification with specialized bibliography and manual adaptation of the code ensured grammatical and functional accuracy, mitigating current limitations of GAI, such as potential biases or contextual errors. The AR animations, projected onto everyday settings (tables, bridges, gardens), exemplified using prepositions in an intuitive and contextualized way, leveraging AR's ability to merge virtual objects with real environments (Azuma, 2015).

The usability results (SUS in students and teachers) validated the resources' pedagogical effectiveness and technological acceptance. "Excellent" scores (≥80.3) reflect that the apps were intuitive, efficient, and satisfying, adhering to user-centered design principles (Bangor et al., 2008). E.g., the animation of "through" (a sphere passing through a 3D donut) and "over" (a flying disc over cylinders) facilitated the understanding of abstract spatial relationships through interactive visualization, reducing the cognitive load (Sweller, 2011). Furthermore, the adaptability of the scenes to multiple contexts (classrooms, streets, gardens) highlighted the potential of AR to create situated experiences where students practice real-time descriptions, linking language and sensory perception (Wu et al., 2023).

Although GAI accelerated development, its initial reliance on human oversight required linguistic accuracy, highlighting the need for human-AI collaboration in educational projects (Zhao & Li, 2022). The slight variability in SUS items related to technical assistance (e.g., "I needed help frequently") suggests the importance of prior teacher training to maximize autonomy in using AR.

This project validates the technical and pedagogical feasibility of integrating GAI and AR in language teaching and sets a precedent for designing immersive, personalized, and accessible educational tools. The combination of excellent usability, situated contextualization, and visual feedback positions these resources as a promising model for revolutionizing grammar teaching in the digital age.

The results demonstrated how the strategic integration of immersive technologies (e.g., AR) and GAI significantly strengthens language education, directly aligning with the targets of SDG 4 and its emphasis on digital innovation. The development of educational resources based on free and open-source tools such as A-Frame and Glitch exemplifies how ICTs can democratize access to advanced pedagogies, enabling the creation of interactive materials for teaching prepositions of motion in English as a second language (L2) without requiring expensive infrastructure. Through experiential learning, AR animations (such as a sphere moving through a three-dimensional donut or a flying saucer over cylinders) materialize abstract grammatical concepts. The usability outcomes (SUS) validate that these resources are technically robust, although their pedagogical validation is not considered adequate. They are also inclusive and scalable, essential for reducing educational gaps in vulnerable contexts. The GAI-AR integration addresses three critical dimensions of SDG 4: (1) accessibility, by removing economic barriers through open platforms; (2) pedagogical relevance, by optimizing grammar instruction through scenario customization and visual feedback; and (3) teacher development, by empowering educators to create tailored materials (as evidenced by SUS scores as high as 97.5 among teachers).

Furthermore, this model promotes digital skills (SDG 4.4), fosters educational equity (SDG 4.5) by adapting to diverse learning styles, and is transferable to other curricular areas. This project substantially enriches foreign language teaching by linking technological innovation with proven pedagogical principles. It offers a replicable model for advancing inclusive, quality, and student-centered education, significantly contributing to the 2030 Agenda for Sustainable Development goals.

Finally, UNESCO (2019) emphasizes the need for regulatory frameworks and interdisciplinary collaboration for SDG4. Research should prioritize models co-designed with educators, as suggested by Zawacki-Richter et al. (2019), so that AI solutions respond to real classroom needs and strengthen, not replace, human agency in education. Additionally, it is crucial to address gaps in large-scale assessment and adaptation of emerging technologies for remote educational settings, ensuring that they are both inclusive and scalable (Lydia et al., 2023; Iqbal et al., 2022). Collaboration among institutions, developers, and governments will be crucial to overcoming these barriers and maximizing the potential of AR and AI in future education.

ACKNOWLEDGMENT

We gratefully acknowledge the support of the Secretariat of Science, Humanities, Technology, and Innovation (SECIHTI by its acronym in Spanish) through the Mexican Postdoctoral Fellowship Program and the National System of Researchers (SNII by its acronym in Spanish). Finally, to the students and teachers who participated in the usability tests.

ChatGPT Generative Artificial Intelligence tools were used in text-to-text and text-to-code modalities. The authors have reviewed and adapted the results.

REFERENCES

Abdalla, I. (2021). Difficulties in using correct English prepositions among EFL students. [Journal of English Educators Society]. *JEES*, *6*(2), 2. DOI: 10.21070/jees.v6i2.1640

Akçayır, M., & Akçayır, G. (2017). Advantages and challenges associated with augmented reality for education: A systematic review of the literature. *Educational Research Review*, *20*, 1–11. DOI: 10.1016/j.edurev.2016.11.002

Aladin, M., Ismail, A., Salam, M., Kumoi, R., & Ali, A. (2020). AR-TO-KID: A speech-enabled augmented reality to engage preschool children in pronunciation learning. *IOP Conference Series. Materials Science and Engineering*, *979*(1), 012011. https://iopscience.iop.org/article/10.1088/1757-899X/979/1/012011/pdf. DOI: 10.1088/1757-899X/979/1/012011

AlBadarin, Y., Tukiainen, M., Saqr, M., & Pope, N. (2023). A Systematic Literature Review of Empirical Research on ChatGPT in Education. DOI: 10.2139/ssrn.4562771

AlNajdi, S. M. (2022). The effectiveness of using augmented Reality (AR) to enhance student performance: Using quick response (QR) codes in student textbooks in the Saudi education system. *Educational Technology Research and Development*, *70*(3), 1105–1124. DOI: 10.1007/s11423-022-10100-4 PMID: 35400977

Azuma, R. T. (2015). *Augmented Reality: Principles and practice*. Addison-Wesley.

Baidoo-Anu, D., & Owusu, L. (2023). Education in the Era of Generative Artificial Intelligence (AI): Understanding the Potential Benefits of ChatGPT in Promoting Teaching and Learning. *Journal of AI*, *7*(1), 52–62. DOI: 10.61969/jai.1337500

Baker, R. S., & Inventado, P. S. (2021). *Educational data mining and learning analytics*. Springer.

Bangor, A., Kortum, P., & Miller, J. (2008). An Empirical Evaluation of the System Usability Scale. *International Journal of Human-Computer Interaction, 24*(6), 574–594. DOI: 10.1080/10447310802205776

Banh, L., & Strobel, G. (2023). Generative artificial intelligence. *Electronic Markets, 33*(1), 63. DOI: 10.1007/s12525-023-00680-1

Baumert, J., Fleckenstein, J., Leucht, M., Köller, O., & Möller, J. (2020). The long-term proficiency of early, middle, and late starters learning English as a foreign language at school: A narrative review and empirical study. *Language Learning, 70*(4), 1091–1135. https://onlinelibrary.wiley.com/doi/full/10.1111/lang.12414. DOI: 10.1111/lang.12414

Brooke, J. (1996). SUS - A quick and dirty usability scale. In P. Jordan, B. Thomas, I. McLelland y B. Weerdmeester (Eds.), *Usability evaluation in industry* (pp. 189–194). Taylor y Francis Ltd. https://hell.meiert.org/core/pdf/sus.pdf

Celce-Murcia, M., & Larsen-Freeman, D. (2015). *The grammar book: An ESL/EFL teacher's course* (3rd ed.). Heinle.

Chapelle, C. A., & Sauro, S. (2017). *The handbook of technology and second language teaching and learning*. Wiley., DOI: 10.1002/9781118914069

Chen, L., Chen, P., & Lin, Z. (2020). Artificial Intelligence in Education: A Review. *IEEE Access : Practical Innovations, Open Solutions, 8*(8), 75264–75278. DOI: 10.1109/ACCESS.2020.2988510

Chen, Y., & Wang, C. (2021). Learning vocabulary in augmented reality environments: Effects of visualization and interaction types. *Journal of Educational Computing Research, 59*(5), 1–24.

Chen, Y., Wang, Y., & Chen, N.-S. (2020). Is FLIP enough? Or should we use the FLIPPED model instead? *Computers & Education, 146*, 103751. DOI: 10.1016/j.compedu.2019.103751

Dalim, C. S. C., Dey, A., Piumsomboon, T., Billinghurst, M., & Sunar, S. (2016). TeachAR: An interactive augmented reality tool for teaching basic English to non-native children. *Simposio Internacional IEEE sobre Realidad Mixta y Aumentada (ISMAR-Adjunct)*, 82-86, https://www.computer.org/csdl/proceedings-article/ismarw/2016/07836467/12OmNxdm4C4

Damayanti, D., & Sundari, H. (2022). The Use of Prepositions among EFL Learners: A Systematic Review. Scope. *Journal of English Language Teaching, 6*(2), 2. DOI: 10.30998/scope.v6i2.11381

Dawoud, N. L. D., & Al Hanaqtah, M. (2021). Difficulties That Face BA Students When Translating Prepositions of Movement from English into Standard Arabic. *Amman Arab University Journal, 6*(2).

Delgado, N., Campo, L., Sainz, M., & Etxabe-Urbieta, J. M. (2024). Aplicación de la Inteligencia Artificial (IA) en Educación: Los beneficios y limitaciones de la IA percibidos por el profesorado de educación primaria, educación secundaria y educación superior. *Revista Electrónica Interuniversitaria de Formación del Profesorado, 27*(1), 207–224. DOI: 10.6018/reifop.577211

Dixon, R. M. (2021). *English prepositions: Their meanings and uses.* Oxford University Press. DOI: 10.1093/oso/9780198868682.001.0001

Dunleavy, M., & Dede, C. (2023). Immersive interfaces for engagement and learning. *Science, 340*(6130), 66–68. PMID: 19119219

Ellis, R. (2020). *Understanding second language acquisition* (2nd ed.). Oxford University Press.

Fuchter, S. K., Schlichting, M. S., & Gurgel, G. (2025). Study on the use of ChatGPT for generating code for web-based augmented reality applications. *Measurement. Sensors, 38*, 101701. DOI: 10.1016/j.measen.2024.101701

García-Martínez, I., Fernández-Batanero, J. M., Fernández-Cerero, J., & León, S. P. (2023). Analysing the Impact of Artificial Intelligence and Computational Sciences on Student Performance: Systematic Review and Meta-analysis. *Journal of New Approaches Educational Research., 12*(1), 171–197. DOI: 10.7821/naer.2023.1.1240

Godwin-Jones, R. (2021). Emerging technologies: Collaborative language learning. *Language Learning & Technology, 25*(3), 4–15.

Grece, E. G., Vidhyavathi, P., & Malathi, P. (2023). A study on "AI in education: Opportunities and challenges for personalized learning. *Industrial Engineering Journal, 52*(05), 750–759. DOI: 10.36893/IEJ.2023.V52I05.750-759

Hattie, J. (2023). *Artificial intelligence in education: Promises and implications.* Routledge.

Hockly, N. (2022). *Digital learning: Principles and tools for teachers.* EdTech Books.

Holmes, W., Porayska-Pomsta, K., Holstein, K., Sutherland, E., Baker, T., Shum, S. B., Santos, O. C., Rodrigo, M. T., Cukurova, M., Bittencourt, I. I., & Koedinger, K. R. (2022). Ethics of AI in education: Towards a community-wide framework. *International Journal of Artificial Intelligence in Education, 32*(3), 504–526. DOI: 10.1007/s40593-021-00239-1

Hsu, T.-C. (2020). Learning English with augmented Reality: Do learning styles matter? *Computers & Education, 160*, 137–149. DOI: 10.1016/j.compedu.2016.12.007

Hwang, G. J., Xie, H., Wah, B. W., & Gašević, D. (2020). Vision, challenges, roles and research issues of AI in education. *Computers & Education: AI, 1*(1), 100001. DOI: 10.1016/j.caeai.2020.100001

IEEE. (2020). IEEE standard for augmented reality learning experience models (AR-LEM) (IEEE Std 1589-2020). https://standards.ieee.org/ieee/1589/6073/

Ilham, I. (2018). An Analysis of The Students' Difficulties in using preposition. *Research in English and Education Journal, 3*(2), 125-129. https://jim.usk.ac.id/READ/article/view/9247

Iqbal, M. Z., Mangina, E., & Campbell, A. G. (2022). Current Challenges and Future Research Directions in Augmented Reality for Education. *Multimodal Technologies and Interaction*, *6*(9), 75. DOI: 10.3390/mti6090075

Jensen, H. P., & Johannesson, H. (2006). Engineering courses taught in English: An experience from Denmark. *European Journal of Engineering Education*, *20*(1), 19–23. DOI: 10.1080/0304379950200103

Kartal, G. (2023). Contemporary language teaching and learning with ChatGPT. *Contemporary Research in Language and Linguistics*, *1*(1), 59–70. DOI: 10.62601/crll.v1i1.10

Koraishi, O. (2023). Teaching English in the age of AI: Embracing ChatGPT to optimize EFL materials and assessment. *Language Education and Technology, 3*(1). https://langedutech.com/letjournal/index.php/let/article/view/48

Krashen, S. (1985). *The input hypothesis: Issues and implications*. Longman.

Lee, M. J. W., & Park, S. Y. (2022). Augmented Reality for enhanced learning environments. In *Innovations in educational technology* (pp. 123–140). Springer.

Lim, J., Leinonen, T., Lipponen, L., Lee, H., DeVita, J., & Murray, D. (2023). Artificial intelligence as relational artifacts in creative learning. *Digital Creativity (Exeter)*, *34*(3), 192–210. DOI: 10.1080/14626268.2023.2236595

Luckin, R. (2018). *Machine learning and human intelligence: The future of education*. UCL Institute of Education Press.

Lydia, E. G., Vidhyavathi, P., & Malathi, P. (2023). A study on "AI in education: Opportunities and challenges for personalized learning". *Industrial Engineering Journal*, *52*(5), 750–759. DOI: 10.36893/IEJ.2023.V52I05.750-759

Mavlyuda, X. (2021). Creation of 3d models of historical monuments application of digital technologies. *Academicia: An International Multidisciplinary Research Journal, 11*(10), 1260–1268. https://www.indianjournals.com/ijor.aspx?target=ijor:aca&volume=11&issue=10&article=188

Mayer, R. E. (2021). *Multimedia learning* (3rd ed.). Cambridge University Press., DOI: 10.1017/9781316941355

Meniado, J. C. (2023). El Impacto de ChatGPT en la enseñanza, el aprendizaje y la evaluación del inglés: Una revisión rápida de la literature. *Arab World English Journal, 14*(4), 3–18. DOI: 10.24093/awej/vol14no4.1

Molenaar, I. (2023). Towards hybrid human-AI learning technologies. *European Journal of Education, 58*(1), 89–104.

Newport, E. L. (2019). Children and adults as language learners: Rules, variation, and maturational change. *Topics in Cognitive Science, 12*(1), 153–169. https://onlinelibrary.wiley.com/doi/epdf/10.1111/tops.12416. DOI: 10.1111/tops.12416 PMID: 30834701

Nitika, N., Sharma, T. K., Rajvanshi, S., & Kishore, K. (2021). A study of Augmented Reality performance in web browsers (WebAR). *2.ª Conferencia Internacional sobre Métodos Computacionales en Ciencia y Tecnología (ICCMST).* 281-286, DOI: 10.1109/ICCMST54943.2021.00065

Norman, D. A. (2013). *The design of everyday things* (Revised and expanded ed.). Basic Books. https://dl.icdst.org/pdfs/files4/4bb8d08a9b309df7d86e62ec4056ceef.pdf

Onggirawan, C. A., Kho, J. M., Kartiwa, A. P., Anderies, , & Gunawan, A. A. S. (2023). Systematic literature review: The adaptation of distance learning process during the COVID-19 pandemic using virtual educational spaces in metaverse. *Procedia Computer Science, 216*, 274–283. DOI: 10.1016/j.procs.2022.12.137 PMID: 36643176

Onishchuk, I., Ikonnikova, M., Antonenko, T., Kharchenko, I., Shestakova, S., Kuzmenko, N., & Maksymchuk, B. (2020). Characteristics of foreign language education in foreign countries and ways of applying foreign experience in pedagogical universities of Ukraine. *Revista Romaneasca Pentru Educatie Multidimensionala, 12*(3), 44–65. DOI: 10.18662/rrem/12.3/308

Open, AI (2023). *GPT-4 Technical Report.* arXiv:2303.08774.

Parmaxi, A. (2023). Collaborative language learning in augmented reality environments. *ReCALL, 35*(1), 45–61.

Patra, B., & Mohanty, A. K. (2016). Importance of English for engineering students: An evaluation of the prevalent teaching-learning system in the Indian context. *International Journal of English and Literature*, *6*(4), 21–34.

Pfenninger, S. E., Festman, J., & Singleton, D. (2023). *Second Language Acquisition and Lifelong Learning*. Routledge., DOI: 10.4324/9781003168935

Pregowska, A., Masztalerz, K., Garlińska, M., & Osial, M. (2021). A worldwide journey through distance education—From the post office to virtual, augmented, and mixed realities, and education during the COVID-19 pandemic. *Education Sciences*, *11*(3), 118. DOI: 10.3390/educsci11030118

Qadir, J. (2022). Engineering Education in the Era of ChatGPT: Promise and Pitfalls of Generative AI for Education. *TechRxiv*. DOI: 10.36227/techrxiv.21789434.v1

Rasul, T., Nair, S., Kalendra, D., Robin, M., de Oliveira Santini, F., Ladeira, W. J., Mingwei, S., Day, I., Rather, R. A., & Heathcote, L. (2023). The role of ChatGPT in higher education: Benefits, challenges, and future research directions. *Journal of Applied Learning and Teaching*, *6*(1). Advance online publication. DOI: 10.37074/jalt.2023.6.1.29

Rusmiyanto, R., Huriati, N., Fitriani, N., Tyas, N. K., Rofi'i, A., & Sari, M. N. (2023). The Role of Artificial Intelligence (AI) In Developing English Language Learner's Communication Skills. *Journal of Education*, *6*(1), 750–757. DOI: 10.31004/joe.v6i1.2990

Sweller, J. (2011). *Cognitive load theory*. Springer., DOI: 10.1007/978-1-4419-8126-4

Tukhtabayeva, A., Kenzhebekova, A., Utemuratova, A., Amanbekova, N., Naubay, B., & Tuzelbayeva, D. (2024). Applying augmented Reality (QR-code) in English language classroom. *Procedia Computer Science*, *251*, 573–578. DOI: 10.1016/j.procs.2024.11.151

Ubal, M., Tambasco, P., Martínez, S., & García Correa, M. (2023). El impacto de la Inteligencia Artificial en la educación. Riesgos y potencialidades de la IA en el aula [The impact of Artificial Intelligence in education. Risks and potentials of AI in the classroom]. *RiiTE Revista interuniversitaria de investigación en Tecnología Educativa,* (15), 41–57. DOI: 10.6018/riite.584501

UNESCO. (2019). *Artificial intelligence in education: Challenges and opportunities for sustainable development*. United Nations Educational, Scientific and Cultural Organization.

UNESCO. (2021). *International Forum on AI and the Futures of Education Developing Competencies for the AI Era*. United Nations Educational, Scientific and Cultural Organization. https://unesdoc.unesco.org/ark:/48223/pf0000377251.locale=en

UNESCO. (2022). *Guidelines for immersive technologies in education*. United Nations Educational, Scientific and Cultural Organization.

UNESCO. (2023). *Guidelines for generative AI in education and research*. United Nations Educational, Scientific and Cultural Organization. https://unesdoc.unesco.org/ark:/48223/pf0000386693.locale=en

Vartiainen, H., & Tedre, M. (2023). Using artificial intelligence in craft education: Crafting with text-to-image generative models. *Digital Creativity (Exeter)*, *34*(1), 1–21. DOI: 10.1080/14626268.2023.2174557

Wei, X., Weng, D., Liu, Y., & Wang, Y. (2015). Teaching based on augmented Reality for a technical creative design course. *Computers & Education*, *81*, 221–234. DOI: 10.1016/j.compedu.2014.10.017

Wu, H. K., Lee, S. W. Y., Chang, H. Y., & Liang, J. C. (2023). Current status, opportunities, and challenges of augmented Reality in education. *Computers & Education*, *182*, 113100.

Yaş, E. (2022). English Prepositions as Function Words Are Not as Easy for Language Learners as Normally Supposed to Be. *Batman University Journal of Life Sciences*, *12*(1), 48–64. DOI: 10.55024/buyasambid.1126711

Yu, H., & Guo, Y. (2023). Generative artificial intelligence empowers educational reform: Current status, issues, and prospects. *Frontiers in Education*, *8*, 1183162. DOI: 10.3389/feduc.2023.1183162

Zawacki-Richter, O., Marín, V. I., Bond, M., & Gouverneur, F. (2019). Systematic review of research on artificial intelligence applications in higher education-where are the educators? *International Journal of Educational Technology in Higher Education*, *16*(1), 39. DOI: 10.1186/s41239-019-0171-0

Zhao, Y., & Li, S. (2022). Generative AI in language education: Opportunities and challenges. *Journal of Educational Technology & Society*, *25*(3), 112–125.

Zhao, Y., Li, S., & Zhang, L. (2023). Adaptive feedback in AI-driven augmented reality language apps. *Educational Technology Research and Development*, *71*(3), 1129–1150.

Compilation of References

Abdalla, I. (2021). Difficulties in using correct English prepositions among EFL students. [Journal of English Educators Society]. *JEES*, *6*(2), 2. DOI: 10.21070/jees.v6i2.1640

Abdi, Y. M., Waititu, M. M., & Mugo, B. C. (2021). Challenges facing teachers' integration of information communication and technology in teaching and learning of welding and fabrication at the vocational training centers in Mandera County. *International Academic Journal of Information Systems and Technology*, *2*(1), 297–310.

Abós Catalán, A. García González, L. & Aibar Solana, A. (2017). El uso del ThatQuiz como recurso de aprendizaje y guía para la evaluación de los estudiantes de Postgrado. En Del Moral Barrigüete, C. (coord. y ed.) Buenas prácticas de E-learning en el contexto de la Educación Permanente y Tecnologías. 129-140. Enciclopedia Virtual umed.net.

Abraham, M., Arficho, Z., & Habtemariam, T. (2022). Effects of Training in ICT-Assisted English Language Teaching on Secondary School English Language Teachers' Knowledge, Skills, and Practice of Using ICT Tools for Teaching English. *Education Research International*, *2022*, 1–10. DOI: 10.1155/2022/6233407

Abraham, M., Arficho, Z., Habtemariam, T., & Demissie, A. (2022). Effects of information communication technology-assisted teaching training on English language teachers' pedagogical knowledge and English language proficiency. *Cogent Education*, *9*(1), 2028336. DOI: 10.1080/2331186X.2022.2028336

Acilo Julita, L.M. (2024). Gardner's Theory of Multiple Intelligences: The Basis for Creating a New Learning Approach. *Psychology and Education: A multidisciplinary Journal, 19*(2), 120-131. DOI: 10.5281/zenodo.10997015

Aguirre Idrogo, Y. M., Vargas Navarro, R., Huamán Guzmán, A. M., & Gutiérrez Narrea, G. S. (2021). Uso de las TIC en la comprensión de textos del idioma inglés en estudiantes de secundaria. *Horizontes Revista de Investigación en Ciencias de la Educación, 5*(21), 1419–1429. DOI: 10.33996/revistahorizontes.v5i21.285

Ahmed, S. T., & Roche, T. (2021). Making the connection: Examining the relationship between undergraduate students' digital literacy and academic success in an English medium instruction (EMI) university. *Education and Information Technologies, 24*(4), 4601–4620. DOI: 10.1007/s10639-021-10443-0

Ahmed, Z., Nathaniel, S. P., & Shahbaz, M. (2021). The criticality of information and communication technology and human capital in environmental sustainability: Evidence from Latin American and Caribbean countries. *Journal of Cleaner Production, 286*, 125529. DOI: 10.1016/j.jclepro.2020.125529

Ai, Y., Hu, Y., & Zhao, E. (2024). Interactive learning: Harnessing technology to alleviate foreign language anxiety in foreign literature education, 1-20. *Interactive Learning Environments*. DOI: 10.1080/10494820.2024.2409990

Akçayır, M., & Akçayır, G. (2017). Advantages and challenges associated with augmented reality for education: A systematic review of the literature. *Educational Research Review, 20*, 1–11. DOI: 10.1016/j.edurev.2016.11.002

Akour, M., & Alenezi, M. (2022). Higher education in the era of digital transformation. *Education Sciences, 12*(11), 784. DOI: 10.3390/educsci12110784

Akram, H., Abdelrady, A. H., Al-Adwan, A. S., & Ramzan, M. (2022). Teachers' perceptions of technology integration in teaching-learning practices: A systematic review. *Frontiers in Psychology, 13*, 920317. DOI: 10.3389/fpsyg.2022.920317 PMID: 35734463

Aladin, M., Ismail, A., Salam, M., Kumoi, R., & Ali, A. (2020). AR-TO-KID: A speech-enabled augmented reality to engage preschool children in pronunciation learning. *IOP Conference Series. Materials Science and Engineering, 979*(1), 012011. https://iopscience.iop.org/article/10.1088/1757-899X/979/1/012011/pdf. DOI: 10.1088/1757-899X/979/1/012011

Alanoglu, M., Aslan, S., & Karabatak, S. (2022). Do teachers' educational philosophies affect their digital literacy? The mediating effect of resistance to change. *Education and Information Technologies, 27*(3), 3447–3466. DOI: 10.1007/s10639-021-10753-3 PMID: 34602847

Alarcón Hernández, P., Vásquez Bustos, V., Díaz Larenas, C., & Venegas Carrasco, C. (2020). El profesor como guía y guerrero: metáforas sobre la profesión docente. *Cuadernos de Lingüística Hispánica,* 36, 105-128. https://doi.org/https://doi.org/10.19053/0121053X.n36.2020.10989

AlBadarin, Y., Tukiainen, M., Saqr, M., & Pope, N. (2023). A Systematic Literature Review of Empirical Research on ChatGPT in Education. DOI: 10.2139/ssrn.4562771

Alenezi, M., Wardat, S., & Akour, M. (2023). The need of integrating digital education in higher education: Challenges and opportunities. *Sustainability (Basel), 15*(6), 4782. DOI: 10.3390/su15064782

Alesandrini, K., & Larson, L. (2020). Teachers bridge to constructivism. *The Clearing House: A Journal of Educational Strategies, Issues and Ideas*, *75*(3), 118–119. DOI: 10.1080/00098650209599249

Alexei, L. A., & Alexei, A. (2021). Cyber security threat analysis in higher education institutions as a result of distance learning. *International Journal of Scientific and Technology Research*, (3), 128–133.

Alfaro-Perez, J. L. (2017). Moderating effect of learning styles on a learning management system's success. *Telematics and Informatics*, *34*(1), 272–286. DOI: 10.1016/j.tele.2016.04.006

Alkhawaldeh, M. A., & Khasawneh, M. A. S. (2023). Exploring virtual reality as a transformative tool for enhancing learning abilities in students with disabilities. *Journal of Namibian Studies: History Politics Culture*, *35*, 861–882.

AlNajdi, S. M. (2022). The effectiveness of using augmented Reality (AR) to enhance student performance: Using quick response (QR) codes in student textbooks in the Saudi education system. *Educational Technology Research and Development*, *70*(3), 1105–1124. DOI: 10.1007/s11423-022-10100-4 PMID: 35400977

Alobaid, A. (2020). Smar multimedia learning of ICT: Role and impact on language learners' writing fluency – YouTube online English learning resources as an example. *Smart Learning Environments, 24.* https://slejournal.springeropen.com/articles/10.1186/s40561-020-00134-7

Alonso, J. L. G., & Samy, D. (2018). Applicability of ICT-supported language teaching in contexts of social integration and international cooperation. *Círculo de Lingüística Aplicada a la Comunicación*, *76*, 101–116. DOI: 10.5209/CLAC.62500

Alotaibi, H., & Salamah, D. (2023). The impact of translation apps on translation students' performance. *Education and Information Technologies*, *28*(8), 10709–10729. DOI: 10.1007/s10639-023-11578-y

Alotaibi, N. S. (2024). The impact of AI and LMS integration on the future of higher education: Opportunities, challenges, and strategies for transformation. *Sustainability (Basel), 16*(23), 10357. DOI: 10.3390/su162310357

Alsayer, A. A. (2023). Learners' experiences in an online environment: An analysis of the impact of international collaboration. *SAGE Open, 13*(4), 21582440231208524. DOI: 10.1177/21582440231208524

Altbach, P. G. (2014). India's higher education challenges. *Asia Pacific Education Review, 15*(4), 503–510. DOI: 10.1007/s12564-014-9335-8

AlTwijri, L., & Alghizzi, T. M. (2024). Investigating the integration of artificial intelligence in English as foreign language classes for enhancing learners' affective factors: A systematic review. *Heliyon, 10*(10), e31053. DOI: 10.1016/j.heliyon.2024.e31053 PMID: 38778968

Álvarez Herrero, J. F. (2021). *Uso de imágenes en redes sociales para la mejora del aprendizaje en alumnos de Secundaria*. Servicio de Publicaciones Universidad de Valladolid.

Ammon, U. (2010). World languages: Trends and futures. In Coupland, N. (Ed.), *The Handbook of Language and Globalization* (pp. 101–122). John Wiley & Sons., DOI: 10.1002/9781444324068.ch4

Amo, D., Torres, R., Canaleta, X., Herrero-Martín, J., Rodríguez-Merino, C., & Fonseca, D. (2020, October). Seven principles to foster privacy and security in educational tools: Local Educational Data Analytics. In *Eighth International Conference on Technological Ecosystems for Enhancing Multiculturality* (pp. 730-737). DOI: 10.1145/3434780.3436637

Anbalagan, M., & Balasubramani, J. (2021). An analysis of NIRF ranked Indian Institute of Technology (IITs) profiles: With special reference to Indian Research Information Network System (IRINS). *Library Philosophy and Practice*, Article 6042.

Anbalagan, M., & Tamizhchelvan, M. T. (2021). Ranking of Indian institutions in global and Indian ranking system: A comparative study. *Library Philosophy and Practice*, Article 5069.

Andreou, S. N., & Koutsampelas, C. (2015). Intergenerational mobility and equality of opportunity in higher education in Cyprus. *International Journal of Educational Development, 41*, 80–87. DOI: 10.1016/j.ijedudev.2015.01.003

Angelaki, M. E., Bersimis, F., Karvounidis, T., & Douligeris, C. (2023). Towards more sustainable higher education institutions: Implementing the sustainable development goals and embedding sustainability into the information and computer technology curricula. *Education and Information Technologies*, *29*(4), 5079–5113. DOI: 10.1007/s10639-023-12025-8

Aparicio Gómez, O. Y., & Ostos Ortiz, O. L. (2021). Pedagogías emergentes en ambientes virtuales de aprendizaje. *Revista Internacional de Pedagogía e Innovación Educativa*, *1*(1), 11–36. DOI: 10.51660/ripie.v1i1.25

Arabit García, J., Prendes Espinosa, P., & Serrano Sánchez, J. L. (2023). Recursos Educativos Abiertos y metodologías activas para la enseñanza de STEM en Educación Primaria. *RELATEC. Revista Latinoamericana de Tecnología Educativa*, *22*(1), 89–106. DOI: 10.17398/1695-288X.22.1.89

Area Moreira, M., & Adell Segura, J. (2021). Tecnologías digitales y cambio educativo: Una aproximación crítica. *REICE. Revista Electrónica Iberoamericana sobre Calidad, Eficacia y Cambio en Educación*, *19*(4), 83–96. DOI: 10.15366/reice2021.19.4.005

Area Moreira, M., Alonso Cano, C., Correa Gorospe, J. M., Moral Pérez, M. E., de Pablos Pons, J., Paredez Labra, J., Peirats Chacón, J., Sanabria Mesa, A. L., San Martín Alonso, A., & Valverde Berrocoso, J. (2024). Las políticas educativas TIC en España después del Programa Escuela 2.0: Las tendencias que emergen. *RELATEC Revista Latinoamericana de Tecnología Educativa*, *13*(2), 11–33. DOI: 10.17398/1695-288X.13.2.11

Area Moreira, M., Cepeda Romero, O., & Feliciano García, L. (2018). El uso escolar de las TIC desde la visión del alumnado de Educación Primaria, ESO y Bachillerato. *Educatio XXI*, *36*(2), 229–276. DOI: 10.6018/j/333071

Ariza Covarrubias, R., & Pons Bonals, L. (2021). Medios y redes sociales en la enseñanza-aprendizaje del inglés. *Revista de Estudios y Experiencias en Educación*, *20*(43), 129–148. DOI: 10.21703/rexe.20212043ariza7

Ashley, S. L. (2016). Unpacking an over-packed agenda for the marginalized: Problematizing sustainable development goal 4, targets 4.6 and 4.7. *Andragoške studije*, (2), 9-19.

Asongu, S., Amari, M., Jarboui, A., & Mouakhar, K. ICT dynamics for gender inclusive intermediary education: Minimum poverty and inequality thresholds in developing countries. *Telecommunications Policy, 45*(5). DOI: 10.1016/j.telpol.2021.102125

Asto Luna, E. L., Chávez Espinoza, P. E., Menacho Vargas, I., Taber De la Cruz, Y. O., & Jáuregui Eléspuru, J. C. (2023). Las plataformas e-learning en el aprendizaje del inglés. Horizontes. *Revista de Investigación en Ciencias de la Educación*, *7*(27), 62–76. DOI: 10.33996/revistahorizontes.v7i27.497

Azuma, R. T. (2015). *Augmented Reality: Principles and practice*. Addison-Wesley.

Baah, C., Govender, I., & Subramaniam, R. (2023). Exploring the role of gamification in motivating students to learn. *Cogent Education*, *10*(1), 2210045. DOI: 10.1080/2331186X.2023.2210045

Baidoo-Anu, D., & Owusu, L. (2023). Education in the Era of Generative Artificial Intelligence (AI): Understanding the Potential Benefits of ChatGPT in Promoting Teaching and Learning. *Journal of AI*, *7*(1), 52–62. DOI: 10.61969/jai.1337500

Baker, R. S., & Inventado, P. S. (2021). *Educational data mining and learning analytics*. Springer.

Bangor, A., Kortum, P., & Miller, J. (2008). An Empirical Evaluation of the System Usability Scale. *International Journal of Human-Computer Interaction*, *24*(6), 574–594. DOI: 10.1080/10447310802205776

Banh, L., & Strobel, G. (2023). Generative artificial intelligence. *Electronic Markets*, *33*(1), 63. DOI: 10.1007/s12525-023-00680-1

Baño Lucio, L., González Quiñones, F., & Tarango Ortiz, J. (2023). Influencia de las TIC en el aprendizaje del idioma inglés en niños. *Tsafiqui Revista Científica en Ciencias Sociales*, *13*(21), 115–125. DOI: 10.29019/tsafiqui.v13i21.1096

Banshal, S. K., Singh, V. K., & Mayr, P. (2019). Comparing research performance of private universities in India with IITs, central universities, and NITs. *Current Science*, *116*(8), 1308–1314. DOI: 10.18520/cs/v116/i8/1304-1313

Barbosa, M. W., & Ferreira-Lopes, L. (2021). Emerging trends in telecollaboration and virtual exchange: A bibliometric study. *Educational Review*, *75*(3), 558–586. DOI: 10.1080/00131911.2021.1907314

BARNUCZ, N., & FÓNAI, M. (. (2020). The use of ICT in language education in schools of disadvantaged students. *Informacios Tarsadalom*, *20*(1), 7–28. DOI: 10.22503/inftars.XX.2020.1.1

Baskara, R. M., & Mukarto, M. (2023). Exploring the implications of ChatGPT for language learning in higher education. *Indonesian Journal of English Language Teaching and Applied Linguistics*, *7*(2), 343–358. https://ijeltal.org/index.php/ijeltal/article/view/1387. DOI: 10.21093/ijeltal.v7i2.1387

Bastani, H., Bastani, O., Sungu, A., Ge, H., Kabakcı, Ö., & Mariman, R. (2024, Jul 15). *Generative AI can harm learning* (The Wharton School Research Paper). DOI: 10.2139/ssrn.4895486

Bates, A. W. (2005). Technology, e-learning and distance education.

Baumert, J., Fleckenstein, J., Leucht, M., Köller, O., & Möller, J. (2020). The long-term proficiency of early, middle, and late starters learning English as a foreign language at school: A narrative review and empirical study. *Language Learning*, *70*(4), 1091–1135. https://onlinelibrary.wiley.com/doi/full/10.1111/lang.12414. DOI: 10.1111/lang.12414

Bautista Zárate, E. J. (2023). Uso de Redes Sociales como Herramienta para Mejorar la Escritura en Inglés Como Lengua Extranjera. *Ciencia Latina Revista Científica Multidisciplinar*, *7*(4), 8367–8387. DOI: 10.37811/cl_rcm.v7i4.7568

Becirovic, S., Brdarevic-Celjo, A. B., & Delic, H. (2021). The use of digital technology in foreign language learning. *Spring Nature, 1*(10), 246. https://pmc.ncbi.nlm.nih.gov/articles/PMC8475434/

Bekele Sime, T., Gencha, M. G., & Olamo, T. G. (2024). Effects of Blended Instruction on students' paragraph writing performances: The case of first year Health science pharmacy students at Pharma College Hawassa Campus, Ethiopia. *Cogent Education, 11*(1), 1–24. DOI: 10.1080/2331186X.2024.2321309

Belda-Medina, J., & Kokošková, V. (2023). Integrating chatbots in education: Insights from the chatbot-human interaction satisfaction model (CHISM). *International Journal of Educational Technology in Higher Education*, *20*(1), 62. DOI: 10.1186/s41239-023-00432-3

Benavente Vera, S. U., Flores Coronado, M. L., Guizado Oscco, F., & Nuñez Lira, L. A. (2021). Desarrollo de las competencias digitales de docentes a través de programas de intervención 2020. *Propósitos y Representaciones*, *9*(1), 1–23. DOI: 10.20511/pyr2021.v9n1.1034

Bentz, J. (2020). Learning about climate change in, with and through art. *Climatic Change*, *162*(3), 1595–1612. DOI: 10.1007/s10584-020-02804-4

Bentz, J., & O'Brien, K. (2019). Art for change: Transformative learning and youth empowerment in a changing climate. *Elementa*, *7*, 52. DOI: 10.1525/elementa.390

Betancur Chicué, V., & García Valcárcel, A. (2022). Training Needs Around Digital Teaching Competence: A Systematic Review. *Fonseca Journal of Communication*, *25*, 133–147. DOI: 10.14201/fjc.29603

Biasutti, M., & Frate, S. (2017). Validity and reliability study of the attitudes toward sustainable development scale. *Environmental Education Research, 23*(2), 214–230. DOI: 10.1080/13504622.2016.1146660

Bicans, J., & Grundspenkis, J. (2017). Student learning style extraction from on-campus learning context data. *Procedia Computer Science, 104*, 272–278. DOI: 10.1016/j.procs.2017.01.135

Bilgin, N. (2014). *Content analysis techniques and case studies in social* (3rd ed.). Siyasal.

Bingham, A. J., & Oluwafolakemi, O. (2017). Staying on track: Examining teachers' experiences in a personalized learning model. *Journal of Ethnographic and Qualitative Research, 12*(2), 75.

Bingimlas, K. A. (2009). Barriers to the successful integration of ICT in teaching and learning environments: A review of the literature. *Eurasia Journal of Mathematics, Science and Technology Education, 5*(3), 235–245. DOI: 10.12973/ejmste/75275

Blake, R. J. (2013). *Brave new digital classroom: Technology and foreign language learning* (2nd ed.). Georgetown University Press.

Blue, J. (2022). *Introducing the Sustainability Framework for ELT: free activity cards.* World of better learning. https://www.cambridge.org/elt/blog/2022/09/30/sustainability-framework-elt-activity-cards/

Bohara, D. K. (2024). Teachers' Perceived Value of Integrating ICT in Transposing English Language Teaching in Nepal. *KMC Journal, 6*(1), 106–121. DOI: 10.3126/kmcj.v6i1.62332

Bonilla del Río, M. & Aguaded Gómez, I. (2018). La escuela en la era digital: smartphones, apps y programación en Educación Primaria y su repercusión en la competencia mediática del alumnado. *Píxel-Bit. Revista de Medios y Educación*, 1-13. DOI: 10.12795/pixelbit.2018

Borromeo García, C.A. & Ramírez Hernández, M. (2018). Uso de redes sociales en docentes de lengua inglesa y pedagogía: ¿Diferencias por disciplina? *Revista Ensayos Pedagógicos*, Edición Especial, 189-205. DOI: 10.15359/rep.esp-16.10

Boyles, B. (2017). Virtual reality and augmented reality in education. *Center For Teaching Excellence, United States Military Academy, West Point, Ny, 67.*

Brautlacht, R. C., Martins, M. L., & Poppi, F. (2022). *Offering 21st century skills training through interactive online collaboration in higher education.* Routledge.

Bringula, R. P. (2017). Influence of usage of e-books, online educational materials, and other programming books and students' profiles on adoption of printed programming textbooks. *Program, 51*(4), 441–457. DOI: 10.1108/PROG-06-2015-0046

Brooke, J. (1996). SUS - A quick and dirty usability scale. In P. Jordan, B. Thomas, I. McLelland y B. Weerdmeester (Eds.), *Usability evaluation in industry* (pp. 189–194). Taylor y Francis Ltd. https://hell.meiert.org/core/pdf/sus.pdf

Brown, E. D., & Sax, K. L. (2013). Arts enrichment and preschool emotions for low-income children at risk. *Early Childhood Research Quarterly, 28*(2), 337–346. DOI: 10.1016/j.ecresq.2012.08.002

Brown, E., Garnett, M., Anderson, K., & Laurenceau, J. (2016). Can the arts get under the skin? Arts and cortisol for economically disadvantaged children. *Child Development, 88*(4), 1368–1381. DOI: 10.1111/cdev.12652 PMID: 27921313

Brown, H. D. (2007). *Principles of language learning and teaching* (5th ed.). Pearson Education.

Brown, M. D. J., & Millichap, N. (2015). The next generation digital learning environment: A report on research. *EDUCASE Learning Initiative Paper, 2015*, 11.

Burov, O. Y., Butnik-Siversky, O. B., Orliuk, O., & Horska, K. A. (2020). Cybersecurity and innovative digital educational environment. *Інформаційні технології і засоби навчання, 6*(80), 414-430.

Burov, O., Lytvynova, S., Lavrov, E., Krylova-Grek, Y., Orliyk, O., Petrenko, S., . . . Tkachenko, O. M. (2020). Cybersecurity in educational networks. In *Intelligent Human Systems Integration 2020: Proceedings of the 3rd International Conference on Intelligent Human Systems Integration (IHSI 2020): Integrating People and Intelligent Systems, February 19-21, 2020, Modena, Italy* (pp. 359-364). Springer International Publishing. DOI: 10.1007/978-3-030-39512-4_56

Cabrera Rodríguez, L.J., Sicilia Suárez, G., Marrero Callico, G., Pérez Sánchez, C.N. & Bethencour Marrero, C. (2022). The Digital Gap in Primary Education in Spain. *Éducation compare, 26*(1), 101-131.

Caines, A., Benedetto, L., Taslimipoor, S., Davis, C., Gao, Y., Andersen, Ø., Yuan, Z., Elliott, M., Moore, R., Bryant, C., Rei, M., Yannakoudakis, H., Mullooly, A., Nicholls, D., & Buttery, P. (2023). On the application of Large Language Models for language teaching and assessment technology. In J.Stamper, R. Tong, C. Cao, Z. Liu, X. Hu, Y. Lu, J. Liang, H. Khosravi, P. Denny, A. Singh, & C. Broos (Eds.), *Proceedings of the Workshop on Empowering Education with LLMs - the Next-Gen Interface and Content Generation 2023 (AIEDLLM 2023)*. Vol.3487. (pp. 173-197). CEUR Workshop Proceedings. DOI: 10.48550/arXiv.2307.08393

Çakır, M. P., Acartürk, C., Alaşehir, O., & Alkan, O. (2015). A comparative analysis of global and national university ranking systems. *Scientometrics*, *103*(3), 813–848. DOI: 10.1007/s11192-015-1586-6

Cambridge (n.d.). *The sustainability framework for ELT.* [Infographics]. https://assets.cambridgeenglish.org/events/sustainability-framework-for-elt.pdf?_gl=1*pqow4k*_gcl_au*OTk4OTc3NDI2LjE3NDE2NzY2OTg

Canese, V., Paez, R., & Amarilla, J. (2023). Critical issues in the English language classroom: ICT and online learning in language education. *International Journal of Technology in Education*, *6*(1), 87–99. DOI: 10.46328/ijte.312

Cardona, M. A., Rodriguez, R. J., & Ishmael, K. (2023). *Artificial intelligence and the future of teaching and learning: Insights and recommendations.* U.S. Department of Education, Office of Educational Technology. https://www.ed.gov/sites/ed/files/documents/ai-report/ai-report.pdf

Carm, E. (2013). Rethinking education for all. *Sustainability (Basel)*, *5*(8), 3447–3472. DOI: 10.3390/su5083447

Carrión Montalván, B. K., Pillajo Angos, C. G., Castellanos Fonseca, J. A., & Vega Aguaiza, R. (2024). WebQuest como herramienta de aprendizaje: Análisis del impacto en la producción y aprendizaje del inglés como lengua extranjera. *Ibero-American Journal of Education & Society Research*, *4*(1), 129–141. DOI: 10.56183/iberoeds.v4i1.661

Casañ Nuñez, J.C., Millán Scheiding, C. & Márquez Baldó, L. (2021). *H5P y Moodle en la enseñanza del inglés: encuesta al alumnado del máster de profesorado*. Dykinson, S.L.

Castillo López, D. (2020). Las TIC en los procesos de enseñanza-aprendizaje desarrollados por maestros tutores de Educación Primaria en la Región de Murcia. *Revista Interuniversitaria de Investigación en Tecnología Educativa*, *9*, 1–14. DOI: 10.6018/riite.432061

Cebrián, G., & Junyent, M. (2015). Competencies in education for sustainable development: Exploring the student teachers' views. *Sustainability (Basel)*, *7*(3), 2768–2786. DOI: 10.3390/su7032768

Celce-Murcia, M., & Larsen-Freeman, D. (2015). *The grammar book: An ESL/EFL teacher's course* (3rd ed.). Heinle.

Çelik, F., Yangın Ersanlı, C., & Arslanbay, G. (2024). Does AI simplification of authentic blog texts improve reading comprehension, inferencing, and anxiety? A one-shot intervention in Turkish EFL context. *International Review of Research in Open and Distance Learning*, *25*(3), 287–303. DOI: 10.19173/irrodl.v25i3.7779

Central Institute of Educational Technology. (n.d.). *ICT for teaching and learning of languages.* https://ciet.ncert.gov.in/

Cha, H. J., Yong, S. K., Park, S. H., Yoon, T. B., Jung, Y. M., & Lee, J. H. (2006). Learning styles diagnosis based on user interface behaviors for the customization of learning interfaces in an intelligent tutoring system. *Lecture Notes in Computer Science*, *4053*, 513–524. DOI: 10.1007/11774303_51

Chakraborty, K., Upadhyay, N., & Upadhyay, S. R. (2021). Explored publication pattern of the top twenty NIRF-2020 ranked Indian institutions: An evaluative study. *Library Philosophy and Practice*, Article 5230.

Chang, A. C.-S., & Read, J. (2012). The effects of listening support on the listening performance of EFL learners. *TESOL Quarterly*, *40*(2), 375–397. DOI: 10.2307/40264527

Chapelle, C. A., & Sauro, S. (2017). *The handbook of technology and second language teaching and learning*. Wiley., DOI: 10.1002/9781118914069

Chattopadhyay, S. (2020). National Education Policy, 2020. *Economic and Political Weekly*, *55*(46), 23–25.

Cheng, H.-F., & Dornyei, Z. (2007). The use of motivational strategies in language instruction: The case of EFL teaching in Taiwan. *Innovation in Language Learning and Teaching*, *1*(1), 153–174. DOI: 10.2167/illt048.0

Cheng, S., & Parker, M. (2023). The role of school socioeconomic status in school-wide technology integration in the U.S. *Contemporary Educational Technology*, *15*(2), 422. DOI: 10.30935/cedtech/13059

Chen, H. J. (2023). Gather in the metaverse: Learning outcomes, virtual presence, and perceptions of high- and low-achieving pre-service teachers of English as foreign language. *Education and Information Technologies, 29*(7), 8549–8577. DOI: 10.1007/s10639-023-12135-3

Chen, L., Chen, P., & Lin, Z. (2020). Artificial intelligence in education: A review. *IEEE Access : Practical Innovations, Open Solutions, 8*, 75264–75278. DOI: 10.1109/ACCESS.2020.2988510

Chen, X., Zou, D., Xie, H., & Cheng, G. (2021). Twenty years of personalized language learning: Topic Modeling and knowledge mapping. *Journal of Educational Technology & Society, 24*(1), 205–222. https://www.jstor.org/stable/26977868

Chen, Y. C. (2022). Effects of technology-enhanced language learning on reducing EFL learners' public speaking anxiety. *Computer Assisted Language Learning, 37*(4), 789–813. DOI: 10.1080/09588221.2022.2055083

Chen, Y., & Wang, C. (2021). Learning vocabulary in augmented reality environments: Effects of visualization and interaction types. *Journal of Educational Computing Research, 59*(5), 1–24.

Chen, Y., Wang, Y., & Chen, N.-S. (2020). Is FLIP enough? Or should we use the FLIPPED model instead? *Computers & Education, 146*, 103751. DOI: 10.1016/j.compedu.2019.103751

Cho, K., Merrienboer, B. V., Bahdanau, D., & Bengio, Y. (2014, Oct 25). On the properties of neural machine translation: Encoder-decoder approaches. In *Proceedings of the Eighth Workshop on Syntax, Semantics and Structure in Statistical Translation, Empirical Methods in Natural Language Processing* (pp. 103–111). Doha, Qatar. DOI: 10.3115/v1/W14-4012

Chong Baque, P. G. (2020). Estrategias pedagógicas innovadoras en entornos virtuales de aprendizaje. *Dominio de las Ciencias, 6*(3), 56–77. DOI: 10.23857/dc.v6i3.1274

Christie, M. J. (2021). Constructivism and the role of the teacher. *Journal of Education, 195*(1), 23–35. DOI: 10.31703/glr.2020(V-III).15

Chugh, K. L., Alekhya, N., & Prabhu Kishore, N. (2017). Quality research publications – A key differentiator in India rankings 2017. *International Journal of Mechanical Engineering and Technology, 8*(6), 117–124.

Chugh, K. L., Alekhya, N., Prabhu Kishore, N., & Shekar, K. (2018). Analysis of national institutional ranking framework: Journey so far. In *Proceedings of the 6th IEEE International Conference on MOOCs, Innovation and Technology in Education (MITE 2018)* (pp. 115–119). IEEE. DOI: 10.1109/MITE.2018.8747105

Coffield, F., Ecclestone, K., Moseley, D., & Hall, E. (2004). *Learning styles and pedagogy in post 16 education: A critical and systematic review*. Learning & Skills Research Centre.

Colás Bravo, M. P., de Pablo Pons, J., & Ballesta Pagán, J. (2018). The Impact of ICT on Teaching in the Spanish Education System: A Literature Review. [RED]. *Revista de Educación a Distancia*, *56*, 1–23. DOI: 10.6018/red/56/2

Consoli, T., Désiorn, J., & Cattaneo, A. (2023). What is "technology integration" and how is it measured in K-12 education? A systematic review of survey instruments from 2010 to 2021. *Computers & Education*, *197*, 104742. DOI: 10.1016/j.compedu.2023.104742

Costa, A. C. F., Silva, A. M., Espuny, M., Rocha, A. B. T. R., & Oliveira, O. J. (2023). Toward quality education: Contributions of EdTech to the achievement of the fourth United Nations sustainable development goal. *Sustainable Development.* DOI: 10.1002/sd.2742

Crompton, H., & Burke, D. (2023). Artificial intelligence in higher education: The state of the field. *International Journal of Educational Technology in Higher Education*, *20*(1), 22. DOI: 10.1186/s41239-023-00392-8

Cruz-Jesus, F., Vicente, M. R., Bacao, F., & Oliveira, T. (2016). The education-related digital divide: An analysis for the EU-28. *Computers in Human Behavior*, *56*, 72–82. DOI: 10.1016/j.chb.2015.11.027

Crystal, D. (2003). *English as a global language* (2nd ed.). Cambridge University. DOI: 10.1017/CBO9780511486999

Culduz, M. (2024). Benefits and Challenges of E-Learning, Online Education, and Distance Learning. In *Incorporating the Human Element in Online Teaching and Learning* (pp. 1–27). IGI Global. DOI: 10.4018/979-8-3693-4131-5.ch001

Culton, K., & Muñoz, J. A. (2016). Lady Gaga meets Ritzer: Using music to teach sociological theory. *Dialogue Interdiscip. J. Pop. Cult. Pedagog.*, *3*, 35–43.

Dadhe, P. P., & Dubey, M. N. (2021). Ranking and research trend: A comparative study of research output of top ten NIRF ranked engineering institutions of India based on scientometric indicators. *Library Philosophy and Practice*, Article 5314.

Dalim, C. S. C., Dey, A., Piumsomboon, T., Billinghurst, M., & Sunar, S. (2016). TeachAR: An interactive augmented reality tool for teaching basic English to non-native children. *Simposio Internacional IEEE sobre Realidad Mixta y Aumentada (ISMAR-Adjunct)*, 82-86, https://www.computer.org/csdl/proceedings-article/ismarw/2016/07836467/12OmNxdm4C4

Damayanti, D., & Sundari, H. (2022). The Use of Prepositions among EFL Learners: A Systematic Review. Scope. *Journal of English Language Teaching*, *6*(2), 2. DOI: 10.30998/scope.v6i2.11381

Dam, M., Majumder, D., Bhattacharjee, R., & Santra, S. S. (2021). Performance measurement model for ranking of educational institutes: A fuzzy reasoning approach. *Journal of Physics: Conference Series*, *1797*(1), 012012. DOI: 10.1088/1742-6596/1797/1/012012

Dar, T. H., Jeelani, S. G. M., Mir, H. A., & Ganaie, S. A. (2017). Use of ICT in IIT and IIM libraries of India. *International Journal of Library and Information Science*, *6*(1), 1–18. https://www.iaeme.com/IJLIS/issues.asp?JType=IJLIS&VType=6&IType=1

Davidson, A. L., & Carliner, S. (2014). E-books for educational uses. *Handbook of research on educational communications and technology*, 713-722.

Davies, B., & Hentschke, G. (2006). Public–private partnerships in education: Insights from the field. *School Leadership & Management*, *26*(3), 205–226. DOI: 10.1080/13632430600736977

Dawoud, N. L. D., & Al Hanaqtah, M. (2021). Difficulties That Face BA Students When Translating Prepositions of Movement from English into Standard Arabic. *Amman Arab University Journal, 6*(2).

Deka, P., & Sarmah, M. (2021). Impact of NIRF ranking on research publications: A study with special reference to North-East Indian universities. *Library Philosophy and Practice*, Article 5233.

Delgado, N., Campo, L., Sainz, M., & Etxabe-Urbieta, J. M. (2024). Aplicación de la Inteligencia Artificial (IA) en Educación: Los beneficios y limitaciones de la IA percibidos por el profesorado de educación primaria, educación secundaria y educación superior. *Revista Electrónica Interuniversitaria de Formación del Profesorado*, *27*(1), 207–224. DOI: 10.6018/reifop.577211

Dhimolea, T. K., Kaplan-Rakowski, R., & Lin, L. (2022). A systematic review of research on high-immersion virtual reality for language learning. *TechTrends*, *66*(5), 810–824. DOI: 10.1007/s11528-022-00717-w

Di Franco, M. (2022). La investigación en formación docente. *Praxis Educativa (Santa Rosa)*, *26*(2), 1–6. https://doi.org/https://dx.doi.org/10.19137/praxiseducativa-2022-260201. DOI: 10.19137/praxiseducativa-2022-260201

Diallo, A. (2014). *The Use of Technology to Enhance The Learning Experience of ESL Students*. Online Submission.

Dias, S. B., & José, A. (2013). FuzzyQoi model: A fuzzy logic-based modelling of users' quality of interaction with a learning management system under blended learning. *Computers & Education*, *69*, 38–59. DOI: 10.1016/j.compedu.2013.06.016

Dissanayake, D., Perera, T., Elladeniya, C., Dissanayake, K., Herath, S., Perera, I., Dissanayake, D., Perera, T., Elladeniya, C., & Dissanayake, K. (2017, May 6–8). Identifying the learning style of students in MOOCs using video interactions. In *Proceedings of the 4th International Conference on Society, Education and Psychology (ICSEP 2017)*. Macau, China. DOI: 10.18178/ijiet.2018.8.3.1029

Dixon, R. M. (2021). *English prepositions: Their meanings and uses*. Oxford University Press. DOI: 10.1093/oso/9780198868682.001.0001

Domenica Espinar, C. (2021). Aplicación de Moodle para fortalecer el proceso de enseñanza de inglés en la educación abierta. *Revista Tecnológica Ciencia y Educación Edwards Deming*, *5*(1), 81–97. DOI: 10.37957/ed.v5i1.73

Dontre, A. J. (2020). The influence of technology on academic distraction: A review. *Human Behavior and Emerging Technologies*. DOI: 10.1002/hbe2.229

Duffy, L. N., Stone, G. A., Townsend, J., & Cathey, J. (2020). Rethinking curriculum internationalization: Virtual exchange as a means to attaining global competencies, developing critical thinking, and experiencing transformative learning. *SCHOLE: A Journal of Leisure Studies and Recreation Education, 37*(1-2), 11-25. DOI: 10.1080/1937156X.2020.1760749

Dunleavy, M., & Dede, C. (2023). Immersive interfaces for engagement and learning. *Science*, *340*(6130), 66–68. PMID: 19119219

Ebrahimi, S. S., & Jiar, Y. K. (2018). Technology at Malaysia public high school. *Merit Res. J. Educ. Rev.*, *6*, 54–60.

Eickelmann, B., & Vennemann, M. (2017). Teachers' attitudes and beliefs regarding ICT in teaching and learning in European countries. *European Educational Research Journal*, *16*(6), 733–761. DOI: 10.1177/1474904117725899

Elahi, F. (2020). *Digital inclusion: Bridging divides*. Cumberland Lodge.

Ellis, R. (1997). *Second language acquisition*. Oxford University.

Ellis, R. (2020). *Understanding second language acquisition* (2nd ed.). Oxford University Press.

Enith Moreno, L., & Bautista Moreno, L. C.Luz Enith MorenoLeidy Constanza Bautista Moreno. (2024). El uso de las Tics en el fortalecimiento del inglés como lengua extranjera. *Línea Imaginaria*, *2*(18), 1–15. DOI: 10.56219/lneaimaginaria.v2i18.2754

Ennouari, A., & Houssaini, K.Ennouari A.Houssaini K. (2023). Transformative Impacts of ICT-Based Gamification on English Language Teaching in Moroccan Education: A Quasi-Experimental Study. *International Journal For Multidisciplinary Research*, *5*(6), 1–24. DOI: 10.36948/ijfmr.2023.v05i06.9649

Ergado, A. A., Desta, A., & Mehta, H. (2021). Determining the barriers contributing to ICT implementation by using technology-organization-environment framework in Ethiopian higher educational institutions. *Education and Information Technologies*, *26*(3), 3115–3133. DOI: 10.1007/s10639-020-10397-9

Etnologue (2025). *What are the top 200 most spoken languages?* https://www.ethnologue.com/insights/ethnologue200/

European Parliament and Council of the European Union. (2006, December). Recommendation 2006/962/EC on key competences for lifelong learning. *Official Journal of the European Union*, *394*, 30.

Eurydice Unit Ukraine. (2025). *Ukraine: Digital transformation of education as a strategic path to resilience and innovation.* Eurydice. https://eurydice.eacea.ec.europa.eu/news/ukraine-digital-transformation-education-strategic-path-resilience-and-innovation

Eusebio Hermira, S. (2023). Los foros como herramienta de aprendizaje y evaluación de los cursos virtuales asíncronos. *Anuari de Filología. Estudis de Lingüística*, *13*(1), 27–54. DOI: 10.1344/AFEL2023.13.2

Evurulobi, C. I., Dagunduro, A. O., & Ajuwon, O. A. (2024). *Language learning technologies: A review of trends in the USA and globally*. World Journal of Advanced Research and Reviews., DOI: 10.30574/wjarr.2024.23.3.2851

Eyyam, R., & Yaratan, H. S. (2014). Impact of use of technology in mathematics lessons on student achievement and attitudes. *Social Behavior and Personality*, *42*(1), 31S–42S. DOI: 10.2224/sbp.2014.42.0.S31

Felder, R. M., & Soloman, B. A. (n.d.). *Index of learning styles questionnaire.* https://www.engr.ncsu.edu/learningstyles/ilsweb.html

Felder, R. M., & Silverman, L. K. (1988). Learning and teaching styles in engineering education. *Eng. Educ.*, *78*, 674–681.

Felder, R. M., & Spurlin, J. E. (2005). Applications, reliability and validity of the index of learning styles. *Int. J. Contin. Eng. Educ. Life-Long Learn.*, *21*, 103–112.

Ferguson, T., Iliško, D., Roofe, C., & Hill, S. (2018). *SDG4–Quality Education: Inclusivity, Equity and Lifelong Learning for All.* Emerald Publishing Limited. DOI: 10.1108/9781787694231

Fernández Mata, R. (2018). *Hacia el aprendizaje autónomo y colectivo mediante la herramienta "documentos" de Google Drive.* Adaya Press.

Fernández Pa, H. (2024). Plataforma Moodle para la enseñanza de las habilidades fundamentales del idioma inglés como lengua extranjera. *Journal of Science and Research*, *5*, 449–453. DOI: 10.5281/zenodo.133848556

Fernández Regueira, U., González Villa, Á., & Gewerc, A. (2021). *Enseñanza en línea bajo pandemia: una experiencia de enseñanza-aprendizaje basada en una WebQuest.* Octaedro Editorial.

Fernández-Batanero, J. M., Montenegro-Rueda, M., Fernández-Cerero, J., & García-Martínez, I. (2022). Assistive technology for the inclusion of students with disabilities: A systematic review. *Educational Technology Research and Development*, *70*(5), 1911–1930. DOI: 10.1007/s11423-022-10127-7

Fitria, T. N. (2021, Dec). Artificial intelligence (AI) in education: Using AI tools for teaching and learning process. In *Prosiding Seminar Nasional & Call for Paper STIE AAS* (Vol. 4, No. 1, pp. 134-147).

Fitria, T. N. (2023). Using Information and Communication Technology (Ict) in the Education Sector: Opportunities and Challenges in English Language Teaching (Elt). *Teaching English as Foreign Language. Literatura y Lingüística*, *3*(1), 9–30. DOI: 10.33752/teflics.v3i1.4038

Flores Banda, J.C., Huerta Patraca, G.A., Solís Peralta, F.M. & Hernández Martínez, C.E. (2024). Influencia de la Competencia Digital Docente en el Aprendizaje en Bachillerato. *Revista Docentes 2.0, 17*(2), 62-73. DOI: 10.37843/rted.v17i2.525

Flores Nessi, E., Loaiza Falcón, A., & Rojas de Ricardo, G. (2020). Rol del docente investigador desde su práctica social. *Revista Scientific*, *5*(15), 106–128. DOI: 10.29394/Scientific.issn.2542-2987.2020.5.15.5.106-128

Fraga Varela, F., & Alonso Ferreiro, A. (2021). El Proyecto Escuela 2.0 en Galicia (España): Percepciones del Profesorado. *Innovación Educativa (México, D.F.)*, *27*(27), 285–301. DOI: 10.15304/ie.27.4330

Fuchter, S. K., Schlichting, M. S., & Gurgel, G. (2025). Study on the use of ChatGPT for generating code for web-based augmented reality applications. *Measurement. Sensors*, *38*, 101701. DOI: 10.1016/j.measen.2024.101701

Galaczi, E. (2023). *English language education in the era of generative AI: our perspective.* Cambridge University Press & Assessment. https://www.cambridgeenglish.org/Images/685411-english-language-education-in-the-era-of-generative-ai-our-perspective.pdf

Galaczi, E., & Luckin, R. (2024). *Generative AI and language education: Opportunities, challenges and the need for critical perspectives.* Cambridge University Press & Assesment. https://www.cambridge.org/sites/default/files/media/documents/CPELE_Generative%20AI%20and%20Language%20Education%20Opportunities%20Challenges%20and%20the%20Need%20for%20Critical%20Perspectives_FINAL%20%281%29.pdf

Gallego Arrufat, M. J., Torres Hernández, N., & Pessoa, T. (2019). Competence of future teachers in the digital area. *Comunicar*, *27*(61), 57–67. DOI: 10.3916/C61-2019-05

Gangopadhyay, S. (2020). Changes in web content in first 20 NIRF ranking institutes during 2010–19: An analysis. *Library Philosophy and Practice*, Article 4414.

Gangopadhyay, S., & Mukherjee, B. (2021). Research productivity of first ten NIRF ranking academic institutes in India during 2015–19: A scientometric analysis. *Library Philosophy and Practice*, Article 5261.

García Delgado, M. A., Rodríguez Cano, S., Delgado Benito, V., & Di Giusto Valle, C. (2023). Digital Teaching Competence among Teachers of Different Educational Stages in Spain. *Education Sciences*, *13*(6), 1–13. DOI: 10.3390/educsci13060581

García Martín, J. & García Martín, S. (2021). Uso de herramientas digitales para la docencia en España durante la pandemia COVID-19. *Revista Española de Educación Comparada, 38*(extra), 151-173. DOI: 10.5944/reec.38.2021.27816

Garcia-López, I. M., Acosta-Gonzaga, E., & Ruiz-Ledesma, E. F. (2023). Investigating the impact of gamification on student motivation, engagement, and performance. *Education Sciences*, *13*(8), 813. DOI: 10.3390/educsci13080813

García-Martínez, I., Fernández-Batanero, J. M., Fernández-Cerero, J., & León, S. P. (2023). Analysing the Impact of Artificial Intelligence and Computational Sciences on Student Performance: Systematic Review and Meta-analysis. *Journal of New Approaches Educational Research.*, *12*(1), 171–197. DOI: 10.7821/naer.2023.1.1240

García, P., Amandi, A., Schiaffino, S., & Campo, M. (2007). Evaluating Bayesian networks' precision for detecting students' learning styles. *Computers & Education, 49*(3), 794–808. DOI: 10.1016/j.compedu.2005.11.017

Gesa, R. F., Lázaro, J. L. M., & Carrillo, C. I. P. D. (2000). *Teaching support units.* Springer.

Ghaus-Pasha, A. (2005, May). Role of civil society organizations in governance. In *Kertas Persidangan 6th Global Forum on Reinventing Government Towards Participatory and Transparent Governance. Seoul* (pp. 24-27).

Ghavifekr, S., & Rosdy, W. A. W. (2015). Teaching and learning with technology: Effectiveness of ICT integration in schools. *International Journal of Research in Education and Science, 1*(2), 175–191. https://files.eric.ed.gov/fulltext/EJ1105224.pdf. DOI: 10.21890/ijres.23596

Ghazali, M., Makrakis, V., Kostoulas-Makrakis, N., Yakob, N., Rashid, R. A. A., Othman, W., & Fitriyanto, N. A. (2024). Predicting teacher's information and communication technology-enabled education for sustainability self-efficacy. *Sustainability (Basel), 16*(3), 5323. DOI: 10.3390/su16135323

Ghaznavi, M. R., Keikha, A., & Yaghoubi, N. M. (2011). The Impact of Information and Communication Technology (ICT) on Educational Improvement. *International Education Studies, 4*(2), 116–125. DOI: 10.5539/ies.v4n2p116

Gil Pérez, A., & Berlanga Fernández, I. (2023). La interactividad en el aula. Un reto de la escuela 2.0. *EDMETIC, 2*(2), 56-75. DOI: 10.21071/edmetic.v2i2.2870

Gillani, N., Eynon, R., Chiabaut, C., & Finkel, K. (2023). Unpacking the "black box" of AI in education. *Journal of Educational Technology & Society, 26*(1), 99–111. DOI: 10.30191/ETS.202301_26(1).0008

Gillen, J., & Kucirkova, N. (2018). Percolating spaces: Creative ways of using digital technologies to connect young children's school and home lives. *British Journal of Educational Technology, 49*(5), 834–846. DOI: 10.1111/bjet.12666

Girón Chávez, A., Cruz Maldonado, E. Y., Bermej del Villar, M. M., & Cancino Zamarrón, R. (2023). Las TIC y el aprendizaje colaborativo para mejorar la pronunciación de inglés de estudiantes universitarios. *Revista Lengua y Cultura, 5*(9), 1–10. DOI: 10.29057/lc.v5i9.11531

Gnanasekaran, D., & Rajkumar, T. (2022). Research productivity and altmetrics of NIRF top ranked medical institutions. *Annals of Library and Information Studies, 69*(2), 120–128.

Godwin-Jones, R. (2021). Emerging technologies: Collaborative language learning. *Language Learning & Technology*, *25*(3), 4–15.

Goel, R. K., & Vishnoi, S. (2022). Urbanization and sustainable development for inclusiveness of using ICTs. *Telecommunications Policy*, *46*(6), 102311. DOI: 10.1016/j.telpol.2022.102311

Gómez Trigueros, I. M., & Bustamante Alonso, C. (2023). Nuevas perspectivas en la formación del profesorado en competencias digitales. *Bordón Revista de Pedagogía*, *75*(4), 11–30. DOI: 10.13042/Bordon.2023.100532

Gough, D., Oliver, S., & Thomas, J. (Eds.). (2017). *An introduction to systematic reviews* (2nd ed.). Sage.

Grabner-Hagan, M. M., & Kingsley, T. (2023). From badges to boss challenges: Gamification through need-supporting scaffolded design to instruct and motivate elementary learners. *Computers and Education Open*, *4*, 100131. DOI: 10.1016/j.caeo.2023.100131

Graf, S. (2007). *Adaptivity in learning management systems focussing on learning styles* (Ph.D. Thesis). Vienna University of Technology, Vienna, Austria.

Graf, S., & Kinshuk, P. (2006, Jul 5–7). An approach for detecting learning styles in learning management systems. In *Proceedings of the IEEE International Conference on Advanced Learning Technologies*, Kerkrade, The Netherlands (pp. 161–163). DOI: 10.1109/ICALT.2006.1652395

Grece, E. G., Vidhyavathi, P., & Malathi, P. (2023). A study on "AI in education: Opportunities and challenges for personalized learning. *Industrial Engineering Journal*, *52*(05), 750–759. DOI: 10.36893/IEJ.2023.V52I05.750-759

Guamán Gómez, V. J., Espinoza Freire, E., & Granda Ayabaca, D. M. (2023). Rol del docente en la era digital. *Portal de la Ciencia*, *4*(3), 364–378. DOI: 10.51247/pdlc.v4i3.398

Gudoniene, D., & Rutkauskiene, D. (2019). Virtual and augmented reality in education. *Baltic Journal of Modern Computing*, *7*(2), 293–300. DOI: 10.22364/bjmc.2019.7.2.07

Guo, P., Jeyaraji, J. J., & Razali, A. B. (2024). A systematic review of collaborative mobile-assisted language learning (C-MALL) practices using bibliometric, content, and scientometric analyses. *Humanities & Social Sciences Communications*, *11*(1), 1435. DOI: 10.1057/s41599-024-03940-3

Gutiérrez-Martín. Pinedo-González, R., & Gil-Puente, C. (2022). ICT and media competencies of teachers. Convergence towards an integrated MIL-ICT model. *Media Education Research Journal, 30*(70), 19-30. https://eric.ed.gov/?id=EJ1320974

Habibu, T., Al-Mamun, A., & Clement, C. (2022). Difficulties Faced by Teachers in Using ICT in Teaching-Learning at Technical and Higher Educational Institutions of Uganda. *International Journal of Engineering Research & Technology (Ahmedabad), 1*(7), 1–9.

Habók, A., & Nguyen, L. A. T. (2024). A comparative study of language learners' ICT attitudes and behavior pre- and post-COVID-19. *Scientific Reports, 14*(1), 1–12. DOI: 10.1038/s41598-023-50872-0 PMID: 38182683

Hadaya, A., & Hanif, M. (2019). The Impact of Using the Interactive E-Book on Students' Learning Outcomes. *International Journal of Instruction, 12*(2), 709–722. DOI: 10.29333/iji.2019.12245a

Hafifah, G. N., & Sulistyo, G. H. (2020a). Teachers' ICT literacy and ICT integration in ELT in the Indonesian higher education setting. *Turkish Online Journal of Distance Education, 21*(3), 186–198. DOI: 10.17718/tojde.762050

Hakim, B. (2021). Role of ICT in the process of EFL teaching and learning in an Arab context. *Humanities and Social Sciences Letters, 9*(1), 58–71. DOI: 10.18488/journal.73.2021.91.58.71

Haleem, A., Javaid, M., Qadri, M. A., & Suman, R. (2022). Understanding the role of digital technologies in education: A review. *Sustainable operations and computers, 3*, 275-285.

Haleem, A., Javaid, M., Qadri, M. A., & Suman, R. (2022). Understanding the role of digital technologies in education: A review. *Sustainable Operations and Computers, 3*, 275–285. DOI: 10.1016/j.susoc.2022.05.004

Halkiopoulos, C., & Gkintoni, E. (2024). Leveraging AI in e-learning: Personalized learning and adaptive assessment through cognitive neuropsychology – a systematic analysis. *Electronics (Basel), 13*(18), 3762. DOI: 10.3390/electronics13183762

Hannaford, J., & Beavis, C. (2018). When will the Internet be connected? Digital worlds and belonging in the lives of globally mobile children. *Literacy, 52*(1), 47–54. DOI: 10.1111/lit.12123

Han, R., Alibakshai, G., Lu, L., & Labbafi, A. (2024). Digital communication activities and EFL learners' willingness to communicate and engagement: Exploring the intermediate language learners' perceptions. *Heliyon, 10*(3), e25213. DOI: 10.1016/j.heliyon.2024.e25213 PMID: 38333790

Hassain, K. I. (2024). Reviewing the role of culture in English language learning: Challenges and opportunities for educators. *Social Sciences & Humanities Open*, *9*, 100781. DOI: 10.1016/j.ssaho.2023.100781

Hassan, M., Mahmud, R., Mohd Ayub, A. F., & Wong, S. L. (2016). Teachers' acceptance of ICT and its integration in the classroom. *Quality Assurance in Education*, *24*(1), 26–40. DOI: 10.1108/QAE-06-2014-0025

Hattie, J. (2023). *Artificial intelligence in education: Promises and implications*. Routledge.

Hemingway, P., & Brereton, N. (2009, Apr). *What is a systematic review?* What is ...? series. https://familymedicine.med.wayne.edu/mph/project/what_is_a_systematic_review.pdf

Heras, M., & Tàbara, J. D. (2014). Let's play transformations! Performative methods for sustainability. *Sustainability Science*, *9*(3), 379–398. DOI: 10.1007/s11625-014-0245-9

Hidasi, B., Karatzoglou, A., Baltrunas, L., & Tikk, D. (2016, May 2–4). Session-based recommendations with recurrent neural networks. In *Proceedings of the International Conference on Learning Representations (ICLR) 2016*, San Juan, Puerto Rico.

High-Level Expert Group on Artificial Intelligence. (2018). *A definition of AI: Main capabilities and scientific disciplines*. European Commission. https://ec.europa.eu/futurium/en/system/files/ged/ai_hleg_definition_of_ai_18_december_1.pdf

Hilty, L. M., & Huber, P. (2018). Motivating students on ICT-related study programs to engage with the subject of sustainable development. *International Journal of Sustainability in Higher Education*, *19*(3), 642–656. DOI: 10.1108/IJSHE-02-2017-0027

Hockly, N. (2022). *Digital learning: Principles and tools for teachers*. EdTech Books.

Holmes, W., Bialik, M., & Fadel, C. (2019). *Artificial intelligence in education: Promises and implications for teaching and learning*. Center for Curriculum Redesign (CCR). https://curriculumredesign.org/wp-content/uploads/AIED-Book-Excerpt-CCR.pdf

Holmes, W., Porayska-Pomsta, K., Holstein, K., Sutherland, E., Baker, T., Shum, S. B., Santos, O. C., Rodrigo, M. T., Cukurova, M., Bittencourt, I. I., & Koedinger, K. R. (2022). Ethics of AI in education: Towards a community-wide framework. *International Journal of Artificial Intelligence in Education*, *32*(3), 504–526. DOI: 10.1007/s40593-021-00239-1

Hopkins, C. (2012). Twenty years of education for sustainable development. *Journal of Education for Sustainable Development, 6*(1), 1–4. DOI: 10.1177/097340821100600101

Howard, S. K., Tondeur, J., Ma, J., & Yang, J. (2021). What to teach? Strategies for developing digital competency in preservice teacher training. *Computers & Education, 165*, 104149. DOI: 10.1016/j.compedu.2021.104149

Hsu, T.-C. (2020). Learning English with augmented Reality: Do learning styles matter? *Computers & Education, 160*, 137–149. DOI: 10.1016/j.compedu.2016.12.007

Huang, Y., & Khan, S. M. (2021). Advances in AI and machine learning for education research. *Computational Psychometrics: New Methodologies for a New Generation of Digital Learning and Assessment: With Examples in R and Python*, 195-208.

Hughes, G., & Dobbins, C. (2015). The utilization of data analysis techniques in predicting student performance in massive open online courses (MOOCs). *Research and Practice in Technology Enhanced Learning, 10*(1), 10. DOI: 10.1186/s41039-015-0007-z PMID: 30613219

Hung, J. L., & Zhang, K. (2012). Examining m-learning trends 2003–2008: A categorical meta-trend analysis using text mining techniques. *Journal of Computing in Higher Education, 24*(1), 1–17. DOI: 10.1007/s12528-011-9044-9

Hunter, L., & Frawley, E. (2023). Engaging students using an arts-based pedagogy: Teaching and learning sociological theory through film, art, and music. *Teaching Sociology, 51*(1), 13–25. DOI: 10.1177/0092055X221096657

Huong, N. L. T. (2021). Teachers' perceptions of ICT integration in English language teaching at the Vietnamese tertiary level. *European Journal of Contemporary Education, 10*(3), 697–710. https://files.eric.ed.gov/fulltext/EJ1324207.pdf

Hwang, G. J., Xie, H., Wah, B. W., & Gašević, D. (2020). Vision, challenges, roles and research issues of AI in education. *Computers & Education: AI, 1*(1), 100001. DOI: 10.1016/j.caeai.2020.100001

IEEE. (2020). IEEE standard for augmented reality learning experience models (AR-LEM) (IEEE Std 1589-2020). https://standards.ieee.org/ieee/1589/6073/

Ilham, I. (2018). An Analysis of The Students' Difficulties in using preposition. *Research in English and Education Journal, 3*(2), 125-129. https://jim.usk.ac.id/READ/article/view/9247

Imran, A. (2022). Why addressing digital inequality should be a priority. *The Electronic Journal on Information Systems in Developing Countries*, *89*(3), e12255. DOI: 10.1002/isd2.12255

Intriago Cedeño, G. (2019). TIC en la enseñanza y autoaprendizaje del idioma inglés. *Skopos Revista Internacional de Traducción e Interpretación*, *10*, 65–85. DOI: 10.21071/skopos.v10i.12759

Iqbal, M. Z., Mangina, E., & Campbell, A. G. (2022). Current Challenges and Future Research Directions in Augmented Reality for Education. *Multimodal Technologies and Interaction*, *6*(9), 75. DOI: 10.3390/mti6090075

Ivanytska, N., Koliasa, O., Kovalevska, T., Matsera, O., & Tkachuk, T. (2024). Analyzing the possibilities of implementation of AI and social networks in teaching foreign language students: Ukrainian universities case study. *Arab World English Journal (AWEJ) Special Issue on ChatGPT*, 306-318. DOI: 10.24093/awej/ChatGPT.21

Jacobs, R. F. (2022). Arts-based critical service-learning experiences as transformative pedagogy. *J. Pedagog.*, *13*(2), 29–53. DOI: 10.2478/jped-2022-0007

Jain, E. (2020). A review study on sustainable development goals: Un 2030 Agenda. *Our Heritage*, *68*(5), 1–13.

Janzen, K. J., Perry, B., & Edwards, M. (2012). Engaging students: Strategies for digital natives. *Academic Exchange Quarterly*, *16*, 116–123.

Jayanthi, C. E. (2023). Challenges In Using ICT Tools Among Student Teachers. *Educational Administration: Theory and Practice*, *29*(4), 3520–3522. DOI: 10.53555/kuey.v29i4.8157

Jensen, H. P., & Johannesson, H. (2006). Engineering courses taught in English: An experience from Denmark. *European Journal of Engineering Education*, *20*(1), 19–23. DOI: 10.1080/0304379950200103

Jhurry, D., & Rampersad, R. D. (2022). From online learning to digital transformation. *Quality Assuring Unknown Territory, 57*.

Ji, H., Han, I., & Ko, Y. (2023). A systematic review of conversational AI in language education: Focusing on the collaboration with human teachers. *Journal of Research on Technology in Education*, *55*(1), 48–63. DOI: 10.1080/15391523.2022.2142873

Jiménez Hernández, D., Muñoz Sánchez, P., & Sánchez Giménez, F. (2021). La Competencia Digital Docente, una revisión sistemática de los modelos más utilizados. *Revista Interuniversitaria de Investigación en Tecnología Educativa*, *10*, 105–112. DOI: 10.6018/riite.472351

Johler, M., & Krumsvik, R. J. (2022). Increasing inclusion through differentiated instruction in a technology-rich primary school in Norway. *International Journal of Primary. Elementary and Early Years Education*, *52*(8), 1207–1221. DOI: 10.1080/03004279.2022.2143721

Jones, G., & Brader-Araje, L. (2022). The impact of constructivism on education: Language, discourse, and meaning. *American Communication Journal*, *5*(3), 1–10.

Joseph, O., Onwuzulike, O., & Shitu, K. (2024). Digital transformation in education: Strategies for effective implementation. *World Journal of Advanced Research and Reviews.*, *2*.DOI: .30574/wjarr

Joshi, S., & Malgan, D. (2017). Missing scholars: Social exclusion at the Indian Institutes of Management. *IIM Bangalore Research Paper*, (554).

Jumani, A. K., Siddique, W. A., Laghari, A. A., Abro, A., & Khan, A. A. (2022). Virtual reality and augmented reality for education. In *Multimedia computing systems and virtual reality* (pp. 189–210). CRC Press. DOI: 10.1201/9781003196686-9

Kamarulzaman, K., Che Anuar, C. A., & Mohd Noor, I. (2017). Integrating ICT in teaching and learning: A preliminary study on Malaysia private preschool. *International Journal of Academic Research in Business & Social Sciences*, *7*, 1236–1248.

Kamenskih, A. (2022). The analysis of security and privacy risks in smart education environments. *Journal of Smart Cities and Society*, *1*(1), 17–29. DOI: 10.3233/SCS-210114

Kaplan, A. M., & Haenlein, M. (2016). Higher education and the digital revolution: About MOOCs, SPOCs, social media, and the cookie monster. *Business Horizons*, *59*(4), 441–450. DOI: 10.1016/j.bushor.2016.03.008

Kapur, R., Byfield, V., Del Frate, F., Higgins, M., & Jagannathan, S. (2018). The digital transformation of education. *Earth observation open science and innovation*, 25-41.

Kartal, G. (2023). Contemporary language teaching and learning with ChatGPT. *Contemporary Research in Language and Linguistics*, *1*(1), 59–70. DOI: 10.62601/crll.v1i1.10

Katamaya Cruz, E., & Rojas Montero, J. A. (2021). WebQuest como escenario para el aprendizaje colaborativo y el desarrollo de competencias digitales. *Hamut'ay*, *8*(3), 54–61. DOI: 10.21503/hamu.v8i3.2332

Kaufmann, H. (2003). Collaborative augmented reality in education. *Institute of Software Technology and Interactive Systems, Vienna University of Technology*, 2-4.

Kaya, O. S., & Ercag, E. (2023). The impact of applying challenge-based gamification program on students' learning outcomes: Academic achievement, motivation, and flow. *Education and Information Technologies*, *28*(8), 10053–10078. DOI: 10.1007/s10639-023-11585-z PMID: 36691635

Kesim, M., & Ozarslan, Y. (2012). Augmented reality in education: Current technologies and the potential for education. *Procedia: Social and Behavioral Sciences*, *47*, 297–302. DOI: 10.1016/j.sbspro.2012.06.654

Kessler, G. (2018). Technology and the future of language teaching. *Foreign Language Annals*, *51*(1), 205–218. DOI: 10.1111/flan.12318

Key Sustainability. (2024, Jul 24). *United Nations sustainable development goals: Together we can make "sustainable future"*. Commitment towards sustainable future. https://www.keysustainability.com/united-nations-sustainable-development-goals-together-we-can-make-sustainable-future/

Khan, N. M., & Kuddus, K. (2020). Integrating ICT in English Language Teaching in Bangladesh: Teachers' Perceptions and Challenges. *Rupkatha Journal on Interdisciplinary Studies in Humanities*, *12*(5), 1–10. DOI: 10.21659/rupkatha.v12n5.rioc1s23n1

Kibar, A. H., Ampa, A. T., & Nappu, S. (2023). A Study on EFL Teacher Strategies in Utilizing ICT for Regional Public Highschool of Indonesia. *Tamaddun*, *22*(1), 1–10. DOI: 10.33096/tamaddun.v22i1.205

Kingma, D., & Ba, J. (2015, May 7). Adam: A method for stochastic optimization. In *Proceedings of the International Conference on Learning Representations (ICLR) 2015*, San Diego, CA, USA.

Kolb, D. (1984). *Experiential learning: Experience as the source of learning and development* (Vol. 1). Prentice Hall.

Koraishi, O. (2023). Teaching English in the age of AI: Embracing ChatGPT to optimize EFL materials and assessment. *Language Education and Technology, 3*(1). https://langedutech.com/letjournal/index.php/let/article/view/48

Krashen, S. D. (2009). *Principles and practice in second language acquisition*. Pergamon Press. https://www.sdkrashen.com/content/books/principles_and_practice.pdf (Original work published 1982).

Krashen, S. (1985). *The input hypothesis: Issues and implications*. Longman.

Kryshtanovych, S., Bekh, Y., Stadnichenko, O., Shevchenko, Z., Maikher, V., & Liubinska, O. (2025). Education 4.0: Development of the Ukrainian education system in the context of artificial intelligence and information technologies. *Journal of Management World, 2025*(2), 315–319. DOI: 10.53935/jomw.v2024i4.927

Kumar, A., & Tiwari, P. K. (2022). Digital accessibility for persons with disabilities: A mixed method study of websites of 15-top ranked universities of India. *Academia: Social Sciences, 29*, 68–82.

Kumar, P. C., Chetty, M., Clegg, T. L., & Vitak, J. (2019, May). Privacy and security considerations for digital technology use in elementary schools. In *Proceedings of the 2019 CHI Conference on Human Factors in Computing Systems* (pp. 1-13). DOI: 10.1145/3290605.3300537

Kurt, G., & Kurt, Y. (2024). Enhancing L2 writing skills: ChatGPT as an automated feedback tool. *Journal of Information Technology Education, 23*, 24. DOI: 10.28945/5370

Kurvinen, E., Järvinen, J. P., & Kaila, E. (2022). Artificial intelligence in education–Where are we now? In Carmo, M. (Ed.), *Education and New Developments 2022* (Vol. 2, pp. 391–395). Science Press., DOI: 10.36315/2022v2end087

Kwihangana, F. (2024). Teacher positioning in educational ICT policies: Implications for digital teacher identity development in under-resourced contexts. *Journal of Education Policy, 40*(2), 242–265. DOI: 10.1080/02680939.2024.2386309

Laabidi, M., Jemni, M., Ayed, L. J. B., Brahim, H. B., & Jemaa, A. B. (2014). Learning technologies for people with disabilities. *Journal of King Saud University. Computer and Information Sciences, 26*(1), 29–45. DOI: 10.1016/j.jksuci.2013.10.005

Laak, K. J., & Aru, J. (2024). AI and personalized learning: bridging the gap with modern educational goals. *arXiv preprint arXiv:2404.02798*.

Labadze, L., Grigolia, M., & Machaidze, L. (2023). Role of AI chatbots in education: Systematic literature review. *International Journal of Educational Technology in Higher Education, 20*(1), 56. DOI: 10.1186/s41239-023-00426-1

Lambert, R. (2006). Foreign language teaching policy. In Brown, K. (Ed.), *Encyclopedia of Language & Linguistics* (2nd ed., pp. 551–558). Elsevier., DOI: 10.1016/B0-08-044854-2/00656-8

Laura de la Cruz, K., Morales Vargas, K., Huanacuni Clavitea, M., & Aza Custodio, P. (2021). Aplicación Quizizz y comprensión de textos en inglés con el contenido de la plataforma educativa "Aprendo en Casa". *Revista Innova Educación, 3*(1), 151–159. DOI: 10.35622/j.rie.2021.01.007

Laura de la Cruz, K., & Tolentino Cotrina, M. P. (2022). Quizizz en el aprendizaje del inglés en estudiantes de la Universidad Nacional Jorge Basadre Grohmann de Tacna. *PURIQ*, *4*, 1–13. DOI: 10.37073/puriq.4.298

Leavy, P. (2015). *Method meets art: Arts-based research practice* (2nd ed.). Guilford.

Lebler, D. (2012). Technology and students' musicking: Enhancing the learning experience. *Theory into Practice*, *51*(3), 204–211. DOI: 10.1080/00405841.2012.690302

Lee, K. (2012). The Future of Learning and Training in Augmented Reality. *InSight: A Journal of Scholarly Teaching, 7*, 31-42.

Lee, M. J. W., & Park, S. Y. (2022). Augmented Reality for enhanced learning environments. In *Innovations in educational technology* (pp. 123–140). Springer.

Leontiev, A. (1975). *Activity, Consciousness, and Personality*. Prentice-Hall.

Ley Leyva, N. V. (2022). El papel del docente de educación básica en el contexto actual. *Portal de la Ciencia*, *3*(1), 27–37. DOI: 10.51247/pdlc.v3i1.308

Liang, G., & Akiba, M. (2021). Teacher evaluation, performance-related pay, and constructivist instruction. *Educational Policy*, *29*(2), 375–401. DOI: 10.1177/0895904813492379

Likovič, A., & Rojko, K. (2022). E-Learning and a Case Study of Coursera and edX Online Platforms. *Research in Social Change*, *14*(1), 94–120. DOI: 10.2478/rsc-2022-0008

Lim, J., Leinonen, T., Lipponen, L., Lee, H., DeVita, J., & Murray, D. (2023). Artificial intelligence as relational artifacts in creative learning. *Digital Creativity (Exeter)*, *34*(3), 192–210. DOI: 10.1080/14626268.2023.2236595

Limna, P., Jakwatanatham, S., Siripipattanakul, S., Kaewpuang, P., & Sriboonruang, P. (2022). A review of artificial intelligence (AI) in education during the digital era. *Advance Knowledge for Executives*, *1*(1), 1–9.

Lin, M. (2018). *"I don't even know where Turkey is: Developing intercultural competence through e-pal exchanges. Journal of Global Education and Research, 2*(2), 68-81. 68-81. https://www.doi.org/10.5038/

Linguistic – Third Year – Lecture One. (n.d.). *Second vs Foreign Language Learning /Acquisition* [Course Notes]. Université Frères Mentouri - Constantine 1. https://fac.umc.edu.dz/fll/images/cours_ang/L3/L3_LING_Lecture%201.pdf

Liu, C. C., & Chen, I. J. (2020). Evolution of constructivism. *Contemporary Issues in Education Research*, *3*(4), 63–66. DOI: 10.19030/cier.v3i4.199

Liu, G. Z., Fathi, J., & Rahimi, M. (2024). Using digital gamification to improve language achievement, foreign language enjoyment, and ideal L2 self: A case of English as a foreign language learners. *Journal of Computer Assisted Learning, 40*(4), 1347–1364. DOI: 10.1111/jcal.12954

Livingstone, S., & Helsper, E. (2007). Gradations in digital inclusion: Children, young people and the digital divide. *New Media & Society, 9*(4), 671–696. DOI: 10.1177/1461444807080335

Loewen, S., Crowther, D., Isbell, D. R., Kim, K. M., Maloney, J., Miller, Z. F., & Rawal, H. (2019). Mobile-assisted language learning: A Duolingo case study. *ReCALL, 31*(3), 293–311. DOI: 10.1017/S0958344019000065

López Aguilar, J., Maza Córdova, J., & Tusa Jumbo, F. (2020). Educar en el contexto digital: el reto de ser edutuber. *risti Revista Ibérica de Sistemas e Tecnologias de Informação, 1*(E25), 188–200.

López Belmonte, J., Pozo Sánchez, S., Fuentes Cabrera, A., & Gómez García, G. (2019). Análisis del efecto de la formación b-learning en el profesorado. *Texto Livre: Linguagem e Tecnologia, 12*(2), 98–115. DOI: 10.17851/1983-3652.12.2.98-115

López-Chila, R., Llerena-Izquierdo, J., Sumba-Nacipucha, N., & Cueva-Estrada, J. (2024). Artificial intelligence in higher education: An analysis of existing bibliometrics. *Education Sciences, 14*(1), 47. DOI: 10.3390/educsci14010047

Lotz-Sisitka, H., Wals, A., Kronlid, D., & McGarry, D. (2015). Transformative, transgressive social learning: Rethinking higher education pedagogy in times of systemic global dysfunction. *Current Opinion in Environmental Sustainability, 16*, 73–80. DOI: 10.1016/j.cosust.2015.07.018

Low, E. L. (2025). Repositioning the English language teacher education for global competence and local realities: Adopting the cline of glocality. *TESOL Journal, 16*(1), e70012. DOI: 10.1002/tesj.70012

Lozano Rodríguez, A. L., Valdés Lozano, D. E., Sánchez Aradillas, A. L., & Esparza Duque, E. E. (2021). Uso de Gogle Docs como herramienta de construcción colaborativa tomando en cuenta los estilos de aprendizaje. *Revista De Estilos De Aprendizaje, 4*(8), 23–39. DOI: 10.55777/rea.v4i8.934

Luan, H., & Tsai, C. C. (2021). A review of using machine learning approaches for precision education. *Journal of Educational Technology & Society, 24*(1), 250–266.

Luckin, R. (2018). *Machine learning and human intelligence: The future of education.* UCL Institute of Education Press.

Lu, D., & Xie, Y. N. (2022). Critical thinking cultivation in TESOL with ICT tools: A systematic review. *Computer Assisted Language Learning*, *37*(1), 222–242. DOI: 10.1080/09588221.2022.2033788

Lune, H., & Berg, B. L. (2017). *Qualitative research methods for the social sciences* (9th ed.). Pearson.

Luo, J. (2024). Validating the impact of gamified technology-enhanced learning environments on motivation and academic performance: Enhancing TELES with digital badges. *Frontiers in Education*, *9*, 1429452. DOI: 10.3389/feduc.2024.1429452

Luo, Z. (2023). The effectiveness of gamified tools for foreign language learning (FLL): A systematic review. *Behavioral Science*, *13*(13), 331. https://pmc.ncbi.nlm.nih.gov/articles/PMC10135444/. DOI: 10.3390/bs13040331 PMID: 37102845

Macas Granda, C. J., Granda Asencio, L. Y., & Carbay Cajamarca, W. A. (2021). Rol del docente en la alfabetización digital en el siglo XXI. *Sociedad & Tecnología*, *4*(S2), 350–363. DOI: 10.51247/st.v4iS2.156

Macinska, S., & Vinkler, A. (2024). *The role of AI in language learning: Research evidence and strategies for success.* Cambridge University Press & Assesment. https://www.cambridge.org/sites/default/files/media/documents/The_Role_of_AI_in_Language_Learning_Research_Evidence_and_Strategies.pdf

Mageira, K., Pittou, D., Papasalouros, A., Kotis, K., Zangogianni, P., & Daradoumis, A. (2022). Educational AI Chatbots for Content and Language Integrated Learning. *Applied Sciences (Basel, Switzerland)*, *12*(7), 1–16. DOI: 10.3390/app12073239

Makki, T. W., O'Neal, L. J., Cotton, S. R., & Rikard, R. V. (2018). When first-order barriers are high: A comparison of second and third order barriers to classroom computing integration. *Computers & Education*, *120*, 90–97. DOI: 10.1016/j.compedu.2018.01.005

Makrakis, V. (2022). From STEM to STEAM and to STREAM enabled through meaningful critical reflective learning. In E. Koleza, C. Panagiotakopoulos, & C. Skordoulis (Eds.), *Innovating STEM education: Increased engagement and best practices* (pp. 161–172). Common Ground Research Network; University of Illinois Research Park.

Makrakis, V. (2023). Using the DREAM methodology for course assessment in the field of ICT-enabled education for sustainability. *European Journal of Investigation in Health, Psychology and Education*, *13*(7), 1378–1391. DOI: 10.3390/ejihpe13070100 PMID: 37504491

Makrakis, V., & Kostoulas-Makrakis, N. (2023). A participatory curriculum approach to ICT-enabled education for sustainability in higher education. *Sustainability (Basel), 15*(5), 3967. DOI: 10.3390/su15053967

Malish, C. M. (2020). Measuring access to higher education. *Economic and Political Weekly, 55*(40), 55–61.

Maliza Muñoz, W., Medina León, A., Vera Mora, G., & Castro Molina, N. (2020). Aprendizaje autónomo en Moodle. *Journal of Science and Research, 5*, 632–652. DOI: 10.5281/zeonodo.4441105

Mallik, S., & Gangopadhyay, A. (2023). Proactive and reactive engagement of artificial intelligence methods for education: A review. *Frontiers in Artificial Intelligence, 6*, 1151391. DOI: 10.3389/frai.2023.1151391 PMID: 37215064

Mariana-Daniela González-Zamar, M.-D., Abad-Segura, E., López-Meneses, E., & Gómez-Galán, J. (2020). Managing ICT for sustainable education: Research analysis in the context of higher education. *Sustainability (Basel), 12*(19), 8254. DOI: 10.3390/su12198254

Marisha. (2021). Analysing the stability of India rankings. *Current Science, 120*(7), 1144–1151.

Martí Climent, A. (2022). *El uso del vídeo en la formación de docentes*. Adaya Press.

Martín Párraga, L., Llorente Cejudo, M. C., & Cabero Almenara, J. (2022). Analysis of teachers' digital competencies from assessment frameworks and instruments. *IJERI: International Journal of Educational Research and Innovation, 18*, 62–79. DOI: 10.46661/ijeri.7444

Martínez Sala, A. M., & Alemany Martínez, D. (2022). Redes sociales educativas para la adquisición de competencias digitales. *Revista Mexicana de Investigación Educativa, 27*(92), 209–234.

Mas García, V., Gabarda Méndez, V., & Peirats Chacón, J. (2023). Formación y competencia digital del profesorado de Educación Secundaria en España. *Texto Livre Linguagem e Tecnología, 16*(79), 1-12. DOI: 10.1590/1983-3652.2023.44581

Mas García, V., Jordá Fabra, T., & Agustí López, A. I. (2023). La importancia de la creación de recursos digitales de calidad destinados a docentes. Una propuesta para su evaluación y mejora. *Praxis Educativa (Santa Rosa), 27*(1), 1–18. DOI: 10.19137/praxiseducativa-2023-270117

Mavlyuda, X. (2021). Creation of 3d models of historical monuments application of digital technologies. *Academicia: An International Multidisciplinary Research Journal, 11*(10), 1260–1268. https://www.indianjournals.com/ijor.aspx?target=ijor:aca&volume=11&issue=10&article=188

Mayer, R. E. (2021). *Multimedia learning* (3rd ed.). Cambridge University Press., DOI: 10.1017/9781316941355

McCarthy, A. M., Maor, D., McConney, A., & Cavanaugh, C. (2023). Digital transformation in education: Critical components for leaders of system change. *Social Sciences & Humanities Open*, *8*(1), 100479. DOI: 10.1016/j.ssaho.2023.100479

McGreal, R. (2017). Special report on the role of open educational resources in supporting the sustainable development goal 4: Quality education challenges and opportunities. *International Review of Research in Open and Distance Learning*, *18*(7). Advance online publication. DOI: 10.19173/irrodl.v18i7.3541

McKay, L., & Barton, G. (2018). Exploring how arts-based reflection can support teachers' resilience and well-being. *Teaching and Teacher Education*, *75*, 356–365. DOI: 10.1016/j.tate.2018.07.012

Mellado Moreno, P. C., Patiño Masó, J., Ramos Pardo, F. J., & Estebanell Minguell, M. (2022). Discursos en Facebook y Twitter sobre el uso educativo de móviles en el aula. *Revista Latina de Comunicación Social*, 80, 225-240. https://www.doi.org/10.4185/RLCS-2022-1541

Meniado, J. C. (2023). El Impacto de ChatGPT en la enseñanza, el aprendizaje y la evaluación del inglés: Una revisión rápida de la literature. *Arab World English Journal*, *14*(4), 3–18. DOI: 10.24093/awej/vol14no4.1

Mhlongo, S., Mbatha, K., Ramatsetse, B., & Dlamini, R. (2023). Challenges, opportunities, and prospects of adopting and using smart digital technologies in learning environments: An iterative review. *Heliyon*, *9*(6), e16348. DOI: 10.1016/j.heliyon.2023.e16348 PMID: 37274691

Mielikainen, M. (2021). Towards blended learning: Stakeholders' perspectives on a project-based integrated curriculum in ICT engineering education. *Industry and Higher Education*, *36*(1), 74–85. DOI: 10.1177/0950422221994471

Mindiola Molina, I. Y., & Castro Mendoza, J. C.Idayris Yiseth Mindiola-MolinaJuan Camilo Castro-Mendoza. (2021). Desarrollo del pensamiento crítico a través de foros de discusión asincrónicos con estudiantes de 8° grado. *Revista UNIMAR*, *39*(1), 126–144. DOI: 10.31948/Rev.unimar/unimar39-1-art9

Mohammed, A., Kumar, S., Saleh, B. M., & Shuaibu, A. (2017). E-learning: A tool for enhancing teaching and learning in educational institutes. *International Journal of Computer Science and Information Technologies*, *8*(2), 217–221.

Molenaar, I. (2023). Towards hybrid human-AI learning technologies. *European Journal of Education*, *58*(1), 89–104.

Molina, A. (2003). The digital divide: The need for a global e-inclusion movement. *Technology Analysis and Strategic Management*, *15*(1), 137–152. DOI: 10.1080/0953732032000046105

Molsalve Franco, A. P., & Valencia Valencia, E. Z. (2023). Impacto de las tecnologías de la información en los estudiantes del grado aceleración del aprendizaje en un curso de inglés. *Revista Virtual Universidad Católica del Norte*, *1*(68), 37–62. DOI: 10.35575/rvucn.n68a3

Monsalve Lorente, L. & Aguasanta Regalado, M. (2020). Nuevas ecologías del aprendizaje en el currículo: la era digital en la escuela. *Revista Latinoamericana de Tecnología Educativa - RELATEC, 19*(1), 139-154. DOI: 10.17398/1695-288X.19.1.139

Montaner Villaba, S. (2018). Aplicación del Blogging y/o Google Docs para fomentar la competencia en producción escrita en la enseñanza del inglés. *Universitas Tarraconensis Revista de Ciencias de la Educación*, *1*(1), 43–59. DOI: 10.17345/ute.2018.1.2116

Moore, R., Vitale, D., & Stawinoga, N. (2018). The digital divide and educational equity. *Insights in Education and Work*, 1-10.

Moreno Morilla, C., Guzmán Simón, F., & García Jiménez, E. (2021). Digital and information literacy inside and outside Spanish primary education schools. *Learning, Culture and Social Interaction*, *28*, 1–13. DOI: 10.1016/j.lcsi.2020.100455

Mosquera Gende, I. (2024). Los foros como elemento dinamizador para la participación activa en una universidad online. *Hachetetepé Revista Científica de Educación y Comunicación*, *28*(28), 1–21. DOI: 10.25267/Hachetetepe.2024.i28.1203

Msambwa, M. M., Daniel, K., & Lianya, C. (2024). Integration of information and communication technology in secondary education for better learning: A systematic literature review. *Social Sciences & Humanities Open*, *10*, 101203. DOI: 10.1016/j.ssaho.2024.101203

Muir, T., Wang, I., Trimble, A., Mainsbridge, C., & Douglas, T. (2022). Using interactive online pedagogical approaches to promote student engagement. *Education Sciences*, *12*(6), 415. DOI: 10.3390/educsci12060415

Mukhopadhyay, M., & Parhar, M. (2014). ICT in Indian higher education administration and management. In R. Huang, Kinshuk, & J. Price (Eds.), *ICT in education in global context* (pp. 191–208). Springer. DOI: 10.1007/978-3-662-43927-2_15

Mukhopadhyay, P., Tapaswi, M. P., Sudarsan, P. K., & Sudarsan, K. (2018). Assessing the quality of higher education institutions in India. *Current Science*, *114*(6), 1167–1173. DOI: 10.18520/cs/v114/i06/1167-1173

Murillo Camacho, G. A., & Rosales Sánchez, R. E. (2024). Incidencia del uso de las TIC en la enseñanza aprendizaje del idioma inglés en estudiantes de bachillerato. *RECIAMUC*, *8*(2), 114–122. DOI: 10.26820/reciamuc/8.(2).abril.2024.114-122

Mustafa, F., Nguyen, H. T. M., & Goa, X. (2024). The challenges and solutions of technology integration in rural schools: A systematic literature review. *International Journal of Educational Research*, *126*, 102380. DOI: 10.1016/j.ijer.2024.102380

Mutammimah, H., Rejeki, S., Kustini, S., & Amelia, R. (2024). Understanding teachers' perspective toward ChatGPT acceptance in English language teaching. [IJTE]. *International Journal of Technology in Education*, *7*(2), 290–307. DOI: 10.46328/ijte.656

Myers, I. B., Mccaulley, M. H., & Most, R. (1985). *Manual: A guide to the development and use of the Myers-Briggs Type Indicator*. Consulting Psychologists Press.

Nafea, I. T. (2018). Machine learning in educational technology. *Machine learning-advanced techniques and emerging applications*, 175-183.

Naghdipour, B. (2022). ICT-enabled informal learning in EFL writing. *Journal of Second Language Writing*, *56*, 100893. DOI: 10.1016/j.jslw.2022.100893

Nasim, S. M., Mujeeba, S., AlShraah, S. M., Khan, I. A., Amir, , & Ali, Z. (2024). Exploring pedagogical perspectives of EFL instructors: Advantages, disadvantages, and implications of Blackboard as an LMS for language instruction. *Cogent Social Sciences*, *10*(1), 1–18. DOI: 10.1080/23311886.2024.2312659

Nassa, A. K., Arora, J., Singh, P., Joorel, J. P., Solanki, H., Kumar, A., & Trivedi, K. (2021). Five years of India rankings and its impact on performance parameters of engineering educational institutions in India. Pt. 1: Teaching, learning and resources, graduate outcome, outreach and inclusivity and perception. *DESIDOC Journal of Library and Information Technology*, *41*(1), 17–26. DOI: 10.14429/djlit.41.1.16675

National Center for Education Statistics. (n.d.). *Technology and K-12 education.* https://nces.ed.gov/resources/edtechequity/

Ndibalema, P., & Mrosso, V. (2024a). Teachers' Perceptions on the Role and Challenges of using ICT in English Language Classrooms. *International Journal of Technology in Education and Science*, *8*(1), 121–137. DOI: 10.46328/ijtes.527

Nemer, D. (2015). From digital divide to digital inclusion and beyond. *The Journal of Community Informatics*, *11*(1). DOI: 10.15353/joci.v11i1.2857

Newport, E. L. (2019). Children and adults as language learners: Rules, variation, and maturational change. *Topics in Cognitive Science*, *12*(1), 153–169. https://onlinelibrary.wiley.com/doi/epdf/10.1111/tops.12416. DOI: 10.1111/tops.12416 PMID: 30834701

Newton, P. M., & Miah, M. (2017). Evidence-based higher education—Is the learning styles 'myth' important? *Frontiers in Psychology*, *8*, 444. DOI: 10.3389/fpsyg.2017.00444 PMID: 28396647

Nikonova, E., Yakhyaeva, K., Pivkina, N., & Schetinina, A. (2023). Using artificial intelligence tools in teaching a foreign language in higher technical institutions. *European Journal of Contemporary Education*, *12*(2), 578–589. DOI: 10.13187/ejced.2023.2.578

Nilubol, K., & Sitthikikul, P. (2023). Gamification: Trends and opportunities in language teaching and learning practices. *PASAA: Journal of Language Teaching and Learning in Thailand, 67,* 378-400. https://files.eric.ed.gov/fulltext/EJ1413891.pdf

Nitika, N., Sharma, T. K., Rajvanshi, S., & Kishore, K. (2021). A study of Augmented Reality performance in web browsers (WebAR). *2.ª Conferencia Internacional sobre Métodos Computacionales en Ciencia y Tecnología (ICCMST)*. 281-286, DOI: 10.1109/ICCMST54943.2021.00065

Norman, D. A. (2013). *The design of everyday things* (Revised and expanded ed.). Basic Books. https://dl.icdst.org/pdfs/files4/4bb8d08a9b309df7d86e62ec4056ceef.pdf

O'Dowd, R. (2018). From telecollaboration to virtual exchange: State-of-the-art and the role of UNICollaboration in moving forward. *Journal of Virtual Exchange*, *1*, 1–23. https://eric.ed.gov/?id=ED592404. DOI: 10.14705/rpnet.2018.jve.1

Ofosu-Asare, Y. (2024). Developing classroom ICT teaching techniques, principles and practice for teachers in rural Ghana without access to computers or internet: A framework based on literature review. *International Journal of Information and Learning Technology*, *41*(3), 262–279. DOI: 10.1108/IJILT-04-2023-0045

Oliveira, W., Hamari, J., Joaquim, S., Toda, A. M., Palomino, P. T., Vassileva, J., & Isotani, S. (2022). The effects of personalized gamification on students' flow experience, motivation, and enjoyment. *Smart Learn. Environ.*, *9*(16), 16. DOI: 10.1186/s40561-022-00194-x

Oliver, S. (2024). *AI prompt writing for ELT teachers: 7 ingredients of a successful prompt.* World of better learning. https://www.cambridge.org/elt/blog/2024/03/09/ai-prompt-writing-for-elt-teachers-7-ingredients-of-a-successful-prompt/

Onggirawan, C. A., Kho, J. M., Kartiwa, A. P., Anderies, , & Gunawan, A. A. S. (2023). Systematic literature review: The adaptation of distance learning process during the COVID-19 pandemic using virtual educational spaces in metaverse. *Procedia Computer Science, 216*, 274–283. DOI: 10.1016/j.procs.2022.12.137 PMID: 36643176

Onishchuk, I., Ikonnikova, M., Antonenko, T., Kharchenko, I., Shestakova, S., Kuzmenko, N., & Maksymchuk, B. (2020). Characteristics of foreign language education in foreign countries and ways of applying foreign experience in pedagogical universities of Ukraine. *Revista Romaneasca Pentru Educatie Multidimensionala, 12*(3), 44–65. DOI: 10.18662/rrem/12.3/308

Open, AI (2023). *GPT-4 Technical Report.* arXiv:2303.08774.

Organization for Economic Co-Operation and Development (2024). *How 15-year-olds learn English. Case studies from Finland, Greece, Israel, the Netherlands and Portugal.* PISA, OECD Publishing DOI: 10.1787/a3fcacd5-en

Ortiz Rodríguez, G. A., & Tejeda Díaz, R. (2023). Uso de las TIC para el aprendizaje del idioma inglés para estudiantes de secundaria. *Revista Cognosis, 8*(EE1), 127–142. DOI: 10.33936/cognosis.v8iEE1.5301

Osipova, A. V., & Lao, R. S. (2022). Breaking the cycle of failure for culturally and linguistically diverse learners with exceptional needs: Recommendations for improvement of teacher preparation programs. *Educational Research and Development Journal, 25*(1), 1-25. https://files.eric.ed.gov/fulltext/EJ1360921.pdf

Otero Rey, E. M., Blanco Carrión, A., & Rivas Mundiña, B. (2022). *Innovación docente: realización de vídeo de captura de pantalla como recurso para la enseñanza universitaria.* Adaya Press.

Ouyang, F., & Jiao, P. (2021). Artificial intelligence in education: The three paradigms. *Computers and Education: Artificial Intelligence, 2*, 100020. DOI: 10.1016/j.caeai.2021.100020

Ouyang, F., Zheng, L., & Jiao, P. (2022). Artificial intelligence in online higher education: A systematic review of empirical research from 2011 to 2020. *Education and Information Technologies, 27*(6), 7893–7925. DOI: 10.1007/s10639-022-10925-9

Ozdemire, E., & Papi, M. (2021). Mindsets as sources of L2 speaking anxiety and self-confidence: The case of international teaching assistants in the U.S. *Innovation in Language Learning and Teaching, 16*(3), 234–248. DOI: 10.1080/17501229.2021.1907750

Palieraki, S., & Koutrouba, K. (2021). Differentiated instruction in information and communications technology teaching and effective learning in primary education. *European Journal of Educational Research, 10*(3), 1487–1504. DOI: 10.12973/eu-jer.10.3.1487

Parai, H., Wahyudanti Saputri, A., & Kartika Sari, L. (2022). Development of Drama Studies Teaching Material Based on 21st Century Skills and It for Students of Indonesian Language and Literature Education Study Program, Faculty of Language and Arts, Universitas Negeri Jakarta. *Aksis : Jurnal Pendidikan Bahasa Dan Sastra Indonesia, 6*(2), 173–182. DOI: 10.21009/AKSIS.060208

Parameswaran, A. N., Hebbale, A. M., Vidya, S. M., & Pakkala, T. P. M. (2020). Impact of research performance and perception on ranking of universities: A study based on NIRF 2019. *Journal of Engineering Education Transformations, 34*(1), 85–92. DOI: 10.16920/jeet/2020/v34i1/150463

Parmaxi, A. (2023). Collaborative language learning in augmented reality environments. *ReCALL, 35*(1), 45–61.

Parsons, C., & Hick, S. F. (2008). Moving from the digital divide to digital inclusion. *Currents: Scholarship in the Human Services, 7*(2).

Parveen, D. S., & Ramzan, S. I. (2024). The role of digital technologies in education: Benefits and challenges. *Int. Res. J. Adv. Eng. Manag, 2*, 2029–2037.

Pashler, H., Mcdaniel, M., Rohrer, D., & Bjork, R. (2008). Learning styles: Concepts and evidence. *Psychological Science in the Public Interest, 9*(3), 105–119. DOI: 10.1111/j.1539-6053.2009.01038.x PMID: 26162104

Pask, G. (1976). Styles and strategies of learning. *The British Journal of Educational Psychology, 46*(2), 128–148. DOI: 10.1111/j.2044-8279.1976.tb02305.x

Patel, I. G., Paul, S., Khandwalla, P. N., Bose, A., Murthy, K. R. S., Vittal, N., Krishnan, R. T., Jain, A. K., & Gupta, A. K. (2004). Social context of management education: Institution building experiences at IIMs. *Vikalpa, 29*(2), 85–110. DOI: 10.1177/0256090920040208

Pathak, P., & Pal, D. A. E-resource utilization in IIMs libraries: Insights from faculties and students' surveys.

Patra, B., & Mohanty, A. K. (2016). Importance of English for engineering students: An evaluation of the prevalent teaching-learning system in the Indian context. *International Journal of English and Literature*, *6*(4), 21–34.

Patrinos, A. (2023). *Designing effective public-private partnerships in education.*

Pavel, A. P. (2015). Global university rankings: A comparative analysis. *Procedia Economics and Finance*, *26*, 54–63. DOI: 10.1016/S2212-5671(15)00838-2

Pedró, F., Subosa, M., Rivas, A., & Valverde, P. (2019). *Artificial intelligence in education: Challenges and opportunities for sustainable development.* (Report No. ED-2019/WS/8), UNESCO, https://www.gcedclearinghouse.org/sites/default/files/resources/190175eng.pdf

Pelargos, P. E., Nagasawa, D. T., Lagman, C., Tenn, S., Demos, J. V., Lee, S. J., Bui, T. T., Barnette, N. E., Bhatt, N. S., Ung, N., Bari, A., Martin, N. A., & Yang, I. (2017). Utilizing virtual and augmented reality for educational and clinical enhancements in neurosurgery. *Journal of Clinical Neuroscience*, *35*, 1–4. DOI: 10.1016/j.jocn.2016.09.002 PMID: 28137372

Peppin Vaughan, R. (2016). Gender equality and education in the Sustainable Development Goals.

Peters, M. A. (2017). Global university rankings: Metrics, performance, governance. *Educational Philosophy and Theory*, *51*(1), 5–13. DOI: 10.1080/00131857.2017.1381472

Peterson, D., Goode, K., & Gehlhaus, D. (2021). *AI education in China and the United States, a comparative assessment.* Center for Security and Emerging Technology (CSET). DOI: 10.51593/20210005

Pfenninger, S. E., Festman, J., & Singleton, D. (2023). *Second Language Acquisition and Lifelong Learning*. Routledge., DOI: 10.4324/9781003168935

Pillay, H., Watters, J. J., & Hoff, L. (2013). Critical attributes of public-private partnerships: A case study in vocational education. *International Journal of Adult Vocational Education and Technology*, *4*(1), 31–45. DOI: 10.4018/javet.2013010103

Pinto Santos, A. R., & Pérez Garcías, A. (2022). Development of teaching digital competence in initial teacher training: A systematic review. *World Journal on Educational Technology: Current Issues*, *14*(1), 1–15. DOI: 10.18844/wjet.v14i1.6250

Pinto, R. D., Peixoto, B., Melo, M., Cabral, L., & Bessa, M. (2021). Foreign language learning gamification using virtual reality – A systematic review of empirical research. *Education Sciences, 11*(5), 222. DOI: 10.3390/educsci11050222

Pitambar, P. (2021). Information and communication technology in foreign language classes in English: Roles and practices. *International Journal of Technology in Education and Science, 5*(1), 37–55. DOI: 10.46328/ijtes.179

Pitts, G., Marcus, V., & Motamedi, S. (2025). *Student perspectives on the benefits and risks of AI in education*. arXiv. https://doi.org//arXiv.2505.02198DOI: 10.48550

Popenici, S. A., & Kerr, S. (2017). Exploring the impact of artificial intelligence on teaching and learning in higher education. *Research and Practice in Technology Enhanced Learning, 12*(1), 22. DOI: 10.1186/s41039-017-0062-8 PMID: 30595727

Poudel, A. P. (2022). Information and communication technology in English language teaching: Some opportunities and challenges. *Journal of Comparative & International Higher Education, 14*(4), 103–116. https://files.eric.ed.gov/fulltext/EJ1363848.pdf. DOI: 10.32674/jcihe.v14i4.3874

Pradhan, P., Trivedi, K., & Singh, P. (2021). Five years of India rankings (2016–2020): An evolutionary study. *DESIDOC Journal of Library and Information Technology, 41*(1), 42–48. DOI: 10.14429/djlit.41.1.16671

Prathap, G. (2019). Construct validity maps and the NIRF 2019 ranking of colleges. *Current Science, 117*(6), 1079–1083. DOI: 10.18520/cs/v117/i6/1079-1083

Pregowska, A., Masztalerz, K., Garlińska, M., & Osial, M. (2021). A worldwide journey through distance education—From the post office to virtual, augmented, and mixed realities, and education during the COVID-19 pandemic. *Education Sciences, 11*(3), 118. DOI: 10.3390/educsci11030118

Prensky, M. (2001). Digital Natives, Digital Immigrants. *On the Horizon, 9*(5), 1–6. DOI: 10.1108/10748120110424816

Qadir, J. (2022). Engineering Education in the Era of ChatGPT: Promise and Pitfalls of Generative AI for Education. *TechRxiv.* DOI: 10.36227/techrxiv.21789434.v1

Qi, S., & Derakhshan, A. (2024). Technology-based collaborative learning: EFL learners' social regulation and modifications in their academic emotions and academic performance. *Education and Information Technologies.* DOI: 10.1007/s10639-024-13167-z

Radiamoda, A.-F. A. R., Ngo, C. G., Budadong, D., & Obiena, C. M. (2024). ICT Engagement and Digital Competence of Preservice English Teachers. *International Journal Corner of Educational Research, 3*(1), 54–64. DOI: 10.54012/ijcer.v3i1.265

Raghavan, R., Fitzsimmons-Craft, E. E., Welch, R. R., Proctor, E. K., Wilson, T., Agras, W. S., & Wilfley, D. E. (2024). Cost-effectiveness of train-the-trainer versus expert consultation training models for implementing interpersonal psychotherapy in college mental health settings: Evidence from a national cluster randomized trail. *Implementation Science : IS, 19*(55), 55. DOI: 10.1186/s13012-024-01388-2 PMID: 39075590

Rahimi, A. R., & Sevilla-Pavón, A. (2024). The role of ChatGPT readiness in shaping language teachers' language teaching innovation and meeting accountability: A bisymmetric approach. *Computers and Education: Artificial Intelligence, 7*, 100258. DOI: 10.1016/j.caeai.2024.100258

Rahimi, R. A., & Oh, G. S. (2024). Rethinking the role of educators in the 21st century: Navigating globalization, technology, and pandemics. *Journal of Marketing Analytics, 12*(2), 182–197. DOI: 10.1057/s41270-024-00303-4

Rahm, L. (2023). Education, automation and AI: A genealogy of alternative futures. *Learning, Media and Technology, 48*(1), 6–24. DOI: 10.1080/17439884.2021.1977948

Ramadass, D. D., & Shah, P. M. (2022). Knowledge, Attitude and Use of Information Communication Technology (ICT) among English Language Teachers. *Creative Education, 13*(02), 658–674. DOI: 10.4236/ce.2022.132041

Ramaswamy, M., Marciniuk, D. D., Csonka, V., Coló, L., & Saso, L. (2021). Reimagining internationalization of higher education through the United Nations Sustainable Development Goals for the betterment of society. *Journal of Studies in International Education, 25*(4), 388–406. DOI: 10.1177/10283153211031046

Rana, K., & Rana, K. (2020). ICT integration in teaching and learning activities in higher education: A case study of Nepal's teacher education. *Malaysian Online Journal of Educational Technology, 8*(1), 36–47. DOI: 10.17220/mojet.2020.01.003

Rasul, T., Nair, S., Kalendra, D., Robin, M., de Oliveira Santini, F., Ladeira, W. J., Mingwei, S., Day, I., Rather, R. A., & Heathcote, L. (2023). The role of ChatGPT in higher education: Benefits, challenges, and future research directions. *Journal of Applied Learning and Teaching, 6*(1). Advance online publication. DOI: 10.37074/jalt.2023.6.1.29

Recio Mayorga, J., Gutiérrez Esteban, P., & Suárez Guerrero, C. (2021). Recursos educativos abiertos en comunidades virtuales docentes. *Apertura (Guadalajara, Jal.)*, *13*(1), 101–117. DOI: 10.32870/Ap.v13n1.1921

Reis Jorge, J., Ferreira, M., & Olcina Sempere, G. (2020). La figura del profesorado-investigador en la reconstrucción de la profesionalidad docente en un mundo en transformación. *Review of Education*, *44*(1), 502–514. https://doi.org/10.15517/revedu.v44i1.39044

Rice, M. F., & Ortiz, K. R. (2021). Evaluating digital instructional materials for K-12 online and blended learning. *TechTrends*, *65*(6), 977–992. DOI: 10.1007/s11528-021-00671-z PMID: 34632461

Rico Gómez, M., & Ponce Gea, A. (2022). El Docente Del Siglo XXI Perspectivas según el rol formativo y profesional. *Revista Mexicana de Investigación Educativa*, *27*(92), 77–101.

Rieger, K. L., & Chernomas, M. (2013). Arts-based learning: Analysis of the concept for nursing education. *International Journal of Nursing Education Scholarship*, *10*(1), 53–62. DOI: 10.1515/ijnes-2012-0034 PMID: 23629466

Rios, R. (2023). *Sustainability in the ELT Classroom: Making a positive change in the world.* World of better learning. https://www.cambridge.org/elt/blog/2023/11/02/sustainability-in-the-elt-classroom/

Robertson, S. L., & Verger, A. (2012). Governing education through public private partnerships. In *Public private partnerships in education*. Edward Elgar Publishing. DOI: 10.4337/9780857930699.00009

Robles-Moral, F. J. (2021). Learning about sustainability and SDG with future primary education teachers in initial training. *Social Sciences (Basel, Switzerland)*, *10*(11), 409. DOI: 10.3390/socsci10110409

Rocu Gómez, P., Blández Ángel, J., & Sierra Zamorano, M. A. (2018). Construyendo aprendizajes en Expresión Corporal a través de WebQuest: Un estudio de caso múltiple. *Revista Complutense de Educación*, *30*(4), 1013–1029. DOI: 10.5209/rced.59905

Rodríguez Peñarroja, M. (2022). *El uso de YouTube en la clase de IFE y sus efectos en la motivación del alumnado*. Adaya Press.

Romero Hermoza, R. (2021). Competencia digital docente: una revisión sistemática. *Eduser, 8*(1), 131-137. https://doi.org/10.18050/eduser.v8i1.2033

Rosa, W. (2017). Goal 4: Ensure inclusive and equitable quality education and promote lifelong learning opportunities for all. *A New Era in Global Health: Nursing and the United Nations 2030 Agenda for Sustainable Development, 283*.

Rose, P. (2013). Achieving Education for All through public–private partnerships? In *Achieving Education for All through Public–Private Partnerships?* (pp. 1–11). Routledge. DOI: 10.4324/9781315879383

Rothe, F. F., Audenhove, L. V., & Loisen, J. (2022). Digital development inequalities & the sustainable development goals: Whad does "leave-no-one behind" mean for ICT4D? *Information Technology for Development*, *29*(1), 9–26. DOI: 10.1080/02681102.2022.2076640

Rowe, D. (2007). Sustainability. Education for a sustainable future. *Science*, *317*(5836), 323–324. DOI: 10.1126/science.1143552 PMID: 17641184

Royero Thomas, R. P. (2024). La Tecnología y su Influencia en la Enseñanza de la Lengua Extranjera Inglés: Una Revisión Sistemática de Literatura. *Ciencia Latina Revista Científica Multidisciplinar*, *8*(2), 7441–7454. DOI: 10.37811/cl_rcm.v8i2.11138

Rubio, A. D. J. (2024). Developing Motivation through an ICT Cooperation Project Plan in English between Spanish and German Students. *Studies in English Language and Education*, *11*(1), 1–22. DOI: 10.24815/siele.v11i1.30995

Rusmiyanto, R., Huriati, N., Fitriani, N., Tyas, N. K., Rofi'i, A., & Sari, M. N. (2023). The Role of Artificial Intelligence (AI) In Developing English Language Learner's Communication Skills. *Journal of Education*, *6*(1), 750–757. DOI: 10.31004/joe.v6i1.2990

Ryan, K. (2016). Incorporating emotional geography into climate change research: A case study in Londonderry, Vermont, USA. *Emotion, Space and Society*, *19*, 12. DOI: 10.1016/j.emospa.2016.02.006

Saini, M., Sengupta, E., Singh, M., Singh, H., & Singh, J. (2023). Sustainable Development Goal for Quality Education (SDG 4): A study on SDG 4 to extract the pattern of association among the indicators of SDG 4 employing a genetic algorithm. *Education and Information Technologies*, *28*(2), 2031–2069. DOI: 10.1007/s10639-022-11265-4 PMID: 35975216

Sala, N. (2021). Virtual reality, augmented reality, and mixed reality in education: A brief overview. *Current and prospective applications of virtual reality in higher education*, 48-73.

Salamah, U., Zaki, A., Rokhyanto, R., & Razak, F. (2024). Leveraging augmented reality for interactive language learning. *Journal of International of Lingua & Technology, 3*(3), 499. DOI: 10.55849/jiltech.v3i3.729

Samoylenko, N., Zharko, L., & Glotova, A. (2022). Designing online learning environment: Ict tools and teaching strategies. *Athens Journal of Education, 9*(1), 49–62. DOI: 10.30958/aje.9-1-4

Santa Medina, R. (2021). El e-Learning en Educación Primaria como consecuencia de la situación generada por el Covid-19: Un estudio de caso. *RIITE Revista Interuniversitaria de Investigación en Tecnología Educativa, 10*, 121–136. DOI: 10.6018/riite.439831

Santiago Campión, R., Navaridas Nalda, F. & Repáraz Abaitua, C. (2023). La escuela 2.0: reflexiones en torno a su eficacia en los centros educativos de La Rioja. *Educación XX1, 17*(1), 243-270. DOI: 10.5944/educxx.17.1.10713

Sarita, P. (2021). Constructivism: A new paradigm in teaching and learning. *International Journal of Academic Research and Development, 2*(4), 183–186. DOI: 10.52700/pjh.v2i2.86

Savolainen, K., & Torney-Purta, J. (2011). Modes of discourse about education, peace and human rights in the 1974 UNESCO Recommendation. *Prospects, 41*(4), 581–596. DOI: 10.1007/s11125-011-9209-3

Sendag, S., Caner, M., Gedik, N., & Toker, S. (2024). Enhancing language proficiency through mobile extensive listening and podcasting: A multifaceted approached to metacognition and critical thinking. *Thinking Skills and Creativity, 54*, 101656. DOI: 10.1016/j.tsc.2024.101656

Senkbeil, M. (2018). Development and validation of the ICT motivation scale for young adolescents. Results of the international school assessment study ICILS 2013 in Germany. *Learning and Individual Differences, 67*, 167–176. DOI: 10.1016/j.lindif.2018.08.007

Serdyukov, P. (2017). Innovation in education: what works, what doesn't, and what to do about it?. *Journal of research in innovative teaching & learning, 10*(1), 4-33.

Serhan, S. A. L., & Yahaya, N. (2022). A systematic review and trend analysis of personal learning environments research. *International Journal of Information and Education Technology (IJIET), 12*(1), 43–53. DOI: 10.18178/ijiet.2022.12.1.1585

Serna González, P., & Santillán Galván, R. (2021). WebQuest: Marcando el futuro de la educación. *Milenaria. Ciencia y Arte, 18*, 8–10. DOI: 10.35830/mcya.vi18.97

Sheeja, N. K., Mathew, S., & Cherukodan, S. (2018). Impact of scholarly output on university ranking. *Global Knowledge, Memory and Communication*, *67*(8/9), 595–611.

Shen, Z., Lai, M., & Wang, F. (2024). Investigating the influence of gamification on motivation and learning outcomes in online language learning. *Frontiers in Psychology*, *15*, 1295709. DOI: 10.3389/fpsyg.2024.1295709 PMID: 38860036

Shi, J., Sitthiworachart, J., & Hong, J. C. (2024). Supporting project-based learning for students' oral English skill and engagement with immersive virtual reality. *Education and Information Technologies*, *29*(11), 14127–14150. DOI: 10.1007/s10639-023-12433-w

Shivaram, B. S., Uma, M., & Sahu, S. R. (2022). A study of research publications of top NIRF ranked engineering institutions in Karnataka. *Annals of Library and Information Studies*, *69*(1), 44–50.

Shonfeld, M., Cotnam-Kappel, M., Judge, M., Yeehan Ng, C., Ntebutse, J. G., Williamson-Leadley, S., & Yildiz, M. (2021). Learning in digital environments: A model for cross-cultural alignment. *Educational Technology Research and Development*, *69*(4), 2151–2170. DOI: 10.1007/s11423-021-09967-6 PMID: 33654347

Shortt, M., Tilak, S., Kuznetcova, I., Martens, B., & Akinkuolie, B. (2023). Gamification in mobile-assisted language learning: A systematic view of Duolingo literature from public release of 2012 to early 2020. *Computer Assisted Language Learning*, *36*(3), 517–554. DOI: 10.1080/09588221.2021.1933540

Singer, J. B., Báez, J. C., & Rios, J. A. (2023). AI creates the message: Integrating AI language learning models into social work education and practice. *Journal of Social Work Education*, *59*(2), 294–302. DOI: 10.1080/10437797.2023.2189878

Singh, A., & Rao, V. R. (2024). Unpacking inconsistencies in the NIRF rankings. *Current Science*, *126*(11), 1473–1479. DOI: 10.18520/cs/v126/i11/1321-1324

Singh, S., & Singh, A. (2021). Importance of perception as a parameter in university rankings: A critical evaluation. *Prabandhan: Indian Journal of Management*, *14*(11), 25–40. DOI: 10.17010/pijom/2021/v14i11/166979

Smiderle, R., Rigo, S. J., Marques, L. B., Peçanha de Miranda Coelho, J. A., & Jaques, P. A. (2020). The impact of gamification on students' learning, engagement and behavior based on their personality traits. *Smart Learning Environments*, *7*(1), 3. DOI: 10.1186/s40561-019-0098-x

Sofi-Karim, M., Bali, A. O., & Rached, K. (2023). Online education via media platforms and applications as an innovative teaching method. *Education and Information Technologies, 28*(1), 507–523. DOI: 10.1007/s10639-022-11188-0 PMID: 35791317

Soto Esteban, R. (2022). *Twitter y el reconocimiento de figuras del trabajo social en el segundo curso del grado*. Adaya Press.

Srimathi, H., & Krishnamoorthy, A. (2020). Review on NIRF. *Journal of Critical Reviews, 7*(4), 259–262.

Srinivasan, R., Jain, V., & Dharmaraja, S. (2020). Perception based performance analysis of higher education institutions: A soft computing approach. *Soft Computing, 24*(1), 513–521. DOI: 10.1007/s00500-019-03931-6

Stahl, W. M., & Karger, J. (2016). Student Data Privacy, Digital Learning, and Special Education: Challenges at the Intersection of Policy and Practice. *Journal of Special Education Leadership, 29*(2), 79–88.

Steck, H. (2015, Sep 16–20). Gaussian ranking by matrix factorization. In *Proceedings of the ACM Conference on Recommender Systems*, Vienna, Austria (pp. 115–122).

Suhrheinrich, J. (2011). Examining the effectiveness of a train-the-trainer model: Training teachers to use pivotal response training. *Society for Research on Educational Effectiveness,* 1-15.

Sweller, J. (2011). *Cognitive load theory*. Springer., DOI: 10.1007/978-1-4419-8126-4

Syifa, S., & Darmahusni. (2019). Designing ICT Competences-Integrated Syllabuses of Research Skills and Professional Administration Courses (Design and Development Study of English Language Education Study Program Syllabuses). *International Journal of Language Education and Cultural Review (IJLECR), 5*(2), 116–123. e-jurnal:https://journal.unj.ac.id/unj/index.php/ijlecr e-ISSN: 2461-131X Volume

Szyszka, M., Tomczyk, Ł., & Kochanowicz, A. M. (2022). Digitalisation of Schools from the Perspective of Teachers' Opinions and Experiences: The Frequency of ICT Use in Education, Attitudes towards New Media, and Support from Management. *Sustainability (Basel), 14*(14), 1–20. DOI: 10.3390/su14148339

Tarman, B. (2003). *The Digital Divide in Education*. Online Submission.

Taskıran, A., & Goksel, N. (2022). Automated feedback and teacher feedback: Writing achievement in learning English as a foreign language at a distance. *Turkish Online Journal of Distance Education, 23*(2), 120–139. DOI: 10.17718/tojde.1096260

Taylor, R. W. (2002). Pros and cons of online learning–a faculty perspective. *Journal of European Industrial Training, 26*(1), 24–37. DOI: 10.1108/03090590210415876

Teng, M. F., Wang, C., & Wu, J. G. (2021). Metacognitive strategies, language learning motivation, self-efficacy belief, and English achievement during remote learning; A structural equation modelling approach. *RELC Journal, 54*(3), 648–666. DOI: 10.1177/00336882211040268

Teo, T., & Zhou, M. (2017). The influence of teachers' conceptions of teaching and learning on their technology acceptance. *Interactive Learning Environments, 25*(4), 513–527. DOI: 10.1080/10494820.2016.1143844

Termit, K., & Hussein, N. (2015). Teachers' readiness to utilize Frog VLE: A case study of a Malaysian secondary school. *J. Educ. Soc. Behav. Sci., 5*(1), 20–29. DOI: 10.9734/BJESBS/2015/11965

Thah, S. S. (2014). Leveraging virtual learning environment to scale up quality teaching and learning in Malaysia. *Asia-Pac. Collab. Educ. J., 10*, 1–17.

Thannimalai, T., Ponniah, K., Nawastheen, F. M., Jose, F. T., & Jaiseelan, S. (2022). Attitudes and acceptance of information and communication technology (ICT) among urban and rural teachers in teaching and facilitation. *International Journal of Advanced and Applied Sciences, 9*(7), 16–23. DOI: 10.21833/ijaas.2022.07.003

The Importance of Foreign Languages. (n.d.). *The International Union of Youth in Prague Blog*. https://msmstudy.eu/the-importance-of-foreign-languages/

The United Nations. (n.d.). *Sustainable development goals*. https://www.un.org/sustainabledevelopment/

Timotheou, S., Miliou, O., Dimitriadis, Y., Sobrino, S. V., Giannoutsou, N., Cachia, R., Monés, A. M., & Ioannou, A. (2023). Impacts of digital technologies on education and factors influencing schools' digital capacity and transformation: A literature review. *Education and Information Technologies, 28*(6), 6695–6726. DOI: 10.1007/s10639-022-11431-8 PMID: 36465416

Tiwari, R. (2023). The integration of AI and machine learning in education and its potential to personalize and improve student learning experiences. *International Journal of Scientific Research in Engineering and Management, 7*.

Toke, N. (2023). The role of ICT in achieving the SDG goal of quality education. *Diversity for Social Impact*. https://diversity.social/the-role-of-ict-in-achieving-the-sdg-goal-of-quality-education

Tooley, M., & Hood, J. (2021). Harnessing micro-credentials for teacher growth. A national review of early best practices. *New America*. https://files.eric.ed.gov/fulltext/ED612409.pdf

Tracey, B., Florian, K., & Marc, F. (2016). *Educational research and innovation education governance in action lessons from case studies: Lessons from case studies*. OECD Publishing.

Treve, M. (2021). What COVID-19 has introduced into education: Challenges facing higher education institutions (HEIs). *Higher Education Pedagogies, 6*(1), 212–227. DOI: 10.1080/23752696.2021.1951616

Tukhtabayeva, A., Kenzhebekova, A., Utemuratova, A., Amanbekova, N., Naubay, B., & Tuzelbayeva, D. (2024). Applying augmented Reality (QR-code) in English language classroom. *Procedia Computer Science, 251*, 573–578. DOI: 10.1016/j.procs.2024.11.151

Twabu, K., & Nakene-Mginiqi, M. (2024). Developing a design thinking artificial intelligence driven auto-marking/grading system for assessments to reduce the workload of lectures at a higher learning institution in South Africa. *Frontiers in Education, 9*(16), 1512569. DOI: 10.3389/feduc.2024.1512569

Tyagi, R., Vishwakarma, S., Alexandrovich, Z. S., & Mohammmed, S. (2020). ICT skills for sustainable development goal 4. In L. Filho, A. M. Azul, L. Brandli, P. G. Özuyar, P.G., & T. Wall (Eds), *Quality education. Encyclopedia of the unsustainable development goals*. Springer. DOI: 10.1007/978-3-319-95870-5_39

Tzafilkou, K., Perifanou, M., & Economides, A. A. (2021). Teachers' trainers' intention and motivation to transfer ICT training: The role of ICT individual factors, gender, and ICT self-efficacy. *Education and Information Technologies, 26*(5), 5563–5589. DOI: 10.1007/s10639-021-10541-z

Ubal, M., Tambasco, P., Martínez, S., & García Correa, M. (2023). El impacto de la Inteligencia Artificial en la educación. Riesgos y potencialidades de la IA en el aula [The impact of Artificial Intelligence in education. Risks and potentials of AI in the classroom]. *RiiTE Revista interuniversitaria de investigación en Tecnología Educativa,* (15), 41–57. DOI: 10.6018/riite.584501

Ulu, H., & Ulusoy, M. (2019). The development of metacognitive awareness of reading strategies through WebQuest based teaching. *Egitim ve Ögretim, 9*(3), 765–818. DOI: 10.14527/pegegog.2019.025

Umida, K., Dilora, A., & Umar, E. (2020). Constructivism in teaching and learning process. *European Journal of Research and Reflection in Educational Sciences, 8*(3), 134–137.

UNESCO. (2019). *Artificial intelligence in education: Challenges and opportunities for sustainable development*. United Nations Educational, Scientific and Cultural Organization.

UNESCO. (2021). *International Forum on AI and the Futures of Education Developing Competencies for the AI Era*. United Nations Educational, Scientific and Cultural Organization. https://unesdoc.unesco.org/ark:/48223/pf0000377251.locale=en

UNESCO. (2022). *Guidelines for immersive technologies in education*. United Nations Educational, Scientific and Cultural Organization.

UNESCO. (2023). *Guidelines for generative AI in education and research*. United Nations Educational, Scientific and Cultural Organization. https://unesdoc.unesco.org/ark:/48223/pf0000386693.locale=en

United Nations Brundtland Commission. (1987). *Report of the world commission on environment and development: Our common future*. (A/42/427). https://www.are.admin.ch/are/en/home/media/publications/sustainable-development/brundtland-report.html#:~:text=It%20developed%20guiding%20principles%20for,and%20production%20in%20the%20North

United Nations Development Programme. (n.d.). *The SDGS in action. Goal 4 quality education*. https://www.undp.org/sustainable-development-goals/quality-education

United Nations. (2015). *Transforming our world: the 2030 agenda for sustainable development*. (A/RRES/70/1). https://docs.un.org/en/A/RES/70/1

United Nations. (n.d.). *Goal 4: Ensure inclusive and equitable quality education and promote lifelong learning opportunities for all*. https://sdgs.un.org/goals/goal4

Vahedi, Z., Zannella, L., & Want, S. C. (2019). Students' use of information and communication technologies in the classroom: Uses, restriction, and integration. *Active Learning in Higher Education*, *22*(3), 215–228. DOI: 10.1177/1469787419861926

Vaillant, D. (2023). *Formación del profesorado en escenarios de tecnologías digitales*. OEI Publishers.

Valverde-Berrorocoso, J., Fernández-Sánchez, M., Dominguez, F. I. R., & Sosa-Díaz, M. (2021). The educational integration of digital technologies preCovid-19: Lessons for teacher education. *PLoS One*, *16*(8), e0256283. DOI: 10.1371/journal.pone.0256283 PMID: 34411161

Vargas-Montoya, L., Gimenez, G., & Fernández-Gutiérrez, M. (2023). ICT use for learning and students' outcomes: Does the country's development level matter? *Socio-Economic Planning Sciences*, *87*, 101550. DOI: 10.1016/j.seps.2023.101550

Vartiainen, H., & Tedre, M. (2023). Using artificial intelligence in craft education: Crafting with text-to-image generative models. *Digital Creativity (Exeter), 34*(1), 1–21. DOI: 10.1080/14626268.2023.2174557

Vasudevan, N. (2020). Development of a common framework for outcome-based accreditation and rankings. *Procedia Computer Science, 172*, 270–276. DOI: 10.1016/j.procs.2020.05.043

Vázquez-Parra, J. C., Gonzalez-Gonzalez, C. S., Amézquita-Zamora, J. A., Cotino Arbelo, A. E., Palomino-Gámez, S., & Cruz-Sandoval, M. (2024). Complex thinking and adopting artificial intelligence tools: A study of university students. *Frontiers in Education, 9*, 1377553. DOI: 10.3389/feduc.2024.1377553

Verger, A., Bona, L. X., & Zancajo, A. (2016). What is the role and impact of public-private partnerships in education? A realistic evaluation of the Chilean education quasi-market. *Comparative Education Review, 60*(2), 223–248. DOI: 10.1086/685557

Verhoef, P. C., Broekhuizen, T., Bart, Y., Bhattacharya, A., Dong, J. Q., Fabian, N., & Haenlein, M. (2021). Digital transformation: A multidisciplinary reflection and research agenda. *Journal of Business Research, 122*, 889–901. DOI: 10.1016/j.jbusres.2019.09.022

Vesselinov, R., & Grego, J. (2012). *Duolingo effectiveness study final report.* https://www.studocu.vn/vn/document/truong-dai-hoc-ngoai-ngu-tin-hoc-thanh-pho-ho-chi-minh/english-language/duolingo-report-final/62581075

Villacres Arias, G. E., Espinoza Freire, E. E., & Rengifo Ávila, G. K. (2020). Empleo de las tecnologías de la información y la comunicación como estrategia innovadora de enseñanza y aprendizaje. *Revista Universidad y Sociedad, 12*(5), 136–142.

Vincent, D. A., Okeowo, R. O., & Ariyo, S. (2024). The use of assistive technology for students with disabilities in technical colleges in Ondo State. *Journal of Educational Research & Practice, 14*(1), 52–67. DOI: 10.5590/JERAP.2024.14.1.04

Vincent-Lancrin, S., & Van der Vlies, R. (2020). *Trustworthy artificial intelligence (AI) in education: Promises and challenges.* (OECD Education Working Papers No. 218), OECD Publishing. DOI: 10.1787/19939019

Viola, S. R., Graf, S., & Leo, T. (2006, Dec 11–13). Analysis of Felder-Silverman Index of Learning Styles by a data-driven statistical approach. In *Proceedings of the 8th IEEE International Symposium on Multimedia*, San Diego, CA, USA (pp. 959–964). DOI: 10.1109/ISM.2006.30

Vyas-Doorgapersad, S. (2022). The use of digitalization (ICTs) in achieving sustainable development goals. *Global Journal of Emerging Market Economies*, *14*(2), 265–278. DOI: 10.1177/09749101211067295

Waes, L. V., Weijen, D. V., & Leijten, M. (2014). Learning to write in an online writing center: The effect of learning styles on the writing process. *Computers & Education*, *73*, 60–71. DOI: 10.1016/j.compedu.2013.12.009

Walker, C. O., Greene, B. A., & Mansell, R. A. (2006). Identification with academics, intrinsic/extrinsic motivation, and self-efficacy as predictors of cognitive engagement. *Learning and Individual Differences*, *16*(1), 1–12. DOI: 10.1016/j.lindif.2005.06.004

Wang, Y. (1999, Nov). Public-private partnerships in health and education: Conceptual issues and options. In *A Manuscript Prepared for Manila Social Policy Forum: The New Social Agenda for East, Southeast and Central Asia. Joint ADB-World Bank Conference* (pp. 9-12).

Wang, D., Zhou, T., & Wang, M. (2021). Information and communication technology (ICT), digital divide and urbanization: Evidence from Chinese cities. *Technology in Society*, *64*, 101516. DOI: 10.1016/j.techsoc.2020.101516

Wang, J., Yang, Y., Mao, J., Huang, Z., Huang, C., & Xu, W. (2016, Jun 27–30). CNN-RNN: A unified framework for multi-label image classification. In *Proceedings of the 2016 IEEE Conference on Computer Vision and Pattern Recognition (CVPR)*, Seattle, WA, USA (pp. 2285–2294). DOI: 10.1109/CVPR.2016.251

Wang, S., Wang, F., Zhu, Z., Wang, J., Tran, T., & Du, Z. (2024). Artificial intelligence in education: A systematic literature review. *Expert Systems with Applications*, *252*, 124167. DOI: 10.1016/j.eswa.2024.124167

Weber, A. M., & Greiff, S. (2023). ICT Skills in the Deployment of 21st Century Skills: A (Cognitive) Developmental Perspective through Early Childhood. In *Applied Sciences (Switzerland)* (Vol. 13, Issue 7, pp. 1–22). DOI: 10.3390/app13074615

Wei, X., Weng, D., Liu, Y., & Wang, Y. (2015). Teaching based on augmented Reality for a technical creative design course. *Computers & Education*, *81*, 221–234. DOI: 10.1016/j.compedu.2014.10.017

Wong, D. (2007). A critical literature review on e-learning limitations. *Journal for the Advancement of Science and Arts*, *2*(1), 55–62.

Wu, H. K., Lee, S. W. Y., Chang, H. Y., & Liang, J. C. (2023). Current status, opportunities, and challenges of augmented Reality in education. *Computers & Education*, *182*, 113100.

Xiao, Y. (2025). The impact of AI-driven speech recognition on EFL listening comprehension, flow experience, and anxiety: A randomized controlled trial. *Humanities & Social Sciences Communications, 12*(1), 425. DOI: 10.1057/s41599-025-04672-8

Xu, J., Lio, A., Dhaliwal, H., Andrei, S., Balakrishnan, S., Nagani, U., & Samadder, S. (2021). Psychological interventions of virtual gamification within academic intrinsic motivation: A systematic review. *Journal of Affective Disorders, 293*(1), 444–465. DOI: 10.1016/j.jad.2021.06.070 PMID: 34252688

Yang, A. (2024). Challenges and opportunities for foreign language teachers in the era of artificial intelligence. *International Journal of Education and Humanities, 4*(1), 39–50. DOI: 10.58557/(ijeh).v4i1.202

Yaş, E. (2022). English Prepositions as Function Words Are Not as Easy for Language Learners as Normally Supposed to Be. *Batman University Journal of Life Sciences, 12*(1), 48–64. DOI: 10.55024/buyasambid.1126711

Yıldırım, A., & Şimşek, H. (2018). *Qualitative research methods in the social sciences*. Seçkin.

Yufei, L., Saleh, S., Jiahui, H., & Sayed, S. M. (2020). Review of the application of artificial intelligence in education. *International Journal of Innovation. Creativity and Change, 12*(8), 548–562. DOI: 10.53333/IJICC2013/12850

Yu, H., & Guo, Y. (2023). Generative artificial intelligence empowers educational reform: Current status, issues, and prospects. *Frontiers in Education, 8*, 1183162. DOI: 10.3389/feduc.2023.1183162

Yumnam, R. (2021). THE USE OF ICT IN ESL CLASSROOMS IN MANIPUR. *Social Sciences* [SHE Journal]. *Humanities and Education Journal, 2*(2). DOI: 10.25273/she.v2i2.8898

Yunus, M. M., Nordin, N., Salehi, H., Sun, C. H., & Embi, M. A. (2013). Pros and cons of using ICT in teaching ESL reading and writing. *International Education Studies, 6*(7), 119–130. DOI: 10.5539/ies.v6n7p119

Zaiarna, I., Zhyhadlo, O., & Dunaievska, O. (2024). ChatGPT in foreign language teaching and assessment: Exploring EFL instructors' experience. *Information Technologies and Learning Tools, 102*(4), 176–191. DOI: 10.33407/itlt.v102i4.5716

Zakaria, Z., Setyosari, P., Sulton, S., & Kuswandi, D. (2019). The effect of art-based learning to improve teaching effectiveness in pre-service teachers. *J. Educ. Gift. Young Sci., 7*(3), 531–545. DOI: 10.17478/jegys.606963

Zampirolli, F. A., Josko, J. M. B., Venero, M. L. F., Kobayashi, G., Fraga, F. J., Goya, D., & Savegnago, H. R. (2021). An experience of automated assessment in a large-scale introduction programming course. *Computer Applications in Engineering Education, 29*(5), 1284–1299. DOI: 10.1002/cae.22385

Zawacki-Richter, O., Marín, V. I., Bond, M., & Gouverneur, F. (2019). Systematic review of research on artificial intelligence applications in higher education-where are the educators? *International Journal of Educational Technology in Higher Education, 16*(1), 39. DOI: 10.1186/s41239-019-0171-0

Zhai, X., Chu, X., Chai, C. S., Jong, M. S. Y., Istenic, A., Spector, M., Liu, J.-B., Yuan, J., & Li, Y. (2021). A Review of Artificial Intelligence (AI) in Education from 2010 to 2020. *Complexity, 2021*(1), 8812542. DOI: 10.1155/2021/8812542

Zhang, X., Sun, J., & Deng, Y. (2023). Design and application of intelligent classroom for English language and literature based on artificial intelligence technology. *Applied Artificial Intelligence, 37*(1), e2216051. DOI: 10.1080/08839514.2023.2216051

Zhang, X., & Umeanowai, K. O. (2025). Exploring the transformative influence of artificial intelligence in EFL context: A comprehensive bibliometric analysis. *Education and Information Technologies, 30*(3), 3183–3198. DOI: 10.1007/s10639-024-12937-z

Zhang, X., & Zhou, M. (2023). Information and digital technology-assisted interventions to improve intercultural competence: A meta-analytical review. *Computers & Education, 194*, 104697. DOI: 10.1016/j.compedu.2022.104697

Zhang, Y., & Dong, C. (2024). Exploring the digital transformation of generative ai-assisted foreign language education: A socio-technical systems perspective based on mixed-methods. *Systems, 12*(11), 462. DOI: 10.3390/systems12110462

Zhan, Z., Fong, P., Mei, H., Chang, X., Liang, T., & Ma, Z. (2015). Sustainability education in massive open online courses: A content analysis approach. *Sustainability (Basel), 7*(3), 2274–2300. DOI: 10.3390/su7032274

Zhao, X., Ren, Y., & Cheah, K. S. (2023). Leading Virtual Reality (VR) and Augmented Reality (AR) in education: Bibliometric and content analysis from the web of science (2018–2022). *SAGE Open, 13*(3), 21582440231190821. DOI: 10.1177/21582440231190821

Zhao, Y., & Li, S. (2022). Generative AI in language education: Opportunities and challenges. *Journal of Educational Technology & Society, 25*(3), 112–125.

Zhao, Y., Li, S., & Zhang, L. (2023). Adaptive feedback in AI-driven augmented reality language apps. *Educational Technology Research and Development*, *71*(3), 1129–1150.

Zhou, A. (2023). Investigating the impact of online language exchanges on second language speaking and willingness to communicate of Chinese EFL learners: A mixed methods study. *Frontiers in Psychology*, *14*, 1177922. DOI: 10.3389/fpsyg.2023.1177922 PMID: 37251019

Zhou, L. (2023). ICT-Aided Education and Professional Development of Foreign Language Teachers. *Research and Advances in Education*, *2*(8), 47–51. DOI: 10.56397/RAE.2023.08.04

Zorba, M. G. (2022). *Understanding English Language Learners' Interpretations of Cultures: The Case of Digital Photographs*. Adaya Press.

Zúñiga Zárate, A. G. (2022). *Implementación de funcionalidades en Moodle para alumnos con dislexia*. Adaya Press.

About the Contributors

Peter Ilic is a Senior Associate Professor in the Center for Language Research at the University of Aizu in Japan. He holds a BA in History from McMaster University, an MEd in TESOL from Temple University, an MSc. in Educational Research from the University of Exeter, and a Ph.D. in Education from the University of Exeter. During his Ph.D. studies, he investigated the use of Mobile Devices for Collaborative Learning. Information and Communications Technology in Education remains the principal focus of his ongoing research, resulting in an edited book on Microlessons and a second published with Springer publishing on the topic of AI in Education. In addition, he has over 20 peer-reviewed publications, presented several keynotes and given numerous contributed presentations. He is a member of several academic societies, including the IEEE and ACM, and serves as the managing editor of the International Journal of Web-Based Learning and Teaching Technologies (IJWLTT) and is on the editorial board of several journals and conference committees.

***

Jose Castillo Mendoza, Graduated from the Escuela Bancaria y Comercial with a Bachelor's degree in Accounting. In addition, I have a Master's degree in Administration from the Universidad del Valle de México and a Doctorate in Educational Sciences from the Colegio de Posgraduados in Mexico City. This academic background has been key to my development in areas such as human capital formation and research, with a special focus on human resource development and educational technology. My preparation is complemented with certifications in both areas, which supports the experience and knowledge throughout my career.

Isabel María Garcia Conesa has a degree in English Studies from the University of Alicante and a PhD from the National University of Distance Education (UNED). She is currently working as a full time lecturer at the Centro Universitario de la Defensa in San Javier (Spain). She has been awarded a scholarship by the Franklin Institute (University of Alcala de Henares, Spain) and the Radcliffe Institute for Advanced Study (Harvard University, USA), where she conducted a pre-doctoral research stay in the year 2012. Among her main lines of research, we can highlight the role of different women in literature and culture of the United States in contrast to Francophone writers with publication in Spanish journals like Revista Estudios Humanísticos (University of León), Tonos Digital (University of Murcia), Dossiers Feministes (University Jaime I), Prisma Social, Raudem (University of Almeria), Camino Real (University of Alcala de Henres), or Nomadas (University Complutense of Madrid). She also focuses on the study of the history of the teaching of English and gender studies with publications in journals such as Revista Feminismo (University of Alicante) or even Quaderns Digitals.

Antonio D.Juan has a degree in English Studies from the University of Murcia and a PhD from the National University of Distance Education (UNED) with the positive accreditation by the ANECA body, being given the Extraordinary Doctorate Award. He is currently working as a professor at the University of Granada. He has been awarded a scholarship by University College (Cork, Ireland), the Franklin Institute (University of Alcala de Henares, Spain) and the Radcliffe Institute for Advanced Study (Harvard University, USA), where he conducted a pre-doctoral research visit in the year 2012. He is currently a member of the scientific committee of several national and international journals as well as a member of the editorial board of several international journals. He also belongs to the organizing and scientific committee of several conferences organized by the Athens Institute for Education and Research (Greece). Among his main lines of research we can emphasize the following aspects: cultural studies in the United States; gender issues associated with the role of women in the Anglo-American literature; or the teaching practice and process of English.

Rupesh Kumar obtained his PhD from the Indian Institute of Technology Roorkee, India. He completed his Post-Doc from the DEG – Departamento Engenharia E Gestao, Instituto Superior Tecnico, Lisboa, Portugal. He is working as a Professor at Jindal Global Business School, O.P. Jindal Global University, Sonipat Haryana. He is having more than 12 years of teaching and research experience. His research interests include supply chain management, operations management, sustainability, environment and analytics.

Ananya Pandey is a Research Scholar in School of Law at Christ University, Bangalore. She has her research interests in the field of Constitutional Law,

Environment Law, Human Rights, Food Security, Intellectual Property Law and Jurisprudence.

Neeraj Sharma has over 15 years of cross-sectoral and cross-functional experience working with various organizations of repute spanning research, education, print media, logistics, supply chain, renewable energy, banking, IT, and KPO/BPO industries. He has successfully handled business planning and analysis, supply chain management, strategy, marketing, operations, green sustainability, and renewable energy initiatives/projects.

Anurag Singh is an accomplished academic specializing in Human Resource Management and Organisational Behaviour, currently serving as an Assistant Professor in the Department of Management Studies at BITS Pilani, Dubai Campus, and as an International Visiting Faculty at the ESPM Business School in Brazil. He holds a Ph.D. in Management from BHU, Varanasi, and an MBA in Human Resource Management from the University of Mysore, providing a strong foundation for his teaching and research endeavors. Dr. Singh has over a decade of teaching and research experience, having served in various academic roles across premier institutions in India and the UAE.

Anabelem Soberanes-Martin, Graduated in Administrative Computer Systems, Teacher in Education, master's in computer science course, Doctor in Educational Sciences has the Desirable Profile Recognition (PRODEP), member of the National System of Researchers (SNI-I), Certified as Distance Activity Coordinator (San Diego Global Knowledge University), Certified as Instructor of face to face Courses (CONOCER), works in the Centro Universitario UAEM Valle de Chalco of the Universidad Autónoma del Estado de México. She has held the positions of Licentiate Coordinator, Academic Sub-Director, and Academic Faculty Leader. She is currently a full-time professor, teaching in the bachelor's degrees in Computer Engineering, Administrative Informatics, in the master's and Doctorate degrees in Computer Science.

Kelly M. Torres, Ph.D. is the Department Chair of the Educational Psychology and Technology program at The Chicago School. Her research interests are focused on international education, teacher certification programs, innovative technologies, and online learning.

Ülkü Ülker at Dicle University, (Instructional Technologies Department of Educational Sciences) Editorial Review Board Member at International Journal of Web-Based Learnihg and Teaching Technologies published by IG Global

Seema Yadav has academic qualifications of M. Sc. (Chemistry), M Ed (RIE), UGC-NET, and PhD in Education. Presently she is working as an Assistant Professor, in the Department of Education at The Bhopal School of Education, Bhopal. She has almost 18 years of teaching experience. Her areas of specialization are educational psychology, environmental education, digital learning, and curriculum development.

Index

A

B

C

D

E

F

H

I

L

M

P

Q

R

S

T

V

www.ingramcontent.com/pod-product-compliance
Lightning Source LLC
LaVergne TN
LVHW062216200926
848484LV00006B/1412